Adventures of Huckleberry Finn

Mark Twain:

- His name from riverboat men
- Born 1835 - died 1910 at 74
- Born in same year as story takes place
- grows up in Hannibal, Missouri
- Dad dies in his early years, and Twain became an apprentice to a printer. Also drops out of school
- Missouri was a former slave state
- racism
- travelled
- married wealthy woman
- built a big house in Hartford, CT
- Someone said he was the first "true" american writer

New Riverside Editions

General Editor for the American Volumes
Paul Lauter

STEPHEN CRANE, *The Red Badge of Courage, Maggie: A Girl of the Streets, and Other Selected Writings*
Edited by Phyllis Frus and Stanley Corkin

RALPH WALDO EMERSON, *Selected Writings* and MARGARET FULLER, *Woman in the Nineteenth Century*
Edited by John Carlos Rowe

OLAUDAH EQUIANO, MARY ROWLANDSON, AND OTHERS, *American Captivity Narratives*
Edited by Gordon M. Sayre

HENRY DAVID THOREAU, *Walden and Civil Disobedience*
Edited by Paul Lauter

MARK TWAIN, *Adventures of Huckleberry Finn*
Edited by Susan K. Harris

EDITH WHARTON, *The Age of Innocence*
Edited by Carol J. Singley

Other Riverside Literature Titles

Call and Response: The Riverside Anthology of the African American Literary Tradition
Edited by Patricia Liggins Hill et al.

The Riverside Anthology of Children's Literature, Sixth Edition
Edited by Judith Saltman

The Riverside Anthology of Literature, Third Edition
Edited by Douglas Hunt

The Riverside Anthology of Short Fiction: Convention and Innovation
Edited by Dean Baldwin

The Riverside Chaucer, Third Edition
Edited by Larry D. Benson

The Riverside Milton
Edited by Roy Flannagan

The Riverside Shakespeare, Second Edition
Edited by G. Blakemore Evans et al.

NEW RIVERSIDE EDITIONS

General Editor for the American Volumes
Paul Lauter, Trinity College

Mark Twain

Adventures of Huckleberry Finn

Complete Text with Introduction
Historical Contexts • Critical Essays

edited by

Susan K. Harris
Pennsylvania State University

with the assistance of
Lyrae Van Clief-Stefanon

HOUGHTON MIFFLIN COMPANY
Boston • *New York*

For Henry Nash Smith and Louis J. Budd

Senior Sponsoring Editor: Suzanne Phelps Weir
Associate Editor: Jennifer Roderick
Senior Project Editor: Kathryn Dinovo
Senior Cover Design Coordinator: Deborah Azerrad Savona
Manufacturing Manager: Florence Cadran
Senior Marketing Manager: Nancy Lyman
Associate Marketing Manager: Carla Gray

Cover design: Steven Cooley
Cover image: © Corbis

Credits appear on page 391, which constitutes a continuation of the copyright page.

Printed in the U.S.A.

Library of Congress Cataloging-in-Publication Data is available on file.

ISBN: 0-395-98078-X

7 8 9-QF-10 09 08 07 06

As part of Houghton Mifflin's ongoing
commitment to the environment, this text
has been printed on recycled paper.

Contents

Part Three: READINGS   321

About This Series

Paul Lauter

The Riverside name dates back well over a century. Readers of this book may have seen—indeed, may own—Riverside Editions of works by the best-known nineteenth-century American writers, such as Emerson, Thoreau, Lowell, Longfellow, and Hawthorne. Houghton Mifflin and its predecessor, Ticknor & Fields, were the primary publishers of the New England authors who constituted much of the undisputed canon of American literature until well into the twentieth century. The Riverside Editions of works by these writers, and of some later writers such as Amy Lowell, became benchmarks for distinguished and useful editions of standard American authors for home, library, and classroom.

In the 1950s and 1960s, the Riverside name was used for another series of texts, primarily for the college classroom, of well-known American and British literary works. These paperback volumes, edited by distinguished critics of that generation, were among the most widely used and appreciated of their day. They provided carefully edited texts in a handsome and readable format, with insightful critical introductions. They were books one kept beyond the exam, the class, or even the college experience.

In the last quarter century, however, ideas about the American literary canon have changed. Many scholars want to see a canon that reflects a broader American heritage, including significant literary works by previously marginalized writers, many of them women or men of color. These changes began to be institutionalized in curricula as well as in textbooks such as *The Heath Anthology of American Literature,* which Houghton Mifflin started publishing in 1998. The older Riverside series, excellent in its day, ran the risk of appearing outdated; the editors were long retired or deceased, and the authors were viewed by some as too exclusive.

Yet the name Riverside and the ideas behind it continued to have appeal. The name stood for distinction and worth in the publication of

America's literary heritage. Houghton Mifflin's New Riverside Series, initiated in the year 2000, is designed to uphold the Riverside reputation for excellence while offering a more inclusive range of authors. The Series also provides today's reader with books that contain, in addition to notable literary works, introductions by influential critics, as well as a variety of stimulating materials that bring alive the debates, the conversations, the social and cultural movements within which America's literary classics were formed.

Thus emerged the book you have in hand. Each volume of the New Riverside Editions will contain the basic elements that we think today's readers find interesting and useful: important literary works by significant authors, incisive introductions, and a variety of contextual materials to make the literary text fully engaging. These books will be useful in many kinds of classrooms, but they are also designed to offer the casual reader the enjoyment of a good read in a fresh and accessible format. Among the first group of New Riverside Editions are familiar titles, such as Henry David Thoreau's *Walden* and Mark Twain's *Adventures of Huckleberry Finn*. There are also works in fresh new combinations, such as the collection of early captivity narratives and the volume that pairs texts by Ralph Waldo Emerson and Margaret Fuller. And there are well-known works in distinctively interesting formats, such as the volume containing Edith Wharton's *The Age of Innocence* and the volume of writings by Stephen Crane. Future books will include classics as well as works drawing renewed attention.

The New Riverside Editions will provide discriminating readers with a wide range of important literary works, contextual materials that vividly illuminate those works, and the best of recent critical commentary and analysis. And because we have not confined our editors to a single monotonous format, we think our readers will find that each volume in this new series has a character appropriate to the literary work it presents.

We expect the New Riverside Editions to bring to the twenty-first century the same literary publishing distinction of its nineteenth- and twentieth-century predecessors.

Introduction

Susan K. Harris

A lthough he was christened Samuel Langhorne Clemens, and his friends and business associates knew him by that name throughout his life, by the mid-1870s Clemens's pen name, "Mark Twain," had become the label by which he was recognized by an increasing number of his compatriots. Over the next century, Twain came to be regarded as an American icon, a writer whose works embodied an essential American spirit that transcended Samuel Clemens's own time and place. In our day, the pseudonym is so ubiquitous that a week rarely passes without "Mark Twain" being evoked in a newspaper or other medium. In the mid-1990s, Twain even appeared as a character in two episodes of the television science fiction series *Star Trek: The Next Generation.* Perhaps the surest sign of our sense of Mark Twain's contemporaneity is the fact that his 1884 classic, *Adventures of Huckleberry Finn,* is periodically banned in our public schools, making it one of the few nineteenth-century novels to be regarded as still threatening.

Yet even though the name "Mark Twain" has come to signal an authorial presence that seems timeless, part of the fabric of our own lives, it is also important for us to understand the ways in which Twain's writings were rooted in the particularities of the nineteenth century. Because *Huckleberry Finn* is the subject of so much controversy, it is especially useful to understand how the book evolved from Twain's own environment. Formally—that is, in the way it is structured and the kinds of characters it features—and thematically—in the issues with which it deals—*Huckleberry Finn* drew on Mark Twain's cultural environment as the writer slowly shaped his novel. Both Twain's nineteenth-century contexts and twentieth-century readers' responses to this book help us understand how—and why—it continues to be vigorously discussed well over one hundred years after its original publication.

When Mark Twain began composing *Huckleberry Finn* in the late 1870s, he wrote to an audience accustomed to a steady fare of short fiction about America's diverse geographical and social populations. Dialect and backwoods tales were especially popular because they brought the peculiarities, the "local color," of the hinterlands to the parlors of the urban middle class. From the eighteenth century onward, readers were introduced to rural, backwoods, and frontier Americans through the eyes of writers who specialized in presenting class and ethnic differences as bizarre aberrations from an implicit norm. Even though the stories seemed to be reporting authentic behaviors, they were not actually objective about their subjects. Contemporary readers were familiar with the conventions of regionalist literature, however, and they understood that despite the liveliness with which the regional characters were presented, they were not intended as positive role models. Rather, such figures were usually beyond the confines of civilized society.

The most typical form for communicating these assumptions featured a double narrative: it began with a framing narrator who told a story about the strange people inhabiting the regions he (or occasionally she) had visited and segued into a story narrated by a native of the region, who always speaks in the vernacular and often in dialect. In this way the author could simultaneously exhibit and control the regional character's voice and attitudes; that is, the author used the framing narrator to mediate the relationship between the vernacular speaker and the reader. At times the framing narrator even told the reader how to evaluate the vernacular-speaking character. Almost inevitably, these strategies meant that regional stories championed middle-class values, reinforcing the status quo. A. B. Longstreet's *Georgia Scenes,* J. B. Thorpe's "The Big Bear of Arkansas," Twain's own "The Celebrated Jumping Frog of Calaveras County," and, much later, Charles Chesnutt's *Conjure Woman* stories are all masterworks of this genre.

By 1884, when *Adventures of Huckleberry Finn* was first published, this tide of regional writing had already ebbed. In its wake, however, it left not only a formal structure for creating regionalist literature but also a series of scenarios and characters, often comic, to which readers had been educated to respond. Picturesque figures such as Mississippi riverboatmen and Kentucky hunters littered the literary landscape, while camp meetings, "frolics," and brawls suggested the level of group dynamics. Most important, perhaps, writers of this genre delighted in representing regional dialects, often pitting the literary dialect of the framing narrator against the oral dialect of the second narrator and his characters. In general, American readers knew that when nonliterary speech forms appeared in a story, they signaled entry into an imaginative realm of colorful local "types."

Samuel Clemens spent his childhood in the antebellum Mississippi River valley, which abounded in both oral and written forms of regional tales, and his young manhood on the river and in the far West, where he became friends with some of the best storytellers of his generation. Although he also read many other kinds of literature, he was deeply influenced by local-color traditions, which formed the structural foundations and provided many of the characters for much of his fiction. Many of the scenes in *Huckleberry Finn* and other works by Mark Twain were intimately related to his predecessors' writings. Anyone who has read Johnson J. Hooper's "Simon Suggs Attends a Camp Meeting," for example, instantly recognizes where Twain got the idea for the King's conning of the Pokeville camp meeting. Additionally, Twain knew that his readers would laugh at Huck's rendition of Hamlet's soliloquy because they were familiar not only with Shakespeare's plays but with the hundreds of Shakespeare parodies and pastiches that were wildly popular on the American stage. However, much of the cultural context that Twain could take for granted has been lost to subsequent generations, and it is difficult for modern readers to appreciate many of the scenes (not to speak of the jokes) that Twain's first readers enjoyed.

The first section of the New Riverside *Adventures of Huckleberry Finn* introduces some of *Huckleberry Finn*'s historical contexts to familiarize readers with some of the issues that concerned Twain's contemporaries. For instance, Steven Mailloux's work on the popularity of "bad boy" books in the late nineteenth century reminds us that some readers (especially parents) resisted this novel because they perceived it as glorifying juvenile delinquency, and in a society that feared loss of control over its young people, the novel seemed to threaten social cohesion. The essay on slavery by Lorenzo Greene, Gary Kremer, and Antonio Holland, in contrast, reminds readers of the conditions under which a slave like Jim lived and shows why he would risk the penalties of escaping. In a lighter vein, the Reverend William Henry Milburn's contemporary, and sympathetic, account of camp meetings highlights the boisterousness of frontier religion, and Lawrence Levine's discussion of Shakespeare productions in Mississippi River towns provides a rich context for some of the shenanigans of the King and the Duke and, more important, for the people who came to see their shows. These selections demonstrate the diverse backgrounds that contemporary readers brought to *Huckleberry Finn*.

Besides essays on the historical contexts of Twain's novel, this edition includes a sampling of twentieth-century critical readings, evidence of the relevance that this classic has had for later generations. As the twentieth century progressed and the United States moved further and further from the material conditions shaping *Huckleberry Finn*, readers brought the concerns of their own eras to the text. For instance, twentieth-century readers were no longer threatened by Huck's behavior; instead, they were increasingly impressed by his voice. Even Twain's contemporaries had noticed that in eliminating the framing narrator and allowing Huck to speak for himself, directly to the reader, Twain had liberated a vernacular sensibility. Perhaps because Huck makes his own case, he seems neither comic nor bizarre; to most twentieth-century critics he is a sensitive, if naive, preadolescent who, unknown to himself, represents a quintessentially moral position in a world that is cruel, selfish, and hypocritical.

Weary of high-culture pretensions, many twentieth-century Americans have wanted to believe that vernacular voices could speak from a moral sensibility. In the second half of the century, white critics such as Henry Nash Smith wrote influential essays on Huck as a representative American spirit, while African American writers and critics, also fascinated by Huck's contribution to the unleashing of the American vernacular, discussed black literature's indebtedness to Twain. David L. Smith, for example, commented on Twain's use of racial discourse to undermine American racism. Recently, critics such as Shelley Fisher Fishkin have taken another tack, tracing Twain's debts to African American voices in his construction of Huck. Also in the late twentieth century, African American readers questioned Twain's constructions of blackness, especially regarding Jim, and protested the book's status as an American classic. Toni Morrison's essay, which begins by disclosing that "fear and alarm are what I remember most about my first encounter with Mark Twain's *Adventures of Huckleberry Finn,*" most cogently presents the emotional and intellectual challenge that the book has presented to many African American readers. All of these essays demonstrate the extent to which twentieth-century readers, whether they focus on Jim's flight from chattel slavery or Huck's escape from the confines of small-town hypocrisies, have debated the "form of freedom" (as Alan Trachtenberg describes it) outlined in *Adventures of Huckleberry Finn.*

Whereas the essays in the contexts section remind us of the relationship between Twain's novel and the writings of his contemporaries, the critical essays expose the concerns of successive generations and the methods through which those generations bring their interests to their readings of any given text. The fact that many of these later readings ignore nineteenth-century conditions and values should alert us to the many ways a literary work can be interpreted. Perhaps one of the reasons most people consider *Adventures of Huckleberry Finn* a classic is that it lends itself to so many readings, so many concerns. Although Mark Twain himself defined a classic as "something everyone wants to have read but nobody wants to read," his own classic has maintained a steady popularity for well over a hundred years, primarily because it provides an occasion for vigorous debates about American characters and values and about American definitions of race and justice, issues at the very heart of our society.

Despite the hundreds of essays written about this work, critics have not yet exhausted its possibilities for commentary, largely because each generation perceives new areas for investigation as its own interests and priorities shift. For instance, although a handful of scholars have examined Edward Winsor Kemble's nearly two hundred illustrations for the original edition of *Adventures of Huckleberry Finn*, there has been little bold discussion of the pictures' racial stereotyping and its effects on readers, either contemporary or modern. Such studies would certainly elucidate nineteenth-century racial dynamics; additionally, they might help to explain why some readers experience a violent antipathy to the book. As *Huckleberry Finn* moves into its third century, we do well to remember its roots in the culture of its time. But as the sample readings reproduced here illustrate, we should not fear using it to illuminate the troubles, and the possibilities, of our own time.

A Note on the Text and Its Illustrations

Susan K. Harris

Adventures of Huckleberry Finn was first published in England, in December 1884; the first American publication followed in February 1885. The New Riverside text is that of the American first edition as emended by Everett Emerson for the supplementary text to the *Heath Anthology of American Literature* in 1998. These changes include a lengthened version of Chapter 16, known as the "Raftsmen's Passage." Although this episode was originally written for inclusion in *Adventures of Huckleberry Finn,* Twain first published it in *Life on the Mississippi* in 1883. He subsequently omitted it from *Huckleberry Finn* because his publisher, Charles L. Webster, suggested he shorten the text.

Edward Winsor Kemble illustrated the American first edition, except for the illustrations for the "Raftsmen's Passage," which were drawn by John Harley for its publication in *Life on the Mississippi.* The New Riverside edition features Kemble's illustrations for the frontispiece and the last page of *Adventures of Huckleberry Finn,* as well as his opening illustration for each chapter. It also features Harley's opening illustration for the "Raftsmen's Passage."

Contexts

Map of the area covered in the novel. Drawn by Charles Dibner.

THE COMPOSITION OF
ADVENTURES OF HUCKLEBERRY FINN

Victor A. Doyno

Twain originally invented Huckleberry Finn in *The Adventures of Tom Sawyer.* These two boys provided a great dramatic contrast; Twain characterized Tom as a reader of romance fiction who was eager for societal fame and success, but he presented Huck as an outsider, an extremely poor, homeless, unfed child who did not attend school. Despite his background, Huck becomes a quite admirable, honest, brave, intelligent, frank character in Tom's *Adventures.* In fact, Huck begins to take over Tom's novel simply because he is a much more intriguing and complex character. Toward the end of *Tom Sawyer* Twain devotes considerable time, space, and attention to Huck's cleverness, integrity, and way of speaking, taking the first steps in his fictional exploration of how such an unsocialized child might both fit into and resist the dominant culture.

1875–1876

When Twain was finishing *The Adventures of Tom Sawyer,* his good friend William Dean Howells suggested that he continue Tom's story into adulthood. But Twain apparently realized that he was no longer quite so interested in Tom. Instead he seemed to feel drawn to a different character and a first-person point of view. Twain replied to Howells, "I have finished the story & didn't take the chap beyond boyhood. I believe it would be fatal to do it in any shape but autobiographically—like Gil Blas. I perhaps made a mistake in not writing it in the first person." [1]

Twain already had a distinct literary tradition in mind. *The Adventures of Gil Blas,* a picaresque novel by Le Sage, presents the experiences of a Spanish country lad, narrated in his own voice, with the immediacy and limited point of view of the originally naive narrator/adventurer. The lad is a marginalized, low-status traveler who observes and comments on society as he tells a sequence of exciting episodes. Gil Blas begins as a moral, ethical youth, trained in his parents' religion, but he quickly notices a great deal of hypocrisy about religion and gradually becomes utterly indifferent to the laws of a society which has no useful or rewarding place

---

From *Adventures of Huckleberry Finn.* New York: Oxford UP, 1996.
[1] *Twain–Howells Letters* I, 91.

for him. This novel includes countless deceptions, impersonations, and inset stories; Gil spends some time in captivity and in prison.

The recent rediscovery of Twain's 665-page holograph manuscript of the first half of the novel provides much new information about the composition process.[2] For his new project Twain decided—famously—to create a first-person point of view; the early working title was "Huck Finn's Autobiography." This massively important decision enabled Twain to use the eyes and voice of a naive, good-hearted, highly intelligent, but relatively unsocialized observer. Huck seems to be extraordinarily perceptive, but he seldom confides anything of his own internal or psychological life to the people he meets. Instead he tells almost everything to us, his listeners/readers, much as the black child in "Sociable Jimmy" entertained Twain with his nonstop talking.[3] Huck's apparent trust in us seems quite engaging. In response, we tend to trust this child because we are completely limited to his unique point of view. Accordingly, we share his fears, his excitements, his experiences; as a result our human ability to share another's life grows.

Probably Twain originally planned to include much satire about religious hypocrisy, as *Gil Blas* had and as Twain's next novel, *A Connecticut Yankee,* would. Huck's innocence and ignorance of cultural norms enabled Twain to put some priceless, naive, sarcastic commentary on American life in his mouth. In the first few chapters Twain explores the world of Tom Sawyer's village from Huck's perspective, with special attention to Huck's humorous observations about adult religious practices. (It is significant and revealing that Twain at first had Jim belong to the Widow Douglas, a sympathetic character, but later made his owner the mean, authoritarian, Bible-teaching Miss Watson, probably after coming up with the plot idea that Jim would run away from slavery.)

---

[2] The manuscript of approximately the first half of the novel was lost until early 1991. The finders of the document initially attempted to sell it, but the Buffalo and Erie County Public Library Board asserted a claim to ownership. The legal issue was settled by negotiation, and now both the first and last halves of the manuscript are on display at the library and available for scholarly investigation. My summary here of the composition of the novel draws upon three and a half years of scholarly exploration. Episodes from the newly discovered manuscript portion and facsimile pages can be found in the 1996 Random House edition of *Huckleberry Finn*. A more complete study of the second half can be found in Victor A. Doyno, *Writing* Huck Finn: *Mark Twain's Creative Process* (Philadelphia: University of Pennsylvania Press, 1991).

[3] See Shelley Fisher Fishkin, *Was Huck Black? Mark Twain and African-American Voices* (New York: Oxford University Press, 1993).

Early on the novelist faced a creative problem. Why would an inexperienced boy like Huck be motivated to leave his familiar town, his friend, and many newfound comforts, to go off to a totally unknown world which he could not even imagine? Twain hit upon the unexpected plot swerve of having Huck's father return to town in order to gain control of the boy's gold. Pap Finn's arrival is announced by the bootprint with a cross, a religious symbol which he uses for no positive worshiping purpose but only to ward off the devil. Perhaps surprised by this plot development, Twain had Huck safeguard his money by "selling" it to Judge Thatcher, a benevolent caretaker. And Twain originally wrote the passage about Jim and the fortune-telling hairball as a separate chapter; only later, after 1880, did he combine Huck's consulting the judge and Jim into one chapter. The evidence suggests that the author at first did not know what his plot would lead to, and that he used the hairball's prognostications to imagine a few long-range Dickensian plot possibilities. Twain revised Jim's dialect in this scene with great care, and the dramatic interaction between Huck and Jim is engaging and amusing, as when they seem to conspire to fool the hairball into accepting a counterfeit coin. Although Twain thought of the judge and Jim as parallel helpful adults, there is no evidence that when he finished writing the first version of manuscript chapter 5 he had imagined that Jim might run away.

Once Twain decided to have Pap Finn, a child abandoner, return to become a violent child abuser, he stumbled upon a motive for Huck to flee. Twain's skill in characterizing Huck's father seems quite remarkable; this repulsive man is a selfish, nasty, advanced alcoholic, a seething mass of hatreds. Pap Finn's rant about education and the government and the "mulatter" college professor who was allowed to vote touched upon the real post-Reconstruction issues facing a compromised federal government, and upon the real problems of Blacks who wished to vote; although voting had been difficult for free Blacks in the 1845 era, it was far more dangerous and confrontational in the 1872 and 1876 elections. American readers in 1885—and in decades to come—might have winced at this reminder of the racist restrictions and continuing violence directed at Black voters.

Twain initially considered having Huck escape from his father's cabin to set off tramping across Illinois. Then the novel would have been a "road" book, like *Gil Blas,* instead of a "river" book. But when he remembered the June rise in the river level, with logs and rafts coming from upriver, he soon had Huck spot a free-floating canoe, and that gave him the mechanism for Huck to travel down the river Twain knew so well.

Manuscript evidence suggests that when Huck arrived by canoe on Jackson's Island, Twain at first thought of having his hero stay there for a while, because the author stocked the island with a lot of unripe fruit which could be eaten a short time later. But Twain may have been a bit puzzled by the *Robinson Crusoe*-like moment when Huck first discovers the campfire on Jackson's Island because he did not yet know in his imagination who else was there. When he finally realized, after much sequential revision, that the person by the campfire was Jim, he was so excited—and, I think, happy—that he wrote "I bet I was glad to see him!" in running script, lifting his pen off the page between words only four times (his habit when writing very rapidly) instead of the normal seven times. Placing Jim by the campfire was a crucial discovery/creation on the part of Twain's imagination, because it gave Huck a companion who would give the book surprising new possibilities.

In the manuscript version of this part of the novel, Huck is eager to hear why Jim is on Jackson's Island and promises to keep Jim's secret. After Jim admits that he has run away because he overheard Miss Watson talking about selling him downriver, Huck seems surprised, and Jim reminds him of his promise. Huck immediately offers to shake Jim's hand, a symbolic sealing of their agreement, as between two equals. But Twain decided to cancel that gesture of reciprocity, probably because the handshake would imply an interpersonal mutuality far too early in the novel. The relationship has to be earned through future shared experiences, and through Huck's struggle with himself in what Twain would later call a battle between "a sound heart and a deformed conscience."[4]

After Jim tells Huck how he came to be on the island, they begin to talk about investments and bank failures, quite an odd topic for these two characters to be discussing in, say, 1845. But many Americans knew in 1876 and in 1885—although very few Americans know now—that the Freedmen's Bank that was set up after the Civil War had failed, costing the Black depositors about $27 million in very hard earned nickels and dimes. Jim's talk about the dangers of "specalat'n'" must have sounded a bittersweet note when written in 1876 or when read in 1885, because there had been no federal reimbursement to the Black depositors. Indeed, many white readers may have lost money themselves—and may therefore have identified with Jim's attitudes—because at least ninety-eight banks had failed in the 1873 panic, and even more would do so over the next few years.

The two fugitives form a cooperative partnership, experiencing nature and danger, but Huck's prank in fooling Jim to think that they were not

---

[4] Notebook entry, August 23, 1895.

separated in the fog is a violation of personal trust—and Huck shows the moral decency to apologize. But then, once a white had apologized to a slave, Twain's novel was different. Huck's clever, misleading lies fool the slave hunters, save Jim, and cause the intuitively decent boy to feel even more confused.

The manuscript reveals that Twain wrote the 1876 portion beyond the steamboat/raft crash, going on to take Huck into the Grangerford home. Then Twain apparently stopped for three or four years, in mid-episode— right where Huck asks Buck what a feud is! Twain, who knew perfectly well what a feud is, was probably trying to decide whether to hurry Huck away from there and continue downriver or to stop Huck's journey long enough to develop in a few chapters precisely how horrible a feud could be. But how could Twain realistically have his narrator both observe a feud closely and escape safely? He set his 446-page manuscript aside.

1879–1880

Between 1876 and 1880 the concept of the Southern slave-based plantation such as the Grangerfords' was undergoing a nostalgia-driven postwar romanticization that was partially political, pro-Southern, and anti-Republican in effect. Twain apparently decided that this family was an appropriate target for multilevel satire. Clearly the Grangerfords are rich enough, with more than a hundred slaves, to give Huck his own personal servant, a generously intended, polite gesture which quietly asserts their wealth. The Grangerford family represents farming and agricultural interests (the Grange movement). Twain revised to have their enemies carry the name Shepherdson, representing grazing interests. This murderous feud symbolizes larger economic and land-use conflicts. Only Mark Twain could begin the episode with sharp satire on the mortuary school of poetry, describe the pride-driven hatreds, narrate the crying of a child in combat, and end with the wrenching, understated emotions of Huck's covering of Buck's face.

Twain's return trip to Europe in 1878–79 had reminded him about the Old World's aristocratic social structures and the resultant abuses of power supposedly based on birth-related privileges. Accordingly, when two con men take over the raft, they grotesquely, comically claim the titles of European nobility. Because Twain's imagination often liked to present both a serious and a comic version of events, the King and the Duke soon begin to rehearse *Romeo and Juliet*—a parodic re-creation of the tragic plight of the young lovers in the Grangerford-Shepherdson feud.

In the 218-page portion of the novel composed in 1879–80, which covered events from the feud to the beginning of the attempted lynching of Colonel Sherburn, Twain lashed out at several satiric targets. The two fraudulent noblemen soon enslave both Huck and Jim, dramatizing the eternal ingenuity of human evil, with an incongruous, humorous European twist. Twain also sketched more criticisms of religion in passages on missionary fundraising and a camp meeting.

Twain presents the Duke's thievery at the printing shop in a caustic tone that has a sharp historical reference. Before the Civil War, slave hunters and kidnappers could come to the free states, write down a precisely detailed physical description of any Black person they saw, and send it to a Southern newspaper. The published "fugitive slave notice" could then be mailed back up north to the slave hunters, who could proceed to seize the Black person, with federal help, and transport that person south to be sold at an immense profit. The Duke's fabricated runaway slave notice was not simply a plot-directed prank; readers cognizant of events in the 1850s would have understood the bitter satire underlying the comedic jesting.

The shooting of Boggs gave Twain a chance to portray and realistically criticize the violences of American small-town life. Twain despised the dueling tradition, and his imagination has Colonel Sherburn, with a posture and gestures which parody the duel, deliberately execute the unarmed, drunken Boggs, before the time limit, with two shots, in front of the victim's daughter. The "code" of a Southern gentleman's "honor" has seldom seemed more cruel and self-indulgent.

During this compositional period, Twain came up with the idea of warning his readers about how to take his book by writing the "Notice" we now find in revised form right after the published title page. But the manuscript form of the "Notice" does not have the middle warning. Significantly, Twain was first concerned about motive, narrative, and plot. By the time he was revising for publication, in 1883 or 1884, he decided to add an ironic warning for any readers wondering about a moral.

1883–1885

After a three-year break which included a trip down the Mississippi, Twain finished and revised the book in a burst of energy in 1883 and 1884.[5] One should not exaggerate or sentimentalize Huck's moral growth

---

[5] A photographic facsimile of the second half of the manuscript has been edited by Louis Budd, with an afterword by William Loos (1983).

in the chapters composed during this time. Although Huck is controlled by circumstances in the Wilks section, he has learned to treat Jim with loyalty and to attempt to protect his friend. But he has not yet reached a stage of wider compassion or moral development which would permit him to extend his sense of justice to all Blacks. It seems quite realistic for a boy to reach this narrow but nevertheless admirable and necessary stage of moral growth, in which he decides to protect or save his friend, the individual he knows and cares about. It would be quite another level of moral awareness to generalize to an entire class of victims. Still, Huck's willingness to go to hell is a brave rejection of the usually unquestioned religious system.

After the two adult scoundrels have sold Jim back into a kind of slavery, Huck's attempts to find and help Jim take him to the Phelps farm, where Twain was able to line up several more satiric targets, almost one behind the other; although these targets seem relatively distinct, an arrow or a bullet through one often pierces another behind it.

Perhaps Twain's most significant target in this book about liberation and "sivilization" was the treatment of Blacks, both before and after emancipation, and after the breakdown of "Reconstruction." Twain knew that the problems confronting many free people of color before the war, and most emancipated slaves and other Blacks after the war, were enormous and extremely complex.[6] Blacks were obstructed from voting in the 1870s as in the 1840s, and they were captured, imprisoned, and leased out for hard labor in both eras as well. The convict-lease system, which Twain's friend George Washington Cable vehemently opposed, was instituted across the post–Civil War South to continue the profitable exploitation of Blacks. Tom Sawyer desires to duplicate the prison "escapes" of European adventurers while participating in the extended unjust imprisonment of the freed slave Jim. The child Tom and the country both, in effect, were keeping the freed slave down. It is revealing that this complex satire on white supremacism did not begin to trouble most American readers until after 1930. Even today, many Americans are perhaps not so different from the easily befuddled, unknowingly hypocritical Uncle Silas, who could not understand the application of the religious message that he was reading in his Bible (Acts 17) to his enslavement of another human being. Even a good man, such as Twain's uncle John Quarles or the fictional Uncle Silas Phelps, could unquestioningly accept slavery.

Twain found another target for satire in Tom Sawyer's naive, foolish trust in European romantic literature featuring nobles in adventures of

---

[6] See Twain's letter to Karl Gerhardt, May 1, 1883, in *Mark Twain: Selected Writings of an American Skeptic*, ed. V. Doyno (Buffalo: Prometheus, 1983), 222.

escape. Twain realized that American publishers could "pirate" and sell European fiction very cheaply. This practice, although legal because the country did not subscribe to any international copyright agreement, put American authors at a disadvantage in getting their books published and purchased. As a result, Twain thought, American youth was being encouraged by cheap "foreign" fiction to develop a completely wrongheaded set of philosophical values about "nobility" and inherited privilege.

The final portion of *Huckleberry Finn,* in which Tom enacts fantasies derived from such fiction, has struck many readers as problematic. After the King and the Duke have sold Jim, whom they have no right to sell, Tom Sawyer happens along and does not reveal that he knows that Jim has already been freed by Miss Watson. Instead he allows Jim to be kept in a prison shanty while he (knowingly) and Huck (unknowingly) act out a complicated, parodic, dangerous escape attempt. Huck protests Tom's elaborate plans but reluctantly goes along because he trusts Tom's superior literacy. Early commentators criticized the length of this escape episode but not the injustice and deceit of Tom's attitudes. But now many readers are utterly outraged by Tom's trickery and by the fiction which keeps a freed Jim imprisoned.

Yet Jim's condition resonates all too accurately with the situation of freed Black people in the South both before and after the Civil War. The Constitution, article 1, section 9, states that habeas corpus cannot be suspended except in time of rebellion or invasion. (The same section also states that titles of nobility shall not be granted by the United States.) The King, the Duke, and Tom have inflicted harm, committing the tort of unlawful imprisonment; Jim, Huck, and America have been damaged by the supremacist violators of these laws, who would replicate forms of slavery. In the postwar period similar illegal and oppressive measures against ex-slaves and other Blacks were commonplace, and Twain certainly knew it. On August 1, 1880, on the occasion of the anniversary of the nonviolent emancipation of the slaves in the British West Indies, Frederick Douglass spoke in Elmira, New York, where Twain was summering at the time; Douglass referred specifically to violations in the American South of the Fourteenth and Fifteenth Amendments.[7] In Twain's fictional treatment the King and the Duke—confident of their inherent power and supremacy—threaten Jim's life and deprive him of his property and liberty, while Tom Sawyer willingly participates in and prolongs Jim's imprisonment. These actions powerfully evoke the unlawful acts committed

---

[7] See *The Life and Times of Frederick Douglass* (1881; reprint, New York: Gramercy, 1993), 491–504.

with impunity by many whites after the breakdown of Reconstruction. Twain was too realistic a social observer to say that all was well in America. The country was forcing many of the recently freed slaves into forms of involuntary servitude.

When Twain had nearly completed his novel, he inserted a long section that became part of chapter 12 and all of chapters 13 and 14, mainly about Huck and Jim on the wreck of the *Walter Scott,* their overhearing the murderous thieves, and Huck's fooling the steam-ferry captain. In the portion of the insertion that is now chapter 14, Huck and Jim discuss "adventures," and kings and aristocrats and the lack of them in America, and the common humanity of a man and a Frenchman—a fine metafictional way for Twain to prepare for the topics that will emerge later in his book. His creative and editorial processes were thorough and recursive. He had probably started the novel with relatively modest goals, but as he wrote and revised he began to discover and construct certain meanings about freedom and imprisonment, individuality and social conventions. Although Twain's early concerns centered on plot and narrative, as he plunged into and through his eventful, picaresque fiction he found and created levels of complexity which still reward careful reading.

BARGES

George E. Bates Jr., et al.

. . . The design for [upper Mississippi barges] came with Western European boat builders who were familiar with the craft that plied their native European canals. Additionally, some of the nineteenth century craft were patterned after the original river craft of the region—the Indian's dugout canoe and bull boat.

The early French fur traders used the *pirogue* (simply a hollowed-out log) and the *bateau*. The *bateau* was a keelless flat-bottomed boat with ends tapering to points. A single *bateau* could carry up to forty tons and was propelled by oars, poles, and—when the wind was right—square sails. Sometimes as many as eighteen or twenty rowers were employed to propel the *bateau*. The cargo was protected by an awning or wooden shelter.

From *Historic Life Styles in the Upper Mississippi River Valley*. Lanham: UP of America, 1983.

Shortly before 1800, a boat builder, perhaps someone familiar with the canal boats of Western Europe, placed a long beam about four inches square, lengthwise to the bottom of a *bateau*. The beam held the boat on course when being towed and protected the bottom from shock if the vessel happened to hit a rock or sandbar.

The ordinary keelboat was forty to eighty feet in length, seven to ten feet at the beam, and drew about two feet when fully loaded. Each keelboat could carry from fifteen to fifty tons of cargo. The average cargo was thirty tons. The center of the keelboat was hollow and frequently covered to protect the freight. Around the sides, one found a walkway, with cleats driven in, which the crew used while poling the craft. At the bow, one found seats for from four to twelve rowers, and, at the stern, one found a long oar, used for steering.

Flatboats were square, with no keel, between twenty and one hundred feet in length, and from twelve to twenty feet in width. When the voyage was completed, the vessels were frequently stripped, and the planking was used for lumber. In general, the overall shape of the flatboat resembled contemporary barges.

Keelboats and flatboats seem to have been indigenous to the Ohio River and the lower Mississippi. Most were built in Pittsburgh and on tributaries of the Ohio River, where artisans from Western Europe and the Atlantic Coast had been gathered to organize and staff the building facilities. Although constructed in the East, these boats were utilized wherever water transportation was needed, including the upper Mississippi.

FROM SUNUP TO SUNDOWN
The Life of the Slave

*Lorenzo J. Greene, Gary R. Kremer,
and Antonio F. Holland*

Slavery was, above all else, an economic institution. Masters were interested in getting as much work out of their slaves as they could year round; consequently, the life of the slave was determined largely by this fact. Contrary to what some historians once believed, slavery remained a profitable and viable institution right down to the Civil War. In some regions, such as Callaway County, slavery was the most important factor in maintaining the economy.

Missouri slaves had a wider range of skills and occupations than slaves in the South because of the different types of farming. Although the land was abundant and fertile, the colder weather meant a shorter growing season that was not suitable for growing cotton in large quantities; therefore, Missouri farmers and their slaves practiced mixed farming. Hemp, tobacco, wheat, oats, hay, corn, and other feed grains were the main staples, but Missouri was also known for its fine cattle, sheep, horses, and pigs.

The majority of Missouri's slaves worked as field hands on farms, but many others were valets, butlers, handymen, carpenters, common laborers, maids, nurses, and cooks. Isabelle Henderson from Saline County worked "in the house of my master and mistress. . . . I was taught to sew and had to help make clothes for the other slaves. I nursed all the children of my mistress and one time I was hired out to the white preacher's family to take care of his children when his wife was sick." Emma Knight, born on the farm of Will and Emily Ely near Florida, Missouri, and her three sisters "cut weeds along the fences, pulled weeds in the garden and helped the mistress with hoeing. We had to feed the stock, sheep, hogs, and calves because the young masters wouldn't do the work. In the evening we were made to knit a finger width, and if we missed a stitch we would have to pull all the yarn out and do it over." Marie Askin Simpson, born about 1854 near Steelville, remembered how her master's family

> kept me busy waiting on them. Carrying water from the spring, hunting eggs and a lot of other little things. . . . Mother did most of the cooking

---

From *Missouri's Black Heritage*. Rev. ed. Columbia: U of Missouri Press, 1993.

and washing and ironing. In those days they did the washing with battlin'
sticks and boards. They layed the clothes on this board and battled them
with battlin sticks. . . . We boiled our clothes in big iron kettles over a fire
in the yard. We made our own lye and soap.

Richard Bruner, a Missouri slave born about 1840, remembered being "a water-boy to de field hands before I were big enough to wuk in
the fields." Another Missouri slave, Mark Discus, born about 1850, recalled: "When I was nine years old I cut all the corn stalks offen a forty-
acre field with a hoe. We had to work from sun up 'til dark too." Lewis
Mundy, who was born five miles north of La Belle, also worked in the
fields as a youth: "When I was small I rode one of the oxen and harrowed
the fields. When I was about ten or eleven I plowed with oxen." Gus
Smith, born in 1845 near Rich Fountain in Osage County, recalled:
"When we didn't have much work, we would get up about five o'clock
every morning, but in busy season we had to be up and ready to work
at daybreak."

Hiring slaves out was also a profitable gain for Missouri masters.
Not only did they receive payment for the slaves' services, but they did
not have to feed or house the slaves since that was the responsibility of
the hirer. Some slaves found themselves working at the Maramec Iron
Works for one hundred dollars a year. When railroads began moving
through Missouri, slaves were hired to lay the rails at the rate of twenty
dollars a month; brickyards paid a similar sum. Many slaves were hired
out to the owners of riverboats where they worked as deck hands, cabin
boys, and stevedores for approximately fifteen dollars a month.

Wages for slaves were usually less than those paid to whites for
similar work. William Black, a slave from Marion County, recalled that
when he was eight years old, he was bonded out to Sam Briggs of
New London. "Mr. Briggs was a good master and I had little to do.
My duty was to take his children to school and go after them in the
evening. In the meantime I just piddled around de fields." Another
slave, Margaret Davis of Cape Girardeau, was hired out as a nurse-
maid to a white family when she was just ten years old. She was so
small that she remembered having to stand on a chair in order to wash
clothes.

Missouri's population grew rapidly during the decades after it became a state. Attracted by the virgin Missouri soil, people from Kentucky,
Tennessee, North Carolina, and Virginia poured into the state. Many of
the settlers brought slaves, and those who did not came with the hope that
they would one day own slaves. The following figures offer some idea of
the rapid growth of slavery in the state before the Civil War:

MISSOURI'S POPULATION, 1810–1860

Year	Total pop.	Whites	Slaves	Free Blacks	% Slaves
1810	20,845	17,227	3,011	607	14.4
1820	66,076	54,903	9,797	376	14.8
1830	140,445	115,364	25,091	569	17.8
1840	383,702	322,295	57,891	1,478	15.2
1850	682,044	592,004	87,422	2,618	12.8
1860	1,182,012	1,063,489	114,509	3,572	9.7

These figures reveal that the white population of Missouri grew by more than sixty-one-fold between 1810 and 1860. The slave population increased more than thirty-seven-fold during the same period. In 1830 slaves represented 17.8 percent of the total Missouri population. By 1860 that percentage had dropped to about 9.8 in large part due to the influx during the 1840s and 1850s of Germans who were against slavery.

In spite of the large numbers of slaves, there were few large slave-holding plantations in Missouri. Only thirty-six of Missouri's 114 counties had one thousand or more slaves. According to Bill Sims, a slave born in 1839 in Osceola, Missouri, "A man who owned ten slaves was considered wealthy." Jabez F. Smith of Jackson County at one time owned 165 blacks. John W. Ragland, the largest slaveholder in Cooper County, owned seventy slaves. Daniel Ligon, the largest slaveholder in Lewis County, owned twenty-six slaves. Most Missourians owned none, and for those who did the average was four blacks per slaveholding family. When there were only one or two slaves, the master and his family often worked alongside them in the fields. . . .

The treatment of slaves varied greatly, depending upon the moods and attitudes of individual masters. Even the best-treated black slave stood in a servile position to all of white society. From the owner's point of view, slavery was justified on economic, spiritual, and social grounds. Blacks were regarded as inferior. The master argued that he was doing them a favor by enslaving and caring for them. (Some slaveholders even went so far as to argue that blacks were grateful to whites for their enslavement.) Nobody expressed this idea better than United States Senator James Green of Lewis County. In 1849 he wrote that of the two races, "one [was] vastly inferior to the other." As the inferior race, blacks were obligated to be subservient to whites in all things. For the black, this arrangement resulted in an "immense good, an incalculable benefit, both moral and physical." According to Green, blacks were not only inferior to whites, but they were "happy inferiors": "Our Negro is a sleek, fat-sided fellow. He loves to eat and to laugh, and give him his bellyfull and he is as happy as a prince. Work is his element. Meat and bread and the banjo are his happiness." Present scholarship does not accept this description of the slave; it is a stereotype invented by slaveowners in response to attacks by abolitionists upon slavery.

Slavery was an inhumane institution. Slaves were supposed to be protected by law from excessively harsh treatment. Any person found guilty of cruel or inhuman treatment of slaves was fined or sent to jail, but slaveholders paid little or no attention to the law. Cruel treatment, such as a female slave whose master had left her hanging by her thumbs in St. Louis in 1839, was not uncommon.

The harsh system of slavery was able to exist only by forcing blacks to stand in awe of whites. Slaveholders as a group were willing to use whatever means they could to instill fear into slaves. They believed a fearful slave would also be an obedient slave. But fear was a double-edged sword. Masters realized that poor treatment of slaves could inspire resentment. Consequently, they sought an elaborate system of laws to protect themselves, their families, and their communities against any semblance of black resistance. They tried to enlist the support of nonslaveholding whites. Through religion, philosophy, law, and social practice, they tried to convince the lowliest white person that he was better than the most cultured and intelligent black. Whites of all classes were encouraged to believe that they could some day enhance their social status by becoming slaveowners, in spite of the fact that seven out of eight Missouri families would never own slaves.

Missouri's slave codes illustrate the general attitude toward blacks during the antebellum period. Slaves were designated as personal property to be taxed, bought, and sold just like any other property. In 1835 Joseph Hardeman of Cole County offered for sale "one Negro man, one Negro woman, and three children ages 10, 12, and 16." Hardeman noted that the "man is a good plowman, woman and children good field hands." Likewise, in 1851 Edward Lewis and his wife listed a young black with animals and other miscellaneous merchandise they had for sale: "One negro boy named Tom aged about fourteen years, one Bay Mare aged three this spring. One yoke of steers aged three years this spring, three young cows, one yearling mule, sixty barrels of corn all for the sum of nine hundred and fifty-five dollars."

Food, clothing, shelter, and medical attention in most cases rested in the capricious hands of the owners. Whether the slave had sufficient food has always been a highly debated question. One student of Cole County slavery says that blacks had an unbalanced diet of cornbread and potatoes.

Another historian says that slaves occasionally had pork, beef, or mutton. Of course, a master might allow the slave a little time on Saturday or Sunday to grow a few vegetables. The enterprising slave might supplement his diet with possums, rabbits, squirrels, or fish. Filmore Taylor Hancock, a slave born near Springfield in 1851, remembered that he and his brothers and sisters got special consideration in terms of food because "our ol' granny was de white folk's cook. . . . We got to eat what de white folks did. Up to de cabins where de odder niggers was, had salt meat, cabbage, 'taters, an' shortenin' bread three times a day. We all had plenty vegetables, we raised ourselves. . . . Onced a week we had hot biscuits." . . .

A few slaves claimed they had to eat rotten or spoiled food. Harriet Casey, born in Farmington, related the following: "To eat we had cornmeal and fried meat dat had been eaten by bugs. We had some gravy and all ate 'round de pan like pigs eating slop. And we had a tin cup of sour milk to drink. Sometimes we would have ginger bread—dis was 'bout twice a year. . . . Once it got so cold dat de chickens froze and fell out of the trees and de mistress gave each of us a chicken to eat." . . .

Housing for slaves varied but was generally inadequate. If one or two slaves were owned, they might sleep in the master's house. If several were owned, they generally lived in cabins where they cooked, slept, and socialized. Their quarters gave them little privacy and were not spacious by any means. Daniel Ligon of Lewis County had only two houses for ten slaves. The quarters of another owner consisted of small log cabins about twelve-to-fourteen-feet square, an area smaller than most present day bedrooms. In Cole County, slaves were herded into cramped quarters like cattle. At one point there were 987 slaves in the county sharing only ninety cabins, an average of nearly eleven slaves per cabin. Harriet Casey claimed that the cabin her family lived in consisted of "one room, one door, and one fireplace."

The quality of the slaves' quarters depended on individual masters. Some masters provided barely livable quarters, while others provided roomy and comfortable living space. Typically, quarters were hot in the summer, cold in the winter, poorly lighted, and unsanitary. Windows were often only holes in a wall, lacking glass panes and covered with paper or cloth. Charlie Richardson remembered the construction of the slave cabins as being "made of good old Missouri logs daubed with mud, and the chimney was made of sticks daubed with mud." Annie Bridges, born in St. Francois County, lived in a log cabin with two rooms, a floor, and "a bed, but hit hadn't no mattress; jus' roped an' cord'd—holes wuz in de side ob de bed, soo's de ropes cud go thru."

Some masters clothed their slaves better than others, but most looked for the cheapest solution. Materials used were largely tow cloth, white and striped linsey-woolsey, and heavy brown jeans. Advertisements for a run-away slaves often described how slaves might be clothed: a slave who ran away in 1835 carried with him "two cotton shirts, one pair of linen pants, one green blanket, a coat, one pair of brown pants, and an old fur coat." A newspaper in 1847 stated that R. C. Cordell of Jefferson City clothed three slaves for seventy-nine dollars: Lydia for twenty-four dollars for two years, Mary Ann for fifteen dollars for two years, and Penney for forty dollars for one year. An old slave related that the Missouri slaves generally received two pairs of trousers, two shirts, and a hat in the summer; a coat, a pair of trousers, and a pair of shoes in the winter.

Boys and girls generally wore a gownlike garment until they were about ten to fourteen years old. Boys who wore such gowns were called "shirttail boys." Louis Hill described the garment as "a straight slip like a night gown and hit fastened round the neck. . . . Tah dis off an we was naked." Many of the slaves reported that their mothers made most of their clothes. George Bollinger's "mammy wus a good cook 'en she cud spin en weave. She made all de clothes we wore. Us chillunns never wore no pants—jes sumpin like a long shirt made o' homespun." Still another slave remembers: "We all wore homespun clothes, made of wool mostly. Mother carded, spun and wove all our clothes." . . .

Blacks who suffered from physical illnesses were generally cared for by their fellow slaves. Sometimes the master might call a doctor. More often than not, however, doctors were not available since the frontier did not lend itself to attracting medical practitioners any more than the rural community does today. The slave midwife generally delivered the children and frequently cared for the master's offspring. Because of the scarcity of doctors, there were often two or three slaves in a surrounding area who served as doctors for the slave population in a county. Many of these slave doctors also treated white patients, such as Gus Smith's grandfather, Godfry, a slave from Osage County, who apparently possessed a rare talent for curing burns. Gus Smith remembered his grandfather as "an old fashion herb doctor. . . . Everybody knew him in that country and he doctored among the white people. . . . He went over thirty miles around to people who sent for him. . . . Lots of cases that other doctors gave up, he went and 'raised them.' He could cure anything." Slave doctors practiced folk medicine using herbs and plants found in the nearby woods, such as white root, remedy weed, sarsaparilla root, cherry tree bark, pennyroyal, chamomile root, and ginseng, to cure an assortment of ailments.

Although Missouri slaves were generally worked from sunup to sundown during the week, they were often allowed Sunday afternoons to themselves. During that time, they might manufacture small articles for sale, perform odd jobs, or tend to a small plot of land adjoining the slave quarters. At times they were allowed to sing, swim, and dance in the evening; occasionally they attended a circus. Days off from work, and the festivities that surrounded them, often fostered a feeling of interdependence and community among the slaves that gave them a sense of identity and sustained them against the dehumanizing conditions of slavery. William Black remembered how the slaves spent the few hours each day that they were allowed to themselves, and how they oftentimes combined work with entertainment: "In the evening when the work was all done we would sit around and play marbles and sing songs. We made our songs up as we went along. Sometimes there would be a corn shuckin' and that is when we had a good time, but we always shucked a lot of that corn." . . .

Master and slave generally attended the same church. The structure of religious worship left no doubt in the slave's mind of his inferiority. Generally, slaves were physically separated from their masters and other whites either in a loft above the rest of the congregation or in a special section of pews at the rear of the meetinghouse. They often heard sermons in which white ministers counseled them to be obedient and submissive to their masters. Black communicants participated in the sacraments only after all the whites had partaken. Even in death the races were generally separated. There were almost always "white" and "colored" cemeteries in every area of the state occupied by blacks. Isabelle Henderson remembered that the blacks were segregated at the church she attended: "I remember j'inin' the white folks church in old Cambridge. They had a gallery for the slaves." Henderson also recalled that in church "sometimes the slaves did funny things. There was one old woman named Aunt Cindy. . . . One Sunday she got 'happy' and commenced shoutin' and throwin' herself about. White folks in the seats below hurried to get out from under the gallery, fearin' Aunt Cindy, was goin' to lose her balance and fall on them."

The segregation made another Missouri slave, Malinda Discus, question the contradictions inherent in the slave system: "Yes, our Master took his slaves to meetin' with him. They had one corner where they sat with the slaves of other people. There was always something about that I couldn't understand. They treated the colored folks like animals and would not hesitate to sell and separate them, yet they seemed to think they had souls and tried to make Christians of them." Richard Bruner attended a church that was less segregated: "We went to dey white folks church on Sundays. When we went to camp meeting we all went to de mourners bench together. De mourners bench stretch clear across de front of de Arbor; de whites and de blacks, we all jest fell down at de mourners bench and got religion at de same place."

The Missouri slave codes forbade the marriage of slaves. Sometimes a man and woman just "took up" with each other. Other times they were ordered to live together by the master. As far as whites were concerned, the sale of one or the other of the marriage partners ended the relationship. Mark Discus remembered that his master, a Presbyterian preacher, separated his mother and father and ten brothers and sisters: "Yes suh, there was ten children of we'uns and we was all separated. I was sold when I was four years old, they said, for three hundred and fifty dollars. . . . I seen my brothers and sisters [after being separated] but they had different names. Then I heard my Pappy had died. I don't remember him. My Mammy was sold down South and I never seen her again 'til after the war was over." Discus also remembered that slaves often "just had a ceremony and a preacher or some officer married 'em, but after awhile they made 'em get a license. I don't think my Pappy and Mammy had a license but their master was a preacher, as I said, and he married them alright."

The slave family, although often separated by sale and death, was the stabilizing unit of the slave community. The slave family socialized children, taught them folklore and folk songs and herbal remedies, buffered them against the dehumanizing effects of slavery, instructed them in schemes of resistance, and trained them how to survive in a hostile society as black slaves. In place of blood relatives sold away, the slave community ingeniously devised patterns of "fictive kinship" in which other slaves who were unrelated would care for and provide for orphaned or parentless children as "grannies," "aunts," or "uncles." . . .

Slaves were degraded by laws that divided them further from the rest of society. Punishments were barbarous. The general crudeness of frontier justice was made even worse by the master's fear of rebellious or disobedient slaves. A slaveowner who was surrounded by free territory on three sides (Illinois, Iowa, and Kansas) was prompted to take strict precautions to keep his slaves secure. To protect the master and community against slave uprisings, Missouri's statutes included restrictions that prohibited slaves from carrying arms without a license from the justice of the peace. If a gun was found on a slave, it could be taken away, and he or she could receive thirty-nine lashes on his or her bare back. Slaves found guilty of crimes such as conspiracy, rebellion, or murder were to be put to death. . . .

Ed Craddock, born about 1858 near Marshall, Missouri, told a story his father had told him about the cruel punishment of a slave: "A slave right here in Marshall angered his master, was chained to a hemp-brake on a cold night and left to freeze to death, which he did." Another slave, Mary Martha Bolden, born in 1861 on John Lindsey's farm six miles east of Troy, Missouri, was a small girl when she saw "the master and two other men whip three men slaves, for running off. The whipping was unmerciful." And Mark Discus's master once "whooped me 'til the blood run offen my heels for breakin' an axe handle. We knowed to step when he yelled at us."

Often a slave was punished in the presence of other slaves as a dramatic lesson of what would happen to disobedient slaves. The most frequent punishment was whipping. The usual instrument was a wooden handle attached to a flat piece of leather belting about a quarter of an inch thick. The number of lashes varied from ten to one hundred. Such a whip caused blisters, frequently drew blood, and sometimes left permanent scars. Occasionally slaves were beaten with sticks or anything else that might come to the master's hand. Usually, however, the master tried to avoid permanently marking a slave. A scarred slave would be regarded by a prospective buyer as mean or having made attempts to escape. His potential value could be lessened considerably.

Slaves were forbidden to have sexual relations with white women. Blacks or mulattoes who assaulted or attempted to assault a white woman could be killed or mutilated, often by castration. Rape of a black woman by a white man was less serious in the eyes of the law, however. Sexual assault of a slave woman by a white man was not considered an offense against the woman: it was only a case of trespassing on the master's "property." Many slave children were the result of interracial sexual unions, sometimes rapes, between white masters and their slave women. George Jackson Simpson was the son of his master: "My mother was quarter Indian. . . . She was only fifteen when I was born. My master, Jim Simpson a white man was also my father. I did not know who my father was until my mother told me when I was seventeen years old. What was done in slavery days, was simply done and not much thought of it."

Slaves who offered resistance to their owners and overseers could receive thirty-nine lashes. A slave guilty of striking a white person, except in self-defense, was to be punished at the discretion of the justice of the peace. The punishment was not to exceed thirty-nine lashes, which was also the penalty for disturbing church service by "noise, riotous or disorderly conduct." Any person providing liquor to a slave got twenty-five lashes on his bare back and time in jail. Blacks were also declared incompetent as witnesses in legal cases involving whites. They could, however, testify against each other.

By 1847 Missouri slaveowners were extremely fearful of slave insurrections. News of uprisings in the southern states further fueled their fears. Convinced that slaves rebelled because they were reading abolitionist literature, whites sought to stop rebellions by adopting an ordinance that specifically prohibited the education of blacks. Anyone operating a school for Negroes or mulattoes, or teaching reading or writing to any Negro or mulatto in Missouri, could be punished with a fine of not less than five hundred dollars and sentenced up to six months in jail. Bill Sims remembered that "slaves were never allowed to talk to white people other than their masters or someone their masters knew, as they were afraid the white man might have the slave run away. The masters aimed to keep their slaves in ignorance." Filmore Taylor Hancock feared being "kotched wid a book, to read or try to be educated." Despite the state law prohibiting the education of blacks, Emma Knight said her "master's girls taught us to read and write."

One of the most important institutions established in the slave states to guard against slave plots and insurrection was the slave patrols. Legislation was designed authorizing each county to set up its own patrols in Missouri in 1823. The patrols were to ensure that slaves were not traveling abroad at night without their master's consent. Patrols also visited slave quarters to guarantee that there were no unlawful assemblies of slaves. Thirty-nine lashes was the punishment for such illegal activity if the patrol took the slave before the justice of the peace; however, without the master's permission punishment by the "patterollers," as some slaves called them, was limited to ten lashes. Richard Bruner recalled: "Whenever us niggas on one plantation got obstreporous, white folks hawns dey blowed. When de neighbors heard dat hawn hyar dey come to hep make dat obstreporous nigga behave."

As the intensity of the antislavery struggle increased in the years immediately preceding the Civil War, strenuous local laws were passed to control the slaves. In most Missouri cities all blacks without a pass had to be off the street at nine o'clock at night unless they were on business for their master. Special permission had to be secured from the master for all special meetings, and all such persons had to be home by ten o'clock. Passes were good for twenty-four hours only, and the city constable had to see that meetings were orderly.

Compensation of patrol members varied. Sometimes they received no pay—except the satisfaction of keeping blacks "in their place." Patrols were mostly made up of poor and working-class whites, young men who excelled in taking undue advantage of blacks, particularly of the women and girls. Occasionally slaveowners served as patrollers. In Cole County, patrolmen were paid eight cents an hour in 1851 and twenty-five cents an hour in 1852. Pay for patrolmen apparently increased as fear engendered by the antislavery movement intensified. Still, five members of the Jefferson City patrol served for the paltry sum of $28.50 for a year's work.

The "intractable" slave always had one major fear that haunted him continuously: the prospect of being sold away from his family, especially "down South." This was the ultimate legal form of social control open to the master. It was also the most brutal. Masters frequently sold intractable or disobedient slaves down South, away from their families. Taylor Hancock's uncle was sold after a confrontation with his master:

> One time my ol marster Hancock, got mad at my uncle, who was a growed up nigger. Ol marse wanted to whup him. He tried to make my uncle put his head twixt his [ol marster's] knees. My uncle didn't offer to fight him, but twisted him roun' an' roun' tryin' to get his head out. He gave one twist dat throwed ol marse down to de groun'. My uncle jumped an' run an' jumped obber de fence. . . . But ol Marse sure got mad when my uncle run. So he sold him to a man named Dokes—a nigger trader ob dat neighborhood. Dokes bought niggers an' sold dem on de block in St. Louis.

The heavy demand for black slaves in the South meant that there was always a buyer from that region ready to purchase a Missouri slave. Several slave dealers carried on the trade in Missouri, buying and selling blacks for the cotton, rice, and sugar fields of the South. St. Louis was the largest slave market in the state. Slave dealers there advertised in various counties for salable slaves. In 1845 W. Edgerton, a St. Louis dealer, advertised in the *Jefferson Inquirer*: "The undersigned proposes remaining a few weeks in this city for the purpose of purchasing a few Negro slaves. Persons having young slaves for sale will find this a favorable opportunity to sell. His rooms are in the national hotel."

St. Louis companies such as Blakey and McAfee kept an agent in the state capital in the early 1850s, offering "highest prices for Negroes of every description." They boasted of their facilities as being "well suited for the boarding and safe keeping of Negroes sent to this market for sale." Competing with them was yet another St. Louis firm, Bolton, Dickens and Company. In 1853 the latter firm advertised in the *Jefferson Examiner* for one thousand slaves.

None of the slave states admitted to the breeding of slaves, and the question of Missouri's involvement in that practice remains debatable. Still, William Wells Brown, an escaped slave who became an antislavery speaker and novelist, argued that slave breeding occurred in Missouri and that the children born of such unions were sold down South. Another former slave claimed that a neighboring master "used to have me come over and father children; you know, I was big and strong and made big strong slaves."

FROM *PIONEERS, PREACHERS AND PEOPLE OF THE MISSISSIPPI VALLEY* (1860)

Rev. William Henry Milburn

The Moravian brethren were the first to bring the Word of Life and Truth into the vast region of the Mississippi Valley; always of course excepting the old Jesuit Fathers and other Catholic missionaries who came with the French. . . .

South of the Ohio, the earliest Christian denomination to enter Kentucky as a field of labor, were the Baptists—a large and exceedingly influential sect in Virginia and North Carolina, from which States most of the early settlers of Kentucky came. While there were few preachers who came with the single purpose of preaching the Word, there were a good many who were licensed to administer the sacraments, or whose object was to instruct the young, or like their secular companions, to take possession of the country, and to secure for themselves farms and estates. These were not long after followed by Presbyterian ministers and missionaries, who came here expressly for the purpose of preaching the Gospel. It is not my desire here to assume a sectional or denominational position. Nevertheless, it is necessary to call special attention to the characteristics, peculiarities, lives, manners, customs, names, and reputations of some of the preachers of my own church, the Methodist. . . .

The Baptists did a noble and excellent work, as did also the Presbyterians, in the early times of the West. The Methodist church was a younger church than these—its first regular preachers having landed on this continent in 1770. Fourteen years after their first teacher, sent out by Wesley, set foot in America—seven years after the first Baptist minister in Kentucky— and three years after the first Presbyterian—they commenced penetrating the wilds of the Far West, and their pioneer missionaries, James Haw and Benjamin Ogden, crossed the Alleghenies and entered the boundless tracts of Kentucky. Others rapidly followed him. At first there was much antagonism—a sort of pugnacious rivalry or "free fight" between these various denominations out in the West—nor has this yet quite passed away. There is an active, rough, resolute courage, independence, and pluck about the western people, which inclines them to close scuffling and grappling, a sort of knockdown attitude visible through all the moods of their life; and their clergy are not free from the same peculiarities. They were therefore great controversialists; and there was an immense din about Baptism and Pedobaptism; Free Grace and Predestination; Falling from Grace and the Perse-

New York: Derby, 1860.

verance of the Saints, etc., etc. Brethren of different denominations often held what they called discussions or debates; where one of one denomination challenged one of another. Meeting together before the people, occupying a temporary pulpit in a grove, they would thus treat—and maltreat—the doctrines and views of each other, to the eminent edification, and oftentimes the entertainment of the assembled multitude. The people, nevertheless, were somewhat insensible to the preached Word during the first twenty years of its dispensation. They were absorbed by Indian wars, and by the pressing demands upon their labor, necessary to maintain physical existence in a new country. Soon afterward came in French infidelity with French politics; and deism and atheism were openly avowed on every hand. Many of the principal citizens of the West were not afraid or ashamed to own themselves skeptical or infidels in regard to the old system of Revelation. Thus the field which these pioneer preachers were called to till was a hard and stony one; and they had much difficulty in pushing their way.

The Presbyterians and Methodists found it necessary, toward the close of the last century, to conjoin their efforts and unite for the furtherance of the common cause. This was in the southern part of the State of Kentucky. They held "union meetings"—sacramental meetings, where the two denominations worked together, kindly and efficient yoke-fellows. Under these efforts the people at length became much excited on the subject of religion, and there then broke out, in the spring of 1800, the most extraordinary revival of religion that ever happened on this continent, or perhaps in the history of the church since the Day of Pentecost. It was called the Cumberland Revival, or the Great Revival. It broke out at one of these sacramental occasions, when the Methodist and Presbyterian ministers were holding a two or three days' meeting, for the purpose of stimulating the attention of the people to the all-important subject of personal holiness. At this, there were strange manifestations. The people were seized as by a sort of superhuman power; their physical energy was lost; their senses refused to perform their functions; all forms of manifesting consciousness were for the time annulled. Strong men fell upon the ground, utterly helpless; women were taken with a strange spasmodic motion, so that they were heaved to and fro, sometimes falling at length upon the floor, their hair dishevelled, and throwing their heads about with a quickness and violence so great as to make their hair crack against the floor as if it were a teamster's whip. Then they would rise up again under this strange power, fall on their faces, and the same violent movements and cracking noise would ensue. Such peculiarities characterized this first meeting.

The meetings went on, and at length there was a grand convocation at Cane Ridge, Kentucky. . . . People came sixty, seventy, a hundred, even three hundred miles to attend . . . , and it is said that on one night there were not less than thirty thousand people present at the Cane Ridge ground. There were present eight or ten preachers of different denominations, standing up on the stumps of trees, fallen logs, or temporary pulpits, all of them holding forth in their loudest tone—and that was a very loud tone, for the lungs of the backwoods preachers were of the strongest. They roared like lions—their tones were absolutely like peals of thunder. The celebrated William Burke . . . was one of the principal orators on that occasion. . . . He took a stand on . . . a fallen log, and here, having rigged up an umbrella as a temporary shelter, a brother standing by to see that it performed its functions properly, he gave out a hymn, and by the time that he had mentioned his text, there were some ten thousand persons about him. Although his voice when he began was like a crash of thunder, after three-quarters of an hour or an hour, it was like an infant's.

It is said that all these people, the whole ten thousand of men and women standing about the preacher, were from time to time shaken as a forest by a tornado, and five hundred were at once prostrated to the earth, like the trees in a "windfall," by some invisible agency. Some were agitated by violent whirling motions, some by fearful contortions; and then came "the jerks." Scoffers, doubters, deniers, men who came to ridicule and sneer at the supernatural agency, were taken up in the air, whirled over upon their heads, coiled up so as to spin about like cart-wheels, catching hold, meantime, of saplings, endeavoring to clasp the trunks of trees in their arms, but still going headlong and helplessly on. These motions were called "the jerks," a name which was current in the West for many a year after; and many an old preacher has described these things accurately to me. It was not the men who were already members of the church, but the scoffing, the blasphemous, the profane, who were taken in this way. Here is one example: A man rode into what was called the "Ring Circle," where five hundred people were standing in a ring, and another set inside. Those inside were on their knees, crying, shouting, praying, all mixed up in heterogeneous style. This man comes riding up at the top of his speed, yelling like a demon, cursing and blaspheming. On reaching the edge of the ring, he falls from his horse, seemingly lifeless, and lies in an apparently unconscious condition for thirty hours; his pulse at about forty, or less. When he opens his eyes and recovers his senses, he says he has retained his consciousness all the time—that he has been aware of what has been passing around—but was seized with some agency which he could not define. I fancy that neither physiology, nor psychology, nor biology, nor any of the ologies or isms, have, thus far, given any satisfactory explanation of the singular manifestations that attended this great revival.

These meetings take place in open woods, and attracting such immense multitudes, no provision could possibly be made for them by the surrounding neighborhood. People came in their carriages, in wagons, in ox-carts, on horses, and, themselves accustomed to pioneer habits and lives, they brought their own food, commonly jerked meat and corn dodgers, and pitched their tents upon the ground.

Such was the origin of camp-meetings. . . .

WILLIAM SHAKESPEARE
AND THE AMERICAN PEOPLE
A Study in Cultural Transformation

Lawrence W. Levine

. . . The humor of a people affords important insights into the nature of their culture. Thus Mark Twain's treatment of Shakespeare in his novel *Huckleberry Finn* helps us place the Elizabethan playwright in nineteenth-century American culture. Shortly after the two rogues, who pass themselves off as a duke and a king, invade the raft of Huck and Jim, they decide to raise funds by performing scenes from Shakespeare's *Romeo and Juliet* and *Richard III*. That the presentation of Shakespeare in small Mississippi River towns could be conceived of as potentially lucrative tells us much about the position of Shakespeare in the nineteenth century. The specific nature of Twain's humor tells us even more. Realizing that they would need material for encores, the "duke" starts to teach the "king" Hamlet's soliloquy, which he recites from memory:

> To be, or not to be; that is the bare bodkin
> That makes calamity of so long life;
> For who would fardels bear, till Birnam Wood do come
>   to Dunsinane,
> 5 But that the fear of something after death Murders the
>   innocent sleep,
> Great nature's second course,
> And makes us rather sling arrows of outrageous fortune
> Than fly to others that we know not of.

Twain's humor relies on his audience's familiarity with *Hamlet* and its ability to recognize the duke's improbable coupling of lines from a variety

From *The Unpredictable Past: Explorations in American Cultural History.* New York: Oxford UP, 1993.

of Shakespeare's plays. Twain was employing one of the most popular forms of humor in nineteenth-century America. Everywhere in the nation burlesques and parodies of Shakespeare constituted a prominent form of entertainment.

Hamlet was a favorite target in numerous travesties imported from England or crafted at home. Audiences roared at the sight of Hamlet dressed in fur cap and collar, snowshoes and mittens; they listened with amused surprise to his profanity when ordered by his father's ghost to "swear" and to his commanding Ophelia, "Get thee to a brewery"; they heard him recite his lines in black dialect or Irish brogue and sing his most famous soliloquy, "To be, or not to be," to the tune of "Three Blind Mice." In the 1820s the British comedian Charles Mathews visited what he called the "Nigger's (or Negroe's) theatre" in New York, where he heard "a black tragedian in the character of Hamlet" recite "To be, or not to be? That is the question; whether it is nobler in *de* mind to suffer, or tak' up arms against a sea of trouble, and by *opossum* end 'em." "No sooner was the word *opossum* out of his mouth," Mathews reported, "than the audience burst forth, in one general cry, '*Opossum! opossum! opossum!*'"—prompting the actor to come forward and sing the popular dialect song "Opossum up a Gum Tree." On the nineteenth-century American stage, audiences often heard Hamlet's lines intricately combined with those of a popular song:

> Oh! 'tis consummation
> Devoutly to be wished
> To end your heart-ache by a sleep,
> When likely to be dish'd.
> 5 Shuffle off your mortal coil,
> Do just so,
> Wheel about, and turn about,
> And jump Jim Crow[1]

---

[1] Laurence Hutton, *Curiosities of the American Stage* (New York, 1891), 157, 181–86; Stanley Wells, ed., *Nineteenth-Century Shakespeare Burlesques,* 5 (London, 1978): xi–xii; Charles Mathews, *Trip to America* (Baltimore, 1824), 9, 25; Charles Haywood, "Negro Minstrelsy and Shakespearean Burlesque," in Bruce Jackson, ed., *Folklore and Society: Essays in Honor of Benj. A. Botkin* (Norwood, Pa., 1976), 88; and Ray B. Browne, "Shakespeare in America: Vaudeville and Negro Minstrelsy," *American Quarterly,* 12 (1960):381–82. For examples of parodies of *Hamlet,* see *An Old Play in a New Garb: Hamlet, Prince of Denmark,* in Wells, *Nineteenth-Century Shakespeare Burlesques;* and *Hamlet the Dainty,* in Gary D. Engle, ed., *This Grotesque Essence: Plays from the Minstrel Stage* (Baton Rouge, 1978). For the popularity of parodies of *Hamlet* in the United States, see Ralph Leslie Rusk, *The Literature of the Middle Western Fron-*

No Shakespearean play was immune to this sort of mutilation. *Richard III,* the most popular Shakespearean play in the nineteenth century, was lampooned frequently in such versions as *Bad Dicky.* In one New York production starring first-rank Shakespearean actors, a stuttering, lisping Othello danced while Desdemona played the banjo and Iago, complete with Irish brogue, ended their revelries with a fire hose. Parodies could also embody a serious message. In Kenneth Bangs's version of *The Taming of the Shrew,* for example, Kate ended up in control, observing that, although "Shakespeare or Bacon, or whoever wrote the play . . . studied deeply the shrews of his day . . . . , the modern shrew isn't built that way," while a chastened Petruchio concluded, "Sweet Katharine, of your remarks I recognize the force: / Don't strive to tame a woman as you would a horse." Serious or slapstick, the punning was endless. In one parody of the famous dagger scene, Macbeth continues to put off his insistent wife by asking, "Or is that dagger but a false Daguerreotype?" Luckily, Desdemona had no brother, or Othello "might look both black and blue," a character in *Othello* remarked, while one in *The Merchant of Venice* observed of Shylock, "This crafty Jew is full of *Jeux d'esprit!*" Throughout the century, the number of parodies with such titles as *Julius Sneezer, Roamy-E-Owe and Julie-Ate,* and *Desdemonum* was impressive.[2]

These full-fledged travesties reveal only part of the story. Nineteenth-century Shakespearean parody most frequently took the form of short skits, brief references, and satirical songs inserted into other modes of entertainment. In one of their routines, for example, the Bryants' Minstrels playfully referred to the famous observation in Act II of *Romeo and Juliet:*

Adolphus Pompey is my name,
    But that don't make no difference,
For as Massa Wm. Shakespeare says,
    A name's of no significance.

---

tier, 2 vols. (New York, 1925), 2:4n; Louis Marder, *His Exits and His Entrances: The Story of Shakespeare's Reputation* (Philadelphia, 1963), 295–96, 316–17; and Esther Cloudman Dunn, *Shakespeare in America* (New York, 1939), 108–12, 215–16.

[2] For examples, see Wells, *Nineteenth-Century Shakespeare Burlesques;* and Engle, *This Grotesque Essence.* For a contemporary view of nineteenth-century parodies, see Hutton, *Curiosities of the American Stage,* 145–204. Also see Marder, *His Exits and His Entrances,* 316–17; Alice I. Perry Wood, *The Stage History of Shakespeare's* King Richard the Third (New York, 1909), 158; Browne, "Shakespeare in America," 380, 385–90; David Grimsted, *Melodrama Unveiled: American Theater and Culture, 1800–1850* (Chicago, 1968), 240; and Constance Rourke, *Troupers of the Gold Coast* (New York, 1928), 221.

The minstrels loved to invoke Shakespeare as an authority: "you know what de Bird of Avon says 'bout de black scandal an' de foul faced reproach!" And they constantly quoted him in appropriately garbled form: "Fust to dine own self be true, an' it must follow night an' day, dou den can be false to any man." The significance of this national penchant for parodying Shakespeare is clear: Shakespeare and his drama had become by the nineteenth century an integral part of American culture. It is difficult to take familiarities with that which is not already familiar; one cannot parody that which is not well known. The minstrels' characteristic conundrums would not have been funny to an audience lacking knowledge of Shakespeare's works:

> When was Desdemona like a ship?
> When she was Moored.[3]

It is not surprising that educated Americans in the eighteenth and nineteenth centuries knew their Shakespeare. What is more interesting is how widely Shakespeare was known to the public in general. In the last half of the eighteenth century, when the reading of Shakespeare's plays was still confined to a relatively small, educated elite, substantial numbers of Americans had the chance to see his plays performed. From the first documented American performance of a Shakespearean play in 1750 until the closing of the theaters in 1778 because of the American Revolution, Shakespeare emerged as the most popular playwright in the colonies. Fourteen or fifteen of his plays were presented at least one hundred and eighty—and one scholar has estimated perhaps as many as five hundred—times. Following the Revolution, Shakespeare retained his position as the most widely performed dramatist, with five more of his plays regularly performed in an increasing number of cities and towns.[4]

---

[3] Haywood, "Negro Minstrelsy and Shakespearean Burlesque," 80, 86–87; and Browne, "Shakespeare in America," 376–79.

[4] John Quincy Adams, who was born in 1767, wrote of Shakespeare, "at ten years of age I was as familiarly acquainted with his lovers and his clowns, as with Robinson Crusoe, the Pilgrim's Progress, and the Bible. In later years I have left Robinson and the Pilgrim to the perusal of the children; but have continued to read the Bible and Shakespeare." Adams to James H. Hackett, printed in Hackett, *Notes and Comments upon Certain Plays and Actors of Shakespeare, with Criticisms and Correspondence* (New York, 1864), 229. See Alfred Van Rensselaer Westfall, *American Shakespearean Criticism, 1607–1865* (New York, 1939), 45–46, 50–55; Wood, *The Stage History of Shakespeare's King Richard the Third*, 134–35; Charles H. Shattuck, *Shakespeare on the American Stage: From the Hallams to Edwin Booth* (Washington, 1976), 3, 15–16; and Hugh Rankin, *The Theater in Colonial America* (Chapel Hill, 1960), 191–92.

Not until the nineteenth century, however, did Shakespeare come into his own—presented and recognized almost everywhere in the country. In the cities of the Northeast and Southeast, Shakespeare's plays dominated the theater. During the 1810–11 season in Philadelphia, for example, Shakespearean plays accounted for twenty-two of eighty-eight performances. The following season lasted 108 nights, of which again one-quarter—27—were devoted to Shakespeare. From 1800 to 1835, Philadelphians had the opportunity to see twenty-one of Shakespeare's thirty-seven plays. The Philadelphia theater was not exceptional; one student of the American stage concluded that in cities on the Eastern Seaboard at least one-fifth of all plays offered in a season were likely to be by Shakespeare.[5] George Makepeace Towle, an American consul in England, returned to his own country just after the Civil War and remarked with some surprise, "Shakespearian dramas are more frequently played and more popular in America than in England." Shakespeare's dominance can be attested to by what Charles Shattuck has called "the westward flow of Shakespearean actors" from England to America. In the nineteenth century, one prominent English Shakespearean actor after another—George Frederick Cooke, Edmund Kean, Junius Brutus Booth, Charles and Fanny Kemble, Ellen Tree, William Charles Macready—sought the fame and financial rewards that awaited them in their tours of the United States.[6]

It is important to understand that their journey did not end with big cities or the Eastern Seaboard. According to John Bernard, the English actor and comedian who worked in the United States from 1797 to 1819, "If an actor were unemployed, want and shame were not before him: he had merely to visit some town in the interior where no theatre existed, but

---

[5] Arthur Hobson Quinn, *A History of the American Drama* (New York, 1943), 162; Dunn, *Shakespeare in America*, 133, 171–72; and Carl Bode, *The Anatomy of American Popular Culture, 1840–1861* (Berkeley and Los Angeles, 1960), 16–17. For the reception of Shakespeare in specific Eastern and Southern cities, the following are useful: T. Allston Brown, *A History of the New York Stage from the First Performance in 1732 to 1901*, 3 vols. (New York, 1903); James H. Dorman, Jr., *Theater in the Ante-Bellum South, 1815–1861* (Chapel Hill, 1967); W. Stanley Hoole, *The Ante-Bellum Charleston Theatre* (Tuscaloosa, Ala., 1946); Reese Davis James, *Cradle of Culture, 1800–1810: The Philadelphia Stage* (Philadelphia, 1957); Martin Staples Shockley, *The Richmond Stage, 1784–1812* (Charlottesville, Va., 1977); Eola Willis, *The Charleston Stage in the XVIII Century* (Columbia, S.C., 1924); and Joseph Patrick Roppolo, "Hamlet in New Orleans," *Tulane Studies in English*, 6 (1956):71–86. For tables showing the popularity of plays in the first half of the nineteenth century, see Grimsted, *Melodrama Unveiled*, apps. 1–2.
[6] Towle, *American Society*, 2 (London, 1870):22. The migration of English stars to America is demonstrated throughout Shattuck's *Shakespeare on the American Stage*.

'readings' were permitted; and giving a few recitations from Shakespeare and Sterne, his pockets in a night or two were amply replenished." During his travels through the United States in the 1830s, Tocqueville found Shakespeare in "the recesses of the forests of the New World. There is hardly a pioneer's hut that does not contain a few odd volumes of Shakespeare. I remember that I read the feudal drama of *Henry V* for the first time in a log cabin." [7] Five decades later, the German visitor Karl Knortz made a similar observation:

> There is, assuredly, no other country on the face of this earth in which Shakespeare and the Bible are held in such general high esteem as in America, the very country so much decried for its lust for money. If you were to enter an isolated log cabin in the Far West and even if its inhabitant were to exhibit many of the traces of backwoods living, he will most likely have one small room nicely furnished in which to spend his few leisure hours and in which you will certainly find the Bible and in most cases also some cheap edition of the works of the poet Shakespeare. [8]

Even if we discount the hyperbole evident in such accounts, they were far from inventions. The ability of the illiterate Rocky Mountain scout Jim Bridger to recite long passages from Shakespeare, which he had learned by hiring someone to read the plays to him, and the formative influence that the plays had upon young Abe Lincoln growing up in Salem, Illinois, became part of the nation's folklore. [9] But if books had become a more important vehicle for disseminating Shakespeare by the nineteenth century, the stage remained the primary instrument. The theater, like the church, was one of the earliest and most important cultural institutions established in frontier cities. And almost everywhere the theater blossomed Shakespeare was a paramount force. In his investigation of the theater in Louisville, Cincinnati, St. Louis, Detroit, and Lexington, Kentucky, from 1800 to 1840, Ralph Leslie Rusk concluded that Shakespeare's plays were performed more frequently than those of any other author. In Mississippi between 1814 and the outbreak of the Civil War, the towns of Natchez and Vicksburg, with only a few thousand inhabitants each, put on at least one hundred and fifty performances of Shakespeare featuring such British

---

[7] Bernard, *Retrospections of America, 1797–1811* (New York, 1887), 263; and Tocqueville, *Democracy in America*, pt. 2 (Vintage edn., New York, 1961), 58.
[8] Knortz, *Shakespeare in Amerika: Eine Literarhistorische Studie* (Berlin, 1882), 47.
[9] James G. McManaway, "Shakespeare in the United States," *Publications of the Modern Language Association of America*, 79 (1964): 514; and Bernard DeVoto, *Mark Twain's America* (Boston, 1932), 142–43.

and American stars as Ellen Tree, Edwin Forrest, Junius Brutus Booth, J. W. Walleck, Charles Kean, J. H. Hackett, Josephine Clifton, and T. A. Cooper. Stars of this and lesser caliber made their way into the interior by boat, along the Ohio and Mississippi rivers, stopping at towns and cities on their way to New Orleans. Beginning in the early 1830s, the rivers themselves became the site of Shakespearean productions, with floating theaters in the form first of flatboats and then steamboats bringing drama to small river towns.[10]

By mid-century, Shakespeare was taken across the Great Plains and over the Rocky Mountains and soon became a staple of theaters in the Far West. During the decade following the arrival of the Forty-niners, at least twenty-two of Shakespeare's plays were performed on California stages, with *Richard III* retaining the predominance it had gained in the East and South. In 1850 the Jenny Lind Theatre, seating two thousand, opened over a saloon in San Francisco and was continuously crowded: "Miners . . . swarmed from the gambling saloons and cheap fandango houses to see *Hamlet* and *Lear*." In 1852 the British star Junius Brutus Booth and two of his sons played *Hamlet, Macbeth, Othello,* and *Richard III* from the stage of the Jenny Lind and packed the house for the two weeks of their stay. In 1856 Laura Keen brought San Franciscans not only old favorites but such relatively uncommon productions as *Coriolanus* and *A Midsummer Night's Dream*. Along with such eminent stars from abroad, American actors like McKean Buchanan and James Stark kept the hunger for Shakespeare satisfied.[11] . . .

Shakespeare was by no means automatically treated with reverence. Nor was he accorded universal acclaim. In Davenport and neighboring areas of Eastern Iowa, where the theater flourished in both English and German, Shakespeare was seldom performed and then usually in the form of

---

[10] Rusk, *The Literature of the Middle Western Frontier*, 1:398–400, 411–14; William Bryan Gates, "Performances of Shakespeare in Ante-Bellum Mississippi," *Journal of Mississippi History*, 5 (1943):28–37; Ashley Thorndike, "Shakespeare in America," in L. Abercrombie et al., eds., *Aspects of Shakespeare* (Oxford, 1933), 116–17; Westfall, *American Shakespearean Criticism,* 59; William G. B. Carson, *The Theatre on the Frontier: The Early Years of the St. Louis Stage* (1932; reprint edn., New York, 1965); West T. Hill, Jr., *The Theatre in Early Kentucky, 1790–1820* (Lexington, Ky., 1971); Sol Smith, *Theatrical Management in the West and South for Thirty Years* (New York, 1868); and Noah Ludlow, *Dramatic Life as I Found It* (St. Louis, 1880).

[11] Rourke, *Troupers of the Gold Coast* 33, 44, 101–02; George R. MacMinn, *The Theater of the Golden Era in California* (Caldwell, Idaho, 1941), 23–24, 84, 87–88; and Margaret G. Watson, *Silver Theatre: Amusements of the Mining Frontier in Early Nevada, 1850–1864* (Glendale, Calif., 1964), 73.

short scenes and soliloquies rather than entire plays. As more than one theater manager learned, producing Shakespeare did not necessarily result in
profits. Theatrical lore often repeated the vow attributed to Robert L.
Place that he would never again produce a play by Shakespeare "no matter how many more he wrote." But these and similar incidents were exceptions to the general rule: from the large and often opulent theaters of
major cities to the makeshift stages in halls, saloons, and churches of small
towns and mining camps, wherever there was an audience for the theater,
there Shakespeare's plays were performed prominently and frequently.
Shakespeare's popularity in frontier communities in all sections of the
country may not fit Frederick Jackson Turner's image of the frontier as a
crucible, melting civilization down into a new amalgam, but it does fit our
knowledge of human beings and their need for the comfort of familiar
things under the pressure of new circumstances and surroundings. James
Fenimore Cooper had this familiarity in mind when he called Shakespeare
"the great author of America" and insisted that Americans had "just as
good a right" as Englishmen to claim Shakespeare as their countryman.[12]

Shakespeare's popularity can be determined not only by the frequency
of Shakespearean productions and the size of the audiences for them but
also by the nature of the productions and the manner in which they were
presented. Shakespeare was performed not merely alongside popular entertainment as an elite supplement to it; Shakespeare was performed as an
integral part of it. Shakespeare *was* popular entertainment in nineteenth-
century America. The theater in the first half of the nineteenth century
played the role that movies played in the first half of the twentieth: it was
a kaleidoscopic, democratic institution presenting a widely varying bill of
fare to all classes and socioeconomic groups.

During the first two-thirds of the nineteenth century, the play may
have been the thing, but it was not the only thing. It was the centerpiece,
the main attraction, but an entire evening generally consisted of a long
play, an afterpiece (usually a farce), and a variety of between-act speciali-
ties. In the spring of 1839, a playbill advertising the appearance of William
Evans Burton in *As You Like It* at Philadelphia's American Theatre announced, "Il Diavolo Antonio and his Sons, Antonio, Lorenzo, Augustus

---

[12] Place, as quoted in Dorman, *Theater in the Ante-Bellum South,* 257n; Cooper, *Notions
of the Americans,* 2 (London, 1828):100, 113. For the theater in Iowa, see Joseph S.
Schick, *The Early Theater in Eastern Iowa: Cultural Beginnings and the Rise of the
Theater in Davenport and Eastern Iowa, 1836–1863* (Chicago, 1939). Schick's appen-
dixes contain a list of all plays performed in either English or German in Iowa during
these years.

and Alphonzo will present a most magnificent display of position in the Science of Gymnastics, portraying some of the most grand and imposing groups from the ancient masters . . . to conclude with a grand Horizontal Pyramid." It was a characteristically full evening. In addition to gymnastics and Shakespeare, "Mr. Quayle (by Desire)" sang "The Swiss Drover Boy," La Petite Celeste danced "a New Grand Pas Seul," Miss Lee danced "La Cachuca," Quayle returned to sing "The Haunted Spring," Mr. Bowman told a "Yankee Story," and "the Whole" concluded "with *Ella Rosenberg* starring Mrs. Hield." [13]

Thus Shakespeare was presented amid a full range of contemporary entertainment. During the Mexican War, a New Orleans performance of *Richard III* was accompanied by "A NEW and ORIGINAL Patriotic Drama in 3 Acts, . . . (founded in part on events which have occurred during the Mexican War,) & called: Palo Alto! Or, Our Army on the Rio Grande! . . . TRIUMPH OF AMERICAN ARMS! Surrender of Gen. Vega to Capt. May! Grand Military Tableau!" It would be a mistake to conclude that Shakespeare was presented as the dry, staid ingredient in this exciting menu. On the contrary, Shakespearean plays were often announced as spectacles in their own right. In 1799 the citizens of Alexandria, Virginia, were promised the following in a production of *Macbeth:* "In Act 3d—A Regal Banquet in which the Ghost of Banquo appears. In Act 4th—A Solemn incantation & dance of Witches. In Act 5th—A grand Battle, with the defeat & death of Macbeth." At mid-century, a presentation of *Henry IV* in Philadelphia featured the "Army of Falstaff on the March! . . . Battlefield, Near Shrewsbury, Occupying the entire extent of the Stage, Alarms! Grand Battle! Single Combat! DEATH OF HOTSPUR! FINALE—Grand Tableau." [14]

Shakespeare's position as part and parcel of popular culture was reinforced by the willingness of Shakespearean actors to take part in the concluding farce. Thus Mr. Parsons followed such roles as Coriolanus, Othello, Macbeth, and Lear by playing Ralph Stackpole, "A Ring-Tailed Squealer & Rip-Staver from Salt River," in *Nick of the Woods*. Even Junius Brutus Booth followed his celebrated portrayal of Richard III with the

---

[13] Playbill, American Theatre, Philadelphia, May 13, 1839, Folger Shakespeare Library, Washington [hereafter, FSL]. For the prevalence of this format in the eighteenth century, see Rankin, *The Theater in Colonial America*, 150, 193–94; Kenneth Silverman, *A Cultural History of the American Revolution* (New York, 1976), 62; and Garff B. Wilson, *Three Hundred Years of American Drama and Theatre* (Englewood Cliffs, N.J., 1973), 19–27.

[14] Playbills, St. Charles Theatre, New Orleans, November 30, 1846, Alexandria, Virginia, July 12, 1799, and Arch Street Theatre, Philadelphia, March 2, 1857, FSL.

role of Jerry Sneak in *The Mayor of Garrat*.[15] In the postbellum years Edward L. Davenport referred to this very ability and willingness to mix genres when he lamented the decline of his profession: "Why, I've played an act from *Hamlet*, one from *Black-Eyed Susan*, and sung 'A Yankee Ship and a Yankee Crew' and danced a hornpipe, and wound up with a 'nigger' part, all in one night. Is there any one you know of today who can do that?"[16] It is clear that, as much as Shakespearean roles were prized by actors, they were not exalted; they did not unfit one for other roles and other tasks; they were not elevated to a position above the culture in which they appeared. Most frequently, the final word of the evening was not Shakespeare's. *Hamlet* might be followed by *Fortune's Frolic*, *The Merchant of Venice* by *The Lottery Ticket*, *Richard III* by *The Green Mountain Boy*, *King Lear* by *Chaos Is Come Again* on one occasion and by *Love's Laughs at Locksmiths: or, The Guardian Outwitted* on another, and, in California, *Romeo and Juliet* by *Did You Ever Send Your Wife to San Jose?*.[17]

These afterpieces and *divertissements* most often are seen as having diluted or denigrated Shakespeare. I suggest that they may be understood more meaningfully as having *integrated* him into American culture. Shakespeare was presented as part of the same milieu inhabited by magicians, dancers, singers, acrobats, minstrels, and comics. He appeared on the same playbills and was advertised in the same spirit. This does not mean that theatergoers were unable to make distinctions between Shakespearean productions and the accompanying entertainment. Of course they were. Shakespeare, after all, was what most of them came to see. But it was a Shakespeare presented as part of the culture they enjoyed, a Shakespeare rendered familiar and intimate by virtue of his context.

---

[15]Playbills, American Theatre, Philadelphia, August 30, 31, September 1, 11, 1838, June 24, 1839, FSL.

[16]Davenport, as quoted in Lloyd Morris, *Curtain Time: The Story of the American Theater* (New York, 1953), 205.

[17]Playbills, Walnut Street Theater, Philadelphia, November 30, 1821, Military Hall, Newark, N.J., August 15, 1852, Montgomery Theatre, Montgomery, Alabama, March 21, 1835, and American Theatre, Philadelphia, June 25, 1839, December 14, 1837, FSL; and MacMinn, *The Theatre of the Golden Era in California*, 90. Nevertheless, it was not uncommon for *Catharine and Petruchio*, an abridged version of *The Taming of the Shrew*, to serve as an afterpiece; see playbills, American Theatre, New Orleans, April 20, 1827, American Theatre, Philadelphia, September 26, 1838, and St. Charles Theatre, New Orleans, March 25, 1864, FSL. *Catherine and Petruchio* also served as an afterpiece when plays other than Shakespeare's were presented; see playbills, American Theatre, New Orleans, April 20, 1827, and American Theatre, Philadelphia, September 26, December 8, 1838. FSL.

THE BAD-BOY BOOM

Steven Mailloux

. . . *Huckleberry Finn* prefigures an aspect of its own reception when it satirically thematizes the potent effect of novels on impressionable young readers. Tom Sawyer's mind is indelibly marked by the romantic adventure stories he admires and then self-consciously imitates throughout the story. During the first meeting of his "highwaymen," Tom guides his gang in their plans for "robbery and murder" and reads an oath binding each member to secrecy under pain of having "his throat cut, and . . . his carcass burnt up and the ashes scattered all around." Responding to Tom's reading, "everybody said it was a real beautiful oath, and asked Tom if he got it out of his own head. He said, some of it, but the rest was out of pirate books, and robber books, and every gang that was high-toned had it."[1] Though sometimes challenging his friend's expertise, Huck is often intimidated by Tom's superior knowledge of book-lore and usually falls in line behind his friend's outlandish schemes. Imitating the imitator, Huck is affected by books at secondhand, as he comes to admire and repeat Tom's book-learned "style" in his own bad-boy escapades. At the end of the novel, Huck reproduces the fantasy of many an 1840s dime-novel reader when he determines to light out for the western territories.

By the 1880s the dime novel had evolved to include urban as well as western settings, detective heroes as well as cowboys.[2] In the westerns still being written, "blood and thunder" increased dramatically, while the detective fictions presented descriptions of crime quite disturbing to parents of boy readers. The turn to increasing violence and crime in dime novels

---

From *Rhetorical Power*. Ithaca: Cornell UP, 1989.

[1] *Adventures of Huckleberry Finn*, ed. Walter Blair and Victor Fischer (Berkeley, 1985), pp. 9–10. Of course, there is a long tradition of fiction about the effects of reading fiction. On the reception of one such work, see Dominick LaCapra, *"Madame Bovary" on Trial* (Ithaca, N.Y., 1982), esp. pp. 23–52, analyzing the interpretive arguments about the novel during the 1857 court trial and its verdict, which censured (but did not convict) the author.

[2] See Albert Johannsen, *The House of Beadle and Adams and Its Dime Novels: The Story of a Vanished Literature* (Norman, Okla., 1950), 1:3; and Edmund Pearson, *Dime Novels; or Following an Old Trail in Popular Literature* (1929; rpt. Port Washington, N.Y., 1968), pp. 138–90. For a suggestive analysis of the dime novel and cultural politics, see Michael Denning, *Mechanic Accents: Dime Novels and Working-Class Culture in America* (London, 1987).

was a response to the sharp decline in the prices of competing books. When cheap reprints of popular classics began to flood the market in the late 1870s, the dime novel needed more than its low price to attract readers.[3] Competition also came from the newspapers, as the *Police Gazette* and other crime weeklies published explicit stories of criminals' practices and their victims' sufferings. In periodical and novel form, then, boys found new, intriguing, and sometimes attractive criminal models to imitate. Or so it seemed to the horrified parents and arbiters of culture in the early 1880s.

An 1884 editorial in the *New York Tribune* began, "The work of the dime novel is being performed with even more than the usual success. The other day three boys robbed their parents and started off for the boundless West." After describing another example of juvenile crime, the writer went on to analyze its causes in detail:

> The class of literature which is mainly responsible for all this folly is distributed all over the country in immense quantities, and it is distinctly evil in its teachings and tendencies. The heroes of the dime novel are almost always thieves, robbers and immoral characters, and the heroines are no better. The stories abound with descriptions of brutality, cruelty and dishonesty. . . . Through reading this pestilent stuff a great many boys are undoubtedly put fairly in the road to ruin. They insensibly acquire a crooked moral vision. . . . They pine for opportunities to emulate the heroes they are reading about. (10 March 1884, p. 4)

Five days before this editorial appeared, Anthony Comstock had spoken in Union Hall, New York City, on the subject "The Curses of Our City." "What I desire most to impress upon you," he said to his listeners, "is the growth of vile literature. . . . Every publisher of the vile sensational papers for boys is shaping the career of the youth of our country. They glorify crime; the hero of each story is a boy who has escaped the restraints of home and entered on a life of crime." Comstock ended his lecture by calling for "public sentiment" to "root out" vile literature and other evils corrupting the young (*New York World,* 5 March 1884, p. 5).

But it was not only fictional and nonfictional descriptions of crime that inspired attempts at cultural censorship. There also appeared in the 1880s a comic culmination of the new tradition of the bad-boy story, *Peck's Bad Boy and His Pa,* published in 1883. George W. Peck, later governor of Wisconsin, created a character who was . . . much more anti-

---

[3] See Raymond Howard Shove, *Cheap Book Production in the United States, 1870 to 1891* (Urbana, Ill., 1937), pp. 1–25.

authority in his attitude and sadistic in his pranks. Readers were meant to laugh not at the boy's innocence but at his success in causing pain for his father and other adults. Peck's Bad Boy came to symbolize the worst fears of middle-class parents, and newspapers encouraged these fears with comments like these from the *Baltimore Day:*

> When we speak of the pernicious influence of the dime novel or the Jesse James style of border drama we should not forget that there are other and more insidious ways of corrupting youth, and no better illustration of this could be given than the fact that when a number of boys in Milwaukee, of respectable parentage, were recently arrested for barn burning and other wanton outrages, the boast of one of them to the magistrate was: "I am Peck's bad boy, and don't you forget it." (11 March 1884; reprinted as "Peck's Bad Play," *New York World,* 13 March 1884, p. 4)

At stake here is the shaping of youthful identity, and this boy "of respectable parentage" boasts about the fashioning already accomplished. The disciplinary techniques of family and reform school are no match, it seems, for the rhetorical self-fashioning that produced this bad-boy imitator.[4]

At least in this newspaper report, Peck's Bad Boy became a trope used by young lawbreakers for self-definition. How widespread such molding of inner lives came to be remains problematic. But if 1880s juvenile voices are hard to hear, adult voices are not. Whatever juvenile subjects made out of Peck's Bad Boy, many adults were convinced that real bad boys were made out of juveniles subjected to bad-boy fiction. Indeed, Peck's Bad Boy became a rhetorical figure marking a growing concern within the cultural conversation of the mid-eighties, a concern with the special dangers of adolescence and the perceived rise in juvenile delinquency. Unlike earlier worry over the link between pauperism and delinquency, the 1880s anxiety included fear for middle-class youths as well as for orphaned street urchins. Of course, concern over lower-class delinquents continued and was simply compounded by fears that the sons of respectable, bourgeois families were also threatened by corrupting models of bad-boy behavior in and out of texts.[5] . . .

---

[4] Cf. Stephen Greenblatt, *Renaissance Self-Fashioning: From More to Shakespeare* (Chicago, 1980), pp. 86–88, 119–20.

[5] See Geo. C. Needham, *Street Arabs and Gutter Snipes: The Pathetic and Humorous Side of Young Vagabond Life in the Great Cities, with Records of Work for Their Reclamation* (Boston, 1884), chap. 3, on "pernicious literature" as a source of "youthful debasement."

In a piece headed "The Bad-Boy Boom," the editors of the [*New York*] *World* analyzed these reports of juvenile crime:

> No one who reads and thinks need be told that the foolish desire on the part of these boys to organize themselves into predatory gangs is not the usual and natural result of mere depravity. Some new influence is at work to produce this comparatively recent symptom. One does not have to look far to find it. The organization of crime has been made fascinating to the undeveloped mind by the novelist and playwright.

The editorial continued: "Thousands of undisciplined youths have imbibed their notions of heroism and their excuse for the violation of law from the tawdry scenes and the precocious Dick Turpins thus represented." The column ended with the question: "What is society doing to stop these poisonous fountains that are sending out their subtle and fetid waters throughout the country?" (26 March 1884, p. 4). . . .

As if in direct response to this challenge, Senator John Gilbert soon introduced into the New York State Legislature a bill prohibiting "the sale or exhibition of indecent publications devoted to criminal and police news and criminal deeds, tending to corrupt the morals of youth (*New York Evening Post*, 27 March 1884, p. 1). At the same session, the New York Society for the Prevention of Cruelty to Children presented a petition that not only supported the bill but advocated a ban on the sale of dime novels as well.[6] The following year the Massachusetts legislature passed a similar bill sponsored by the New England Society for the Suppression of Vice.[7] Obviously, intense concern over the textual production of real bad boys was not restricted to the popular press in the eighties.

But that press, which soon would review Twain's bad-boy book, did provide the broadest forum for constructing the social linkage between literary effects and juvenile delinquency. Throughout the nation, not only in New York and Boston, newspapers called for cultural censorship of texts that threatened to corrupt minors. In " 'The Bad Boy' of the Period," the *Detroit Free Press* editorialized: "Most excellent is the intent of the law

---

[6] "New York Legislature," *New York Evening Post*, 27 March 1884, p. 1. The society, incorporated in 1875, aimed to prevent such abuses as "the endangering of the health or morals" of children as well as "kidnapping, abduction, abandonment, improper guardianship, begging, the use of unnatural violence," according to William Pryor Letchworth, "The History of Child-Saving Work in the State of New York," in *History of Child Saving in the United States* (Boston, 1893), p. 199.

[7] Chap. 305, *Acts and Resolves of Massachusetts* (1885), p. 758; *Annual Report of the N. E. Society for the Suppression of Vice, for the Year 1885–1886* (Boston, 1886), p. 11.

proposed in the New York Assembly for prohibiting the vicious literature which is turning American boys into savages and rendering it problematical whether the next generation will be either Jesse Jameses or Jay Goulds." Citing the *New York World*'s reports of "sad juvenile depravity" . . . the editorial began its analysis:

> In the large majority of these cases the boys were readers of the newspapers and books whose heroes are of the type of Jesse James, "Peck's Bad Boy," or some other infernal scamp who figures in the vile trash that waylays boys on nearly every street corner. . . . They are insidiously assailed by this literature, which is either vulgar or vicious. They become "bad boys," insolent little vandals, without regard for the rights of person or property. They indulge in what they call the "tricks" of the "bad boy"—which are really odious and lawless assaults upon common rights and common decency. (30 March 1884, p. 4)

Within a year, another bad boy began to tell the public about his delinquent tricks. Huck Finn's reception is best understood in the interpretive and evaluative context typified by these newspaper editorials. Not surprisingly, the *New York World*, which had been so vocal a few months earlier, headed its review "Mark Twain's Bad Boy." It began by attacking Twain at his strongest yet also his most vulnerable point, his status as a "humorist." Though not yet the cultural institution he was to become, Mark Twain in the early 1880s was an extremely popular comic satirist. But being called a humorist was not an unproblematic compliment. Humorous writing had considerably less cultural prestige than more serious literary modes in late-nineteenth-century America, a fact that Samuel Clemens recognized and sometimes worried about. Also, as the *World* reviewer argued, there are humorists and then there are "humorists": "Were Mark Twain's reputation as a humorist less well founded and established, we might say that this cheap and pernicious stuff is conclusive evidence that its author has no claim to be ranked with Artemus Ward, Sydney Smith, Dean Swift . . . or any other recognized humorist above the grade of the author of that outrageous fiction, 'Peck's Bad Boy.'" *Huckleberry Finn*, the reviewer went on, "is the story (told by himself) of a wretchedly low, vulgar, sneaking and lying Southern country boy of forty years ago." The review condemned the book's "irreverence which makes parents, guardians and people who are at all good and proper [look] ridiculous" (2 March 1885, p. 6). This judgment by no means represents the opinions of most reviewers of *Huckleberry Finn*, which received high praise for its realism and humor in many quarters. But the *New York World* review does typify a significant phase of the novel's contemporary reception. . . .

About two weeks after the *World* review, . . . the Concord Free Public Library removed *Huckleberry Finn* from its shelves. This act of cultural censorship received national publicity and inspired debate throughout the country. The *St. Louis Globe-Democrat* quoted one member of the Concord Library committee: Twain's novel "deals with a series of adventures of a very low grade of morality. . . . It is also very irreverent. . . . The whole book is of a class that is more profitable for the slums than it is for respectable people, and it is trash of the veriest sort" (17 March 1885, p. 1). An editorial in the *Springfield* (Massachusetts) *Republican* heartily approved of the library's action in "banishing" the book "on the ground that it is trashy and vicious," and called parts of the book "offensive," comparing their tone to that of a dime novel. Again echoing the rhetoric of earlier attacks on bad-boy literature and periodicals, the editorial concluded by claiming that sample sections of the novel have a low "moral level" and "their perusal cannot be anything less than harmful" (17 March 1885, p. 4).

Not surprisingly, the *New York World* gave its support to the Concord ban. Citing the library committee's judgment of the novel as "trashy and vicious," the newspaper replayed its earlier review in a more understated register: "It is very possible that the book may be as bad as the Concordians pronounce it" (18 March 1885, p. 4). The *World* followed up this editorial with several lighthearted "news items" that kept reminding its readers about the ban. For example, two days after its show of support for the library's action, this notice appeared: "Mark Twain is believed to be in concord with the Concordians in their gratuitous advertisement of 'Huckleberry Finn' as a 'bad' book, but Mr. Comstock has not yet been heard from." [8]

Comstock's voice might not have been heard on this occasion, but Mark Twain's certainly was. In a facetious public letter thanking the Concord Free Trade Club for its invitation to become an honorary member, Clemens also thanked the library committee for its "generous action" in having "condemned and excommunicated" his book, thus doubling its sales (*Boston Daily Advertiser*, 2 April 1885, p. 2). . . . Clemens' responses to the negative criticism indicate that he read it as a manifestation of the literary-ethical linkage most cultural arbiters assumed as given. . . . [H]e fully recognized how seriously his critics took literary reading as child

---

[8] *New York World*, 20 March 1885, p. 4. Mark Twain items also appeared in the *World* on 19 March, p. 4; 2 April, p. 1; 4 April, p. 4; 5 April, p. 4; 6 April, p. 4; and 9 April, p. 4. In some of these items, the *World* took philosophical and political swipes at the Concordians, underlining the fact that the newspaper's agreement with the Concord Library committee was primarily aesthetic-ethical in nature.

rearing. Even some of *Huckleberry Finn*'s defenders accepted the premises of the cultural censors. Although he was professionally concerned about juvenile delinquents, Franklin Sanborn still praised the novel in one of its most favorable reviews: "I cannot subscribe to the extreme censure passed upon this volume, which is no coarser than Mark Twain's books usually are, while it has a vein of deep morality beneath its exterior of falsehood and vice, that will redeem it in the eyes of mature persons. It is not adapted to Sunday-school libraries, and should perhaps be left unread by growing boys; but the mature in mind may read it, without distinction of age or sex, and without material harm." [9] While he vigorously rejected the judgment of the Concord Library committee, Sanborn nonetheless accepted the assumptions about juvenile reading that supported its act of censorship.

In perhaps the most rhetorically incisive analysis of the controversy, the *San Francisco Chronicle* did the best job of exposing the interpretation supporting the negative evaluations of *Huckleberry Finn*:

> The action of the Concord Public Library in excluding Mark Twain's new book . . . is absurd. The managers of this library evidently look on this book as written for boys, whereas we venture to say that upon nine boys out of ten much of the humor, as well as the pathos, would be lost. . . . When the boy under 16 reads a book he wants adventure and plenty of it. He doesn't want any moral thrown in or even implied; the elaborate jokes worked out with so much art, which are Mark Twain's specialty, are wasted upon him. (29 March 1885, p. 41)

Clearly, this reviewer thought that the Concord Library committee had misread Twain's novel—not only missed its moral but also misidentified its intended audience. Still other reviewers could see no moral appropriate for young readers, whatever the intended audience. The *Cleveland Leader and Herald,* in its approval of the Concord ban, added its opinion that the novel "cannot be said to have a very high moral tone, but records the adventures of a lot of fishy people who try to outdo each other in mischievousness; very amusing, no doubt, but hardly suitable for a Sunday school, as Horace Greeley remarked about Byron's poems" (26 April 1885, p. 4).

In light of these contemporary comments, we can see that a significant part of *Huckleberry Finn*'s reception participated in the ongoing cultural discussion of literary effects and juvenile delinquency. . . . [C]ertainly, as I have tried to show, a novel's relationship to [this discussion] functioned as a dominant criterion for judging any 1885 book about boys. Anxiety over

---

[9] Franklin B. Sanborn, "Our Boston Literary Letter," *Springfield* (Mass.) *Daily Republican,* 27 April, 1885, p. 2.

the bad-boy boom and assumptions about vulnerable readers formed an inextricable part of the rhetorical context in which such books as *Huckleberry Finn* were written, read, and evaluated in mid-1880s America. . . .

FROM *WAS HUCK BLACK? MARK TWAIN AND AFRICAN-AMERICAN VOICES*

Shelley Fisher Fishkin

The Negro looks at the white man and finds it difficult to believe that the "grays"—a Negro term for white people—can be so absurdly self-deluded over the true interrelatedness of blackness and whiteness.
—*Ralph Ellison*[1]

The range of models critics cite when they probe the sources of Mark Twain's *Adventures of Huckleberry Finn* is wide. It includes the picaresque novel, the Southwestern humorists, the Northeastern literary comedians, the newspapers Twain contributed to and read, and the tradition of the "boy book" in American popular culture. Twain himself weighed in with a clear statement about the roots of his main character, claiming that Huck Finn was based on Tom Blankenship, a poor-white outcast child Twain remembered from Hannibal, and on Tom's older brother Bence, who once helped a runaway slave.[2] These sources may seem quite different. On one

---

New York: Oxford UP, 1993.

The notes for this essay have been edited and reduced because of space restrictions. Interested readers should consult the text and Works Cited section of *Was Huck Black? Mark Twain and African-American Voices* for more complete bibliographic discussions.

[1] Ralph Ellison, "Change the Joke and Slip the Yoke," from *Shadow and Act* (New York: Random House, 1953), 55.
[2] Twain said, "'Huckleberry Finn,' was Tom Blankenship." *The Autobiography of Mark Twain*, ed. Charles Neider (New York: Harper and Row, Perennial Library, 1966), 73. [See also notes on Tom and Bence Blankenship in *Huck Finn and Tom Sawyer among the Indians and Other Unfinished Stories* by Mark Twain. Foreword and notes by Dahlia Armon and Walter Blair. Texts established by Dahlia Armon, Paul Baender, Walter Blair, William M. Gibson, and Franklin R. Rogers. The Mark Twain Library (Berkeley: U of California P, 1989), 302–03.

level, however, they are the same: they all give Twain's book a genealogy
that is unequivocally white.

Although commentators differ on the question of which models and
sources proved most significant, they tend to concur on the question of
how *Huckleberry Finn* transformed American literature. Twain's innovation of having a vernacular-speaking child tell his own story *in his
own words* was the first stroke of brilliance; Twain's awareness of the
power of satire in the service of social criticism was the second. Huck's
voice combined with Twain's satiric genius changed the shape of fiction
in America.

In this book I will suggest that Twain himself and the critics have ignored or obscured the African-American roots of his art. Critics, for the
most part, have confined their studies of the relationship between Twain's
work and African-American traditions to examinations of his depiction of
African-American folk beliefs or to analyses of the dialects spoken by his
black characters.[3] But by limiting their field of inquiry to the periphery,
they have missed the ways in which African-American voices shaped
Twain's creative imagination at its core.

Compelling evidence indicates that the model for Huck Finn's voice
was a black child instead of a white one and that this child's speech sparked
in Twain a sense of the possibilities of a vernacular narrator. The record
suggests that it may have been yet another black speaker who awakened
Twain to the power of satire as a tool of social criticism. This may help us
understand why Richard Wright found Twain's work "strangely familiar,"
and why [writers] Langston Hughes, Ralph Ellison, and David Bradley

---

[3] The notable exceptions to this rule are William Andrews, "Mark Twain and James
W. C. Pennington: Huckleberry Finn's Smallpox Lie," *Studies in American Fiction* 9
(Spring 1981), 103–12; David Bradley, "The First 'Nigger' Novel," Speech to Annual
Meeting of the Mark Twain Memorial and the New England American Studies Asso-
ciation, Hartford, Connecticut, 1985; Ralph Ellison, "What America Would Be Like
without Blacks" in *Going to the Territory* (New York: Random House, 1987), 104–12;
Lucinda MacKethan, "*Huck Finn* and the Slave Narratives: Lighting Out as Design"
Southern Review 20 (1984), 247–64; and Arnold Rampersad, "*Adventures of Huckle-
berry Finn* and Afro-American Literature" in *Satire or Evasion? Black Perspectives on
Huckleberry Finn*, ed. James S. Leonard, Thomas A. Tenney, and Thadious M. Davis
(Durham: Duke U P, 1991), 216–27. . . .

By far the most important publications on Twain's racial attitudes and on the portrayal of black characters in his work are contained in the 1984 special issue of the *Mark
Twain Journal*, "Black Writers on *Adventures of Huckleberry Finn* One Hundred Years
Later," guest-edited by Thadious M. Davis, and the book in which these and other essays were collected, *Satire or Evasion? Black Perspectives on Huckleberry Finn*.

all found Twain so empowering in their own efforts to convert African-American experience into art.[4]

As Ralph Ellison put it in 1970, *"the black man [was] a co-creator of the language that Mark Twain raised to the level of literary eloquence."* [5] But his comment sank like a stone, leaving barely a ripple on the placid surface of American literary criticism. Neither critics from the center nor critics from the margins challenged the reigning assumption that mainstream literary culture in America is certifiably "white."

[*Was Huck Black*] suggests that we need to revise our understanding of the nature of the mainstream American literary tradition. The voice we have come to accept as the vernacular voice in American literature — the voice with which Twain captured our national imagination in *Huckleberry Finn,* and that empowered Hemingway, Faulkner, and countless other writers in the twentieth century — is in large measure a voice that is "black."

Mark Twain was unusually attuned to the nuances of cadence, rhythm, syntax, and diction that distinguish one language or dialect from another, and he had a genius for transferring the oral into print. Twain, whose preferred playmates had been black, was what J. L. Dillard might have called "bidialectal"; as an engaging black child he encountered in the early 1870s helped reconnect Twain to the cadences and rhythms of black speakers from Twain's own childhood, he inspired him to liberate a language that lay buried within Twain's own linguistic repertoire and to apprehend its stunning creative potential. Twain, in turn, would help make that language available as a literary option to both white and black writers who came after him. As Ellison put it in 1991, "he made it possible for many of us to find our own voices." [6]

Mark Twain helped open American literature to the multicultural polyphony that is its birthright and special strength. He appreciated the creative vitality of African-American voices and exploited their potential in his art. In the process, he helped teach his countrymen new lessons

[4] Richard Wright, "Memories of My Grandmother," quoted in Michel Fabre, *Richard Wright: Books and Writers* (Jackson: U P of Mississippi, 1990), 161; Langston Hughes, "Introduction" to Mark Twain, *Pudd'nhead Wilson* (New York: Bantam, 1959), vii-xiii; Ralph Ellison, unpublished interview with Shelley Fisher Fishkin, 16 July 1991; David Bradley, "The First 'Nigger' Novel" (speech to the Annual Meeting of the Mark Twain Memorial and the New England American Studies Association, Hartford, Connecticut, May 1985).
[5] Ellison, "What America Would Be Like without Blacks," 109. Italics added.
[6] Ralph Ellison in Fishkin interview, 16 July 1991.

about the lyrical and exuberant energy of vernacular speech, as well as about the potential of satire and irony in the service of truth. Both of these lessons would ultimately make the culture more responsive to the voices of African-American writers in the twentieth century. They would also change its definitions of what "art" ought to look and sound like to be freshly, wholly "American." . . . In *Huckleberry Finn* something new happened that would have an enormous impact on the future of American literature. . . . [H]ere, more than in any other work, Twain allowed African-American voices to play a major role in the creation of his art. This fact may go a long way toward clarifying what makes this novel so fresh and so distinctive.

Twain's responsiveness to African-American speaking voices should come as no surprise to us, for the intense and visceral nature of his response to African-American *singing* voices has been widely documented. . . . Twain identified with [African American spirituals] in ways that went to the core of his being; they spoke uniquely to a part of himself that no other art could touch.

African-American speaking voices played much the same role, on a subliminal level, in Twain's consciousness. Twain never expressed his admiration for the power of African-American speaking voices as publicly as he expressed his admiration for the Fisk Jubilee Singers, but many such voices . . . made deep impressions on him during the years preceding *Huckleberry Finn*. During his childhood, Twain had stood in awe of the storytelling powers of a slave named Uncle Dan'l, whom he remembered from summers spent on his uncle's farm in Florida, Missouri. In his autobiography, when Twain described "the white and black children grouped on the hearth" listening to Uncle Dan'l's folk tales, he recalled "the creepy joy which quivered through me when the time for the ghost story of the 'Golden Arm' was reached—and the sense of regret, too, which came over me for it was always the last story of the evening."

In the late 1860s and 1870s, Twain was impressed by the narrative skills of black speakers like Frederick Douglass and Mary Ann Cord (a servant at the Clemenses' summer home in Elmira, New York). In 1869, the "simple language" in which Douglass told a story in the course of social conversation struck Twain as so remarkably "effective" that he described it in detail in a letter to his future wife:

> Had a talk with Fred Douglas [sic], to-day, who seemed exceedingly glad to see me—& I certainly was glad to see *him,* for I do so admire his "spunk." He told the history of his child's expulsion from Miss Tracy's school, & his simple language was very effective. Miss Tracy said the

pupils did not want a colored child among them—which he did not believe, & challenged the proof. She put it at once to a vote of the school, and asked "How many of you are willing to have this colored child be with you?" And they *all* held up their hands! Douglas added: "The children's hearts were right." There was pathos in the way he said it. I would like to hear him make a speech. . . .[7]

And in 1874, the "vigorous eloquence" with which former slave Mary Ann Cord told the story of her reunion with her son after the Civil War inspired Twain's first contribution to the esteemed *Atlantic Monthly;* a quarter-century later, Twain would still recall her stunning "gift of strong & simple speech."[8] Twain wrote that he found the story she told a "curiously strong piece of *literary work* to come unpremeditated from lips untrained in the literary art," showing his awareness of the close relationship between speaking voices and "literature." "The untrained tongue is usually wandering, wordy & vague," Twain wrote; "but this is clear, compact & coherent—yes, & vivid also, & perfectly simple & unconscious."[9] Throughout his career as a lecturer and as a writer, Twain aspired to have the effect upon his listeners and readers that speakers like Frederick Douglass and Mary Ann Cord had upon *him.* . . .

Acknowledging the African-American roots of Twain's art in *Huckleberry Finn* does not make the novel any easier to teach; on the contrary, it may raise more questions than it answers. What correlation is there between listening carefully and appreciatively to African-American voices and recognizing the full humanity of the speakers to whom those voices belong? What connection is there between seeing beyond "race" to qualities that are at root simply "human," and actively challenging the racist social and political mechanisms that prevent large numbers of people in one's society from fulfilling their human potential? Can satire play a catalytic role in shaping people's awareness of the dynamics of racism, or do satire's inherent ambiguities invite too much evasion and denial?

---

[7] Samuel L. Clemens to Olivia L. Langdon, 15 and 16 December 1869, Victor Fischer and Michael B. Frank, eds., *Mark Twain's Letters*, vol. 3, *1869*, Mark Twain Papers, gen. ed. Robert H. Hirst (Berkeley: U of California P, 1992), 426.
[8] Photocopy of manuscript of Mark Twain, "A Family Sketch," 59, 61. Mark Twain Papers. Original in Mark Twain Collection, James S. Copley Library, La Jolla, Ca. Quoted with permission.
[9] Typescript of Mark Twain's notebook 35, May–Oct. 1895, 8. Mark Twain Papers. Quoted with permission. Emphasis added.

Some of Twain's contemporaries—George Washington Cable comes immediately to mind—launched full frontal attacks against racism in the 1880s. Twain did not. Twain's attacks were more subtle, less risky, less courageous. They are also more lasting. Cable's polemics, *The Silent South* and "The Freedman's Case in Equity," for all their forceful directness, are forgotten, except among a handful of scholars. *Huckleberry Finn*, on the other hand, remains one of the most widely read and taught works by an American writer. Has it lasted despite or because of its capacity to be simultaneously all things to all people? Do its complexities contain the power of its social critique or unleash that power?

These questions remain to disturb and provoke us. . . . *Huckleberry Finn* may be more subversive, ultimately, than we might have suspected. For Twain's imaginative blending of black voices with white ones (whether conscious or unconscious) effectively deconstructs "race" as a meaningful category. "Race," for Mark Twain, far from being the "ultimate trope of difference," was often simply irrelevant. The problem of racism, on the other hand, was for Twain, and continues to be for us, undeniably real. . . .

HUCK FINN REVIEWED
The Reception of *Huckleberry Finn* in the United States, 1885–1897

Victor Fischer

. . . *Adventures of Huckleberry Finn* was not ignored by American critics in the way or to the extent supposed, nor were the reviews that did appear in the United States as uniformly unfavorable or as ignorant of what Mark Twain had achieved as has been thought. More than twenty contemporary reviews and well over a hundred contemporary comments on the book have now been found, and more than that certainly appeared and may yet be found in American newspapers and magazines. Although this number is small when compared with the more than fifty reviews that greeted both *The Innocents Abroad* (1869) and *The Gilded Age* (1873), the modest size of the critical arena was not the result of timid critics, bad publicity, and subscription publishing: it can be traced almost wholly to the author himself. Although disapproval of subscription publishing and

American Literary Realism: 1870–1910, Spring, 1983.

the bad publicity affected some contemporary reaction, they did so prin-
cipally in Massachusetts. Critics in Boston and New York did deplore the
book, and their attitudes to some extent influenced opinions expressed in
other cities around the country. However, *Huck* was also well received and
intelligently praised in New York, Connecticut, Georgia, California, and
even Massachusetts. Moreover, the Concord Library ban, which drew out
so many hostile comments on the book, was also well and repeatedly denounced by editors who had already reviewed the book favorably, or who
took this opportunity to defend it for the first time. Finally, although Mark
Twain found the hostile reaction emanating from Boston disturbing, he
also discovered that his book was selling very well. In fact, the intrinsic
merits of the book combined with this large sale to unify its readers over
the next ten years. By 1896, the Philadelphia *Public Ledger* could say, "We
are suspicious of the middle-aged person who has not read 'Huckleberry
Finn'; we envy the young person who has it still in store." [1]

I

Huckleberry Finn was one of the most thoroughly publicized of Mark
Twain's books, and some account of this publicity—much of it adven-
titious—forms a necessary background to the contemporary reaction.
On the three-month speaking tour that immediately preceded publication
(November 1884–early February 1885), Mark Twain often read excerpts
from it that were reviewed, quoted, and paraphrased by reporters. During
this same period, he frequently gave interviews that were in part about his
book.[2] Excerpts from it were syndicated in newspapers independently of
the *Century's* selections.[3] And just before (and after) publication, several
much publicized crises involving the manufacture and sale of the book
kept it in the news—not always favorably: (1) The obscene engraving. In

---

[1] *Harper's Monthly*, 93 (September 1896), *Advertiser*, p. 3.
[2] For accounts of the readings, see Paul Fatout, *Mark Twain on the Lecture Circuit*
(Bloomington: Indiana Univ. Press, 1960), pp. 214–29, and Guy A. Cardwell, *Twins of
Genius* (Michigan State College Press, 1953). In addition, Paul Fatout has generously left
on deposit in the Mark Twain Papers [hereafter MTP] a large collection of photocopies
of contemporary newspaper accounts of the tour. For a list of contemporary interviews,
see Louis J. Budd, "A Listing of and Selection from Newspaper and Magazine Interviews
with Samuel L. Clemens, 1874–1910," *American Literary Realism*, 10 (Winter 1977),
3–5.
[3] An account of the syndication is given in *Adventures of Huckleberry Finn*, ed. Walter
Blair and Victor Fischer (Berkeley, Los Angeles, London: Univ. of California Press,
1984).

late November 1884, Charles L. Webster (Mark Twain's nephew recently appointed head of the author's publishing firm) was alerted to an engraving in the book that had been surreptitiously altered to make it obscene; the defective illustration had already been distributed in copies of the salesmen's prospectus, but not in copies of the book. On 27 November 1884 the *New York World* told the story of this embarrassment, and its account was reprinted and rehashed by other newspapers, particularly in New York City. (2) The Estes & Lauriat lawsuit. In December 1884, even before Mark Twain's agents had copies of the book in hand, the Boston booksellers Estes & Lauriat published a catalog that advertised the book at a price below the standard agents' price. By 3 January 1885 Mark Twain had instituted a lawsuit, the progress of which was carefully followed in the press, with the Boston papers printing especially full accounts.[4] (3) The Concord Library ban. As Vogelback pointed out, the banning of *Huckleberry Finn* by the Concord Public Library in mid-March 1885, together with Mark Twain's subsequent letter to the Concord Free Trade Club published on 2 April, stimulated newspaper comment because editors took the opportunity to reflect on the book itself.

Even before these events, however, some newspapers had commented on the selections published in the *Century* magazine in its December 1884, January and February 1885 issues, each of which appeared up to two weeks before the first of the month. (Many newspapers and magazines routinely surveyed the monthly magazines for their readers, sometimes merely listing the contents, sometimes commenting article by article.) Some of these notices were, of course, perfunctory: the *Boston Daily Advertiser,* reviewing the third installment on 20 January 1885, said only that "Mark Twain amuses his readers with Huckleberry Finn's chronicles of 'Royalty on the Mississippi.'" Some, however, were not so impartial: the *Boston Herald,* reviewing the same issue on 1 February, said "Mark Twain's 'Royalty on the Mississippi' has a trifle of 'too muchness of that sort of thing,' which is the prevailing characteristic of this kind of writing. It is pitched in one key, and that is the key of a vulgar and abhorrent life."[5]

---

[4] See Arthur Lawrence Vogelback, "The Publication and Reception of *Huckleberry Finn* in America," *American Literature,* 11 (November 1939), pp. 262–63, for quotations from the *World* story and citations to others. Merle Johnson, *A Bibliography of the Works of Mark Twain,* rev. ed. (New York: Harper and Brothers, 1935), pp. 47–49, and Walter Blair, *Mark Twain and Huck Finn* (Berkeley and Los Angeles: Univ. of California Press, 1960), pp. 364–67, give accounts of the discovery and subsequent flurry when the publisher demanded the return of the mutilated page from the distributed prospectuses, and the printer was forced to replace the page in "thousands" of already printed volumes.
[5] *Boston Daily Advertiser,* 20 January 1885, p. 2; *Boston Herald,* 1 February 1885, p. 17.

It may have been the negative tone of some of the Estes & Lauriat stories or a review of the *Century* selections such as the *Boston Herald*'s that alerted Mark Twain to the possibility of a bad critical reception and reminded him of the necessity of sending out review copies of the book. On 23 January, three weeks before publication, he began to advise Webster about how best to distribute the book for review: "A day or two after the book issues, you want to send a cloth copy to the prominent journals & magazines of the country. Perhaps you better send to the prominent magazines NOW (with unbound copies to make extracts from.)" On 26 January he re-emphasized his wish that unbound copies be sent to the magazines "now," suggesting that Webster "ask Gilder if he can't review it in next Century." The next day he refined his strategy: "Send no copy of the book to any newspaper until after the <ser> Century or the Atlantic shall have reviewed it. <I make an exception in New York.> [¶] What we want is a favorable review, by an authority—then immediately distribute the book among the press."[6] . . .

> As to notices, I suggest this plan: Send immediately, copies (bound & unbound) to the [New York] Evening Post, Sun, World, & the Nation; the Hartford Courant, Post & Times; & the principal Boston dailies; Baltimore American. (Never send any to N.Y. Graphic.)
>
> Keep a sharp lookout, & if the general tone of the resulting notices is favorable, then send out your 300 press copies over the land. . . .

If we suppose that Webster distributed review copies only in accord with this plan, the question cannot any longer be why *Huckleberry Finn* was neglected by almost every major American journal (as it appears to have been), but rather whether it was seriously reviewed by the three magazines (*Century, Atlantic,* and *Nation*) and by the newspapers that were sent review copies—and beyond that, whether the "300 press copies" were ever subsequently distributed "over the land." Most of the magazines and newspapers specified by Mark Twain did in fact review the book. Both the *Century* and the *Atlantic* printed favorable reviews, while the *Nation* confined itself to listing *Huck* among its "Books of the Week," and announcing the English-language German edition (published with

---

[6] Clemens to Webster, 23 January, 26 January, and 27 January 1885, in *Mark Twain: Business Man*, ed. Samuel Charles Webster (Boston: Little, Brown and Co., 1946) [hereafter MTBus], pp. 294, 297, 298. These and subsequent letters from MTBus have been corrected where possible against the original manuscripts in the Jean Webster McKinney Family Papers, Francis Fitz Randolph Rare Book Room, Vassar College Library, Poughkeepsie, New York. Angle brackets enclose Mark Twain's cancellations.

Mark Twain's blessing by Bernhard Tauchnitz).[7] The *Century* and *Atlantic* reviews appeared too late to influence the newspapers in the way Mark Twain had hoped; but their praise was surely not without some effect. The *Century* review, by Thomas Sergeant Perry, appeared in the May issue (that is, mid-April) and is well known.[8] The *Atlantic* review was unsigned, briefer, but also favorable; it appeared in the April issue (mid-March) and has not been previously identified:

> Mark Twain's new book for young folks, The Adventures of Huckleberry Finn (C. L. Webster & Co.), is in some sense a sequel to The Adventures of Tom Sawyer, though each of the two stories is complete in itself. Huckleberry Finn, Tom Sawyer's old comrade, is not only the hero but the historian of his adventures, and certainly Mr. Clemens himself could not have related them more amusingly. The work is sold only by subscription.[9]

The hostility of trade-house reviewers toward subscription publishers has been advanced as a possible reason for the neglect of *Huck Finn* in the *Atlantic* and the newspapers. Although this review was more perfunctory than Mark Twain might have wished, it shows no evident bias against the book because it was published by subscription. Moreover, of the eight newspapers Mark Twain mentioned by name in his 10 February letter, reviews appeared in five: the *New York Sun* and *World* and the *Hartford Courant, Post,* and *Times.* In addition, three of the four or five "principal" Boston dailies—the *Evening Traveller,* the *Daily Advertiser,* and the *Globe*—printed reviews. The remaining papers—the *New York Evening Post,* the *Baltimore American,* and the other Boston papers that may have received review copies—failed to publish an original review, but even they demonstrated familiarity with the book in shorter notices, particularly after the Concord Library ban.[10]

---

[7] *Nation,* 40 (26 February 1885), 181, 182.
[8] It is reprinted in full in *Mark Twain: The Critical Heritage,* ed. Frederick Anderson, with the assistance of Kenneth M. Sanderson (New York: Barnes and Noble, 1971), 128–30.
[9] *Atlantic,* 55 (April 1885), 576.
[10] The *New York Post* printed the following curious story on 21 February (p. 2), showing the author's knowledge of the Royal Nonesuch episode:

> We apprehend that Mr. Henry Irving has been made the victim of Huckleberry Fenn [sic] or some other designing joker of the Western country. In an article in the *Fortnightly Review* . . . Mr. Irving tells us of the narrow escape which a travelling

The *New York Sun* began its review of 15 February by calling Mark
Twain "the greatest living authority on the Mississippi River and on juvenile cussedness," and said that despite Mark Twain's notice about what
will happen to persons "attempting to find a motive, a moral, or a plot in
the narrative," his

> last story can brag of both a motive and a fairish plot, while a beautiful
> moral decorates nearly every one of its shining pages, namely, that it is
> better and nobler to lie simply and directly to the purpose than to put on
> frills of overelaborate mendacity, or to wander from the main chance into
> the byways of unnecessary prevarication. That is what is taught by the
> careers of Huckleberry Finn and Tom Sawyer; and along with the lesson
> we get no end of stirring incident, river lore, human nature, philology,
> and fun.[11]

The reviewer quoted at length from the book, including passages about
Huck's life at the widow's, Pap's speech about the "govment," Jim's investments, and Judith Loftus's encounter with Huck disguised as a girl[.]

> Thus it always was with Huckleberry Finn. His fabrications lay in strata,
> and if any penetrating person, like this woman, succeeded in getting
> through one thickness it was only to strike a subjacent layer, which usu-
> ally proved satisfactory. Huck was never stumped. In the course of the
> varied and entertaining adventures with which the historian has filled this
> book the hero frequently indulges in bursts of candor; but it is always a
> voluntary performance on his part. He is never forced, beguiled, or sur-
> prised into telling the truth when from his point of view a fiction is the
> proper thing for the occasion. His resources are unfailing; and at times,

---

dramatic company made from sudden death in Colorado. The manager, he says,
had been obliged on one occasion to cut short the performance by half an hour, in
a certain town, in order to catch the train to the next place. He was not aware how
much dissatisfaction had been caused by this curtailment of the programme until
some time afterward, when the course of business brought him back to the same
town. On approaching it he was met, some miles out, by the Sheriff, who warned
him not to come nearer because the people were waiting for him with shot-guns.
Of course he cancelled the engagement without an instant's hesitation.

[11] *New York Sun*, 15 February 1885, p. 3. Charles A. Dana, editor of the *Sun*, had a pol-
icy of guarding the identity of his writers, as did many other newspaper editors and publishers of the time. Most book reviews were written by the literary editor, Mayo W.
Hazeltine, whose specialties were "prodigious book reviews which filled an entire page of
the Sunday *Sun*" and "were considered compulsory reading for those who wished to keep
abreast of literary trends" (Candace Stone, *Dana and the Sun* [New York: Dodd, Mead
& Co., 1938], pp. 35, 40). However, Louis J. Budd suggests as a more likely candidate
Edward Mitchell, author of one or two burlesque interviews with Clemens in the *Sun*.

in the more complicated situations into which his fortunes bring him as he makes his way down the Mississippi with Jim, his statements become marvels of ingenious complexity, like a series of carved ivory balls within balls, or a nest of Japanese boxes. And yet each individual lie is perfectly simple and generally plausible. For this reason his achievements are really more artistic, although much less elaborate and showy, than those of the better-known Tom Sawyer, who possessed a far livelier imagination and a far greater fund of general information on which to draw in an emergency. Tom's school was the ornate, Huckleberry's the practical; and yet the latter, perhaps for this very reason, persisted in looking u[p] to his comrade as to a superior being, his master in the art.

Introducing the incident near Cairo where Huck nearly turns in Jim, the reviewer noted that "Huck's moral nature began to experience a singular reawakening. A conscience that was sufficiently elastic on the subject of mendacity, and that never kicked when Huck stole chickens or watermelons, . . . was strongly agitated by the thought that here he was helping a slave to escape to freedom." After quoting the later, related incident, where Huck tries to pray and finds he cannot because "You can't pray a lie," the reviewer defended the truth of the passage and the book: "Although this seems like an audacious burlesque of religious sentiment, reaching quite to the limits of the permissible, the reflections attributed to Huckleberry on the enormity of his transgression are probably as true as anything else in the book to the Missouri creed of forty years ago." The *Sun* reviewer also quoted briefly from the feud chapters, which he called "the most interesting episode in the story," and at greater length from the murder of Boggs and the Wilks funeral episodes. Commending Mark Twain's achievement and, somewhat obscurely, his "good English," the reviewer concluded:

> Who on earth except Mark Twain would ever cotton to a youth like Huckleberry Finn for the hero of what is neither a boys' book nor a grown-up novel? And who else, having elected to record the scrapes of this uncommonly able descendant of Ananias, and without mitigating any of his innumerable lies, or blinking any of his countless sins against the common decencies of literature, could so present his character and misdeeds as to hold the reader through four hundred pages and then dismiss him Huck's friend for life? We want to say something, too, about Mark Twain's good English. His book, for the most part, is made up of words of one syllable.

The *New York World* of 2 March was not so sympathetic. Offended both by the subject of the book and its subversive and "irreverent" treatment, the *World* headed its review "'Humor' of a Very Low Order—Wit and Literary Ability Wasted on a Pitiable Exhibition of Irreverence and Vulgarity," and attacked the author as well as his book:

> Were Mark Twain's reputation as a humorist less well founded and es-
> tablished, we might say that this cheap and pernicious stuff is conclusive
> evidence that its author has no claim to be ranked with Artem[u]s Ward,
> Sydney Smith, Dean Swift, John Hay, or any other recognized humorist
> above the grade of the author of that outrageous fiction, "Peck's Bad Boy."
> "Huckleberry Finn" is the story (told by himself) of a wretchedly low,
> vulgar, sneaking and lying Southern country boy of forty years ago. He
> runs away from a drunken father in company with a runaway negro.
> They are joined by a couple of rascally impostors. . . . The humor of the
> work, if it can be called such, depends almost wholly on the scrapes
> into which the quartet are led by the rascality of the impostors, "Huck's"
> lying, the negro's superstition and fear and on the irreverence which
> makes parents, guardians and people who are at all good and proper
> ridiculous. That such stuff should be considered humor is more than a
> pity. Even the author objects to it being considered literature. But what
> can be said of a man of Mr. Clemens's wit, ability and position deliber-
> ately imposing upon an unoffending public a piece of careless hack-work
> in which a few good things are dropped amid a mass of rubbish. . . .
> There is an abundance of moving accidents by fire and flood, a number
> of situations more or less unpleasant in which he involves his dramatis
> personae and then leaves them to lie themselves out of it, a series of epi-
> sodes and digressions apparently introduced to give Mr. Twain's peculiar
> sense of humor a breathing spell, and finally two or three unusually atro-
> cious murders in cold blood, thrown in by way of incidental diversion.[12]

The reviewer went on to describe the plot with mock approval, noting, for instance, that the "various doings and sayings of [Huck and Pap] are told with infinite grace and fancy and an excruciating funny account of an attack of delirium tremens . . . is introduced with thrilling effect." He said that "the entertainment which the two frauds, who are known as the 'King' and the 'Duke,' give at one of the river towns is also extremely elevated in character, and the 'Royal Nonesuch' should find a favored place in the list of parlor exhibitions." Charging that the "cream" of the Wilks episode had been "cleverly skimmed off for the *Century*," he quoted from the "orgies/ obsequies" episode at the Wilks funeral and from the description of Jim's cabin after it had been filled with spiders, rats, and snakes. And he con-cluded on a scornful note about Mark Twain's use of "seven dialects": "Dis-criminating which is which in this extraordinary assortment will be found a pleasant literary amusement for people who are fond of puzzles." . . .

---

[12] *New York World,* 2 March 1885, p. 3.

II

In mid-March 1885, just after the first newspaper reviews had appeared, *Huck Finn* became news once again when it was banned by the Concord Free Public Library in Massachusetts. Many editorials appeared in answer to this action: some were written for papers which had already reviewed the book and took the occasion to reassess it, but more were for papers which had not previously expressed an opinion, but did so now. On the whole, the papers that had reviewed the book favorably remained favorable. Those that had been critical—the *New York World* and the Boston papers—took the incident and Mark Twain's subsequent letter to the Concord Free Trade Club as an opportunity to criticize the author's character as well as his book. The negative reaction in Boston, in fact, was so strong and so widely publicized that it has been mistakenly represented as typifying the book's American reception.

When the Concord Library Committee—Edward W. Emerson, Henry M. Grout, George A. King, Reuben N. Rice, and James L. Whitney—decided not to circulate a copy of *Huck Finn* that had been purchased by the library, and made public their reasons, the *Boston Transcript* published a brief account of the action on 17 March, noting that the "librarian and the other members of the committee" characterized the whole book as being "more suited to the slums than to intelligent, respectable people." [13] Fuller accounts, clearly from the same source as the *Transcript* story, appeared in the *St. Louis Globe-Democrat* of 17 March and the *New York Herald* of 18 March. The *Globe-Democrat,* after noting the library's action, quoted the committee members at length, without comment:

> Said one member of the committee: "While I do not wish to state it as my opinion that the book is absolutely immoral in its tone, still it seems to me that it contains but very little humor, and that little is of a very coarse type. If it were not for the author's reputation the book would undoubtedly meet with severe criticism. I regard it as the veriest trash." Another member says: "I have examined the book and my objections to it are these: It deals with a series of adventures of a very low grade of morality; it is couched in the language of a rough, ignorant dialect, and all through its pages there is a systematic use of bad grammar and an employment of rough, coarse, inelegant expressions. It is also very irreverent. To sum up,

---

[13] *Boston Transcript,* 17 March 1885, p. 4; reprinted in Kenneth S. Lynn, *Huckleberry Finn: Text, Sources, Criticism* (New York, Burlingame: Harcourt, Brace & World, 1961), p. 171. Concord librarian was Ellen F. Whitney. Three of the more prominent men of the Concord Library Committee were: Edward Waldo Emerson, son of Ralph Waldo, an

the book is flippant and irreverent in its style. It deals with a series of experiences that are certainly not elevating. The whole book is of a class that is more profitable for the slums than it is for respectable people, and it is trash of the veriest sort."[14]

The *Herald,* which also quoted the committee, was clearly amused by the ban:

The sage censors of the Concord public library have unanimously reached the conclusion that "Huckleberry Finn" is not the sort of reading matter for the knowledge seekers of a town which boasts the only "summer school of philosophy" in the universe. They have accordingly banished it from the shelves of that institution.

The reasons which moved them to this action are weighty and to the point. One of the Library Committee, while not prepared to hazard the opinion that the book is "absolutely immoral in its tone," does not hesitate to declare that to him "it seems to contain but very little humor." Another committeeman perused the volume with great care and discovered that it was "couched in the language of a rough, ignorant dialect" and that "all through its pages there is a systematic use of bad grammar and an employment of inelegant expressions." The third member voted the book "flippant" and "trash of the veriest sort." They all united in the verdict that "it deals with a series of experiences that are certainly not elevating," and voted that it could not be tolerated in the public library.

The committee very considerately explain the mystery of how this unworthy production happened to find its way into the collection under their charge. "Knowing the author's reputation," and presumably being familiar with the philosophic pages of "The Innocents Abroad," "Roughing It," "The Adventures of Tom Sawyer," "The Jumping Frog," &c., they deemed it "totally unnecessary to make a very careful examination of 'Huckleberry Finn' before sending it to Concord." But the learned librarian, probably seizing upon it on its arrival to peruse it with eager zest, "was not particularly pleased with it." He promptly communicated his feelings to the committee, who at once proceeded to enter upon a critical reading of the suspected volume, with the results that are now laid before the public.[15]

instructor at the Museum of Fine Arts in Boston in 1885; George Augustus King, lawyer and former state senator; and James Lyman Whitney, librarian at the Boston Library, and chairman of the School Committee of Concord. Albert Tolman was secretary to the Library Committee. I thank Marcia E. Moss of the Concord Public Library for her help in uncovering the information about the membership of the 1885 Library Committee.
[14] *St. Louis Globe-Democrat,* 17 March 1885, p. 1.
[15] *New York Herald,* 18 March 1885, p. 6.

News of the ban, often reported without editorial comment, spread immediately, appearing within two days in papers as far away as California. On 18 March the *San Jose Times-Mercury* noted that the "Concord Public Library Committee has unanimously decided to exclude Mark Twain's new book."[16] The following day, the *Stockton Evening Mail* printed a similar dispatch, adding that the book was excluded "as flippant, irreverent and trashy."[17] Most papers, however, could not resist editorial comment. The *Boston Daily Globe* of 17 March used the occasion to mock not only the library committee but the town's reputation for obscure Transcendental thought:

> Members of the Concord public library committee have drawn the line on literature, and pronounced Mark Twain's "Huckleberry Finn" too "coarse" for a place among the classic tomes that educate and edify the people. They do not pick out any particular passage, but just sit on the book in general. When Mark writes another book he should think of the Concord School of Philosophy and put a little more whenceness of the hereafter among his nowness of the here.[18]

The *New York World* of 18 March mistakenly thought the book had been "repudiated by the Concord Public Schools," but similarly joked that *Huck Finn* would be "immensely popular with the Concord School of Philosophy, which will find in it no end of Henceness of the Which and Thingness of the Unknowable."[19] A few of the papers immediately called attention to the great advertising potential of the Concord ban, and implicit in their stories was a defense of the book. On 17 March the *St. Louis Post-Dispatch* wrote that the directors of the library had "joined in the general scheme to advertise Mark Twain's new book 'Huckleberry Finn'. They have placed it on the *Index Expurgatorius,* and this will compel every citizen of Concord to read the book in order to see why the guardians of his morals prohibited it. Concord keeps up its recent reputation of being the home of speculative philosophy and of practical nonsense."[20] On 18 March the *Hartford Courant* was more explicit: "The result [of the ban] will be that people in Concord will buy the book instead of drawing it from the library, and

---

[16] *San Jose Times-Mercury,* 18 March 1885, p. 4.
[17] *Stockton Evening Mail,* 19 March 1885, p. 2.
[18] *Boston Daily Globe,* 17 March 1885, p. 2.
[19] *New York World,* 18 March 1885, p. 4.
[20] *St. Louis Post-Dispatch,* 17 March 1885, p. 4.

those who do will smile not only at the book but at the idea that it is not for respectable people."[21] On the same day, and in the same vein, the *New York Sun* wrote:

> People who have watched the alarming rise and progress of the Concord Summer School of Philosophy will not be surprised that Mark Twain's delightful and healthful humor should be driven out of that unhappy village. Transcendentalism, even before it was second hand, and humor never got along with each other, and Concord has pampered its Oversoul at the expense of its understanding. In objecting to "Huckleberry Finn" as frivolous and what not, the authorities of the Concord Public Library have unconsciously and for the first time been humorous with a humor equal to that of Mr. Clemens, who, by the way, ought to send them a small check in acknowledgment of the compliment and the advertising they have given him.[22]

Even the Concord newspaper, the *Freeman,* reprinted on 20 March the mocking story that had appeared in the *Boston Daily Globe* (and evidently the *Record*) on 17 March, and noted: "Of course the committee are to be commended for their intentions, but, haven't they drawn the line a little inconsistently? As it is, however, the sale of the pr[o]scribed book has largely increased in Concord this week."[23]

Mark Twain's initial reaction, perhaps after reading some of these earlier accounts, was almost exultant. "The Committee," he wrote to Webster on 18 March, ". . . have given us a rattling tip-top puff which will go into every paper in the country. They have expelled Huck from their library as 'trash & suitable only for the slums.' That will sell 25,000 copies for us, sure."[24] . . .

---

[21] *Hartford Courant,* 18 March 1885, p. 2.
[22] *New York Sun,* 18 March 1885, p. 2
[23] *Concord Freeman,* 20 March 1885, n.p.
[24] Clemens to Webster, 18 March 1885, MTP. This now famous letter of Mark Twain's has been printed or quoted in a number of places; for the full text see *Mark Twain's Letters,* II, ed. Albert Bigelow Paine (New York: Harper and Brothers, 1917), pp. 452–53.

PART TWO

The Text

published in 1884

Setting: 1835 - 1845 : ~~before~~ civil war
Mississippi Valley : Heart of America

Tone : satirical, humorous

Voice : (dialectic, mostly true with "stretchers")
1st person narrator (Huck)

genre: novel, fictional autobiography

HUCKLEBERRY FINN.

ADVENTURES OF HUCKLEBERRY FINN

(Tom Sawyer's Comrade)

Scene: The Mississippi Valley
Time: Forty to Fifty Years Ago
[Sometime between 1835 and 1845]

By *Mark Twain*

Notes by Lyrae Van Clief-Stefanon

NOTICE

Persons attempting to find a motive in this narrative will be prosecuted; persons attempting to find a moral in it will be banished; persons attempting to find a plot in it will be shot.

—*By Order of the Author,*
 Per G. G., Chief of Ordnance.

EXPLANATORY

In this book a number of dialects are used, to wit: the Missouri negro dialect; the extremest form of the backwoods South-Western dialect; the ordinary "Pike-County" dialect; and four modified varieties of this last. The shadings have not been done in a haphazard fashion, or by guess-work; but pain-stakingly, and with the trustworthy guidance and support of personal familiarity with these several forms of speech.

I make this explanation for the reason that without it many readers would suppose that all these characters were trying to talk alike and not succeeding.

—*The Author.*

Chapter I
Civilizing Huck—Miss Watson—
Tom Sawyer Waits

You don't know about me, without you have read a book[1] by the name of "The Adventures of Tom Sawyer," but that ain't no matter. That book was made by Mr. Mark Twain, and he told the truth, mainly. There was things which he stretched, but mainly he told the truth. That is nothing. I never seen anybody but lied, one time or another, without it was Aunt Polly, or the widow, or maybe Mary.

THE WIDOW'S.

Aunt Polly—Tom's Aunt Polly, she is—and Mary, and the Widow Douglas, is all told about in that book—which is mostly a true book; with some stretchers, as I said before.

Now the way that the book winds up, is this: Tom and me found the money that the robbers hid in the cave, and it made us rich. We got six thousand dollars apiece—all gold. It was an awful sight of money when it was piled up. Well, Judge Thatcher, he took it and put it out at interest, and it fetched us a dollar a day apiece, all the year round—more than a body could tell what to do with. The Widow Douglas, she took me for her son, and allowed she would sivilize me; but it was rough living in the house all the time, considering

---

[1] By the time of its official American publication in 1876, excerpts of *The Adventures of Tom Sawyer* had already appeared in several American newspapers and a pirated Canadian edition was in circulation. New printings of *Tom Sawyer*, issued "every two to three years during the 1880s," allowed Twain's audience plenty of opportunity to get to know Huck by the 1885 publication of *Adventures of Huckleberry Finn*.

how dismal regular and decent the widow was in all her ways; and so when I couldn't stand it no longer, I lit out. I got into my old rags, and my sugar-hogshead[2] again, and was free and satisfied. But Tom Sawyer, he hunted me up and said he was going to start a band of robbers, and I might join if I would go back to the widow and be respectable. So I went back.

The widow she cried over me, and called me a poor lost lamb, and she called me a lot of other names, too, but she never meant no harm by it. She put me in them new clothes again, and I couldn't do nothing but sweat and sweat, and feel all cramped up. Well, then, the old thing commenced again. The widow rung a bell for supper, and you had to come to time. When you got to the table you couldn't go right to eating, but you had to wait for the widow to tuck down her head and grumble a little over the victuals, though there warn't really anything the matter with them. That is, nothing only everything was cooked by itself. In a barrel of odds and ends it is different; things get mixed up, and the juice kind of swaps around, and the things go better.

After supper she got out her book and learned me about Moses and the Bulrushers;[3] and I was in a sweat to find out all about him; but by-and-by she let it out that Moses had been dead a considerable long time; so then I didn't care no more about him; because I don't take no stock in dead people.

Pretty soon I wanted to smoke, and asked the widow to let me. But she wouldn't. She said it was a mean practice and wasn't clean, and I must try to not do it any more. That is just the way with some people. They get down on a thing when they don't know nothing about it. Here she was a bothering about Moses, which was no kin to her, and no use to anybody, being gone, you see, yet finding a power of fault with me for doing a thing that had some good in it. And she took snuff too; of course that was all right, because she done it herself.

Her sister, Miss Watson, a tolerable slim old maid, with goggles on, had just come to live with her, and took a set at me now, with a spelling-book. She worked me middling hard for about an hour, and then the widow made her ease up. I couldn't stood it much longer. Then for an hour it was deadly

---

[2] A large cask or barrel with a capacity of 63 to 140 gallons.

[3] Exod. 2.3. In the Old Testament, Pharaoh, king of Egypt, demands that all the male children of Israel be killed by being cast into the river. However, Moses' mother builds an ark of bulrushes and sets him afloat. Pharaoh's own daughter finds and adopts Moses, who later leads his people out of Egypt to freedom. Moses' story of adoption parallels Huck's and reveals Twain's use of biblical myths to comment on the moral dilemma Huck faces in hiding Jim.

dull, and I was fidgety. Miss Watson would say, "Don't put your feet up there, Huckleberry;" and "don't scrunch up like that, Huckleberry—set up straight;" and pretty soon she would say, "Don't gap and stretch like that, Huckleberry—why don't you try to behave?" Then she told me all about the bad place, and I said I wished I was there. She got mad, then, but I didn't mean no harm. All I wanted was to go somewheres; all I wanted was a change, I warn't particular. She said it was wicked to say what I said; said she wouldn't say it for the whole world; *she* was going to live so as to go to the good place. Well, I couldn't see no advantage in going where she was going, so I made up my mind I wouldn't try for it. But I never said so, because it would only make trouble, and wouldn't do no good.

Now she had got a start, and she went on and told me all about the good place. She said all a body would have to do there was to go around all day long with a harp and sing, forever and ever. So I didn't think much of it. But I never said so. I asked her if she reckoned Tom Sawyer would go there, and, she said, not by a considerable sight. I was glad about that, because I wanted him and me to be together.

Miss Watson she kept pecking at me, and it got tiresome and lonesome. By-and-by they fetched the niggers in and had prayers,[4] and then everybody was off to bed. I went up to my room with a piece of candle and put it on the table. Then I set down in a chair by the window and tried to think of something cheerful, but it warn't no use. I felt so lonesome I most wished I was dead. The stars was shining, and the leaves rustled in the woods ever so mournful; and I heard an owl, away off, who-whooing about somebody that was dead, and a whippowill and a dog crying about somebody that was going to die; and the wind was trying to whisper something to me and I couldn't make out what it was, and so it made the cold shivers run over me. Then away out in the woods I heard that kind of a sound that a ghost makes when it wants to tell about something that's on its mind and can't make itself understood, and so can't rest easy in its grave and has to go about that way every night grieving. I got so down-hearted and scared, I did wish I had some company. Pretty soon a spider went crawling up my shoulder, and I flipped it off and it lit in the candle; and before I could budge it was all shriveled up. I didn't need anybody to tell me that that was an awful bad sign and would fetch me some bad luck, so I was scared and most shook the clothes off of me. I got up and turned around in my tracks three times and crossed my breast every time; and

---

[4] *Narrative of William W. Brown, A Fugitive Slave* (1848) states, "My master had family worship, night and morning. At night the slaves were called in to attend; but in the mornings they had to be at their work, and master did all the praying" (Weeks 13).

then I tied up a little lock of my hair with a thread to keep witches away. But I hadn't no confidence. You do that when you've lost a horse-shoe that you've found, instead of nailing it up over the door, but I hadn't ever heard anybody say it was any way to keep off bad luck when you'd killed a spider.

I set down again, a shaking all over, and got out my pipe for a smoke; for the house was all as still as death, now, and so the widow wouldn't know. Well, after a long time I heard the clock away off in the town go boom—boom—boom—twelve licks—and all still again—stiller than ever. Pretty soon I heard a twig snap, down in the dark amongst the trees—something was a stirring. I set still and listened. Directly I could just barely hear a *"me-yow! me-yow!"* down there. That was good! Says I, *"me-yow! me-yow!"* as soft as I could, and then I put out the light and scrambled out of the window onto the shed. Then I slipped down to the ground and crawled in among the trees, and sure enough there was Tom Sawyer waiting for me.

Chapter II
The Boys Escape Jim—Tom Sawyer's Gang— Deep-laid Plans

We went tip-toeing along a path amongst the trees back towards the end of the widow's garden, stooping down so as the branches wouldn't scrape our heads. When we was passing by the kitchen I fell over a root and made a noise. We scrouched down and laid still. Miss Watson's big nigger, named Jim, was setting in the kitchen door; we could see him pretty clear, because there was a light behind him. He got up and stretched his neck out about a minute, listening. Then he says,

"Who dah?"

He listened some more; then he come tip-toeing down and stood right between us; we could a touched him, nearly. Well, likely it was minutes and minutes that there warn't a sound, and we all there so close together. There was a place on my ankle that got to itching; but I dasn't scratch it; and then my ear begun to itch; and next my back, right between my shoulders. Seemed like I'd die if I couldn't scratch. Well, I've noticed that thing plenty of times since. If you are with the quality, or at a funeral, or trying to go to sleep when you ain't sleepy—if you are anywheres where it won't do for you to scratch, why you will itch all over in upwards of a thousand places. Pretty soon Jim says:

"Say—who is you? Whar is you? Dog my cats ef I didn' hear sumf'n. Well, I knows what I's gwyne to do: I's gwyne to set down here and listen tell I hears it agin."

THEY TIP-TOED ALONG.

So he set down on the ground betwixt me and Tom. He leaned his back up against a tree, and stretched his legs out till one of them most touched one of mine. My nose begun to itch. It itched till the tears come into my eyes. But I dasn't scratch. Then it begun to itch on the inside. Next I got to itching underneath. I didn't know how I was going to set still. This miserableness went on as much as six or seven minutes; but it seemed a sight longer than that. I was itching in eleven different places now. I reckoned I couldn't stand it more'n a minute longer, but I set my teeth hard and got ready to try. Just then Jim begun to breathe heavy; next he begun to snore—and then I was pretty soon comfortable again.

Tom he made a sign to me— kind of a little noise with his mouth—and we went creeping away on our hands and knees. When we was ten foot off, Tom whispered to me and wanted to tie Jim to the tree for fun; but I said no; he might wake and make a disturbance, and then they'd find out I warn't in. Then Tom said he hadn't got candles enough, and he would slip in the kitchen and get some more. I didn't want him to try. I said Jim might wake up and come. But Tom wanted to resk it; so we slid in there and got three candles, and Tom laid five cents on the table for pay. Then we got out, and I was in a sweat to get away; but nothing would do Tom but he must crawl to where Jim was, on his hands and knees, and play something on him. I waited, and it seemed a good while, everything was so still and lonesome.

As soon as Tom was back, we cut along the path, around the garden fence, and by-and-by fetched up on the steep top of the hill the other side of the house. Tom said he slipped Jim's hat off of his head and hung it on a limb right over him, and Jim stirred a little, but he didn't wake. After-

wards Jim said the witches bewitched him and put him in a trance, and
rode him all over the State, and then set him under the trees again and hung
his hat on a limb to show who done it. And next time Jim told it he said
they rode him down to New Orleans; and after that, every time he told it
he spread it more and more, till by-and-by he said they rode him all over
the world, and tired him most to death, and his back was all over saddle-
boils. Jim was monstrous proud about it, and he got so he wouldn't hardly
notice the other niggers. Niggers would come miles to hear Jim tell about
it, and he was more looked up to than any nigger in that country. Strange
niggers would stand with their mouths open and look him all over, same as
if he was a wonder. Niggers is always talking about witches in the dark by
the kitchen fire; but whenever one was talking and letting on to know all
about such things, Jim would happen in and say, "Hm! What you know
'bout witches?" and that nigger was corked up and had to take a back seat.
Jim always kept that five-center piece around his neck [5] with a string and
said it was a charm the devil give to him with his own hands and told him
he could cure anybody with it and fetch witches whenever he wanted to, just
by saying something to it; but he never told what it was he said to it. Niggers would come from all around there and give Jim anything they had, just
for a sight of that five-center piece; but they wouldn't touch it, because the
devil had had his hands on it. Jim was most ruined, for a servant, because he
got so stuck up on account of having seen the devil and been rode by witches. [6]

Well, when Tom and me got to the edge of the hill-top, we looked away
down into the village and could see three or four lights twinkling, where
there was sick folks, may be; and the stars over us was sparkling ever so
fine; and down by the village was the river, a whole mile broad, and awful
still and grand. We went down the hill and found Jo Harper, and Ben Rogers,

---

[5] In this passage Jim, instead of remaining the butt of the joke, uses Tom's trick to his
own advantage. Victor Doyno writes, "Modern readers may need to know that in some
regions of the country it was common for slaves to have to wear a neck-token or badge,
specifying the slave's name, owner, and usual duty or job. . . . Twain may have created
a satirical jab at the slave-identification system, demonstrating Jim's transformative cleverness" (Doyno, "Economics").
[6] The belief in witches and their ability to commandeer human beings to ride during the
night appears in both American and European folklore. David L. Smith points out the
way in which Jim uses the superstition to his advantage: "By constructing a fictitious
narrative of his own experience, Jim elevates himself above his prescribed station in
life. . . . In assessing Jim's character, we should keep in mind that forethought, creativity, and shrewdness are qualities that racial discourse . . . denies to 'the Negro.' Viewed
in this way, the fact of superstition, which traditionally connotes ignorance and unso-
phistication, becomes far less important than the ends to which superstition is put"
(109–10).

and two or three more of the boys, hid in the old tanyard. So we unhitched a skiff and pulled down the river two mile and a half, to the big scar on the hillside, and went ashore.

We went to a clump of bushes, and Tom made everybody swear to keep the secret, and then showed them a hole in the hill, right in the thickest part of the bushes. Then we lit the candles and crawled in on our hands and knees. We went about two hundred yards, and then the cave opened up. Tom poked about amongst the passages and pretty soon ducked under a wall where you wouldn't a noticed that there was a hole. We went along a narrow place and got into a kind of room, all damp and sweaty and cold, and there we stopped. Tom says:

"Now we'll start this band of robbers and call it Tom Sawyer's Gang. Everybody that wants to join has got to take an oath, and write his name in blood."

Everybody was willing. So Tom got out a sheet of paper that he had wrote the oath on, and read it. It swore every boy to stick to the band, and never tell any of the secrets; and if anybody done anything to any boy in the band, whichever boy was ordered to kill that person and his family must do it, and he mustn't eat and he mustn't sleep till he had killed them and hacked a cross in their breasts, which was the sign of the band. And nobody that didn't belong to the band could use that mark, and if he did he must be sued; and if he done it again he must be killed. And if anybody that belonged to the band told the secrets, he must have his throat cut, and then have his carcass burnt up and the ashes scattered all around, and his name blotted off of the list with blood and never mentioned again by the gang, but have a curse put on it and be forgot, forever.

Everybody said it was a real beautiful oath, and asked Tom if he got it out of his own head. He said, some of it, but the rest was out of pirate books, and robber books, and every gang that was high-toned had it.

Some thought it would be good to kill the *families* of boys that told the secrets. Tom said it was a good idea, so he took a pencil and wrote it in. Then Ben Rogers says:

"Here's Huck Finn, he hain't got no family—what you going to do 'bout him?"

"Well, hain't he got a father?" says Tom Sawyer.

"Yes, he's got a father, but you can't never find him, these days. He used to lay drunk with the hogs in the tanyard, but he hain't been seen in these parts for a year or more."

They talked it over, and they was going to rule me out, because they said every boy must have a family or somebody to kill, or else it wouldn't be fair and square for the others. Well, nobody could think of anything to do—everybody was stumped, and set still. I was most ready to cry; but all at once I thought of a way, and so I offered them Miss Watson—they could kill her. Everybody said:

"Oh, she'll do, she'll do. That's all right. Huck can come in."

Then they all stuck a pin in their fingers to get blood to sign with, and I made my mark on the paper.

"Now," says Ben Rogers, "what's the line of business of this Gang?"

"Nothing only robbery and murder," Tom said.

"But who are we going to rob?—houses—or cattle—or —"

"Stuff! stealing cattle and such things ain't robbery, it's burglary," says Tom Sawyer. "We ain't burglars. That ain't no sort of style. We are highwaymen. We stop stages and carriages on the road, with masks on, and kill the people and take their watches and money."

"Must we always kill the people?"

"Oh, certainly. It's best. Some authorities think different, but mostly it's considered best to kill them. Except some that you bring to the cave here and keep them till they're ransomed."

"Ransomed? What's that?"

"I don't know. But that's what they do. I've seen it in books; and so of course that's what we've got to do."

"But how can we do it if we don't know what it is?"

"Why blame it all, we've *got* to do it. Don't I tell you it's in the books? Do you want to go to doing different from what's in the books, and get things all muddled up?"

"Oh, that's all very fine to *say,* Tom Sawyer, but how in the nation are these fellows going to be ransomed if we don't know how to do it to them? that's the thing I want to get at. Now what do you *reckon* it is?"

"Well I don't know. But per'aps if we keep them till they're ransomed, it means that we keep them till they're dead."

"Now, that's something *like.* That'll answer. Why couldn't you said that before? We'll keep them till they're ransomed to death—and a bothersome lot they'll be, too, eating up everything and always trying to get loose."

"How you talk, Ben Rogers. How can they get loose when there's a guard over them, ready to shoot them down if they move a peg?"

"A guard. Well, that *is* good. So somebody's got to set up all night and never get any sleep, just so as to watch them. I think that's foolishness. Why can't a body take a club and ransom them as soon as they get here?"

"Because it ain't in the books so—that's why. Now Ben Rogers, do you want to do things regular, or don't you?—that's the idea. Don't you reckon that the people that made the books knows what's the correct thing to do? Do you reckon *you* can learn 'em anything? Not by a good deal. No, sir, we'll just go on and ransom them in the regular way."

"All right. I don't mind; but I say it's a fool way, anyhow. Say—do we kill the women, too?"

"Well, Ben Rogers, if I was as ignorant as you I wouldn't let on. Kill the women? No—nobody ever saw anything in the books like that. You fetch them to the cave, and you're always as polite as pie to them; and by-and-by they fall in love with you and never want to go home any more."

"Well, if that's the way, I'm agreed, but I don't take no stock in it. Mighty soon we'll have the cave so cluttered up with women, and fellows waiting to be ransomed, that there won't be no place for the robbers. But go ahead, I ain't got nothing to say."

Little Tommy Barnes was asleep, now, and when they waked him up he was scared, and cried, and said he wanted to go home to his ma, and didn't want to be a robber any more.

So they all made fun of him, and called him cry-baby, and that made him mad, and he said he would go straight and tell all the secrets. But Tom give him five cents to keep quiet, and said we would all go home and meet next week and rob somebody and kill some people.

Ben Rogers said he couldn't get out much, only Sundays, and so he wanted to begin next Sunday; but all the boys said it would be wicked to do it on Sunday, and that settled the thing. They agreed to get together and fix a day as soon as they could, and then we elected Tom Sawyer first captain and Jo Harper second captain of the Gang, and so started home.

I clumb up the shed and crept into my window just before day was breaking. My new clothes was all greased up and clayey, and I was dog-tired.

Chapter III
A Good Going-over—Grace Triumphant—
"One of Tom Sawyer's Lies"

Well, I got a good going-over in the morning, from old Miss Watson, on account of my clothes; but the widow she didn't scold, but only cleaned off the grease and clay and looked so sorry that I thought I would behave a while if I could. Then Miss Watson she took me in the closet and prayed, but nothing come of it. She told me to pray every day, and whatever I asked for I would get it. But it warn't so. I tried it. Once I got a fish-line, but no hooks. It warn't any good to me without hooks. I tried for the hooks three or four times, but somehow I couldn't make it work. By-and-by, one day, I asked Miss Watson to try for me, but she said I was a fool. She never told me why, and I couldn't make it out no way.

I set down, one time, back in the woods, and had a long think about it. I says to myself, if a body can get anything they pray for, why don't Deacon Winn get back the money he lost on pork? Why can't the widow get back her silver snuff-box that was stole? Why can't Miss Watson fat up? No, says I to myself, there ain't nothing in it. I went and told the widow about it, and she said the thing a body could get by praying for it was "spiritual gifts." This was too many for me, but she told me what she meant—I must help other people, and do everything I could for other people, and look out for them all the time, and never think about myself. This was including Miss Watson, as I took it. I went out in the woods and turned it over in my mind a long time, but I

MISS WATSON'S LECTURE.

couldn't see no advantage about it—except for the other people—so at last I reckoned I wouldn't worry about it any more, but just let it go. Sometimes the widow would take me one side and talk about Providence in a way to make a body's mouth water; but maybe next day Miss Watson would take hold and knock it all down again. I judged I could see that there was two Providences, and a poor chap would stand considerable show with the widow's Providence, but if Miss Watson's got him there warn't no help for him any more. I thought it all out, and reckoned I would belong to the widow's, if he wanted me, though I couldn't make out how he was agoing to be any better off then than what he was before, seeing I was so ignorant and so kind of low-down and ornery.

Pap he hadn't been seen for more than a year, and that was comfortable for me; I didn't want to see him no more. He used to always whale me when he was sober and could get his hands on me; though I used to take to the woods most of the time when he was around. Well, about this time he was found in the river drowned, about twelve mile above town, so people said. They judged it was him, anyway; said this drowned man was just his size, and was ragged, and had uncommon long hair—which was all like pap—but they couldn't make nothing out of the face, because it had been in the water so long it warn't much like a face at all. They said he was floating on his back in the water. They took him and buried him on the bank. But I warn't comfortable long, because I happened to think of something.

I knowed mighty well that a drownded man don't float on his back, but on
his face. So I knowed, then, that this warn't pap, but a woman dressed up
in a man's clothes. So I was uncomfortable again. I judged the old man
would turn up again by-and-by, though I wished he wouldn't.

We played robber now and then about a month, and then I resigned.
All the boys did. We hadn't robbed nobody, we hadn't killed any people,
but only just pretended. We used to hop out of the woods and go charging
down on hog-drovers and women in carts taking garden stuff to market,
but we never hived any of them. Tom Sawyer called the hogs "ingots," and
he called the turnips and stuff "julery" and we would go to the cave and
pow-wow over what we had done and how many people we had killed and
marked. But I couldn't see no profit in it. One time Tom sent a boy to run
about town with a blazing stick, which he called a slogan (which was the
sign for the Gang to get together), and then he said he had got secret news
by his spies that next day a whole parcel of Spanish merchants and rich A-
rabs was going to camp in Cave Hollow with two hundred elephants, and
six hundred camels, and over a thousand "sumter" mules, all loaded down
with di'monds, and they didn't have only a guard of four hundred soldiers,
and so we would lay in ambuscade, as he called it, and kill the lot and
scoop the things. He said we must slick up our swords and guns, and get
ready. He never could go after even a turnip-cart but he must have the
swords and guns all scoured up for it; though they was only lath and
broom-sticks, and you might scour at them till you rotted and then they
warn't worth a mouthful of ashes more than what they was before. I didn't
believe we could lick such a crowd of Spaniards and A-rabs, but I wanted
to see the camels and elephants, so I was on hand next day, Saturday, in
the ambuscade; and when we got the word, we rushed out of the woods and
down the hill. But there warn't no Spaniards and A-rabs, and there warn't
no camels nor no elephants. It warn't anything but a Sunday-school picnic, and only a primer-class at that. We busted it up, and chased the children up the hollow; but we never got anything but some doughnuts and
jam, though Ben Rogers got a rag doll, and Jo Harper got a hymn-book
and a tract; and then the teacher charged in and made us drop everything
and cut. I didn't see no di'monds, and I told Tom Sawyer so. He said there
was loads of them there, anyway; and he said there was A-rabs there, too,
and elephants and things. I said, why couldn't we see them, then? He said
if I warn't so ignorant, but had read a book called "Don Quixote," [7] I
would know without asking. He said it was all done by enchantment. He

---

[7] Cervantes's novel, which Twain admired, first appeared in 1605. The story centers on
"conflict in the hero's mind between decayed immoral modernity and the noble, chivalric

said there was hundreds of soldiers there, and elephants and treasure, and so on, but we had enemies which he called magicians, and they had turned the whole thing into an infant Sunday school, just out of spite. I said, all right, then the thing for us to do was to go for the magicians. Tom Sawyer said I was a numskull.

"Why," says he, "a magician could call up a lot of genies, and they would hash you up like nothing before you could say Jack Robinson. They are as tall as a tree and as big around as a church."

"Well," I says, "s'pose we got some genies to help *us*—can't we lick the other crowd then?"

"How you going to get them?"

"I don't know. How do *they* get them?"

"Why they rub an old tin lamp or an iron ring, and then the genies come tearing in, with the thunder and lightning a-ripping around and the smoke a-rolling, and everything they're told to do they up and do it. They don't think nothing of pulling a shot tower up by the roots, and belting a Sunday-school superintendent over the head with it—or any other man."

"Who makes them tear around so?"

"Why, whoever rubs the lamp or the ring. They belong to whoever rubs the lamp or the ring, and they've got to do whatever he says. If he tells them to build a palace forty miles long, out of di'monds, and fill it full of chewing gum, or whatever you want, and fetch an emperor's daughter from China for you to marry, they've got to do it—and they've got to do it before sun-up next morning, too. And more—they've got to waltz that palace around over the country wherever you want it, you understand."

"Well," says I, "I think they are a pack of flatheads for not keeping the palace themselves 'stead of fooling them away like that. And what's more—if I was one of them I would see a man in Jericho[8] before I would drop my business and come to him for the rubbing of an old tin lamp."

---

past celebrated in song and story" and "the interplay between the wildly idealistic, impractical hero, . . . and his worldly, intensely practical page, Sancho Panza" (Lemaster and Wilson 137–38). *Huckleberry Finn*, with its concentration on the relationships between Tom and Huck and between Huck and Jim can be read in terms of Cervantes's work.

[8] Josh. 6.15–27, Luke 10.30. In the Old Testament, the city of Jericho and its citizens are destroyed. In the New Testament, the story of the "Good Samaritan" begins, "A certain man went down . . . to Jericho, and fell among thieves, which stripped him of his raiment, and wounded him, and departed, leaving him half dead." To "see a man in Jericho" is to put oneself in harm's way. Huck resists Tom's suggestion that the genies must obey because those who rub the lamps "own" them. He insists that he would rather "see a man in Jericho" than submit to such an arrangement, establishing his sympathies with Jim.

"How you talk, Huck Finn. Why, you'd *have* to come when he rubbed it, whether you wanted to or not."

"What, and I as high as a tree and as big as a church? All right, then; I *would* come; but I lay I'd make that man climb the highest tree there was in the country."

"Shucks, it ain't no use to talk to you, Huck Finn. You don't seem to know anything, somehow—perfect sap-head."

I thought all this over for two or three days, and then I reckoned I would see if there was anything in it. I got an old tin lamp and an iron ring and went out in the woods and rubbed and rubbed till I sweat like an Injun, calculating to build a palace and sell it; but it warn't no use, none of the genies come. So then I judged that all that stuff was only just one of Tom Sawyer's lies. I reckoned he believed in the A-rabs and the elephants, but as for me I think different. It had all the marks of a Sunday school.

Chapter IV
Huck and the Judge—Superstition

Well, three or four months run along, and it was well into the winter, now. I had been to school most all the time, and could spell, and read, and write just a little, and could say the multiplication table up to six times seven is thirty-five, and I don't reckon I could ever get any further than that if I was to live forever. I don't take no stock in mathematics, anyway.

At first I hated the school, but by-and-by I got so I could stand it. Whenever I got uncommon tired I played hookey, and the hiding I got next day done me good and cheered me up. So the longer I went to school the easier it got to be. I was getting sort of used to the widow's ways, too, and they warn't so raspy on me. Living in a house, and sleeping in a bed, pulled on me pretty tight, mostly, but before the cold weather I used to slide out and sleep in the woods, sometimes, and so that was a rest to me. I liked the old ways best, but I was getting so I liked the new ones, too, a little bit. The widow said I was coming along slow but sure, and doing very satisfactory. She said she warn't ashamed of me.

One morning I happened to turn over the salt-cellar at breakfast. I reached for some of it as quick as I could, to throw over my left shoulder and keep off the bad luck, but Miss Watson was in ahead of me, and crossed me off. She says, "Take your hands away, Huckleberry—what a mess you are always making." The widow put in a good word for me, but that warn't going to keep off the bad luck, I knowed that well enough.

I started out, after breakfast, feeling worried and shaky, and wondering where it was going to fall on me, and what it was going to be. There is ways to keep off some kinds of bad luck, but this wasn't one of them kind; so I never tried to do anything, but just poked along low-spirited and on the watch-out.

I went down the front garden and clumb over the stile, where you go through the high board fence. There was an inch of new snow on the ground, and I seen somebody's tracks. They had come up from the quarry and stood around the stile a while, and then went on around the garden fence. It was funny

! ! ! ! !

they hadn't come in, after standing around so. I couldn't make it out. It was very curious, somehow. I was going to follow around, but I stooped down to look at the tracks first. I didn't notice anything at first, but next I did. There was a cross in the left boot-heel made with big nails, to keep off the devil.

I was up in a second and shinning down the hill. I looked over my shoulder every now and then, but I didn't see nobody. I was at Judge Thatcher's as quick as I could get there. He said:

"Why, my boy, you are all out of breath. Did you come for your interest?"

"No sir," I says; "is there some for me?"

"Oh, yes, a half-yearly is in, last night. Over a hundred and fifty dollars. Quite a fortune for you. You better let me invest it along with your six thousand, because if you take it you'll spend it."

"No sir," I says, "I don't want to spend it. I don't want it at all—nor the six thousand, nuther. I want you to take it; I want to give it to you— the six thousand and all."

He looked surprised. He couldn't seem to make it out. He says:

"Why, what can you mean, my boy?"

I says, "Don't you ask me no questions about it, please. You'll take it—won't you?"

He says:

"Well I'm puzzled. Is something the matter?"

"Please take it," says I, "and don't ask me nothing—then I won't have to tell no lies."

He studied a while, and then he says:

"Oho-o! I think I see. You want to *sell* all your property to me—not give it. That's the correct idea."

Then he wrote something on a paper and read it over, and says:

"There—you see it says 'for a consideration.' That means I have bought it of you and paid you for it. Here's a dollar for you. Now, you sign it."

So I signed it, and left.

Miss Watson's nigger, Jim, had a hair-ball[9] as big as your fist, which had been took out of the fourth stomach of an ox, and he used to do magic with it. He said there was a spirit inside of it, and it knowed everything. So I went to him that night and told him pap was here again, for I found his tracks in the snow. What I wanted to know, was, what he was going to do, and was he going to stay? Jim got out his hair-ball, and said something over it, and then he held it up and dropped it on the floor. It fell pretty solid, and only rolled about an inch. Jim tried it again, and then another time, and it acted just the same. Jim got down on his knees and put his ear against it and listened. But it warn't no use; he said it wouldn't talk. He said sometimes it wouldn't talk without money. I told him I had an old slick counterfeit quarter that warn't no good because the brass showed through the silver a little, and it wouldn't pass nohow, even if the brass didn't show, because it was so slick it felt greasy, and so that would tell on it every time. (I reckoned I wouldn't say nothing about the dollar I got from the judge.) I said it was pretty bad money, but maybe the hair-ball would take it, because maybe it wouldn't know the difference. Jim smelt it, and bit it, and rubbed it, and said he would manage so the hair-ball would think it was good. He said he would split open a raw Irish potato and stick the quarter in between and keep it there all night, and next morning, you couldn't see no brass, and it wouldn't feel greasy no more, and so anybody in town would take it in a minute, let alone a hair-ball. Well, I knowed a potato would do that, before, but I had forgot it.

---

[9] The use of the hair-ball to tell fortunes derives from African voodoo. As with the story of the witches, Jim works toward his own advantage. "He takes a slug which is worthless to Huck, and through the alchemy of his own cleverness contrives to make it worth twenty-five cents to himself. That, in antebellum America, is not a bad price for telling a fortune" (Smith 110).

Jim put the quarter under the hair-ball and got down and listened again. This time he said the hair-ball was all right. He said it would tell my whole fortune if I wanted it to. I says, go on. So the hair-ball talked to Jim, and Jim told it to me. He says:

"Yo' ole father doan' know, yit, what he's a-gwyne to do. Sometimes he spec he'll go 'way, en den agin he spec he'll stay. De bes' way is to res' easy en let de ole man take his own way. Dey's two angels hoverin' roun' 'bout him. One uv 'em is white en shiny, en 'tother one is black. De white one gits him to go right, a little while, den de black one sail in en bust it all up. A body can't tell, yit, which one gwyne to fetch him at de las'. But you is all right. You gwyne to have considable trouble in yo' life, en considable joy. Sometimes you gwyne to git hurt, en sometimes you gwyne to git sick; but every time you's gwyne to git well agin. Dey's two gals flyin' 'bout you in yo' life. One uv 'em's light en 'tother one is dark. One is rich en t'other is po'. You's gwyne to marry de po' one fust en de rich one by-en-by. You wants to keep 'way fum de water as much as you kin, en don't run no resk, 'kase it's down in de bills dat you's gwyne to git hung."

When I lit my candle and went up to my room that night, there set pap, his own self!

Chapter V
Huck's Father—The Fond Parent—Reform

I had shut the door to. Then I turned around, and there he was. I used to be scared of him all the time, he tanned me so much. I reckoned I was scared now, too; but in a minute I see I was mistaken. That is, after the first jolt, as you may say, when my breath sort of hitched—he being so unexpected; but right away after, I see I warn't scared of him worth bothering about.

He was most fifty, and he looked it. His hair was long and tangled and greasy, and hung down, and you could see his eyes shining through like he was behind vines. It was all black, no gray; so was his long, mixed-up whiskers. There warn't no color in his face, where his face showed; it was white; not like another man's white, but a white to make a body sick, a white to make a body's flesh crawl—a tree-toad white, a fish-belly white. As for his clothes—just rags, that was all. He had one ankle resting on 'tother knee; the boot on that foot was busted, and two of his toes stuck through, and he worked them now and then. His hat was laying on the floor; an old black slouch with the top caved in, like a lid.

I stood a-looking at him; he set there a-looking at me, with his chair tilted back a little. I set the candle down. I noticed the window

"PAP."

was up; so he had clumb in by the shed. He kept a-looking me all over. By-and-by he says:

"Starchy clothes—very. You think you're a good deal of a big-bug, *don't* you?"

"Maybe I am, maybe I ain't," I says.

"Don't you give me none o' your lip," says he. "You've put on considerble many frills since I been away. I'll take you down a peg before I get done with you. You're educated, too, they say; can read and write. You think you're better'n your father, now, don't you, because he can't? *I'll* take it out of you. Who told you you might meddle with such hi-falut'n foolishness, hey?—who told you you could?"

"The widow. She told me."

"The widow, hey?—and who told the widow she could put in her shovel about a thing that ain't none of her business?"

"Nobody never told her."

"Well, I'll learn her how to meddle. And looky here—you drop that school, you hear? I'll learn people to bring up a boy to put on airs over his own father and let on to be better'n what *he* is. You lemme catch you fool-ing around that school again, you hear? Your mother couldn't read, and she couldn't write, nuther, before she died. None of the family couldn't, be-fore *they* died. *I* can't; and here you're a-swelling yourself up like this. I ain't the man to stand it—you hear? Say—lemme hear you read."

I took up a book and begun something about General Washington and the wars. When I'd read about a half a minute, he fetched the book a whack with his hand and knocked it across the house. He says:

"It's so. You can do it. I had my doubts when you told me. Now looky here; you stop that putting on frills. I won't have it. I'll lay for you, my smarty; and if I catch you about that school I'll tan you good. First you know you'll get religion, too. I never see such a son.

He took up a little blue and yaller picture of some cows and a boy, and says:

"What's this?"

"It's something they give me for learning my lessons good."

He tore it up, and says—

"I'll give you something better—I'll give you a cowhide."

He set there a-mumbling and a-growling a minute, and then he says—

"*Ain't* you a sweet-scented dandy, though? A bed; and bedclothes; and a look'n-glass; and a piece of carpet on the floor—and your own father got to sleep with the hogs in the tanyard. I never see such a son. I bet I'll take some o' these frills out o' you before I'm done with you. Why there ain't no end to your airs—they say you're rich. Hey?—how's that?"

"They lie—that's how."

"Looky here—mind how you talk to me; I'm a-standing about all I can stand, now—so don't gimme no sass. I've been in town two days, and I hain't heard nothing but about you bein' rich. I heard about it away down the river, too. That's why I come. You git me that money to-morrow—I want it."

"I hain't got no money."

"It's a lie. Judge Thatcher's got it. You git it. I want it."

"I hain't got no money, I tell you. You ask Judge Thatcher; he'll tell you the same."

"All right. I'll ask him; and I'll make him pungle, too, or I'll know the reason why. Say—how much you got in your pocket? I want it."

"I hain't got only a dollar, and I want that to—"

"It don't make no difference what you want it for—you just shell it out."

He took it and bit it to see if it was good, and then he said he was going down town to get some whisky; said he hadn't had a drink all day. When he had got out on the shed, he put his head in again, and cussed me for putting on frills and trying to be better than him; and when I reckoned he was gone, he come back and put his head in again, and told me to mind about that school, because he was going to lay for me and lick me if I didn't drop that.

Next day he was drunk, and he went to Judge Thatcher's and bully-ragged him and tried to make him give up the money, but he couldn't, and then he swore he'd make the law force him.

The judge and the widow went to law to get the court to take me away from him and let one of them be my guardian; but it was a new judge that had just come, and he didn't know the old man; so he said courts mustn't interfere and separate families if they could help it; said he'd druther not take a child away from its father. So Judge Thatcher and the widow had to quit on the business.

That pleased the old man till he couldn't rest. He said he'd cowhide me till I was black and blue if I didn't raise some money for him. I borrowed three dollars from Judge Thatcher, and pap took it and got drunk and went a-blowing around and cussing and whooping and carrying on; and he kept it up all over town, with a tin pan, till most midnight; then they jailed him, and next day they had him before court, and jailed him again for a week. But he said *he* was satisfied; said he was boss of his son, and he'd make it warm for *him*.

When he got out the new judge said he was agoing to make a man of him. So he took him to his own house, and dressed him up clean and nice, and had him to breakfast and dinner and supper with the family, and was just old pie to him, so to speak. And after supper he talked to him about temperance and such things till the old man cried, and said he'd been a fool, and fooled away his life; but now he was agoing to turn over a new leaf and be a man nobody wouldn't be ashamed of, and he hoped the judge would help him and not look down on him. The judge said he could hug him for them words; so *he* cried, and his wife she cried again; pap said he'd been a man that had always been misunderstood before, and the judge said he believed it. The old man said that what a man wanted that was down, was sympathy; and the judge said it was so; so they cried again. And when it was bedtime, the old man rose up and held out his hand, and says:

"Look at it gentlemen, and ladies all; take ahold of it; shake it. There's a hand that was the hand of a hog; but it ain't so no more; it's the hand of a man that's started in on a new life, and 'll die before he'll go back. You mark them words—don't forget I said them. It's a clean hand now; shake it—don't be afeard."

So they shook it, one after the other, all around, and cried. The judge's wife she kissed it. Then the old man he signed a pledge—made his mark. The judge said it was the holiest time on record, or something like that. Then they tucked the old man into a beautiful room, which was the spare room, and in the night sometime he got powerful thirsty and clumb out onto the porch-roof and slid down a stanchion and traded his new coat for a jug of forty-rod, and clumb back again and had a good old time; and towards daylight he crawled out again, drunk as a fiddler, and rolled off the porch and broke his left arm in two places and was most froze to death when somebody found him after sun-up. And when they come to look at that spare room, they had to take soundings before they could navigate it.

The judge he felt kind of sore. He said he reckoned a body could reform the old man with a shot-gun, maybe, but he didn't know no other way.

Chapter VI
He Went for Judge Thatcher—Huck Decided to
Leave—Political Economy—Thrashing Around

Well, pretty soon the old man was up and around again, and then he went for Judge Thatcher in the courts to make him give up that money, and he went for me, too, for not stopping school. He catched me a couple of times and thrashed me, but I went to school just the same, and dodged him or out-run him most of the time. I didn't want to go to school much, before, but I reckoned I'd go now to spite pap. That law trial was a slow business; appeared like they warn't ever going to get started on it; so every now and then I'd borrow two or three dollars off of the judge for him, to keep from getting a cowhiding. Every time he got money he got drunk; and every time he got drunk he raised Cain around town; and every time he raised Cain he got jailed. He was just suited—this kind of thing was right in his line.

He got to hanging around the widow's too much, and so she told him at last, that if he didn't quit using around there she would make trouble for him. Well, *wasn't*

GETTING OUT OF THE WAY.

he mad? He said he would show who was Huck Finn's boss. So he watched out for me one day in the spring, and catched me, and took me up the river about three mile, in a skiff, and crossed over to the Illinois shore where it was woody and there warn't no houses but an old log hut in a place where the timber was so thick you couldn't find it if you didn't know where it was.

He kept me with him all the time, and I never got a chance to run off. We lived in that old cabin, and he always locked the door and put the key under his head, nights. He had a gun which he had stole, I reckon, and we fished and hunted, and that was what we lived on. Every little while he locked me in and went down to the store, three miles, to the ferry, and traded fish and game for whisky and fetched it home and got drunk and had a good time, and licked me. The widow she found out where I was, by-and-by, and she sent a man over to try to get hold of me, but pap drove him off with the gun, and it warn't long after that till I was used to being where I was, and liked it, all but the cowhide part.

It was kind of lazy and jolly, laying off comfortable all day, smoking and fishing, and no books nor study. Two months or more run along, and my clothes got to be all rags and dirt, and I didn't see how I'd ever got to like it so well at the widow's, where you had to wash, and eat on a plate, and comb up, and go to bed and get up regular, and be forever bothering over a book and have old Miss Watson pecking at you all the time. I didn't want to go back no more. I had stopped cussing, because the widow didn't like it; but now I took to it again because pap hadn't no objections. It was pretty good times up in the woods there, take it all around.

But by-and-by pap got too handy with his hick'ry, and I couldn't stand it. I was all over welts. He got to going away so much, too, and locking me in. Once he locked me in and was gone three days. It was dreadful lonesome. I judged he had got drowned and I wasn't ever going to get out any more. I was scared. I made up my mind I would fix up some way to leave there. I had tried to get out of that cabin many a time, but I couldn't find no way. There warn't a window to it big enought for a dog to get through. I couldn't get up the chimbly, it was too narrow. The door was thick solid oak slabs. Pap was pretty careful not to leave a knife or anything in the cabin when he was away; I reckon I had hunted the place over as much as a hundred times; well, I was 'most all the time at it, because it was about the only way to put in the time. But this time I found something at last; I found an old rusty wood-saw without any handle; it was laid in between a rafter and the clapboards of the roof. I greased it up and went to work. There was an old horse-blanket nailed against the logs at the far end of the cabin behind the table, to keep the wind from blowing through the chinks and putting the candle out. I got under the table and raised the blanket and went to work to saw a section of the big bottom log out, big enough to let me through. Well, it was a good long job, but I was getting towards the end of it when I heard pap's gun in the woods. I got rid of the signs of my work, and dropped the blanket and hid my saw, and pretty soon pap come in.

Pap warn't in a good humor—so he was his natural self. He said he was down to town, and everything was going wrong. His lawyer said he reckoned he would win his lawsuit and get the money, if they ever got started on the trial; but then there was ways to put it off a long time, and Judge Thatcher knowed how to do it. And he said people allowed there'd be another trial to get me away from him and give me to the widow for my guardian, and they guessed it would win, this time. This shook me up considerable, because I didn't want to go back to the widow's any more and be so cramped up and sivilized, as they called it. Then the old man got to cussing, and cussed everything and everybody he could think of, and then cussed them all over again to make sure he hadn't skipped any, and after that he polished off with a kind of a general cuss all round, including a considerable parcel of people which he didn't know the names of, and so called them what's-his-name when he got to them, and went right along with his cussing.

He said he would like to see the widow get me. He said he would watch out, and if they tried to come any such game on him he knowed of a place six or seven mile off, to stow me in, where they might hunt till they dropped and they couldn't find me. That made me pretty uneasy again, but only for a minute; I reckoned I wouldn't stay on hand till he got that chance.

The old man made me go to the skiff and fetch the things he had got. There was a fifty-pound sack of corn meal, and a side of bacon, ammunition, and a four-gallon jug of whisky, and an old book and two newspapers for wadding, besides some tow. I toted up a load, and went back and set down on the bow of the skiff to rest. I thought it all over, and I reckoned I would walk off with the gun and some lines, and take to the woods when I run away. I guessed I wouldn't stay in one place, but just tramp right across the country, mostly night times, and hunt and fish to keep alive, and so get so far away that the old man nor the widow couldn't ever find me any more. I judged I would saw out and leave that night if pap got drunk enough, and I reckoned he would. I got so full of it I didn't notice how long I was staying, till the old man hollered and asked me whether I was asleep or drownded.

I got the things all up to the cabin, and then it was about dark. While I was cooking supper the old man took a swig or two and got sort of warmed up, and went to ripping again. He had been drunk over in town, and laid in the gutter all night, and he was a sight to look at. A body would a thought he was Adam, he was just all mud. Whenever his liquor begun to work, he most always went for the govment. This time he says:

"Call this a govment! why, just look at it and see what it's like. Here's the law a-standing ready to take a man's son away from him—a man's own son, which he has had all the trouble and all the anxiety and all the expense of raising. Yes, just as that man has got that son raised at last, and ready to go to work and begin to do suthin' for *him* and give him a rest, the law up and goes for him. And they call *that* govment! That ain't all, nuther. The law backs that old Judge Thatcher up and helps him to keep me out o' my property. Here's what the law does. The law takes a man worth six thousand dollars and upards, and jams him into an old trap of a cabin like this, and lets him go round in clothes that ain't fitten for a hog. They call that govment! A man can't get his rights in a govment like this. Sometimes I've a mighty notion to just leave the country for good and all. Yes, and *told* 'em so; I told old Thatcher so to his face. Lots of 'em heard me, and can tell what I said. Says I, for two cents I'd leave the blamed country and never come anear it agin. Them's the very words. I says, look at my hat—if you call it a hat—but the lid raises up and the rest of it goes down till it's below my chin, and then it ain't rightly a hat at all, but more like my head was shoved up through a jint o' stove-pipe. Look at it, says I—such a hat for me to wear—one of the wealthiest men in this town, if I could git my rights.

"Oh, yes, this is a wonderful govment, wonderful. Why, looky here. There was a free nigger there, from Ohio; a mulatter, most as white as a white man. He had the whitest shirt on you ever see, too, and the shiniest hat; and there ain't a man in that town that's got as fine clothes as what he had; and he had a gold watch and chain, and a silver-headed cane—the awfulest old gray-headed nabob in the State. And what do you think? they said he was a p'fessor in a college, and could talk all kinds of languages, and knowed everything. And that ain't the wust. They said he could *vote*,[10] when he was at home. Well, that let me out. Thinks I, what is the country a-coming to? It was 'lection day, and I was just about to go and vote, myself, if I warn't too drunk to get there; but when they told me there was a State in this country where they'd let that nigger vote, I drawed out. I says I'll never vote agin. Them's the very words I said; they all heard me; and the country may rot for all me—I'll never vote agin as long as I live. And to see the cool way of that nigger—why, he wouldn't a give me the road if I hadn't shoved him out o' the way. I says to the people, why ain't this nigger put up at auction and sold?—that's what I want to know. And what do you reckon they said? Why, they said he couldn't be sold till he'd been in the State six months, and he hadn't been there that long yet. There, now—that's a specimen. They call that a govment[11] that can't sell

---

[10] Pap is mistaken about the voting issue. Free blacks could not vote in Ohio. However, Wilberforce University in Ohio did hire John G. Mitchell (1827–1900), a black professor of Greek, Latin, and mathematics, during the 1860s.

[11] Missouri law necessitated that free blacks carry passes lest they be mistaken as fugitive slaves. A suspected fugitive could be held in prison and sold after twelve months. According to an 1823 code, "Any person had the right to apprehend a slave." However, a white man causing the arrest of a nonfugitive black could, under law, be fined $100 plus all costs (see Trexler). Pap's tirade reflects the view of "not only poor whites but all 'right thinking' southerners, regardless of their social class" (Smith 107). It also reflects

a free nigger till he's been in the State six months. Here's a govment that calls itself a govment, and lets on to be a govment, and thinks it is a govment, and yet's got to set stock-still for six whole months before it can take ahold of a prowling, thieving, infernal, white-shirted free nigger, and—"

Pap was agoing on so, he never noticed where his old limber legs was taking him to, so he went head over heels over the tub of salt pork, and barked both shins, and the rest of his speech was all the hottest kind of language—mostly hove at the nigger and the govment, though he give the tub some, too, all along, here and there. He hopped around the cabin considerable, first on one leg and then on the other, holding first one shin and then the other one, and at last he let out with his left foot all of a sudden and fetched the tub a rattling kick. But it warn't good judgment, because that was the boot that had a couple of his toes leaking out of the front end of it; so now he raised a howl that fairly made a body's hair raise, and down he went in the dirt, and rolled there, and held his toes; and the cussing he done then laid over anything he had ever done previous. He said so his own self afterwards. He had heard old Sowberry Hagan in his best days, and he said it laid over him, too; but I reckon that was sort of piling it on, maybe.

After supper pap took the jug, and said he had enough whisky there for two drunks and one delirium tremens. That was always his word. I judged he would be blind drunk in about an hour, and then I would steal the key, or saw myself out, one or 'tother. He drank, and drank, and tumbled down on his blankets, by-and-by; but luck didn't run my way. He didn't go sound asleep, but was uneasy. He groaned, and moaned, and thrashed around this way and that, for a long time. At last I got so sleepy I couldn't keep my eyes open, all I could do, and so before I knowed what I was about I was sound asleep, and the candle burning.

I don't know how long I was asleep, but all of a sudden there was an awful scream and I was up. There was pap, looking wild and skipping around every which way and yelling about snakes. He said they was crawling up his legs; and then he would give a jump and scream, and say one had bit him on the cheek—but I couldn't see no snakes. He started and run round and round the cabin, hollering "take him off! take him off! he's biting me on the neck!" I never see a man look so wild in the eyes. Pretty soon he was all fagged out, and fell down panting; then he rolled over and over, wonderful fast, kicking things every which way, and striking and grabbing at the air with his hands, and screaming, and saying there was devils ahold

---

the precarious position of the free black man, who constantly ran the risk of detainment and sale.

of him. He wore out, by-and-by, and laid still a while, moaning. Then he laid stiller, and didn't make a sound. I could hear the owls and the wolves, away off in the woods, and it seemed terrible still. He was laying over by the corner. By-and-by he raised up, part way, and listened, with his head to one side. He says very low:

"Tramp—tramp—tramp; that's the dead; tramp—tramp—tramp; they're coming after me; but I won't go—Oh, they're here! don't touch me—don't! hands off—they're cold; let go—Oh, let a poor devil alone!" *him*

Then he went down on all fours and crawled off begging them to let him alone, and he rolled himself up in his blanket and wallowed in under the old pine table, still a-begging; and then he went to crying. I could hear him through the blanket.

By-and-by he rolled out and jumped up on his feet looking wild, and he see me and went for me. He chased me round and round the place, with a clasp-knife, calling me the Angel of Death and saying he would kill me and then I couldn't come for him no more. I begged, and told him I was only Huck, but he laughed *such* a screechy laugh, and roared and cussed, and kept on chasing me up. Once when I turned short and dodged under his arm he made a grab and got me by the jacket between my shoulders, and I thought I was gone; but I slid out of the jacket quick as lightning, and saved myself. Pretty soon he was all tired out, and dropped down with his back against the door, and said he would rest a minute and then kill me. He put his knife under him, and said he would sleep and get strong, and then he would see who was who.

So he dozed off, pretty soon. By-and-by I got the old split-bottom chair and clumb up, as easy as I could, not to make any noise, and got down the gun. I slipped the ramrod down it to make sure it was loaded, and then I laid it across the turnip barrel, pointing towards pap, and set down behind it to wait for him to stir. And how slow and still the time did drag along.

Chapter VII
Laying for Him—Locked in the Cabin—
Sinking the Body—Resting

"Git up! what you 'bout!"

I opened my eyes and looked around, trying to make out where I was. It was after sun-up, and I had been sound asleep. Pap was standing over me, looking sour—and sick, too. He says—

"What you doin' with this gun?"

I judged he didn't know nothing about what he had been doing, so I says:

"Somebody tried to get in, so I was laying for him."

"Why didn't you roust me out?"

"Well I tried to, but I couldn't; I couldn't budge you."

"Well, all right. Don't stand there palavering all day, but out with you and see if there's a fish on the lines for breakfast. I'll be along in a minute."

He unlocked the door and I cleared out, up the river bank. I noticed some pieces of limbs and such things floating down, and a sprinkling of bark; so I knowed the river had begun to rise. I reck-

"GIT UP!"

oned I would have great times, now, if I was over at the town. The June rise[12] used to be always luck for me; because as soon as that rise begins, here comes cord-wood floating down, and pieces of log rafts—sometimes a dozen logs together; so all you have to do is to catch them and sell them to the wood yards and the sawmill.

I went along up the bank with one eye out for pap and 'tother one out for what the rise might fetch along. Well, all at once, here comes a canoe; just a beauty, too, about thirteen or fourteen foot long, riding high like a duck. I shot head first off of the bank, like a frog, clothes and all on, and struck out for the canoe. I just expected there'd be somebody laying down in it, because people often done that to fool folks, and when a chap had pulled a skiff out most to it they'd raise up and laugh at him. But it warn't so this time. It was a drift-canoe, sure enough, and I clumb in and paddled her ashore. Thinks I, the old man will be glad when he sees this—she's worth ten dollars. But when I got to shore pap wasn't in sight yet, and as I was running her into a little creek like a gully, all hung over with vines

---

[12] The Mississippi rises, flooding its banks and collecting debris, in June and December. Twain gained his knowledge of the river as a steamboat pilot. He describes the challenges of navigating the river, crowded with driftwood and logs during the rise, in *Old Times on the Mississippi*.

and willows, I struck another idea; I judged I'd hide her good, and then, stead of taking to the woods when I run off, I'd go down the river about fifty mile and camp in one place for good, and not have such a rough time tramping on foot.

It was pretty close to the shanty, and I thought I heard the old man coming, all the time; but I got her hid; and then I out and looked around a bunch of willows, and there was the old man down the path apiece just drawing a bead on a bird with his gun. So he hadn't seen anything.

When he got along, I was hard at it taking up a "trot" line. He abused me a little for being so slow, but I told him I fell in the river and that was what made me so long. I knowed he would see I was wet, and then he would be asking questions. We got five cat-fish off of the lines and went home.

While we laid off, after breakfast, to sleep up, both of us being about wore out, I got to thinking that if I could fix up some way to keep pap and the widow from trying to follow me, it would be a certainer thing than trusting to luck to get far enough off before they missed me; you see, all kinds of things might happen. Well, I didn't see no way for a while, but by-and-by pap raised up a minute, to drink another barrel of water, and he says:

"Another time a man comes a-prowling round here, you roust me out, you hear? That man warn't here for no good. I'd a shot him. Next time, you roust me out, you hear?"

Then he dropped down and went to sleep again—but what he had been saying give me the very idea I wanted. I says to myself, I can fix it now so nobody won't think of following me.

About twelve o'clock we turned out and went along up the bank. The river was coming up pretty fast, and lots of drift-wood going by on the rise. By-and-by, along comes part of a log raft—nine logs fast together. We went out with the skiff and towed it ashore. Then we had dinner. Anybody but pap would a waited and seen the day through, so as to catch more stuff; but that warn't pap's style. Nine logs was enough for one time; he must shove right over to town and sell. So he locked me in and took the skiff and started off towing the raft about half-past three. I judged he wouldn't come back that night. I waited till I reckoned he had got a good start, then I out with my saw and went to work on that log again. Before he was 'tother side of the river I was out of the hole; him and his raft was just a speck on the water away off yonder.

I took the sack of corn meal and took it to where the canoe was hid, and shoved the vines and branches apart and put it in; then I done the same with the side of bacon; then the whisky jug; I took all the coffee and sugar there was, and all the ammunition; I took the wadding; I took the bucket and gourd, I took a dipper and a tin cup, and my old saw and two blankets, and the skillet and the coffee-pot. I took fish-lines and matches and other things—everything that was worth a cent. I cleaned out the place. I wanted an axe, but there wasn't any, only the one out at the wood pile, and I knowed why I was going to leave that. I fetched out the gun, and now I was done.

I had wore the ground a good deal, crawling out of the hole and dragging out so many things. So I fixed that as good as I could from the outside by scattering dust on the place, which covered up the smoothness and the sawdust. Then I fixed the piece of log back into its place, and put two rocks under it and one against it to hold it there—for it was bent up at that place, and didn't quite touch ground. If you stood four or five foot away and didn't know it was sawed, you wouldn't ever notice it; and besides, this was the back of the cabin and it warn't likely anybody would go fooling around there.

It was all grass clear to the canoe; so I hadn't left a track. I followed around to see. I stood on the bank and looked out over the river. All safe. So I took the gun and went up a piece into the woods and was hunting around for some birds, when I see a wild pig; hogs soon went wild in them bottoms after they had got away from the prairie farms. I shot this fellow and took him into camp.

I took the axe and smashed in the door—I beat it and hacked it considerable, a-doing it. I fetched the pig in and took him back nearly to the table and hacked into his throat with the axe, and laid him down on the ground to bleed—I say ground, because it *was* ground—hard packed, and no boards. Well, next I took an old sack and put a lot of big rocks in it— all I could drag—and I started it from the pig and dragged it to the door and through the woods down to the river and dumped it in, and down it sunk, out of sight. You could easy see that something had been dragged over the ground. I did wish Tom Sawyer was there, I knowed he would take an interest in this kind of business, and throw in the fancy touches. Nobody could spread himself like Tom Sawyer in such a thing as that.

Well, last I pulled out some of my hair, and bloodied the axe good, and stuck it on the back side, and slung the axe in the corner. Then I took up the pig and held him to my breast with my jacket (so he couldn't drip) till I got a good piece below the house and then dumped him into the river. Now I thought of something else. So I went and got the bag of meal and my old saw out of the canoe and fetched them to the house. I took the bag to where it used to stand, and ripped a hole in the bottom of it with the saw, for there warn't no knives and forks on the place—pap done everything with his clasp-knife, about the cooking. Then I carried the sack about a hundred yards across the grass and through the willows east of the house, to a shallow lake that was five mile wide and full of rushes—and ducks too, you might say, in the season. There was a slough or a creek leading out of it on the other side, that went miles away, I don't know where, but it didn't go to the river. The meal sifted out and made a little track all the way to the lake. I dropped pap's whetstone there too, so as to look like it had been done by accident. Then I tied up the rip in the meal sack with a string, so it wouldn't leak no more, and took it and my saw to the canoe again.

It was about dark, now; so I dropped the canoe down the river under some willows that hung over the bank, and waited for the moon to rise. I made fast to a willow; then I took a bite to eat, and by-and-by laid down in the canoe to smoke a pipe and lay out a plan. I says to myself, they'll follow the track of that sackful of rocks to the shore and then drag the river for me. And they'll follow that meal track to the lake and go browsing down the creek that leads out of it to find the robbers that killed me and took the things. They won't ever hunt the river for anything but my dead carcass. They'll soon get tired of that, and won't bother no more about me. All right; I can stop anywhere I want to. Jackson's Island[13] is good enough for me; I know that island pretty well, and nobody ever comes there. And then I can paddle over to town, nights, and slink around and pick up things I want. Jackson's Island's the place.

I was pretty tired, and the first thing I knowed, I was asleep. When I woke up I didn't know where I was, for a minute. I set up and looked around, a little scared. Then I remembered. The river looked miles and miles across. The moon was so bright I could a counted the drift logs that went a slipping along, black and still, hundreds of yards out from shore. Everything was dead quiet, and it looked late, and *smelt* late. You know what I mean—I don't know the words to put it in.

I took a good gap and a stretch, and was just going to unhitch and start, when I heard a sound away over the water. I listened. Pretty soon I made it out. It was that dull kind of a regular sound that comes from oars working in rowlocks when it's a still night. I peeped out through the willow branches, and there it was—a skiff, away across the water. I couldn't tell how many was in it. It kept a-coming, and when it was abreast of me I see there warn't but one man in it. Thinks I, maybe it's pap, though I warn't expecting him. He dropped below me, with the current, and by-and-by he come a-swinging up shore in the easy water, and he went by so close

---

[13] Twain based Jackson's Island on Glasscock's Island. Once located three miles downstream of Hannibal, the island has since eroded away.

I could a reached out the gun and touched him. Well, it *was* pap, sure enough—and sober, too, by the way he laid to his oars.

I didn't lose no time. The next minute I was a-spinning down stream soft but quick in the shade of the bank. I made two mile and a half, and then struck out a quarter of a mile or more towards the middle of the river, because pretty soon I would be passing the ferry landing and people might see me and hail me. I got out amongst the drift-wood and then laid down in the bottom of the canoe and let her float. I laid there and had a good rest and a smoke out of my pipe, looking away into the sky, not a cloud in it. The sky looks ever so deep when you lay down on your back in the moonshine; I never knowed it before. And how far a body can hear on the water such nights! I heard people talking at the ferry landing. I heard what they said, too, every word of it. One man said it was getting towards the long days and the short nights, now. 'Tother one said *this* warn't one of the short ones, he reckoned—and then they laughed, and he said it over again and they laughed again; then they waked up another fellow and told him, and laughed, but he didn't laugh; he ripped out something brisk and said let him alone. The first fellow said he 'lowed to tell it to his old woman— she would think it was pretty good; but he said that warn't nothing to some things he had said in his time. I heard one man say it was nearly three o'clock, and he hoped daylight wouldn't wait more than about a week longer. After that, the talk got further and further away, and I couldn't make out the words any more, but I could hear the mumble; and now and then a laugh, too, but it seemed a long ways off.

I was away below the ferry now. I rose up, and there was Jackson's Island, about two mile and a half down stream, heavy-timbered and standing up out of the middle of the river, big and dark and solid, like a steamboat without any lights. There warn't any signs of the bar at the head—it was all under water, now.

It didn't take me long to get there. I shot past the head at a ripping rate, the current was so swift, and then I got into the dead water and landed on the side towards the Illinois shore. I run the canoe into a deep dent in the bank that I knowed about; I had to part the willow branches to get in; and when I made fast nobody could a seen the canoe from the outside.

I went up and set down on a log at the head of the island and looked out on the big river and the black driftwood, and away over to the town, three mile away, where there was three or four lights twinkling. A monstrous big lumber raft was about a mile up stream, coming along down, with a lantern in the middle of it. I watched it come creeping down, and when it was most abreast of where I stood I heard a man say, "Stern oars, there! heave her head to stabboard!" I heard that just as plain as if the man was by my side.

There was a little gray in the sky, now; so I stepped into the woods and laid down for a nap before breakfast.

Chapter VIII
Sleeping in the Woods—Raising the Dead—
Exploring the Island—Finding Jim—
Jim's Escape—Signs—Balum

The sun was up so high when I waked, that I judged it was after eight o'clock. I laid there in the grass and the cool shade, thinking about things and feeling rested and ruther comfortable and satisfied. I could see the sun out at one or two holes, but mostly it was big trees all about, and gloomy in there amongst them. There was freckled places on the ground where the light sifted down through the leaves, and the freckled places swapped about a little, showing there was a little breeze up there. A couple of squirrels set on a limb and jabbered at me very friendly.

IN THE WOODS.

I was powerful lazy and comfortable—didn't want to get up and cook breakfast. Well, I was dozing off again, when I thinks I hears a deep sound of "boom!" away up the river. I rouses up and rests on my elbow and listens; pretty soon I hears it again. I hopped up and went and looked out at a hole in the leaves, and I see a bunch of smoke laying on the water a long ways up—about abreast the ferry. And there was the ferry-boat full of people, floating along down. I knowed what was the matter, now. "Boom!" I see the white smoke squirt out of the ferry-boat's side. You see, they was firing cannon over the water,[14] trying to make my carcass come to the top.

I was pretty hungry, but it warn't going to do for me to start a fire, because they might see the smoke. So I set there and watched the cannon-smoke and listened to the boom. The river was a mile wide, there, and it always looks pretty on a summer morning—so I was having a good enough time seeing them hunt for my remainders, if I only had a bite to eat. Well, then I happened to think how they always put quicksilver in loaves of bread and float them off because they always go right to the drownded carcass and stop there. So says I, I'll keep a lookout, and if any of them's floating around after me, I'll give them a show. I changed to the Illinois edge of the island to see what luck I could have, and I warn't disappointed. A big double loaf come along, and I most got it, with a long stick, but my foot slipped and she floated out further. Of course I was where the current set in the closest to the shore—I knowed enough for that. But by-and-by along comes another one, and this time I won. I took out the plug and shook out the little dab of quicksilver, and set my teeth in. It was "baker's bread"—what the quality eat—none of your low-down cornpone.

I got a good place amongst the leaves, and set there on a log, munching the bread and watching the ferry-boat, and very well satisfied. And then something struck me. I says, now I reckon the widow or the parson or somebody prayed that this bread would find me, and here it has gone and done it. So there ain't no doubt but there is something in that thing. That is, there's something in it when a body like the widow or the parson prays, but it don't work for me, and I reckon it don't work for only just the right kind.

I lit a pipe and had a good long smoke and went on watching. The ferry-boat was floating with the current, and I allowed I'd have a chance to see who was aboard when she come along, because she would come in close, where the bread did. When she'd got pretty well along down towards me, I put out my pipe and went to where I fished out the bread, and laid down behind a log on the bank in a little open place. Where the log forked I could peep through.

By-and-by she come along, and she drifted in so close that they could a run out a plank and walked ashore. Most everybody was on the boat. Pap, and Judge Thatcher, and Becky Thatcher, and Jo Harper, and Tom

---

[14]European and American superstition suggested that firing a cannon could raise a corpse from the bottom of a body of water.

Sawyer, and his old Aunt Polly, and Sid and Mary, and plenty more. Everybody was talking about the murder, but the captain broke in and says:

"Look sharp, now; the current sets in the closest here, and maybe he's washed ashore and got tangled amongst the brush at the water's edge. I hope so, anyway."

I didn't hope so. They all crowded up and leaned over the rails, nearly in my face, and kept still, watching with all their might. I could see them first-rate, but they couldn't see me. Then the captain sung out:

"Stand away!" and the cannon let off such a blast right before me that it made me deef with the noise and pretty near blind with the smoke, and I judged I was gone. If they'd a had some bullets in, I reckon they'd a got the corpse they was after. Well, I see I warn't hurt, thanks to goodness. The boat floated on and went out of sight around the shoulder of the island. I could hear the booming, now and then, further and further off, and by-and-by after an hour, I didn't hear it no more. The island was three mile long. I judged they had got to the foot, and was giving it up. But they didn't yet a while. They turned around the foot of the island and started up the channel on the Missouri side, under steam, and booming once in a while as they went. I crossed over to that side and watched them. When they got abreast the head of the island they quit shooting and dropped over to the Missouri shore and went home to the town.

I knowed I was all right now. Nobody else would come a-hunting after me. I got my traps out of the canoe and made me a nice camp in the thick woods. I made a kind of a tent out of my blankets to put my things under so the rain couldn't get at them. I catched a cat-fish and haggled him open with my saw, and towards sundown I started my camp fire and had supper. Then I set out a line to catch some fish for breakfast.

When it was dark I set by my camp fire smoking, and feeling pretty satisfied; but by-and-by it got sort of lonesome, and so I went and set on the bank and listened to the currents washing along, and counted the stars and drift-logs and rafts that come down, and then went to bed; there ain't no better way to put in time when you are lonesome; you can't stay so, you soon get over it.

And so for three days and nights. No difference—just the same thing. But the next day I went exploring around down through the island. I was boss of it; it all belonged to me, so to say, and I wanted to know all about it; but mainly I wanted to put in the time. I found plenty strawberries, ripe and prime; and green summergrapes, and green razberries; and the green blackberries was just beginning to show. They would all come handy by-and-by, I judged.

Well, I went fooling along in the deep woods till I judged I warn't far from the foot of the island. I had my gun along, but I hadn't shot nothing;

it was for protection; thought I would kill some game nigh home. About this time I mighty near stepped on a good sized snake, and it went sliding off through the grass and flowers, and I after it, trying to get a shot at it. I clipped along, and all of a sudden I bounded right on to the ashes of a camp fire that was still smoking.

My heart jumped up amongst my lungs. I never waited for to look further, but uncocked my gun and went sneaking back on my tip-toes as fast as ever I could. Every now and then I stopped a second, amongst the thick leaves, and listened; but my breath come so hard I couldn't hear nothing else. I slunk along another piece further, then listened again; and so on, and so on; if I see a stump, I took it for a man; if I trod on a stick and broke it, it made me feel like a person had cut one of my breaths in two and I only got half, and the short half, too.

When I got to camp I warn't feeling very brash, there warn't much sand in my craw; but I says, this ain't no time to be fooling around. So I got all my traps into my canoe again so as to have them out of sight, and I put out the fire and scattered the ashes around to look like an old last year's camp, and then clumb a tree.

I reckon I was up in the tree two hours; but I didn't see nothing, I didn't hear nothing—I only *thought* I heard and seen as much as a thousand things. Well, I couldn't stay up there forever; so at last I got down, but I kept in the thick woods and on the lookout all the time. All I could get to eat was berries and what was left over from breakfast.

By the time it was night I was pretty hungry. So when it was good and dark, I slid out from shore before moonrise and paddled over to the Illinois bank—about a quarter of a mile. I went out in the woods and cooked a supper, and I had about made up my mind I would stay there all night, when I hear a *plunkety-plunk, plunkety-plunk,* and says to myself, horses coming; and next I hear people's voices. I got everything into the canoe as quick as I could, and then went creeping through the woods to see what I could find. I hadn't got far when I hear a man say:

"We better camp here, if we can find a good place; the horses is about beat out. Let's look around."

I didn't wait, but shoved out and paddled away easy. I tied up in the old place, and reckoned I would sleep in the canoe.

I didn't sleep much. I couldn't, somehow, for thinking. And every time I waked up I thought somebody had me by the neck. So the sleep didn't do me no good. By-and-by I says to myself, I can't live this way; I'm agoing to find out who it is that's here on the island with me; I'll find it out or bust. Well, I felt better, right off.

So I took my paddle and slid out from shore just a step or two, and then let the canoe drop along down amongst the shadows. The moon was shining, and outside of the shadows it made it most as light as day. I poked along well onto an hour, everything still as rocks and sound asleep. Well by this time I was most down to the foot of the island. A little ripply, cool breeze begun to blow, and that was as good as saying the night was about done. I give her a turn with the paddle and brung her nose to shore; then I got my gun and slipped out and into the edge of the woods. I set down there on a log and looked out through the leaves. I see the moon go off watch and the darkness begin to blanket the river. But in a little while I see a pale streak over the tree-tops, and knowed the day was coming. So I took my gun and slipped off towards where I had run across that camp fire, stopping every minute or two to listen. But I hadn't no luck, somehow; I couldn't seem to find the place. But by-and-by, sure enough, I catched a glimpse of fire, away through the trees. I went for it, cautious and slow. By-and-by I was close enough to have a look, and there laid a man on the ground. It most give me the fan-tods. He had a blanket around his head, and his head was nearly in the fire. I set there behind a clump of bushes, in about six foot of him, and kept my eyes on him steady. It was getting gray daylight, now. Pretty soon he gapped, and stretched himself, and hove off the blanket, and it was Miss Watson's Jim! I bet I was glad to see him. I says:

"Hello, Jim!" and skipped out.

He bounced up and stared at me wild. Then he drops down on his knees, and puts his hands together and says:

"Doan' hurt me—don't! I hain't ever done no harm to a ghos'. I awluz liked dead people, en done all I could for 'em. You go en git in de river agin, whah you b'longs, en doan' do nuffn to Ole Jim, 'at 'uz awluz yo' fren'."

Well, I warn't long making him understand I warn't dead. I was ever so glad to see Jim. I warn't lonesome, now. I told him I warn't afraid of *him* telling the people where I was. I talked along, but he only set there and looked at me; never said nothing. Then I says:

"It's good daylight. Le's get breakfast. Make up your camp fire good."

"What's de use er makin' up de camp fire to cook strawbries en sich truck? But you got a gun, hain't you? Den we kin git sumfn better den strawbries."

"Strawberries and such truck," I says. "Is that what you live on?"

"I couldn' get nuffn else," he says.

"Why, how long you been on the island, Jim?"

"I come heah de night arter you's killed."

"What, all that time?"

"Yes-indeedy."

"And ain't you had nothing but that kind of rubbage to eat?"

"No, sah—nuffn else."

"Well, you must be most starved, ain't you?"

"I reck'n I could eat a hoss. I think I could. How long you ben on de islan'?"

"Since the night I got killed."

"No! W'y, what has you lived on? But you got a gun. Oh, yes, you got a gun. Dat's good. Now you kill sumfn en I'll make up de fire."

So we went over to where the canoe was, and while he built a fire in a grassy open place amongst the trees, I fetched meal and bacon and coffee, and coffee-pot and frying-pan, and sugar and tin cups, and the nigger was set back considerable, because he reckoned it was all done with witchcraft. I catched a good big cat-fish, too, and Jim cleaned him with his knife, and fried him.

When breakfast was ready, we lolled on the grass and eat it smoking hot. Jim laid it in with all his might, for he was most about starved. Then when we had got pretty well stuffed, we laid off and lazied.

By-and-by Jim says:

"But looky here, Huck, who wuz it dat 'uz killed in dat shanty, ef it warn't you?"

Then I told him the whole thing, and he said it was smart. He said Tom Sawyer couldn't get up no better plan than what I had. Then I says:

"How do you come to be here, Jim, and how'd you get here?"

He looked pretty uneasy, and didn't say nothing for a minute. Then he says:

"Maybe I better not tell."

"Why, Jim?"

"Well, dey's reasons. But you wouldn' tell on me ef I 'uz to tell you, would you, Huck?"

"Blamed if I would, Jim."

"Well, I b'lieve you, Huck. I—I *run off*."

"Jim!"

"But mind, you said you wouldn't tell—you know you said you wouldn't tell, Huck."

"Well, I did. I said I wouldn't, and I'll stick to it. Honest *injun* I will. People would call me a low down Ablitionist[15] and despise me for keeping

---

[15] The argument between abolitionists and those who supported slavery grew violent in the 1840s and 1850s. The Kansas-Nebraska Act (which nullified the Missouri Compromise), John Brown's raid, and the Fugitive Slave Act fueled the heated debate. Those who supported slavery saw abolitionists as bent on robbing slaveholders of their livelihood and property. James Henry Hammond wrote in a letter to abolitionists: "You would deem a man insane, whose keen sense of equity would lead him to denounce your right to the lands you hold. . . . And so would the New-England abolitionist regard any one

mum—but that don't make no difference. I ain't agoing to tell, and I ain't agoing back there anyways. So now, le's know all about it."

"Well, you see, it 'uz dis way. Ole Missus—dat's Miss Watson—she pecks on me all de time, en treats me pooty rough, but she awluz said she wouldn' sell me down to Orleans. But I noticed dey wuz a nigger trader roun' de place[16] considable, lately, en I begin to git oneasy. Well, one night I creeps to de do', pooty late, en de do' warn't quite shet, en I hear old missus tell de widder she gwyne to sell me down to Orleans, but she didn' want to, but she could git eight hund'd dollars for me, en it 'uz sich a big stack o' money she couldn' resis'. De widder she try to git her to say she wouldn' do it, but I never waited to hear de res'. I lit out mighty quick, I tell you.

"I tuck out en shin down de hill en 'spec to steal a skift 'long de sho' som'ers 'bove de town, but dey wuz people a-stirrin' yit, so I hid in de ole tumble-down cooper shop on de bank to wait for everybody to go 'way. Well, I wuz dah all night. Dey wuz somebody roun' all de time. 'Long 'bout six in de mawnin', skifts begin to go by, en 'bout eight er nine every skift dat went 'long wuz talkin' 'bout how yo' pap come over to de town en say you's killed. Dese las' skifts wuz full o' ladies en genlmen agoin' over for to see de place. Sometimes dey'd pull up at de sho' en take a res' b'fo' dey started acrost, so by de talk I got to know all 'bout de killin'. I 'uz powerful sorry you's killed, Huck, but I ain't no mo', now.

"I laid dah under de shavins all day. I 'uz hungry, but I warn't afeard; bekase I knowed ole missus en de widder wuz goin' to start to de campmeetn'[17] right arter breakfas' en be gone all day, en dey knows I goes off

---

who would insist that he should restore his farm to the descendants of the slaughtered red men. . . . The means, therefore, whatever they may have been, by which the African race now in this country have been reduced to Slavery, cannot affect us, since they are our property, as your land is yours, by inheritance or purchase and prescriptive right" (Johnson 132).

[16] Missouri slave narratives abound with references to slave traders. Slaves sold to traders were often bound and driven to auction. Former slave Joe Higgerson's narrative provides the following description: "One trader, name of Henry Moore, he used to handcuff all the niggahs together to put 'em on the boat for Noo Orleans. Dey always carried whips and they'd crack dem to see how far de darkies could jump" (Rawick 176). Jim faces separation from his family and the probability of harsh conditions "down the river." Fear of being sold often precipitated escapes.

[17] Camp meetings, outdoor religous gatherings held in wooded clearings, began in the late 1790s or early 1800s. Common characteristics of the camp meeting included a four-day duration, extremely large crowds, fiery sermons, and highly emotional conversion experiences, marked by such physical displays as rolling, jerking, running, and falling. Generally occurring right after harvest, camp meetings provided a much needed social

wid de cattle 'bout daylight, so dey wouldn' 'spec to see me roun' de place, en so dey wouldn' miss me tell arter dark in de evenin'. De yuther servants wouldn' miss me, kase dey'd shin out en take holiday, soon as de ole folks 'uz out'n de way.

"Well, when it come dark I tuck out up de river road, en went 'bout two mile er more to whah dey warn't no houses. I'd made up my mine 'bout what I's agwyne to do. You see ef I kep' on tryin' to git away afoot, de dogs 'ud track me; ef I stole a skift to cross over, dey'd miss dat skift, you see, en dey'd know 'bout whah I'd lan' on de yuther side en whah to pick up my track. So I says, a raff is what I's arter; it doan' *make* no track.

"I see a light a-comin' roun' de p'int, bymeby, so I wade' in en shove' a log ahead o' me, en swum more'n half-way acrost de river, en got in 'mongst de driftwood, en kep' my head down low, en kinder swum agin de current tell de raff come along. Den I swum to de stern uv it, en tuck aholt. It clouded up en 'uz pooty dark for a little while. So I clumb up en laid down on de planks. De men 'uz all 'way yonder in de middle, whah de lantern wuz. De river wuz arisin' en dey wuz a good current; so I reck'n'd 'at by fo' in de mawnin' I'd be twenty-five mile down de river, en den I'd slip in, jis' b'fo' daylight, en swim asho' en take to de woods on de Illinois side.[18]

"But I didn' have no luck. When we 'uz mos' down to de head er de islan', a man begin to come aft wid de lantern, I see it warn't no use fer to wait, so I slid overboad, en struck out fer de islan'. Well, I had a notion I could lan' mos' anywhers, but I couldn'—bank too bluff. I 'uz mos' to de foot er de islan' b'fo' I foun' a good place. I went into de woods en jedged I wouldn' fool wid raffs no mo', long as dey move de lantern roun' so. I had my pipe en a plug er dog-leg, en some matches in my cap, en dey warn't wet, so I 'uz all right."

"And so you ain't had no meat nor bread to eat all this time? Why didn't you get mud-turkles?"

"How you gwyne to git 'm? You can't slip up on um en grab um; en how's a body gwyne to hit um wid a rock? How could a body do it in de night? en I warn't gwyne to show myself on de bank in de daytime."

---

outlet for their participants. Camp meetings also often provided slaves with the courage or the opportunity to develop plans of escape.

[18] Freedom for Jim is not as easy as swimming to Illinois, a state in which the Fugitive Slave Act of 1793 was enforced. Rewards offered for fugitives (as chattel, Jim is "worth" $800) attracted kidnappers and bounty hunters to the state. Also, without a registration certificate or "pass," Jim faces the possibility of imprisonment and indentured servitude until claimed by his "rightful owner."

"Well, that's so. You've had to keep in the woods all the time, of course. Did you hear 'em shooting the cannon?"

"Oh, yes. I knowed dey was arter you. I see um go by heah; watched um thoo de bushes."

Some young birds come along, flying a yard or two at a time and lighting. Jim said it was a sign it was going to rain. He said it was a sign[19] when young chickens flew that way, and so he reckoned it was the same way when young birds done it. I was going to catch some of them, but Jim wouldn't let me. He said it was death. He said his father laid mighty sick once, and some of them catched a bird, and his old granny said his father would die, and he did.

And Jim said you mustn't count the things you are going to cook for dinner, because that would bring bad luck. The same if you shook the table-cloth after sun-down. And he said if a man owned a bee-hive, and that man died, the bees must be told about it before sun-up next morning, or else the bees would all weaken down and quit work and die. Jim said bees wouldn't sting idiots; but I didn't believe that, because I had tried them lots of times myself, and they wouldn't sting me.

I had heard about some of these things before, but not all of them. Jim knowed all kinds of signs. He said he knowed most everything. I said it looked to me like all the signs was about bad luck, and so I asked him if there warn't any good-luck signs. He says:

"Mighty few—an' *dey* ain' no use to a body. What you want to know when good luck's a-comin' for? want to keep it off?" And he said: "Ef you's got hairy arms en a hairy breas', it's a sign dat you's agwyne to be rich. Well, dey's some use in a sign like dat, 'kase it's so fur ahead. You see, maybe you's got to be po' a long time fust, en so you might git discourage' en kill yo'sef 'f you didn' know by de sign dat you gwyne to be rich bymeby."

"Have you got hairy arms and a hairy breast, Jim?"

"What's de use to axe dat question? don' you see I has?"

---

[19] Jim establishes himself as an authority on signs by accurately predicting the storm, revealing his knowledge of the natural world. The narrative of former slave Gus Smith reveals ways in which such knowledge proved useful for escaping slaves: "Indian turnip grows by de thousands in de woods here. Colored folks used to use de Indian turnip in slave times. Dey would take dis and dry it, pulverize it and tie it in big quantities around their feet to keep off the trail of bloodhounds. No bloodhound could trail a bit further after smelling it. It was strong like red pepper, burns like everything and colored folks running away use it all de time" (Rawick 332). Jim's knowledge of signs also cements his relationship with Huck.

"Well, are you rich?"

"No, but I ben rich wunst, and gwyne to be rich agin. Wunst I had fo-teen dollars, but I tuck to specalat'n', en got busted out."

"What did you speculate in, Jim?"

"Well, fust I tackled stock."

"What kind of stock?"

"Why, live stock. Cattle, you know. I put ten dollars in a cow. But I ain' gwyne to resk no mo' money in stock. De cow up 'n' died on my han's."

"So you lost the ten dollars."

"No, I didn' lose it all. I on'y los' 'bout nine of it. I sole de hide en taller for a dollar en ten cents."

"You had five dollars and ten cents left. Did you speculate any more?"

"Yes. You know dat one-laigged nigger dat b'longs to old Misto Bradish? well, he sot up a bank,[20] en say anybody dat put in a dollar would git fo' dollars mo' at de en' er de year. Well, all de niggers went in, but dey didn' have much. I wuz de on'y one dat had much. So I stuck out for mo' dan fo' dollars, en I said 'f I didn' git it I'd start a bank mysef. Well, o' course dat nigger want' to keep me out er de business, bekase he say dey warn't business 'nough for two banks, so he say I could put in my five dollars en he pay me thirty-five at de en' er de year.

"So I done it. Den I reck'n'd I'd inves' de thirty-five dollars right off en keep things a-movin'. Dey wuz a nigger name' Bob, dat had ketched a wood-flat, en his marster didn' know it; en I bought it off'n him en told him to take de thirty-five dollars when de en' er de year come; but some-body stole de wood-flat dat night, en nex' day de one-laigged nigger say de bank's busted. So dey didn' none uv us git no money."

"What did you do with the ten cents, Jim?"

"Well, I 'uz gwyne to spen' it, but I had a dream, en de dream tole me to give it to a nigger name' Balum—Balum's Ass[21] dey call him for short, he's one er dem chuckle-heads, you know. But he's lucky, dey say,

---

[20] Jim's economic ventures reflect the dire situation of free blacks during the period. Victor Doyno notes, "After the Civil War a National Freedmen's Bank was established and began to receive deposits. . . . [T]he Freedmen's Bank received about 27 million dollars, mostly of very small deposits, before it crashed in 1873. Many recently liberated individuals who were relatively new to banking were, in effect, robbed severely again. . . . Jim's lack of knowledge has comic aspects, but the historical situation casts a long dark shadow over the humor" (Doyno, "Economics").

[21] Num. 22.21–34. In this strange and comic Old Testament story, Balaam's ass saves the life of the prophet Balaam. Balaam beats the ass for stubbornness when she refuses to travel down a road, not realizing that the ass can see the angel of the Lord standing in

en I see I warn't lucky. De dream say let Balum inves' de ten cents en he'd make a raise for me. Well, Balum he tuck de money, en when he wuz in church he hear de preacher say dat whoever give to de po' len' to de Lord, en boun' to git his money back a hund'd times. So Balum he tuck en give de ten cents to de po', en laid low to see what wuz gwyne to come of it."

"Well, what did come of it, Jim?"

"Nuffn' never come of it. I couldn' manage to k'leck dat money no way; en Balum he couldn'. I ain' gwyne to len' no mo' money 'dout I see de security. Boun' to git yo' money back a hund'd times, de preacher says! Ef I could git de ten *cents* back, I'd call it squah, en be glad er de chanst."

"Well, it's all right, anyway, Jim, long as you're going to be rich again some time or other."

"Yes—en I's rich now, come to look at it. I owns mysef, en I's wuth eight hund'd dollars. I wisht I had de money, I wouldn' want no mo'."

Chapter IX
The Cave—The Floating House ~huh?

I wanted to go and look at a place right about the middle of the island, that I'd found when I was exploring; so we started, and soon got to it, because the island was only three miles long and a quarter of a mile wide.

This place was a tolerable long steep hill or ridge, about forty foot high. We had a rough time getting to the top, the sides was so steep and the bushes so thick. We tramped and clumb around all over it, and by-and-by found a good big cavern in the rock, most up to the top on the side towards Illinois. The cavern was as big as two or three rooms bunched together, and Jim could stand up straight in it. It was cool in there. Jim was for putting our traps in there, right away, but I said we didn't want to be climbing up and down there all the time.

Jim said if we had the canoe hid in a good place, and had all the traps in the cavern, we could rush there if anybody was to come to the island,

---

the way. The animal protests the beating, demanding, "Am I not thine ass, upon which thou has ridden ever since I was thine unto this day? was I ever wont to do so unto thee?" Twain contrasts the comic specter of the animal giving advice not only with Jim's investment strategies but with his ability to read "signs." Jim reaps the benefits of "lending to the Lord" in that he now owns himself. Further, Jim's advice always proves sound.

and they would never find us without dogs. And besides, he said them little birds had said it was going to rain, and did I want the things to get wet?

So we went back and got the canoe and paddled up abreast the cavern, and lugged all the traps up there. Then we hunted up a place close by to hide the canoe in, amongst the thick willows. We took some fish off of the lines and set them again, and begun to get ready for dinner.

The door of the cavern was big enough to roll a hogshead in, and on one side of the door the floor stuck out a little bit and was flat and a good place to build a fire on. So we built it there and cooked dinner.

We spread the blankets inside for a carpet, and eat our dinner in there. We put

EXPLORING THE CAVE.

all the other things handy at the back of the cavern. Pretty soon it darkened up and begun to thunder and lighten; so the birds was right about it. Directly it begun to rain, and it rained like all fury, too, and I never see the wind blow so. It was one of these regular summer storms. It would get so dark that it looked all blue-black outside, and lovely; and the rain would thrash along by so thick that the trees off a little ways looked dim and spider-webby; and here would come a blast of wind that would bend the trees down and turn up the pale underside of the leaves; and then a perfect ripper of a gust would follow along and set the branches to tossing their arms as if they was just wild; and next, when it was just about the bluest and blackest—*fst!* it was as bright as glory and you'd have a little glimpse of tree-tops a-plunging about, away off yonder in the storm, hundreds of yards further than you could see before; dark as sin again in a second, and now you'd hear the thunder let go with an awful crash and then go rumbling, grumbling, tumbling down the sky towards the under side of the world, like rolling empty barrels down stairs, where it's long stairs and they bounce a good deal, you know.

"Jim, this is nice," I says. "I wouldn't want to be nowhere else but here. Pass me along another hunk of fish and some hot corn-bread."

"Well, you wouldn't a ben here, 'f it hadn't a ben for Jim. You'd a been down dah in de woods widout any dinner, en gittn' mos' drownded, too, dat you would, honey. Chickens knows when it's gwyne to rain, en so do de birds, chile.") - *spiritual*

The river went on raising and raising for ten or twelve days, till at last it was over the banks. The water was three or four foot deep on the island in the low places and on the Illinois bottom. On that side it was a good many miles wide; but on the Missouri side it was the same old distance across—a half a mile—because the Missouri shore was just a wall of high bluffs.

Daytimes we paddled all over the island in the canoe. It was mighty cool and shady in the deep woods even if the sun was blazing outside. We went winding in and out amongst the trees; and sometimes the vines hung so thick we had to back away and go some other way. Well, on every old broken-down tree, you could see rabbits, and snakes, and such things; and when the island had been overflowed a day or two, they got so tame, on account of being hungry, that you could paddle right up and put your hand on them if you wanted to; *funny* — but not the snakes and turtles—they would slide off in the water. The ridge our cavern was in, was full of them. We could a had pets enough if we'd wanted them.

One night we catched a little section of a lumber raft—nice pine planks. It was twelve foot wide and about fifteen or sixteen foot long, and the top stood above water six or seven inches, a solid level floor. We could see saw-logs go by in the daylight, sometimes, but we let them go; we didn't show ourselves in daylight.

Another night, when we was up at the head of the island, just before daylight, here comes a frame house down, on the west side. She was a two-story, and tilted over, considerable. We paddled out and got aboard—clumb in at an up-stairs window. But it was too dark to see yet, so we made the canoe fast and set in her to wait for daylight.

all of a sudden supplies fall from the sky The light begun to come before we got to the foot of the island. Then we looked in at the window. We could make out a bed, and a table, and two old chairs, and lots of things around about on the floor; and there was clothes hanging against the wall. There was something laying on the floor in the far corner that looked like a man. So Jim says:

"Hello, you!"

But it didn't budge. So I hollered again, and then Jim says:

"De man ain't asleep—he's dead. You hold still—I'll go en see."

He went and bent down and looked, and says:

"It's a dead man. Yes, indeed; naked, too. He's ben shot in de back. I reck'n he's ben dead two er three days. Come in, Huck, but doan' look at his face—it's too gashly." *~ he cares about Huck*

I didn't look at him at all. Jim threw some old rags over him, but he needn't done it; I didn't want to see him. There was heaps of old greasy cards scattered around over the floor, and old whisky bottles, and a couple of masks made out of black cloth; and all over the walls was the ignorantest kind of words and pictures, made with charcoal. There was two old dirty calico dresses, and a sun-bonnet, and some women's under-clothes, hanging against the wall, and some men's clothing, too. We put the lot into the canoe; it might come good. There was a boy's old speckled straw hat on the floor; I took that too. And there was a bottle that had had milk in it; and it had a rag stopper for a baby to suck. We would a took the bottle, but it was broke. There was a seedy old chest, and an old hair trunk with the hinges broke. They stood open, but there warn't nothing left in them that was any account. The way things was scattered about, we reckoned the people left in a hurry and warn't fixed so as to carry off most of their stuff. *from the picture*

We got an old tin lantern, and a butcher knife without any handle, and a bran-new Barlow knife[22] worth two bits in any store, and a lot of tallow candles, and a tin candlestick, and a gourd, and a tin cup, and a ratty old bed-quilt off the bed, and a reticule with needles and pins and beeswax and buttons and thread and all such truck in it, and a hatchet and some nails, and a fish-line as thick as my little finger, with some monstrous hooks on it, and a roll of buckskin, and a leather dog-collar, and a horse-shoe, and some vials of medicine that didn't have no label on them; and just as we was leaving I found a tolerable good curry-comb, and Jim he found a ratty old fiddle-bow, and a wooden leg. The straps was broke off of it, but barring that, it was a good enough leg, though it was too long for me and not long enough for Jim, and we couldn't find the other one, though we hunted all around. *longer sentence #2*

And so, take it all around, we made a good haul. When we was ready to shove off, we was a quarter of a mile below the island, and it was pretty broad day; so I made Jim lay down in the canoe and cover up with the quilt, because if he set up, people could tell he was a nigger a good ways

---

[22] A large pocketknife with one blade, named after a family of Sheffield cutlers who allegedly produced this kind of knife before 1700.

off. I paddled over to the Illinois shore, and drifted down most a half a mile doing it. I crept up the dead water under the bank, and hadn't no accidents and didn't see nobody. We got home all safe.

Chapter X
The Find—Old Hank Bunker—In Disguise

After breakfast I wanted to talk about the dead man and guess out how he come to be killed, but Jim didn't want to. He said it would fetch bad luck; and besides, he said, he might come and ha'nt us; he said a man that warn't buried was more likely to go a-ha'nting around than one that was planted and comfortable. That sounded pretty reasonable, so I didn't say no more; but I couldn't keep from studying over it and wishing I knowed who shot the man, and what they done it for.

We rummaged the clothes we'd got, and found eight dollars in silver sewed up in the lining of an old blanket overcoat. Jim said he reckoned the people in that house stole the coat, because if they'd a knowed the money was there they wouldn't a left it. I said I reckoned they killed him, too; but Jim didn't want to talk about that. I says:

"Now you think it's bad luck; but what did you say when I fetched in the snake-skin that I found on the top of the ridge day before yesterday? You said it was the worst bad luck in the world to touch a snake-skin with my hands. Well, here's your bad luck! We've raked in all this truck and eight dollars besides. I wish we could have some bad luck like this every day, Jim."

"Never you mind, honey, never you mind. Don't you git too peart. It's a-comin'. Mind I tell you, it's a-comin'."

THEY FOUND EIGHT DOLLARS.

It did come, too. It was a Tuesday that we had that talk. Well, after dinner Friday, we was laying around in the grass at the upper end of the ridge, and got out of tobacco. I went to the cavern to get some, and found a rattlesnake in there. I killed him, and curled him up on the foot of Jim's blanket, ever so natural, thinking there'd be some fun when Jim found him there. Well, by night I forgot all about the snake, and when Jim flung himself down on the blanket while I struck a light, the snake's mate was there, and bit him.

He jumped up yelling, and the first thing the light showed was the varmint curled up and ready for another spring. I laid him out in a second with a stick, and Jim grabbed pap's whisky jug and begun to pour it down.

He was barefooted, and the snake bit him right on the heel. That all comes of my being such a fool as to not remember that wherever you leave a dead snake its mate always comes there and curls around it. Jim told me to chop off the snake's head and throw it away, and then skin the body and roast a piece of it. I done it, and he eat it and said it would help cure him. He made me take off the rattles and tie them around his wrist, too. He said that that would help. Then I slid out quiet and throwed the snakes clear away amongst the bushes; for I warn't going to let Jim find out it was all my fault, not if I could help it.

Jim sucked and sucked at the jug, and now and then he got out of his head and pitched around and yelled; but every time he come to himself he went to sucking at the jug again. His foot swelled up pretty big, and so did his leg; but by-and-by the drunk begun to come, and so I judged he was all right; but I'd druther been bit with a snake than pap's whisky.

Jim was laid up for four days and nights. Then the swelling was all gone and he was around again. I made up my mind I wouldn't ever take a-holt of a snake-skin again with my hands, now that I see what had come of it. Jim said he reckoned I would believe him next time. And he said that handling a snake-skin was such awful bad luck that maybe we hadn't got to the end of it yet. He said he druther see the new moon over his left shoulder as much as a thousand times than take up a snake-skin in his hand. Well, I was getting to feel that way myself, though I've always reckoned that looking at the new moon over your left shoulder is one of the carelessest and foolishest things a body can do. Old Hank Bunker done it once, and bragged about it; and in less than two years he got drunk and fell off of the shot tower and spread himself out so that he was just a kind of a layer, as you may say; and they slid him edgeways between two barn doors for a coffin, and buried him so, so they say, but I didn't see it. Pap told me. But anyway, it all come of looking at the moon that way, like a fool.

Well, the days went along, and the river went down between its banks again; and about the first thing we done was to bait one of the big hooks with a skinned rabbit and set it and catch a cat-fish that was as big as a man, being six foot two inches long, and weighed over two hundred pounds. We couldn't handle him, of course; he would a flung us into Illinois. We just set there and watched him rip and tear around till he drownded. We found a brass button in his stomach, and a round ball, and lots of rubbage. We split the ball open with the hatchet, and there was a spool in it. Jim said he'd had it there a long time, to coat it over so and make a ball of it. It was as big a fish as was ever catched in the Mississippi, I reckon. Jim said he hadn't ever seen a bigger one. He would a been worth a good deal over at the village. They peddle out such a fish as that by the pound in the market house there; everybody buys some of him; his meat's as white as snow and makes a good fry.

Next morning I said it was getting slow and dull, and I wanted to get a stirring up, some way. I said I reckoned I would slip over the river and find out what was going on. Jim liked that notion; but he said I must go in the dark and look sharp. Then he studied it over and said, couldn't I put on some of them old things and dress up like a girl? That was a good notion, too. So we shortened up one of the calico gowns and I turned up my trouser-legs to my knees and got into it. Jim hitched it behind with the hooks, and it was a fair fit. I put on the sun-bonnet and tied it under my chin, and then for a body to look in and see my face was like looking down a joint of stove-pipe. Jim said nobody would know me, even in the daytime, hardly. I practiced around all day to get the hang of the things, and by-and-by I could do pretty well in them, only Jim said I didn't walk like a girl; and he said I must quit pulling up my gown to get at my britches pocket. I took notice, and done better.

I started up the Illinois shore in the canoe just after dark.

I started across to the town from a little below the ferry landing, and the drift of the current fetched me in at the bottom of the town. I tied up and started along the bank. There was a light burning in a little shanty that hadn't been lived in for a long time, and I wondered who had took up quarters there. I slipped up and peeped in at the window. There was a woman about forty year old in there, knitting by a candle that was on a pine table. I didn't know her face; she was a stranger, for you couldn't start a face in that town that I didn't know. Now this was lucky, because I was weakening; I was getting afraid I had come; people might know my voice and find me out. But if this woman had been in such a little town two days she could tell me all I wanted to know; so I knocked at the door, and made up my mind I wouldn't forget I was a girl.

Chapter XI
Huck and the Woman—The Search—
Prevarication—Going to Goshen

"Come in," says the woman, and I did. She says:
"Take a cheer."
I done it. She looked me all over with her little shiny eyes, and says:
"What might your name be?"
"Sarah Williams."
"Where 'bouts do you live? In this neighborhood?"
"No'm. In Hookerville, seven mile below. I've walked all the way and I'm all tired out."
"Hungry, too, I reckon. I'll find you something."
"No'm. I ain't hungry. I was so hungry I had to stop two miles below here at a farm; so I ain't hungry no more. It's what makes me so late. My mother's down sick, and out of money and everything, and I come to tell my uncle Abner Moore. He lives at the upper end of the town, she says. I hain't ever been here before. Do you know him?"

"No; but I don't know every-body yet. I haven't lived here quite two weeks. It's a consider-able ways to the upper end of the town. You better stay here all night. Take off your bonnet."

"No," I says; "I'll rest a while, I reckon, and go on. I ain't afeared of the dark."

She said she wouldn't let me go by myself, but her husband would be in by-and-by, maybe in a hour and a half, and she'd send him along with me. Then she got to talking about her hus-band, and about her relations up the river, and her relations down the river, and about how much better off they used to was, and how they didn't know but they'd

"COME IN."

made a mistake coming to our town, instead of letting well alone—and so on and so on, till I was afeard *I* had made a mistake coming to her to find out what was going on in the town; but by-and-by she dropped onto pap and the murder, and then I was pretty willing to let her clatter right along. She told about me and Tom Sawyer finding the six thousand dollars (only she got it ten) and all about pap and what a hard lot he was, and what a hard lot I was, and at last she got down to where I was murdered. I says:

"Who done it? We've heard considerable about these goings on, down in Hookerville, but we don't know who 'twas that killed Huck Finn."

"Well, I reckon there's a right smart chance of people *here* that'd like to know who killed him. Some think old Finn done it himself."

"No—is that so?"

"Most everybody thought it at first. He'll never know how nigh he come to getting lynched. But before night they changed around and judged it was done by a runaway nigger named Jim."

"Why *he*—"

I stopped. I reckoned I better keep still. She run on, and never noticed I had put in at all.

"The nigger run off the very night Huck Finn was killed. So there's a reward out for him—three hundred dollars. And there's a reward out for old Finn, too—two hundred dollars. You see, he come to town the morning after the murder, and told about it, and was out with 'em on the ferry-boat hunt, and right away after he up and left. Before night they wanted to lynch him, but he was gone, you see. Well, next day they found out the nigger was gone; they found out he hadn't ben seen sence ten o'clock the night the murder was done. So then they put it on him, you see, and while they was full of it, next day back comes old Finn and went boohooing to Judge Thatcher to get money to hunt for the nigger all over Illinois with. The judge give him some, and that evening he got drunk and was around till after midnight with a couple of mighty hard looking strangers, and then went off with them. Well, he hain't come back sence, and they ain't looking for him back till this things blows over a little, for people thinks now that he killed his boy and fixed things so folks would think robbers done it, and then he'd get Huck's money without having to bother a long time with a lawsuit. People do say he warn't any good to do it. Oh, he's sly, I reckon. If he don't come back for a year, he'll be all right. You can't prove anything on him, you know; everything will be quieted down then, and he'll walk into Huck's money as easy as nothing."

"Yes, I reckon so, 'm. I don't see nothing in the way of it. Has everybody quit thinking the nigger done it?"

"Oh, no, not everybody. A good many thinks he done it. But they'll get the nigger pretty soon, now, and maybe they can scare it out of him."

"Why, are they after him yet?"

"Well, you're innocent, ain't you! Does three hundred dollars lay around every day for people to pick up? Some folks thinks the nigger ain't far from here. I'm one of them—but I hain't talked it around. A few days ago I was talking with an old couple that lives next door in the log shanty, and they happened to say hardly anybody ever goes to that island over yonder that they call Jackson's Island. Don't anybody live there? says I. No, nobody, says they. I didn't say any more, but I done some thinking. I was pretty near certain I'd seen smoke over there, about the head of the island, a day or two before that, so I says to myself, like as not that nigger's hiding over there; anyway, says I, it's worth the trouble to give the place a hunt. I hain't seen any smoke sence, so I reckon maybe he's gone, if it was him; but husband's going over to see—him and another man. He was gone up the river; but he got back to-day and I told him as soon as he got here two hours ago."

I had got so uneasy I couldn't set still. I had to do something with my hands; so I took up a needle off of the table and went to threading it. My hands shook, and I was making a bad job of it. When the woman stopped talking, I looked up, and she was looking at me pretty curious, and smiling a little. I put down the needle and thread and let on to be interested—and I was, too—and says:

"Three hundred dollars is a power of money. I wish my mother could get it. Is your husband going over there to-night?"

"Oh, yes. He went up town with the man I was telling you of, to get a boat and see if they could borrow another gun. They'll go over after midnight."

"Couldn't they see better if they was to wait till daytime?"

"Yes. And couldn't the nigger see better, too? After midnight he'll likely be asleep, and they can slip around through the woods and hunt up his camp fire all the better for the dark, if he's got one."

"I didn't think of that."

The woman kept looking at me pretty curious, and I didn't feel a bit comfortable. Pretty soon she says:

"What did you say your name was, honey?"

"M-Mary Williams."

Somehow it didn't seem to me that I said it was Mary before, so I didn't look up; seemed to me I said it was Sarah; so I felt sort of cornered, and was afeared maybe I was looking it, too. I wished the woman would say something more; the longer she set still, the uneasier I was. But now she says:

"Honey, I thought you said it was Sarah when you first come in?"

"Oh, yes'm, I did. Sarah Mary Williams. Sarah's my first name. Some calls me Sarah, some calls me Mary." *lie*

"Oh, that's the way of it?"

"Yes'm."

I was feeling better, then, but I wished I was out of there, anyway. I couldn't look up yet.

Well, the woman fell to talking about how hard times was, and how poor they had to live, and how the rats was as free as if they owned the place, and so forth, and so on, and then I got easy again. She was right about the rats. You'd see one stick his nose out of a hole in the corner every little while. She said she had to have things handy to throw at them when she was alone, or they wouldn't give her no peace. She showed me a bar of lead, twisted up into a knot, and said she was a good shot with it generly, but she'd wrenched her arm a day or two ago, and didn't know whether she could throw true, now. But she watched for a chance, and directly she banged away at a rat, but she missed him wide, and said "Ouch!" it hurt her arm so. Then she told me to try for the next one. I wanted to be getting away before the old man got back, but of course I didn't let on. I got the thing, and the first rat that showed his nose I let drive, and if he'd a stayed where he was he'd a been a tolerable sick rat. She said that that was first-rate, and she reckoned I would hive the next one. She went and got the lump of lead and fetched it back and brought along a hank of yarn, which she wanted me to help her with. I held up my two hands and she put the hank over them and went on talking about her and her husband's matters. But she broke off to say:

"Keep your eye on the rats. You better have the lead in your lap, handy."

So she dropped the lump into my lap, just at that moment, and I clapped my legs together on it and she went on talking. But only about a minute. Then she took off the hank and looked me straight in the face, but very pleasant, and says:

"Come, now—what's your real name?"

uh-oh "Wh-what, mum?"

"What's your real name? Is it Bill, or Tom, or Bob?—or what is it?"

I reckon I shook like a leaf, and I didn't know hardly what to do. But I says:

"Please to don't poke fun at a poor girl like me, mum. If I'm in the way, here, I'll—"

"No, you won't. Set down and stay where you are. I ain't going to hurt you, and I ain't going to tell on you, nuther. You just tell me your secret, and trust me. I'll keep it; and what's more, I'll help you. So'll my old man, if you want him to. You see, you're a runaway 'prentice—that's all. It ain't anything. There ain't any harm in it. You've been treated bad, and you made up your mind to cut. Bless you, child, I wouldn't tell on you. Tell me all about it, now—that's a good boy."

So I said it wouldn't be no use to try to play it any longer, and I would just make a clean breast and tell her everything, but she musn't go back on her promise. Then I told her my father and mother was dead, and the law had bound me out to a mean old farmer in the country thirty mile back from the river, and he treated me so bad I couldn't stand it no longer; he went away to be gone a couple of days, and so I took my chance and stole some of his daughter's old clothes, and cleared out, and I had been three nights coming the thirty miles; I traveled nights, and hid day-times and slept, and the bag of bread and meat I carried from home lasted me all the way and I had a plenty. I said I believed my uncle Abner Moore would take care of me, and so that was why I struck out for this town of Goshen. *huge lie*

"Goshen, child? This ain't Goshen. This is St. Petersburg. Goshen's ten mile further up the river. Who told you this was Goshen?"

"Why, a man I met at day-break this morning, just as I was going to turn into the woods for my regular sleep. He told me when the roads forked I must take the right hand, and five mile would fetch me to Goshen."

"He was drunk I reckon. He told you just exactly wrong."

"Well, he did act like he was drunk, but it ain't no matter now. I got to be moving along. I'll fetch Goshen before day-light."

"Hold on a minute. I'll put you up a snack to eat. You might want it." So she put me up a snack, and says:

"Say—when a cow's laying down, which end of her gets up first? Answer up prompt, now—don't stop to study over it. Which end gets up first?"

"The hind end, mum."

"Well, then, a horse?"

"The for'rard end, mum."

"Which side of a tree does the most moss grow on?"

"North side."

"If fifteen cows is browsing on a hillside, how many of them eats with their heads pointed the same direction?"

"The whole fifteen, mum."

"Well, I reckon you *have* lived in the country. I thought maybe you was trying to hocus me again. What's your real name, now?"

"George Peters, mum." *lie*

"Well, try to remember it, George. Don't forget and tell me it's Elexander before you go, and then get out by saying it's George-Elexander when

she knew he lied then also

I catch you. And don't go about women in that old calico. You do a girl tolerable poor, but you might fool men, maybe. Bless you, child, when you set out to thread a needle, don't hold the thread still and fetch the needle up to it; hold the needle still and poke the thread at it—that's the way a woman most always does; but a man always does 'tother way. And when you throw at a rat or anything, hitch yourself up a tip-toe, and fetch your hand up over your head as awkward as you can, and miss your rat about six or seven foot. Throw stiff-armed from the shoulder, like there was a pivot there for it to turn on—like a girl; not from the wrist and elbow, with your arm out to one side, like a boy. And mind you, when a girl tries to catch anything in her lap, she throws her knees apart; she don't clap them together, the way you did when you catched the lump of lead. Why, I spotted you for a boy when you was threading the needle; and I contrived the other things just to make certain. Now trot along to your uncle, Sarah Mary Williams George Elexander Peters, and if you get into trouble you send word to Mrs. Judith Loftus, which is me, and I'll do what I can to get you out of it. Keep the river road, all the way, and next time you tramp, take shoes and socks with you. The river road's a rocky one, and your feet 'll be in a condition when you get to Goshen, I reckon."

I went up the bank about fifty yards, and then I doubled on my tracks and slipped back to where my canoe was, a good piece below the house. I jumped in and was off in a hurry. I went up stream far enough to make the head of the island, and then started across. I took off the sun-bonnet, for I didn't want no blinders on, then. When I was about the middle, I hear the clock begin to strike; so I stops and listens; the sound come faint over the water, but clear—eleven. When I struck the head of the island I never waited to blow, though I was most winded, but I shoved right into the timber where my old camp used to be, and started a good fire there on a high-and-dry spot.

Then I jumped in the canoe and dug out for our place a mile and a half below, as hard as I could go. I landed, and slopped through the timber and up the ridge and into the cavern. There Jim laid, sound asleep on the ground. I roused him out and says:

"Git up and hump yourself, Jim! There ain't a minute to lose. They're after us!"

Jim never asked no questions, he never said a word; but the way he worked for the next half an hour showed about how he was scared. By that time everything we had in the world was on our raft and she was ready to be shoved out from the willow cove where she was hid. We put out the camp fire at the cavern the first thing, and didn't show a candle outside after that.

I took the canoe out from shore a little piece and took a look, but if there was a boat around I couldn't see it, for stars and shadows ain't good to see by. Then we got out the raft and slipped along down in the shade, past the foot of the island dead still, never saying a word.

Chapter XII
Slow Navigation—Borrowing Things—Boarding the Wreck—The Plotters—Hunting for the Boat

It must a been close onto one o'clock when we got below the island at last, and the raft did seem to go mighty slow. If a boat was to come along, we was going to take to the canoe and break for the Illinois shore; and it was well a boat didn't come, for we hadn't ever thought to put the gun in the canoe, or a fishing-line or anything to eat. We was in ruther too much of a sweat to think of so many things. It warn't good judgment to put *everything* on the raft.

If the men went to the island, I just expect they found the camp fire I built, and watched it all night for Jim to come. Anyways, they stayed away from us, and if my building the fire never fooled them it warn't no fault of mine. I played it as lowdown on them as I could.

When the first streak of day began to show, we tied up to a tow-head in a big bend on the Illinois side, and hacked off cotton-wood branches with the hatchet and covered up the raft with them so she looked like there had been a cave-in in the bank there. A tow-head is a sand-bar that has cotton-woods on it as thick as harrow-teeth.

ON THE RAFT.

We had mountains on the Missouri shore and heavy timber on the
Illinois side, and the channel was down the Missouri shore at that place,
so we warn't afraid of anybody running across us. We laid there all day
and watched the rafts and steamboats spin down the Missouri shore, and
up-bound steamboats fight the big river in the middle. I told Jim all about
the time I had jabbering with that woman; and Jim said she was a smart
one, and if she was to start after us herself *she* wouldn't set down and watch
a camp fire—no, sir, she'd fetch a dog. Well, then, I said, why couldn't she
tell her husband to fetch a dog? Jim said he bet she did think of it by the
time the men was ready to start, and he believed they must a gone up town
to get a dog and so they lost all that time, or else we wouldn't be here on
a tow-head sixteen or seventeen mile below the village—no, indeedy, we
would be in that same old town again. So I said I didn't care what was the
reason they didn't get us, as long as they didn't.

When it was beginning to come on dark, we poked our heads out of
the cotton-wood thicket and looked up, and down, and across; nothing in
sight; so Jim took up some of the top planks of the raft and built a snug
wigwam to get under in blazing weather and rainy, and to keep the things
dry. Jim made a floor for the wigwam, and raised it a foot or more above
the level of the raft, so now the blankets and all the traps was out of the
reach of steamboat waves. Right in the middle of the wigwam we made a
layer of dirt about five or six inches deep with a frame around it for to hold
it to its place; this was to build a fire on in sloppy weather or chilly; the
wigwam would keep it from being seen. We made an extra steering oar,
too, because one of the others might get broke, on a snag or something. We
fixed up a short forked stick to hang the old lantern on; because we must
always light the lantern whenever we see a steamboat coming down stream,
to keep from getting run over; but we wouldn't have to light it for up-
stream boats unless we see we was in what they call a "crossing"; for the
river was pretty high yet, very low banks being still a little under water; so
up-bound boats didn't always run the channel, but hunted easy water.

This second night we run between seven and eight hours, with a current that was making over four mile an hour. We catched fish, and talked,
and we took a swim now and then to keep off sleepiness. It was kind of
solemn, drifting down the big still river, laying on our backs looking up at
the stars, and we didn't ever feel like talking loud, and it warn't often that
we laughed, only a little kind of a low chuckle. We had mighty good
weather, as a general thing, and nothing ever happened to us at all, that
night, nor the next, nor the next.

Every night we passed towns, some of them away up on black hill-
sides, nothing but just a shiny bed of lights, not a house could you see. The
fifth night we passed St. Louis, and it was like the whole world lit up. In

St. Petersburg they used to say there was twenty or thirty thousand people in St. Louis, but I never believed it till I see that wonderful spread of lights at two o'clock that still night. There warn't a sound there; everybody was asleep.

Every night, now, I used to slip ashore, towards ten o'clock, at some little village, and buy ten or fifteen cents' worth of meal or bacon or other stuff to eat; and sometimes I lifted a chicken that warn't roosting comfortable, and took him along. Pap always said, take a chicken when you get a chance, because if you don't want him yourself you can easy find somebody that does, and a good deed ain't ever forgot. I never see pap when he didn't want the chicken himself, but that is what he used to say, anyway.

Mornings, before daylight, I slipped into corn fields and borrowed a watermelon, or a mushmelon, or a punkin, or some new corn, or things of that kind. Pap always said it warn't no harm to borrow things, if you was meaning to pay them back, sometime; but the widow said it warn't anything but a soft name for stealing, and no decent body would do it. Jim said he reckoned the widow was partly right and pap was partly right; so the best way would be for us to pick out two or three things from the list and say we wouldn't borrow them any more—then he reckoned it wouldn't be no harm to borrow the others. So we talked it over all one night, drifting along down the river, trying to make up our minds whether to drop the watermelons, or the cantelopes, or the mushmelons, or what. But towards daylight we got it all settled satisfactory, and concluded to drop crabapples and p'simmons. We warn't feeling just right, before that, but it was all comfortable now. I was glad the way it come out, too, because crabapples ain't ever good, and the p'simmons wouldn't be ripe for two or three months yet.

We shot a water-fowl, now and then, that got up too early in the morning or didn't go to bed early enough in the evening. Take it all around, we lived pretty high.

The fifth night below St. Louis we had a big storm after midnight, with a power of thunder and lightning, and the rain poured down in a solid sheet. We stayed in the wigwam and let the raft take care of itself. When the lightning glared out we could see a big straight river ahead, and high rocky bluffs on both sides. By-and-by says I, "Hel-*lo*, Jim, looky yonder!" It was a steamboat that had killed herself[23] on a rock. We was drifting straight down for her. The lightning showed her very distinct. She was leaning over, with part of her upper deck above water, and you could see

---

[23] In *Life on the Mississippi*, Twain writes about dangerous stretches of the river where steamboats often crashed on hidden rocks.

every little chimbly-guy clean and clear, and a chair by the big bell, with an old slouch hat hanging on the back of it when the flashes come.

Well, it being away in the night, and stormy, and all so mysterious-like, I felt just the way any other boy would a felt when I see that wreck laying there so mournful and lonesome in the middle of the river. I wanted to get aboard of her and slink around a little, and see what there was there. So I says:

"Le's land on her, Jim."

But Jim was dead against it, at first. He says:

"I doan' want to go fool'n 'long er no wrack. We's doin' blame' well, en we better let blame' well alone, as de good book says. Like as not dey's a watchman on dat wrack."

"Watchman your grandmother," I says; "there ain't nothing to watch but the texas and the pilot-house; and do you reckon anybody's going to resk his life for a texas and pilot-house such a night as this, when it's likely to break up and wash off down the river any minute?" Jim couldn't say nothing to that, so he didn't try. "And besides," I says, "we might borrow something worth having, out of the captain's stateroom. Seegars, I bet you—and cost five cents apiece, solid cash. Steamboat captains is always rich, and get sixty dollars a month, and they don't care a cent what a thing costs, you know, long as they want it. Stick a candle in your pocket; I can't rest, Jim, till we give her a rummaging. Do you reckon Tom Sawyer would ever go by this thing? Not for pie, he wouldn't. He'd call it an adventure—that's what he'd call it; and he'd land on that wreck if it was his last act. And wouldn't he throw style into it?—wouldn't he spread himself, nor nothing? Why, you'd think it was Christopher C'lumbus discovering Kingdom-Come. I wish Tom Sawyer was here."

Jim he grumbled a little, but give in. He said we mustn't talk any more than we could help, and then talk mighty low. The lightning showed us the wreck again, just in time, and we fetched the stabboard derrick, and made fast there.

The deck was high out, here. We went sneaking down the slope of it to labboard, in the dark, towards the texas, feeling our way slow with our feet, and spreading our hands out to fend off the guys, for it was so dark we couldn't see no sign of them. Pretty soon we struck the forward end of the skylight, and clumb onto it; and the next step fetched us in front of the captain's door, which was open, and by Jimminy, away down through the texas-hall we see a light! and all in the same second we seem to hear low voices in yonder!

Jim whispered and said he was feeling powerful sick, and told me to come along. I says, all right; and was going to start for the raft; but just then I heard a voice wail out and say:

"Oh, please don't, boys; I swear I won't ever tell!"

Another voice said, pretty loud:

"It's a lie, Jim Turner. You've acted this way before. You always want more'n your share of the truck, and you've always got it, too, because you've swore 't if you didn't you'd tell. But this time you've said it jest one time too many. You're the meanest, treacherousest hound in this country."

By this time Jim was gone for the raft. I was just a-biling with curiosity; and I says to myself, Tom Sawyer wouldn't back out now, and so I won't either; I'm agoing to see what's going on here. So I dropped on my hands and knees, in the little passage, and crept aft in the dark, till there warn't but one stateroom betwixt me and the cross-hall of the texas. Then, in there I see a man stretched on the floor and tied hand and foot, and two men standing over him, and one of them had a dim lantern in his hand, and the other one had a pistol. This one kept pointing the pistol at the man's head on the floor, and saying— ~ intense

"I'd *like* to! And I orter, too, a mean skunk!"

The man on the floor would shrivel up and say: "Oh, please don't, Bill—I hain't ever goin' to tell."

And every time he said that, the man with the lantern would laugh, and say:

"'Deed you *ain't!* You never said no truer thing 'n that, you bet you." And once he said: "Hear him beg! and yit if we hadn't got the best of him and tied him, he'd a killed us both. And what *for?* Jist for noth'n. Jist because we stood on our *rights*—that's what for. But I lay you ain't agoin' to threaten nobody any more, Jim Turner. Put *up* that pistol, Bill."

Bill says:

"I don't want to, Jake Packard. I'm for killin' him—and didn't he kill old Hatfield jist the same way—and don't he deserve it?"

"But I don't *want* him killed, and I've got my reasons for it."

"Bless yo' heart for them words, Jake Packard! I'll never forget you, long's I live!" says the man on the floor, sort of blubbering.

Packard didn't take no notice of that, but hung up his lantern on a nail, and started towards where I was, there in the dark, and motioned Bill to come. I crawfished as fast as I could, about two yards, but the boat slanted so that I couldn't make very good time; so to keep from getting run over and catched I crawled into a stateroom on the upper side. The man come a-pawing along in the dark, and when Packard got to my stateroom, he says:

"Here—come in here."

And in he come, and Bill after him. But before they got in, I was up in the upper berth, cornered, and sorry I come. Then they stood there, with their hands on the ledge of the berth, and talked. I couldn't see them, but

I could tell where they was, by the whisky they'd been having. I was glad I didn't drink whisky; but it wouldn't made much difference, anyway, because most of the time they couldn't a treed me because I didn't breathe. I was too scared. And besides, a body *couldn't* breathe, and hear such talk. They talked low and earnest. Bill wanted to kill Turner. He says:

"He's said he'll tell, and he will. If we was to give both our shares to him *now*, it wouldn't make no difference after the row, and the way we've served him. Shore's you're born, he'll turn State's evidence; now you hear *me*. I'm for putting him out of his troubles."

"So'm I," says Packard, very quiet.

"Blame it, I'd sorter begun to think you wasn't. Well, then, that's all right. Le's go and do it."

"Hold on a minute; I hain't had my say yit. You listen to me. Shooting's good, but there's quieter ways if the thing's *got* to be done. But what I say, is this: it ain't good sense to go court'n around after a halter, if you can git at what you're up to in some way that's jist as good and at the same time don't bring you into no resks. Ain't that so?"

"You bet it is. But how you goin' to manage it this time?"

"Well, my idea is this: we'll rustle around and gather up whatever pickins we've overlooked in the staterooms, and shove for shore and hide the truck. Then we'll wait. Now I say it ain't agoin' to be more'n two hours befo' this wrack breaks up and washes off down the river. See? He'll be drownded, and won't have nobody to blame for it but his own self. I reckon that's a considerble sight better 'n killin' of him. I'm unfavorable to killin' a man as long as you can git around it; it ain't good sense, it ain't good morals. Ain't I right?"

"Yes—I reck'n you are. But s'pose she *don't* break up and wash off?"

"Well, we can wait the two hours, anyway, and see, can't we?"

"All right, then; come along."

So they started, and I lit out, all in a cold sweat, and scrambled forward. It was dark as pitch there; but I said in a kind of a coarse whisper, "Jim!" and he answered up, right at my elbow, with a sort of a moan, and I says:

"Quick, Jim, it ain't no time for fooling around and moaning; there's a gang of murderers in yonder, and if we don't hunt up their boat and set her drifting down the river so these fellows can't get away from the wreck there's one of 'em going to be in a bad fix. But if we find their boat we can put *all* of 'em in a bad fix—for the Sheriff'll get 'em. Quick—hurry! I'll hunt the labboard side, you hunt the stabboard. You start at the raft, and—"

"Oh, my lordy, lordy! *Raf'?* Dey ain' no raf' no mo', she done broke loose en gone!—'en here we is!"

Chapter XIII
Escaping from the Wreck—
The Watchman—Sinking

Well, I catched my breath and most fainted. Shut up on a wreck with such a gang as that! But it warn't no time to be sentimentering. We'd *got* to find that boat, now—had to have it for ourselves. So we went a-quaking and shaking down the stabboard side, and slow work it was, too—seemed a week before we got to the stern. No sign of a boat. Jim said he didn't believe he could go any further—so scared he hadn't hardly any strength left, he said. But I said come on, if we get left on this wreck, we are in a fix, sure. So on we prowled, again. We struck for the stern of the texas, and found it, and then scrabbled along forwards on the skylight, hanging on from shutter to shutter, for the edge of the skylight was in the water. When we got pretty close to the cross-hall door, there was the skiff, sure enough! I could just barely see her. I felt ever so thankful. In another second I would a been aboard of

IN A FIX.

her; but just then the door opened. One of the men stuck his head out, only about a couple of foot from me, and I thought I was gone; but he jerked it in again, and says:

"Heave that blame lantern out o' sight, Bill!"

He flung a bag of something into the boat, and then got in himself, and set down. It was Packard. Then Bill *he* come out and got in. Packard says, in a low voice:

"All ready—shove off!"

I couldn't hardly hang onto the shutters, I was so weak. But Bill says:

"Hold on—'d you go through him?"

"No. Didn't you?"

"No. So he's got his share o' the cash, yet."

"Well, then, come along—no use to take truck and leave money."

"Say—won't he suspicion what we're up to?"

"Maybe he won't. But we got to have it anyway. Come along."

So they got out and went in.

The door slammed to, because it was on the careened side; and in a half second I was in the boat, and Jim come a tumbling after me, I out with my knife and cut the rope, and away we went! *that's funny*

We didn't touch an oar, and we didn't speak nor whisper, nor hardly even breathe. We went gliding swift along, dead silent, past the tip of the paddlebox, and past the stern; then in a second or two more we was a hundred yards below the wreck, and the darkness soaked her up, every last sign of her, and we was safe, and knowed it.

When we was three or four hundred yards down stream, we see the lantern show like a little spark at the texas door, for a second, and we knowed by that that the rascals had missed their boat, and was beginning to understand that they was in just as much trouble, now, as Jim Turner was.

Then Jim manned the oars, and we took out after our raft. Now was the first time that I begun to worry about the men—I reckon I hadn't had time to before. I begun to think how dreadful it was, even for murderers, to be in such a fix. I says to myself, there ain't no telling but I might come to be a murderer myself, yet, and then how would *I* like it? So says I to Jim: *you timed to think!*

"The first light we see, we'll land a hundred yards below it or above it, in a place where it's a good hiding-place for you and the skiff, and then I'll go and fix up some kind of a yarn, and get somebody to go for that gang and get them out of their scrape, so they can be hung when their time comes."

But that idea was a failure; for pretty soon it begun to storm again, and this time worse than ever. The rain poured down, and never a light showed; everybody in bed, I reckon. We boomed along down the river, watching for lights and watching for our raft. After a long time the rain let up, but the clouds staid, and the lightning kept whimpering, and by-and-by a flash showed us a black thing ahead, floating, and we made for it.

It was the raft, and mighty glad was we to get aboard of it again. We seen a light, now, away down to the right, on shore. So I said I would go for it. The skiff was half full of plunder which that gang had stole, there on the wreck. We hustled it onto the raft in a pile, and I told Jim to float along down, and show a light when he judged he had gone about two mile, and keep it burning till I come; then I manned my oars and shoved for the light. As I got down towards it, three or four more showed—up on a hillside. It was a village. I closed in above the shore-light, and laid on my oars and floated. As I went by, I see it was a lantern hanging on the jackstaff of a double-hull ferry-boat. I skimmed around for the watchman, a-wondering whereabouts he slept; and by-and-by I found him roosting on the bitts, forward, with his head down between his knees. I gave his shoulder two or three little shoves, and begun to cry.

He stirred up, in a kind of a startlish way; but when he see it was only me, he took a good gap and stretch, and then he says:

"Hello, what's up? Don't cry, bub. What's the trouble?"

I says:

"Pap, and mam, and sis, and—" *lie*

Then I broke down. He says:

"Oh, dang it, now, *don't* take on so, we all has to have our troubles and this'n 'll come out all right. What's the matter with 'em?"

"They're—they're—are you the watchman of the boat?" *— Oh he's good*

"Yes," he says, kind of pretty-well-satisfied like. "I'm the captain and the owner, and the mate, and the pilot, and watchman, and head deckhand; and sometimes I'm the freight and passengers. I ain't as rich as old Jim Hornback, and I can't be so blame' generous and good to Tom, Dick and Harry as what he is, and slam around money the way he does; but I've told him a many a time 't I wouldn't trade places with him; for, says I, a sailor's life's the life for me, and I'm derned if *I'd* live two mile out o' town, where there ain't nothing ever goin' on, not for all his spondulicks and as much more on top of it. Says I—"

I broke in and says:

"They're in an awful peck of trouble, and—"

"*Who* is?"

"Why, pap, and mam, and sis, and Miss Hooker; and if you'd take your ferry-boat and go up there—"

"Up where? Where are they?"

"On the wreck."

"What wreck?"

"Why, there ain't but one."

"What, you don't mean the *Walter Scott?*"[24]

"Yes."

"Good land! what are they doin' *there,* for gracious sakes?"

---

[24]Twain scorned the novels of Sir Walter Scott, popular in the South during the nineteenth century. Scott's writings romanticize rules of chivalry and codes of conduct that Tom Sawyer finds so compelling and Huck finds so bewildering.

"Well, they didn't go there a-purpose."

"I bet they didn't! Why, great goodness, there ain't no chance for 'em if they don't git off mighty quick! Why, how in the nation did they ever git into such a scrape?"

"Easy enough. Miss Hooker was a-visiting, up there to the town—"

"Yes, Booth's Landing—go on."

"She was a-visiting, there at Booth's Landing, and just in the edge of the evening she started over with her nigger woman in the horse-ferry, to stay all night at her friend's house, Miss What-you-may-call-her, I disremember her name, and they lost their steering-oar, and swung around and went a-floating down, stern-first, about two mile, and saddle-baggsed on the wreck, and the ferry man and the nigger woman and the horses was all lost, but Miss Hooker she made a grab and got aboard the wreck. Well, about an hour after dark, we come along down in our trading-scow, and it was so dark we didn't notice the wreck till we was right on it; and so *we* saddle-baggsed; but all of us was saved but Bill Whipple—and oh, he *was* the best cretur!—I most wish't it had been me, I do."

"My George! It's the beatenest thing I ever struck. And *then* what did you all do?"

"Well, we hollered and took on, but it's so wide there, we couldn't make nobody hear. So pap said somebody got to get ashore and get help somehow. I was the only one that could swim, so I made a dash for it, and Miss Hooker she said if I didn't strike help sooner, come here and hunt up her uncle, and he'd fix the thing. I made the land about a mile below, and been fooling along ever since, trying to get people to do something, but they said, 'What, in such a night and such a current? there ain't no sense in it; go for the steam-ferry.' Now if you'll go, and—"

"By Jackson, I'd *like* to, and blame it I don't know but I will; but who in the dingnation's agoin' to *pay* for it? Do you reckon your pap—"

"Why *that's* all right. Miss Hooker she told me, *particular,* that her uncle Hornback—"

"Great guns! is *he* her uncle? Looky here, you break for that light over yonder-way, and turn out west when you git there, and about a quarter of a mile out you'll come to the tavern; tell 'em to dart you out to Jim Hornback's and he'll foot the bill. And don't you fool around any, because he'll want to know the news. Tell him I'll have his niece all safe before he can get to town. Hump yourself, now; I'm agoing up around the corner here, to roust out my engineer."

I struck for the light, but as soon as he turned the corner I went back and got into my skiff and bailed her out and then pulled up shore in the easy water about six hundred yards, and tucked myself in among some woodboats; for I couldn't rest easy till I could see the ferry-boat start. But take it all around, I was feeling ruther comfortable on accounts of taking all this trouble for that gang, for not many would a done it. I wished the widow knowed about it. I judged she would be proud of me for helping these rapscallions, because rapscallions and dead beats is the kind the widow and good people takes the most interest in.

Well, before long, here comes the wreck, dim and dusky, sliding along down! A kind of cold shiver went through me, and then I struck out for her. She was very deep, and I see in a minute there warn't much chance for anybody being alive in her. I pulled all around her and hollered a little, but there wasn't any answer; all dead still. I felt a little bit heavy-hearted about the gang, but not much, for I reckoned if they could stand it, I could.

Then here comes the ferry-boat; so I shoved for the middle of the river on a long down-stream slant; and when I judged I was out of eye-reach, I laid on my oars, and looked back and see her go and smell around the wreck for Miss Hooker's remainders, because the captain would know her uncle Hornback would want them; and then pretty soon the ferry-boat give it up and went for shore, and I laid into my work and went a-booming down the river.

It did seem a powerful long time before Jim's light showed up; and when it did show, it looked like it was a thousand mile off. By the time I got there the sky was beginning to get a little gray in the east; so we struck for an island, and hid the raft, and sunk the skiff, and turned in and slept like dead people. _very odd_

Chapter XIV
A General Good Time—The Harem—French

By-and-by, when we got up, we turned over the truck the gang had stole off of the wreck, and found boots, and blankets, and clothes, and all sorts of other things, and a lot of books, and a spyglass, and three boxes of see-gars. We hadn't ever been this rich before, in neither of our lives. The see-gars was prime. We laid off all the afternoon in the woods talking, and me reading the books, and having a general good time. I told Jim all about what happened inside the wreck, and at the ferry-boat; and I said these kinds of things was adventures; but he said he didn't want no more adventures. He said that when I went in the texas and he crawled back to get on the raft and found her gone, he nearly died; because he judged it was all up with *him*, anyway it could be fixed; for if he didn't get saved he would get drownded; and if he did get saved, whoever saved him would send him back home so as to get the reward, and then Miss Watson would sell him

confusing section

TURNING OVER THE TRUCK.

South, sure. Well, he was right; he was most always right; he had an uncommon level head, for a nigger.

I read considerable to Jim about kings, and dukes, and earls, and such, and how gaudy they dressed, and how much style they put on, and called each other your majesty, and your grace, and your lordship, and so on, 'stead of mister; and Jim's eyes bugged out, and he was interested. He says:

"I didn' know dey was so many un um. I hain't hearn 'bout none un um, skasely, but ole King Sollermun, onless you counts dem kings dat's in a pack er k'yards. How much do a king git?"

"Get?" I says; "why, they get a thousand dollars a month if they want it; they can have just as much as they want; everything belongs to them."

"Ain' dat gay? En what dey got to do, Huck?"

"They don't do nothing! Why how you talk! They just set around."

"No—is dat so?"

"Of course it is. They just set around. Except maybe when there's a war; then they go to the war. But other times they just lazy around; or go hawking—just hawking and sp—Sh!—d' you hear a noise?"

We skipped out and looked; but it warn't nothing but the flutter of a steamboat's wheel, away down coming around the point; so we come back.

"Yes," says I, "and other times, when things is dull, they fuss with the parlyment; and if everybody don't go just so he whacks their heads off. But mostly they hang round the harem."

"Roun' de which?"

"Harem."

"What's de harem?"

"The place where he keeps his wives. Don't you know about the harem? Solomon had one; he had about a million wives."

"Why, yes, dat's so; I—I'd done forgot it. A harem's a bo'd'n-house, I reck'n. Mos' likely dey has rackety times in de nussery. En I reck'n de wives quarrels considable; en dat 'crease de racket. Yit dey say Sollermun de wises' man dat ever live'. I doan' take no stock in dat. Bekase why would a wise man want to live in de mids' er sich a blimblammin' all de time? No—'deed he wouldn't. A wise man 'ud take en buil' a biler-factry; en den he could shet *down* de biler-factry when he want to res'."

"Well, but he *was* the wisest man, anyway; because the widow she told me so, her own self."

"I doan k'yer what de widder say, he *warn't* no wise man, nuther. He had some er de dad-fetchedes' ways I ever see. Does you know 'bout dat chile dat he 'uz gwyne to chop in two?" [25]

"Yes, the widow told me all about it."

"*Well,* den! Warn' dat de beatenes' notion in de worl'? You jes' take en look at it a minute. Dah's de stump, dah—dat's one er de women; heah's you—dat's de yuther one; I's Sollermun; en dish-yer dollar bill's de chile. Bofe un you claims it. What does I do? Does I shin aroun' mongs' de neighbors en fine out which un you de bill *do* b'long to, en han' it over to de right one, all safe en soun', de way dat anybody dat had any gumption would? No—I take en whack de bill in *two,* en give half un it to you, en de yuther half to de yuther woman. Dat's de way Sollermun was gwyne to do wid de chile. Now I want to ast you: what's de use er dat half a bill?—can't buy noth'n wid it. En what use is a half a chile? I wouldn't give a dern for a million un um."

"But hang it, Jim, you've clean missed the point—blame it, you've missed it a thousand mile."

"Who? Me? Go 'long. Doan' talk to *me* 'bout yo' pints. I reck'n I knows sense when I sees it; en dey ain' no sense in sich doin's as dat. De 'spute warn't 'bout a half a chile, de 'spute was 'bout a whole chile; en de man dat think he kin settle a 'spute 'bout a whole chile wid a half a chile, doan' know enough to come in out'n de rain. Doan' talk to me 'bout Sollermun, Huck, I knows him by de back."

"But I tell you you don't get the point."

"Blame de pint! I reck'n I knows what I knows. En mine you, de *real* pint is down furder—it's down deeper. It lays in de way Sollermun was raised. You take a man dat's got on'y one er two chillen; is dat man gwyne to be waseful o' chillen? No, he ain't; he can't 'ford it. *He* know how to value 'em. But you take a man dat's got 'bout five million chillen runnin' roun' de house, en it's diffunt. *He* as soon chop a chile in two as a cat. Dey's

---

[25] 1 Kings 3.16–28. In the Old Testament, King Solomon establishes himself as a wise judge by settling a dispute between two women. When both women claim to be the mother of a child, Solomon suggests they cut the child in half. The true mother begs for the child's life.

plenty mo'. A chile er two, mo' er less, warn't no consekens to Sollermun, dad fatch him!"

I never see such a nigger. If he got a notion in his head once, there warn't no getting it out again. He was the most down on Solomon of any nigger I ever see. So I went to talking about other kings, and let Solomon slide. I told about Louis Sixteenth that got his head cut off in France long time ago; and about his little boy the dolphin, that would a been a king, but they took and shut him up in jail, and some say he died there.

"Po' little chap." *huh?*

"But some says he got out and got away, and come to America." *there was no America*

"Dat's good! But he'll be pooty lonesome—dey ain' no kings here, is dey, Huck?"

"No."

"Den he cain't git no situation. What he gwyne to do?"

"Well, I don't know. Some of them gets on the police, and some of them learns people how to talk French."

"Why, Huck, doan' de French people talk de same way we does?"

"No, Jim; you couldn't understand a word they said—not a single word."

"Well, now, I be ding-busted! How do dat come?"

"I don't know; but it's so. I got some of their jabber out of a book. Spose a man was to come to you and say Polly-voo-franzy—what would you think?"

"I wouldn' think nuff'n; I'd take en bust him over de head. Dat is, if he warn't white. I wouldn't 'low no nigger to call me dat." *—wow.*

"Shucks, it ain't calling you anything. It's only saying do you know how to talk French?"

"Well, den, why couldn't he *say* it?"

"Why, he *is* a-saying it. That's a Frenchman's *way* of saying it."

"Well, it's a blame' ridicklous way, en I doan' want to hear no mo' 'bout it. Dey ain' no sense in it."

"Looky here, Jim; does a cat talk like we do?"

"No, a cat don't."

"Well, does a cow?"

"No, a cow don't, nuther."

"Does a cat talk like a cow, or a cow talk like a cat?"

"No, dey don't."

"It's natural and right for 'em to talk different from each other, ain't it?"

"'Course."

"And ain't it natural and right for a cat and a cow to talk different from *us?*"

"Why, mos' sholy it is."

"Well, then, why ain't it natural and right for a *Frenchman* to talk different from us? You answer me that."

"Is a cat a man, Huck?"

"No."

"Well, den, dey ain't no sense in a cat talkin' like a man. Is a cow a man?—er is a cow a cat?"

"No, she ain't either of them."

"Well, den, she ain' got no business to talk like either one er the yuther of 'em. Is a Frenchman a man?"

"Yes."

"*Well*, den! Dad blame it, why doan' he *talk* like a man? You answer me *dat!*"

I see it warn't no use wasting words—you can't learn a nigger to argue. So I quit.]– very racist

Chapter XV
Huck Loses the Raft—In the Fog—
Huck Finds the Raft—Trash

We judged that three nights more would fetch us to Cairo, at the bottom of Illinois,[26] where the Ohio River comes in, and that was what we was after. We would sell the raft and get on a steamboat and go way up the Ohio amongst the free States, and then be out of trouble.

Well, the second night a fog begun to come on, and we made for a towhead to tie to, for it wouldn't do to try to run in fog; but when I paddled ahead in the canoe, with the line, to make fast, there warn't anything but little saplings to tie to. I passed the line around one of them right on the edge of the cut bank, but there was a stiff current, and the raft come booming down so lively she tore it out by the roots and away she went. I see the fog closing down, and it made me so sick and scared I couldn't budge for most a half a minute it seemed to me—and then there warn't no raft in sight; you couldn't see twenty yards. I jumped into the canoe and run back to the stern and grabbed the paddle and set her back a stroke. But she didn't come. I was in such a hurry I hadn't untied her. I got up and tried to

"in a hurry bc he was scared?

---

[26] Though the Ohio River provided a common escape route for escaping slaves, even the plan to head north from Cairo was risky during this period. Jim's need to keep Huck with him is highlighted by the continuous threat of bounty hunters and kidnappers.

"WE WOULD SELL THE RAFT."

he is freakin'

untie her, but I was so excited my hands shook so I couldn't hardly do anything with them. *how odd!*

As soon as I got started I took out after the raft, hot and heavy, right down the tow-head. That was all right as far as it went, but the tow-head warn't sixty yards long, and the minute I flew by the foot of it I shot out into the solid white fog, and hadn't no more idea which way I was going than a dead man. *3rd time*

Thinks I, it won't do to paddle; first I know I'll run into the bank or a tow-head or something; I got to set still and float, and yet it's mighty fidgety business to have to hold your hands still at such a time. I whooped and listened. Away down there, somewheres, I hears a small whoop, and up comes my spirits. *?* I went tearing after it, listening sharp to hear it again. The next time it come, I see I warn't heading for it but heading away to the right of it. And the next time, I was heading away to the left of it—and not gaining on it much, either, for I was flying around, this way and that and 'tother, but it was going straight ahead all the time.

I did wish the fool would think to beat a tin pan, and beat it all the time, but he never did, and it was the still places between the whoops that was making the trouble for me. Well, I fought along, and directly I hears the whoop *behind* me. I was tangled good, now. That was somebody else's whoop, or else I was turned around.

I throwed the paddle down. I heard the whoop again; it was behind me yet, but in a different place; it kept coming, and kept changing its place, and I kept answering, till by-and-by it was in front of me again and I knowed the current had swung the canoe's head down stream and I was all right, if that was Jim and not some other raftsman hollering. I couldn't tell nothing about voices in a fog, for nothing don't look natural nor sound natural in a fog. *— it seems fog changes life*

The whooping went on, and in about a minute I come a booming down on a cut bank with smoky ghosts of big trees on it, and the current throwed me off to the left and shot by, amongst a lot of snags that fairly roared, the current was tearing by them so swift.

In another second or two it was solid white and still again. I set perfectly still, then, listening to my heart thump, and I reckon I didn't draw a breath while it thumped a hundred.

I just give up, then. I knowed what the matter was. That cut bank was an island, and Jim had gone down t'other side of it. It warn't no tow-head, that you could float by in ten minutes. It had the big timber of a regular island; it might be five or six miles long and more than half a mile wide.

I kept quiet, with my ears cocked, about fifteen minutes, I reckon. I was floating along, of course, four or five miles an hour; but you don't ever think of that. No, you *feel* like you are laying dead still on the water; and if a little glimpse of a snag slips by, you don't think to yourself how fast *you're* going, but you catch your breath and think, my! how that snag's tearing along. If you think it ain't dismal and lonesome out in a fog that way, by yourself, in the night, you try it once—you'll see.

Next, for about a half an hour, I whoops now and then; at last I hears the answer a long ways off, and tries to follow it, but I couldn't do it, and directly I judged I'd got into a nest of tow-heads, for I had little dim glimpses of them on both sides of me, sometimes just a narrow channel between; and some that I couldn't see, I knowed was there, because I'd hear the wash of the current against the old dead brush and trash that hung over the banks. Well, I warn't long losing the whoops, down amongst the tow-heads; and I only tried to chase them a little while, anyway, because it was worse than chasing a Jack-o-lantern. You never knowed a sound dodge around so, and swap places so quick and so much.

I had to claw away from the bank pretty lively, four or five times, to keep from knocking the islands out of the river; and so I judged the raft must be butting into the bank every now and then, or else it would get further ahead and clear out of hearing—it was floating a little faster than what I was.

Well, I seemed to be in the open river again, by-and-by, but I couldn't hear no sign of a whoop nowheres. I reckoned Jim had fetched up on a snag, maybe, and it was all up with him. I was good and tired, so I laid down in the canoe and said I wouldn't bother no more. I didn't want to go to sleep, of course; but I was so sleepy I couldn't help it; so I thought I would take just one little cat-nap.

But I reckon it was more than a cat-nap, for when I waked up the stars was shining bright, the fog was all gone, and I was spinning down a big bend stern first. First I didn't know where I was; I thought I was dreaming; and when things begun to come back to me they seemed to come up dim out of last week.

It was a monstrous big river here, with the tallest and the thickest kind of timber on both banks; just a solid wall, as well as I could see, by the stars.

I looked away down stream, and seen a black speck on the water. I took out after it; but when I got to it it warn't nothing but a couple of saw-logs made fast together. Then I see another speck, and chased that; then another, and this time I was right. It was the raft.

When I got to it Jim was setting there with his head down between his knees, asleep, with his right arm hanging over the steering oar. The other oar was smashed off, and the raft was littered up with leaves and branches and dirt. So she'd had a rough time.

I made fast and laid down under Jim's nose on the raft, and begun to gap, and stretch my fists out against Jim, and says:

"Hello, Jim, have I been asleep? Why didn't you stir me up?"

"Goodness gracious, is dat you, Huck? En you ain' dead—you ain' drownded—you's back agin? It's too good for true, honey, it's too good for true. Lemme look at you chile, lemme feel o' you. No, you ain' dead! you's back agin, 'live en soun', jis de same ole Huck—de same ole Huck, thanks to goodness!"

"What's the matter with you, Jim? You been a drinking?"

"Drinkin'? Has I ben a drinkin'? Has I had a chance to be a drinkin'?"

"Well, then, what makes you talk so wild?"

"How does I talk wild?"

"*How?* why, hain't you been talking about my coming back, and all that stuff, as if I'd been gone away?"

"Huck—Huck Finn, you look me in de eye; look me in de eye. *Hain't* you ben gone away?"

"Gone away? Why, what in the nation do you mean? *I* hain't been gone anywheres. Where would I go to?"

"Well, looky here, boss, dey's sumf'n wrong, dey is. Is I *me*, or who *is* I? Is I heah, or whah *is* I? Now dat's what I wants to know." *- Just stop Jim*

"Well, I think you're here, plain enough, but I think you're a tangle-headed old fool, Jim."

"I is, is I? Well, you answer me dis. Didn't you tote out de line in de canoe, fer to make fas' to de tow-head?"

"No, I didn't. What tow-head? I hain't seen no tow-head."

"You hain't seen no tow-head? Looky here—didn't de line pull loose en de raf' go a hummin' down de river, en leave you en de canoe behine in de fog?"

"What fog?" *how could he forget!?*

"Why, *de* fog. De fog dat's ben aroun' all night. En didn't you whoop, en didn't I whoop, tell we got mix' up in de islands en one un us got los' en t'other one was jis' as good as los', 'kase he didn' know whah he wuz? En didn't I bust up agin a lot er dem islands en have a turrible time en mos' git drownded? Now ain' dat so, boss—ain't it so? You answer me dat."

"Well, this is too many for me, Jim. I hain't seen no fog, nor no islands, nor no troubles, nor nothing. I been setting here talking with you all night till you went to sleep about ten minutes ago, and I reckon I done the same. You couldn't a got drunk in that time, so of course you've been dreaming."

"Dad fetch it, how is I gwyne to dream all dat in ten minutes?"

"Well, hang it all, you did dream it, because there didn't any of it happen."

"But Huck, it's all jis' as plain to me as—"

"It don't make no difference how plain it is, there ain't nothing in it. I know, because I've been here all the time."

Jim didn't say nothing for about five minutes, but set there studying over it. Then he says:

"Well, den, I reck'n I did dream it, Huck; but dog my cats ef it ain't de powerfullest dream I ever see. En I hain't ever had no dream b'fo' dat's tired me like dis one."

"Oh, well, that's all right, because a dream does tire a body like everything, sometimes. But this one was a staving dream—tell me all about it, Jim."

So Jim went to work and told me the whole thing right through, just as it happened, only he painted it up considerable. Then he said he must start in and "'terpret" it, because it was sent for a warning. He said the first tow-head stood for a man that would try to do us some good, but the current was another man that would get us away from him. The whoops was warnings that would come to us every now and then, and if we didn't try hard to make out to understand them they'd just take us into bad luck, 'stead of keeping us out of it. The lot of tow-heads was troubles we was going to get into with quarrelsome people and all kinds of mean folks, but if we minded our business and didn't talk back and aggravate them, we would pull through and get out of the fog and into the big clear river, which was the free States, and wouldn't have no more trouble.

It had clouded up pretty dark just after I got onto the raft, but it was clearing up again, now.

"Oh, well, that's all interpreted well enough, as far as it goes, Jim," I says; "but what does *these* things stand for?"

It was the leaves and rubbish on the raft, and the smashed oar. You could see them first rate, now.

Jim looked at the trash, and then looked at me, and back at the trash again. He had got the dream fixed so strong in his head that he couldn't seem to shake it loose and get the facts back into its place again, right away. But when he did get the thing straightened around, he looked at me steady, without ever smiling, and says:

"What do dey stan' for? I's gwyne to tell you. When I got all wore out wid work, en wid de callin' for you, en went to sleep, my heart wuz mos' broke bekase you wuz los', en I didn' k'yer no mo' what become er me en de raf'. En when I wake up en fine you back agin, all safe en soun', de tears come en I could a got down on my knees en kiss' yo' foot, I's so thankful. En all you wuz thinkin' 'bout wuz how you could make a fool uv ole Jim wid a lie. Dat truck dah is *trash;* en trash is what people is dat puts dirt on de head er dey fren's en makes 'em ashamed."

Then he got up slow, and walked to the wigwam, and went in there, without saying anything but that. But that was enough. It made me feel so mean I could almost kissed *his* foot to get him to take it back.

It was fifteen minutes before I could work myself up to go and humble myself to a nigger—but I done it, and I warn't ever sorry for it afterwards, neither. I didn't do him no more mean tricks, and I wouldn't done that one if I'd a knowed it would make him feel that way.

Chapter XVI
Expectation—A White Lie—
Floating Currency—Running by Cairo—
Swimming Ashore

We slept most all day, and started out at night, a little ways behind a monstrous long raft that was as long going by as a procession. She had four long sweeps at each end, so we judged she carried as many as thirty men, likely. She had five big wigwams aboard, wide apart, and an open camp fire in the middle, and a tall flag-pole at each end. There was a power of style about her. It *amounted* to something being a raftsman on such a craft as that.

We went drifting down into a big bend, and the night clouded up and got hot. The river was very wide, and was walled with solid timber on both sides; you couldn't see a break in it hardly ever, or a light. We talked about Cairo, and wondered whether we would know it when we got to it. I said likely we wouldn't, because I had heard say there warn't but about a dozen houses there, and if they didn't happen to have them lit up, how was we going to know we was passing a town? Jim said if the two big rivers joined together there, that would show. But I said maybe we might think we was passing the foot of an island and coming into the same old river again.

That disturbed Jim—and me too. So the question was, what to do? I said, paddle ashore the first time a light showed, and tell them pap was behind, coming along with a trading-scow, and was a green hand at the business, and wanted to know how far it was to Cairo, Jim thought it was a good idea, so we took a smoke on it and waited.

But you know a young person can't wait very well when he is impatient to find a thing out.[27] We talked it over, and by-and-by Jim said it was such a black night, now, that it wouldn't be no risk to swim down to the big raft and crawl aboard and listen—they would talk about Cairo, because they would be calculating to go

"IT *AMOUNTED* TO SOMETHING
BEING A RAFTSMAN."

ashore there for a spree, maybe, or anyway they would send boats ashore to buy whiskey or fresh meat or something. Jim had a wonderful level head, for a nigger: he could most always start a good plan when you wanted one.

I stood up and shook my rags off and jumped into the river, and struck out for the raft's light. By and by, when I got down nearly to her, I eased up and went slow and cautious. But everything was all right—nobody at the sweeps. So I swum down along the raft till I was most abreast the camp fire in the middle, then I crawled aboard and inched along and got in amongst some bundles of shingles on the weather side of the fire. There was thirteen men there—they was the watch on deck of course. And a mighty roughlooking lot, too. They had a jug, and tin cups, and they kept

[27]The "Raftsmen's Passage," originally written for *Huckleberry Finn* but omitted from early editions, begins here. Twain first published this passage in 1883 in *Life on the Mississippi*, after his publisher convinced him to remove it from *Huckleberry Finn* in order to market the novel as a companion to *Tom Sawyer*. Modern editions include the passage because Twain originally intended its inclusion and because it contains information integral to the novel.

the jug moving. One man was singing—roaring, you may say; and it wasn't a nice song—for a parlor anyway. He roared through his nose, and strung out the last word of every line very long. When he was done they all fetched a kind of Injun war-whoop, and then another was sung. It begun:

> "There was a woman in our towdn,
>   In our towdn did dwed'l (dwell),
> She loved her husband dear-i-lee,
>   But another man twyste as wed'l.

> 5   Singing too, riloo, riloo, riloo,
>   Ri-too, riloo, rilay—e,
> She loved her husband dear-i-lee,
>   But another man twyste as wed'l.

And so on—fourteen verses. It was kind of poor, and when he was going to start on the next verse one of them said it was the tune the old cow died on; and another one said, "Oh, give us a rest." And another one told him to take a walk. They made fun of him till he got mad and jumped up and begun to cuss the crowd, and said he could lam any thief in the lot.

They was all about to make a break for him, but the biggest man there jumped up and says:

"Set whar you are, gentlemen. Leave him to me; he's my meat."

Then he jumped up in the air three times and cracked his heels together every time. He flung off a buckskin coat that was all hung with fringes, and says, "You lay thar tell the chawin-up's done," and flung his hat down, which was all over ribbons, and says, "You lay thar tell his sufferins is over."

Then he jumped up in the air and cracked his heels together again and shouted out:

"Whoo-oop! I'm the old original[28] iron-jawed, brass-mounted, copper-bellied corpse-maker from the wilds of Arkansaw! Look at me! I'm the man they call Sudden Death and General Desolation! Sired by a hurricane, dam'd by an earthquake, half-brother to the cholera, nearly related to the small-pox on the mother's side! Look at me! I take nineteen alligators and a bar'l of whiskey for breakfast when I'm in robust health, and a bushel of rattlesnakes and a dead body when I'm ailing! I split the everlasting rocks with my glance, and I squench the thunder when I speak!

---

[28] Boasts such as those traded by Bob and the Child of Calamity appear frequently in the works of the Southwest humorists. These writers attempted to portray authentically the harsh frontier experience and the oral tradition that grew out of it.

Whoo-oop! Stand back and give me room according to my strength! Blood's my natural drink, and the wails of the dying is music to my ear! Cast your eye on me, gentlemen!—and lay low and hold your breath, for I'm bout to turn myself loose!"

All the time he was getting this off, he was shaking his head and looking fierce, and kind of swelling around in a little circle, tucking up his wrist-bands, and now and then straightening up and beating his breast with his fist, saying, "Look at me, gentlemen!" When he got through, he jumped up and cracked his heels together three times, and let off a roaring "whoo-oop! I'm the bloodiest son of a wildcat that lives!"

Then the man that had started the row tilted his old slouch hat down over his right eye; then he bent stooping forward, with his back sagged and his south end sticking our far, and his fists a-shoving out and drawing in in front of him, and so went around in a little circle about three times, swelling himself up and breathing hard. Then he straightened, and jumped up and cracked his heels together three times before he lit again (that made them cheer), and he begun to shout like this:

"Whoo-oop! bow your neck and spread, for the kingdom of sorrow's a-coming! Hold me down to the earth, for I feel my powers a-working! whoo-oop! I'm a child of sin, *don't* let me get a start! Smoked glass, here, for all! Don't attempt to look at me with the naked eye, gentlemen! When I'm playful I use the meridians of longitude and parallels of latitude for a seine, and drag the Atlantic Ocean for whales! I scratch my head with the lightning and purr myself to sleep with the thunder! When I'm cold, I bile the Gulf of Mexico and bathe in it; when I'm hot I fan myself with an equinoctial storm; when I'm thirsty I reach up and suck a cloud dry like a sponge; when I range the earth hungry, famine follows in my tracks! Whoo-oop! Bow your neck and spread! I put my hands on the sun's face and make it night in the earth; I bite a piece out of the moon and hurry the seasons; I shake myself and crumble the mountains! Contemplate me through leather—*don't* use the naked eye! I'm the man with a petrified heart and biler-iron bowels! The massacre of isolated communities is the pastime of my idle moments, the destruction of nationalities the serious business of my life! The boundless vastness of the great American desert is my enclosed property, and I bury my dead on my own premises!" He jumped up and cracked his heels together three times before he lit (they cheered him again), and as he come down he shouted out: "Whoo-oop! bow your neck and spread, for the pet child of calamity's a-coming!"

Then the other one went to swelling around and blowing again—the first one—the one they called Bob; next, the Child of Calamity chipped in again, bigger than ever; then they both got at it at the same time, swelling round and round each other and punching their fists most into each other's faces, and whooping and jawing like Injuns; then Bob called the Child names, and the Child called him names back again: next, Bob called him a heap rougher names and the Child come back at him with the very worst kind of language; next, Bob knocked the Child's hat off, and the Child picked it up and kicked Bob's ribbony hat about six foot; Bob went and got it and said never mind, this war n't going to be the last of this thing, because he was a man that never forgot and never forgive, and so the Child better look out, for there was a time a-coming, just as sure as he was a living man, that he would have to answer to him with the best blood in his body. The Child said no man was willinger than he was for that time to come, and he would give Bob fair warning, *now,* never to cross his path again, for he could never rest till he had waded in his blood, for such was his nature, though he was sparing him now on account of his family, if he had one.

Both of them was edging away in different directions, growling and shaking their heads and going on about what they was going to do; but a little black-whiskered chap skipped up and says:

"Come back here, you couple of chicken-livered cowards, and I'll thrash the two of ye!"

And he done it, too. He snatched them, he jerked them this way and that, he booted them around, he knocked them sprawling faster than they could get up. Why, it war n't two minutes till they begged like dogs—and how the other lot did yell and laugh and clap their hands all the way through, and shout "Sail in, Corpse-Maker!" "Hi! at him again, Child of Calamity!" "Bully for you, little Davy!" Well, it was a perfect pow-wow for a while. Bob and the Child had red noses and black eyes when they got through. Little Davy made them own up that they was sneaks and cowards and not fit to eat with a dog or drink with a nigger; then Bob and the Child shook hands with each other, very solemn, and said they had always respected each other and was willing to let bygones be bygones. So then they washed their faces in the river, and just then there was a loud order to stand by for a crossing, and some of them went forward to man the sweeps there, and the rest went aft to handle the after-sweeps.

I laid still and waited for fifteen minutes, and had a smoke out of a pipe that one of them left in reach; then the crossing was finished, and they stumped back and had a drink around and went to talking and singing again. Next they got out an old fiddle, and one played, and another patted juba, and the rest turned themselves loose on a regular old-fashioned keelboat break-down. They couldn't keep that up very long without getting winded, so by-and-by they settled around the jug again.

They sung "jolly, jolly raftsman's the life for me," with a rousing cho-
rus, and then they got to talking about differences betwixt hogs, and their
different kinds of habits; and next about women and their different ways;
and next about the best ways to put out houses that was afire; and next
about what ought to be done with the Injuns; and next about what a king
had to do, and how much he got; and next about how to make cats fight;
and next about what to do when a man has fits; and next about differences
betwixt clear-water rivers and muddy-water ones. The man they called Ed
said the muddy Mississippi water was wholesomer to drink than the clear
water of the Ohio; he said if you let a pint of this yaller Mississippi water
settle, you would have about a half to three quarters of an inch of mud in
the bottom, according to the stage of the river, and then it warn't no better than Ohio water—what you wanted to do was to keep it stirred up—
and when the river was low, keep mud on hand to put in and thicken the
water up the way it ought to be.

The Child of Calamity said that was so; he said there was nutritious-
ness in the mud, and a man that drunk Mississippi water could grow corn
in his stomach if he wanted to. He says:

"You look at the graveyards; that tells the tale. Trees won't grow
worth shucks in a Cincinnati graveyard, but in a Sent Louis graveyard they
grow upwards of eight hundred foot high. It's all on account of the water
the people drunk before they laid up. A Cincinnati corpse don't richen a
soil any."

And they talked about how Ohio water didn't like to mix with Mississippi water. Ed said if you take the Mississippi on a rise when the Ohio
is low, you'll find a wide band of clear water all the way down the east side
of the Mississippi for a hundred mile or more, and the minute you get out
a quarter of a mile from shore and pass the line, it is all thick and yaller
the rest of the way across. Then they talked about how to keep tobacco
from getting mouldy, and from that they went into ghosts and told about
a lot that other folks had seen; but Ed says:

"Why don't you tell something that you've seen yourselves? Now let
me have a say. Five years ago I was on a raft as big as this, and right along
here it was a bright moonshiny night, and I was on watch and boss of
the stabboard oar forrard, and one of my pards was a man named Dick
Allbright, and he come along to where I was sitting, forrard—gaping and
stretching, he was—and stooped down on the edge of the raft and washed
his face in the river, and come and set down by me and got out his pipe,
and had just got it filled, when he looks up and says,

" 'Why looky-here,' he says, 'ain't that Buck Miller's place, over yan-
der in the bend?'

"'Yes,' says I, 'it is—why?' He laid his pipe down and leant his head on his hand, and says,

"'I thought we'd be furder down.' I says,

"'I thought it too, when I went off watch'—we was standing six hours on and six off—'but the boys told me,' I says, 'that the raft didn't seem to hardly move, for the last hour,'—says I, 'though she's a slipping along all right, now,' says I. He give a kind of a groan, and says,

"'I've seed a raft act so before, along here,' he says, ''pears to me the current has most quit above the head of this bend durin' the last two years,' he says.

"Well, he raised up two or three times, and looked away off and around on the water. That started me at it, too. A body is always doing what he sees somebody else doing, though there mayn't be no sense in it. Pretty soon I see a black something floating on the water away off to stabboard and quartering behind us. I see he was looking at it, too. I says,

"'What's that?' He says, sort of pettish,

"''Tain't nothing but an old empty bar'l.'

"'An empty bar'l!' says I, 'why,' says I, 'a spy-glass is a fool to *your* eyes. How can you tell it's an empty bar'l?' he says,

"'I don't know; I reckon it ain't a bar'l, but I thought it might be,' says he.

"'Yes,' I says, 'so it might be, and it might be anything else, too; a body can't tell nothing about it, such a distance as that,' I says.

"We hadn't nothing else to do, so we kept on watching it. By-and-by I says,

"'Why looky-here, Dick Allbright, that thing's a-gaining on us, I believe.'

"He never said nothing. The thing gained and gained, and I judged it must be a dog that was about tired out. Well, we swung down into the crossing, and the thing floated across the bright streak of the moonshine, and, by George, it *was* a bar'l. Says I,

"'Dick Allbright, what made you think that thing was a bar'l, when it was a half a mile off,' says I. Says he,

"'I don't know.' Says I,

"'You tell me, Dick Allbright,' He says,

"'Well, I knowed it was a bar'l; I've seen it before; lots has seen it; they says it's a hanted bar'l.'

"I called the rest of the watch, and they come and stood there, and I told them what Dick said. It floated right along abreast, now, and didn't gain any more. It was about twenty foot off. Some was for having it aboard, but the rest didn't want to. Dick Allbright said rafts that had fooled with it had got bad luck by it. The captain of the watch said he didn't believe in it. He said he reckoned the bar'l gained on us because it was in a little better current than what we was. He said it would leave by-and-by.

"So then we went to talking about other things, and we had a song, and then a breakdown; and after that the captain of the watch called for another song; but it was clouding up, now, and the bar'l stuck right thar in the same place, and the song didn't seem to have much warm-up to it, somehow, and so they didn't finish it, and there warn't any cheers, but it sort of dropped flat, and nobody said anything for a minute. Then everybody tried to talk at once, and one chap got off a joke, but it warn't no use, they didn't laugh, and even the chap that made the joke didn't laugh at it, which ain't usual. We all just settled down glum, and watched the bar'l, and was oneasy and oncomfortable. Well, sir, it shut down black and still, and then the wind begin to moan around, and next the lightning begin to play and the thunder to grumble. And pretty soon there was a regular storm, and in the middle of it a man that was running aft stumbled and fell and sprained his ankle so that he had to lay up. This made the boys shake their heads. And every time the lightning come, there was that bar'l with the blue lights winking around it. We was always on the look-out for it. But by-and-by, towards dawn, she was gone. When the day come we couldn't see her anywhere, and we warn't sorry, neither.

"But next night about half-past nine, when there was songs and high jinks going on, here she comes again, and took her old roost on the stabboard side. There warn't no more high jinks. Everybody got solemn; nobody talked; you couldn't get anybody to do anything but set around moody and look at the bar'l. It begun to cloud up again. When the watch changed, the off watch stayed up, stead of turning in. The storm ripped and roared around all night, and in the middle of it another man tripped and sprained his ankle, and had to knock off. The bar'l left towards day, and nobody see it go.

"Everybody was sober and down in the mouth all day. I don't mean the kind of sober that comes of leaving liquor alone—not that. They was quiet, but they all drunk more than usual—not together—but each man sidled off and took it private, by himself.

"After dark the off watch didn't turn in; nobody sung, nobody talked; the boys didn't scatter around, neither; they sort of huddled together, forrard; and for two hours they set there, perfectly still, looking steady in the one direction, and heaving a sigh once in a while. And then, here comes the bar'l again. She took up her old place. She staid there all night; nobody turned in. The storm come on again, after midnight. It got awful dark; the rain poured down; hail, too; the thunder boomed and roared and bellowed; the wind blowed a hurricane; and the lightning spread over everything in big sheets of glare, and showed the whole raft as plain as day; and the river lashed up white as milk as far as you could see for miles, and there was that bar'l jiggering along, same as ever. The captain ordered the watch to man the after sweeps for a crossing, and nobody would go—no more sprained ankles for them, they said. They wouldn't even *walk* aft. Well then, just then the sky split wide open, with a crash, and the lightning killed two men of the after watch, and crippled two more. Crippled them how, says you? Why, *sprained their ankles!* ⌐ w ha l ⁊

"The bar'l left in the dark betwixt lightnings, towards dawn. Well, not a body eat a bite at breakfast that morning. After that the men loafed around, in twos and threes, and talked low together. But none of them herded with Dick Allbright. They all give him the cold shake. If he come around where any of the men was, they split up and sidled away. They wouldn't man the sweeps with him. The captain had all the skiffs hauled up on the raft, alongside of his wigwam, and wouldn't let the dead men be took ashore to be planted; he didn't believe a man that got ashore would come back; and he was right.

"After night come, you could see pretty plain that there was going to be trouble if that bar'l come again; there was such a muttering going on. A good many wanted to kill Dick Allbright, because he'd seen the bar'l on other trips, and that had an ugly look. Some wanted to put him ashore. Some said, let's all go ashore in a pile, if the bar'l comes again.

"This kind of whispers was still going on, the men being bunched together forrard watching for the bar'l, when, lo and behold you, here she comes again, Down she comes, slow and steady, and settles into her old tracks. You could a heard a pin drop. Then up comes the captain, and says:

"'Boys, don't be a pack of children and fools; I don't want this bar'l to be dogging us all the way to Orleans, and *you* don't; well, then, how's the best way to stop it? Burn it up—that's the way. I'm going to fetch it aboard,' he says. And before anybody could say a word, in he went.

"He swum to it, and as he come pushing it to the raft, the men spread to one side. But the old man got it aboard and busted in the head, and there was a baby in it! Yes sir, a stark naked baby. It was Dick Allbright's baby; he owned up and said so.

"'Yes,' he says, a-leaning over it, 'yes, it is my own lamented darling, my poor lost Charles William Allbright deceased,' says he—for he could curl his tongue around the bulliest words in the language when he was a mind to, and lay them before you without a jint started, anywheres. Yes, he said he used to live up at the head of this bend, and one night he choked his child, which was crying, not intending to kill it—which was prob'ly a lie—and then he was scared, and buried it in a bar'l, before his wife got home, and off he went, and struck the northern trail and went to rafting; and this was the third year that the bar'l had chased him. He said the bad

luck always begun light, and lasted till four men was killed, and then the
bar'l didn't come any more after that. He said if the men would stand it
one more night—and was a-going on like that—but the men had got
enough. They started to get out a boat and take him ashore and lynch him,
but he grabbed the little child all of a sudden and jumped overboard with
it hugged up to his breast and shedding tears, and we never see him again
in this life, poor old suffering soul, nor Charles William neither."

"*Who* was shedding tears?" says Bob; "was it Allbright or the baby?"

"Why, Allbright, of course; didn't I tell you the baby was dead? Been
dead three years—how could it cry?"

"Well, never mind how it could cry—how could it *keep* all that time?"
says Davy. "You answer me that."

"I don't know how it done it," says Ed. "It done it though—that's all
I know about it."

"Say—what did they do with the bar'l?" says the Child of Calamity.

"Why, they hove it overboard, and it sunk like a chunk of lead."

"Edward, did the child look like it was choked?" says one.

"Did it have its hair parted?" says another.

"What was the brand on that bar'l, Eddy?" says a fellow they called
Bill.

"Have you got the papers for them statistics, Edmund?" says Jimmy.

"Say, Edwin, was you one of the men that was killed by the lightning?"
says Davy.

"Him? O, no, he was both of 'em," says Bob. Then they all haw-hawed.

"Say, Edward, don't you reckon you'd better take a pill? You look
bad—don't you feel pale?" says the Child of Calamity.

"O, come, now, Eddy," says Jimmy, "show up; you must a kept part
of that bar'l to prove the thing by. Show us the bunghole—*do*—and we'll
all believe you."

"Say, boys," says Bill, "less divide it up. Thar's thirteen of us. I can
swaller a thirteenth of the yarn, if you can worry down the rest."

Ed got up mad and said they could all go to some place which he
ripped out pretty savage, and then walked off aft cussing to himself, and
they yelling and jeering at him, and roaring and laughing so you could
hear them a mile.

"Boys, we'll split a watermelon on that," says the Child of Calamity;
and he come rummaging around in the dark amongst the shingle bundles
where I was, and put his hand on me. I was warm and soft and naked; so
he says "Ouch!" and jumped back.

"Fetch a lantern or a chunk of fire here, boys—there's a snake here as
big as a cow!"

So they run there with a lantern and crowded up and looked in on me.

"Come out of that, you beggar!" says one.

"Who are you?" says another.

"What are you after here? Speak up prompt, or overboard you go."

"Snake him out, boys. Snatch him out by the heels."

I began to beg, and crept out amongst them trembling. They looked me over, wondering, and the Child of Calamity says:

"A cussed thief! Lend a hand and less heave him overboard!"

"No," says Big Bob, "less get out the paint-pot and paint him a sky blue all over from head to heel, and *then* heave him over!"

"Good! that's it. Go for the paint, Jimmy."

When the paint come, and Bob took the brush and was just going to begin, the others laughing and rubbing their hands, I begun to cry, and that sort of worked on Davy, and he says:

"'Vast there! He's nothing but a cub. I'll paint the man that tetches him!"

So I looked around on them, and some of them grumbled and growled, and Bob put down the paint, and the others didn't take it up.

"Come here to the fire, and less see what you're up to here," says Davy. "Now set down there and give an account of yourself. How long have you been aboard here?"

"Not over a quarter of a minute, sir," says I.

"How did you get dry so quick?"

"I don't know, sir. I'm always that way, mostly."

"Oh, you are, are you? What's your name?"

I warn't going to tell my name. I didn't know what to say, so I just says:

"Charles William Allbright, sir."

Then they roared—the whole crowd; and I was mighty glad I said that, because maybe laughing would get them in a better humor.

When they got done laughing, Davy says:

"It won't hardly do, Charles William. You couldn't have growed this much in five year, and you was a baby when you come out of the bar'l, you know, and dead at that. Come, now, tell a straight story, and nobody'll hurt you, if you ain't up to anything wrong. What *is* your name?"

"Aleck Hopkins, sir. Aleck James Hopkins."

"Well, Aleck, where did you come from, here?"

"From a trading scow. She lays up the bend yonder. I was born on her. Pap has traded up and down here all his life; and he told me to swim off here, because when you went by he said he would like to get some of you to speak to a Mr. Jonas Turner, in Cairo, and tell him—"

"Oh, come!"

"Yes, sir, it's as true as the world; Pap he says—"

"Oh, your grandmother!"

They all laughed, and I tried again to talk, but they broke in on me and stopped me.

he always talks wild

"Now, looky-here," says Davy: "you're scared, and so you talk wild. Honest, now, do you live in a scow, or is it a lie?"

"Yes, sir, in a trading scow. She lays up at the head of the bend. But I warn't born in her. It's her first trip."

"Now you're talking! What did you come aboard here, for? To steal?"

"No, sir, I didn't. It was only to get a ride on the raft. All boys does that."

"Well, I know that. But what did you hide for?"

"Sometimes they drive the boys off."

"So they do. They might steal. Looky-here; if we let you off this time, will you keep out of these kind of scrapes hereafter?"

"'Deed I will, boss. You try me."

"All right, then. You ain't but little ways from shore. Overboard with you, and don't you make a fool of yourself another time this way. Blast it, boy, some raftsmen would rawhide you till you were black and blue!"

I didn't wait to kiss good-bye, but went overboard and broke for shore. When Jim come along by-and-by, the big raft was away out of sight around the point. I swum out and got aboard, and was mighty glad to see home again.

There warn't nothing to do, now, but to look out sharp for the town, and not pass it without seeing it. He said he'd be mighty sure to see it, because he'd be a free man the minute he seen it, but if he missed it he'd be in the slave country again and no more show for freedom. Every little while he jumps up and says:

"Dah she is!"

But it warn't. It was Jack-o-lanterns, or lightning-bugs; so he set down again, and went to watching, same as before. Jim said it made him all over trembly and feverish to be so close to freedom. Well, I can tell you it made me all over trembly and feverish, too, to hear him, because I begun to get it through my head that he *was* most free—and who was to blame for it? Why, me. I couldn't get that out of my conscience, no how nor no way. It got to troubling me so I couldn't rest; I couldn't stay still in one place. It hadn't ever come home to me before, what this thing was that I was doing. But now it did; and it stayed with me, and scorched me more and more. I tried to make out to myself that *I* warn't to blame, because *I* didn't run Jim off from his rightful owner; but it warn't no use, conscience up and says, every time, "But you knowed he was running for his freedom, and you could a paddled ashore and told somebody." That was so—I couldn't get around that noway. That was where it pinched. Conscience says to me, "What had poor Miss Watson done to you, that you could see her nigger go off right under your eyes and never say one single word? What did that poor old woman do to you, that you could treat her so mean? Why, she tried to learn you your book, she tried to learn you your manners, she tried to be good to you every way she knowed how. *That's* what she done."

I got to feeling so mean and so miserable I most wished I was dead. I fidgeted up and down the raft, abusing myself to myself, and Jim was fidgeting up and down past me. We neither of us could keep still. Every time he danced around and says, "Dah's Cairo!" it went through me like a shot, and I thought if it *was* Cairo I reckoned I would die of miserableness.

Jim talked out loud all the time while I was talking to myself. He was saying how the first thing he would do when he got to a free State he would go to saving up money and never spend a single cent, and when he got enough he would buy his wife, which was owned on a farm close to where Miss Watson lived; and then they would both work to buy the two children, and if their master wouldn't sell them, they'd get an Ab'litionist to go and steal them.

It most froze me to hear such talk. He wouldn't ever dared to talk such talk in his life before. Just see what a difference it made in him the minute he judged he was about free. It was according to the old saying, "give a nigger an inch and he'll take an ell." Thinks I, this is what comes of my not thinking. Here was this nigger which I had as good as helped to run away, coming right out flat-footed and saying he would steal his children—children that belonged to a man I didn't even know; a man that hadn't ever done me no harm.

I was sorry to hear Jim say that, it was such a lowering of him. My conscience got to stirring me up hotter than ever, until at last I says to it, "Let up on me—it ain't too late, yet—I'll paddle ashore at the first light, and tell." I felt easy, and happy, and light as a feather, right off. All my troubles was gone. I went to looking out sharp for a light, and sort of singing to myself. By-and-by one showed. Jim sings out:

"We's safe, Huck, we's safe! Jump up and crack yo' heels! Dat's de good ole Cairo at las', I jis knows it!"

I says:

"I'll take the canoe and go see, Jim. It mightn't be, you know."

He jumped and got the canoe ready, and put his old coat in the bottom for me to set on, and give me the paddle; and as I shoved off, he says:

"Pooty soon I'll be a-shout'n for joy, en I'll say, it's all on accounts o' Huck; I's a free man, en I couldn't ever ben free ef it hadn' ben for Huck;

Huck done it. Jim won't ever forgit you, Huck; you's de bes' fren' Jim's ever had; en you's de *only* fren' ole Jim's got now."

I was paddling off, all in a sweat to tell on him; but when he says this, it seemed to kind of take the tuck all out of me. I went along slow then, and I warn't right down certain whether I was glad I started or whether I warn't. When I was fifty yards off, Jim says:

"Dah you goes, de ole true Huck; de on'y white genlman dat ever kep' his promise to ole Jim."

Well, I just felt sick. But I says, I *got* to do it—I can't get *out* of it. Right then, along comes a skiff with two men in it, with guns, and they stopped and I stopped. One of them says:

"What's that yonder?"

"A piece of a raft," I says.

"Do you belong on it?"

"Yes, sir."

"Any men on it?"

"Only one, sir."

"Well, there's five niggers run off to-night, up yonder above the head of the bend. Is your man white or black?"

I didn't answer up prompt. I tried to, but the words wouldn't come. I tried, for a second or two, to brace up and out with it, but I warn't man enough—hadn't the spunk of a rabbit. I see I was weakening; so I just give up trying, and up and says—

"He's white."

"I reckon we'll go and see for ourselves."

"I wish you would," says I, "because it's pap that's there, and maybe you'd help me tow the raft ashore where the light is. He's sick—and so is mam and Mary Ann."

"Oh, the devil! we're in a hurry, boy. But I s'pose we've got to. Come—buckle to your paddle, and let's get along."

I buckled to my paddle and they laid to their oars. When we had made a stroke or two, I says:

"Pap'll be mighty much obleeged to you, I can tell you. Everybody goes away when I want them to help me tow the raft ashore, and I can't do it by myself."

"Well, that's infernal mean. Odd, too. Say, boy, what's the matter with your father?"

"It's the—a—the—well, it ain't anything, much."

They stopped pulling. It warn't but a mighty little ways to the raft, now. One says:

"Boy, that's a lie. What *is* the matter with your pap? Answer up square, now, and it'll be the better for you."

"I will, sir, I will, honest—but don't leave us, please. It's the—the—gentlemen, if you'll only pull ahead, and let me heave you the head-line, you won't have to come a-near the raft—please do."

"Set her back, John, set her back!" says one. They backed water. "Keep away, boy—keep to looard. Confound it, I just expect the wind has blowed it to us. Your pap's got the small-pox, and you know it precious well. Why didn't you come out and say so? Do you want to spread it all over?"

"Well," says I, a-blubbering, "I've told everybody before, and then they just went away and left us."

"Poor devil, there's something in that. We are right down sorry for you, but we—well, hang it, we don't want the small-pox, you see. Look here, I'll tell you what to do. Don't you try to land by yourself, or you'll smash everything to pieces. You float along down about twenty miles and you'll come to a town on the left-hand side of the river. It will be long after sun-up then, and when you ask for help, you tell them your folks are all down with chills and fever. Don't be a fool again, and let people guess what is the matter. Now we're trying to do you a kindness; so you just put twenty miles between us, that's a good boy. It wouldn't do any good to land yonder where the light is—it's only a wood-yard. Say—I reckon your father's poor, and I'm bound to say he's in pretty hard luck. Here—I'll put a twenty dollar gold piece on this board, and you get it when it floats by. I feel mighty mean to leave you, but my kingdom! it won't do to fool with small-pox, don't you see?"

"Hold on, Parker," says the other man, "here's a twenty to put on the board for me. Good-bye, boy, you do as Mr. Parker told you, and you'll be all right."

"That's so, my boy—good-bye, good-bye. If you see any runaway niggers, you get help and nab them, and you can make some money by it."

"Good-bye, sir," says I, "I won't let no runaway niggers get by me if I can help it."

They went off, and I got aboard the raft, feeling bad and low, because I knowed very well I had done wrong, and I see it warn't no use for me to try to learn to do right; a body that don't get *started* right when he's little, ain't got no show—when the pinch comes there ain't nothing to back him up and keep him to his work, and so he gets beat. Then I thought a minute, and says to myself, hold on—s'pose you'd a done right and give Jim up; would you felt better than what you do now? No, says I, I'd feel bad—I'd feel just the same way I do now. Well, then, says I, what's the use you learning to do right, when it's troublesome to do right and ain't no trouble to do wrong, and the wages is just the same? I was stuck. I couldn't answer that. So I reckoned I wouldn't bother no more about it, but after this always do whichever come handiest at the time.

I went into the wigwam; Jim warn't there. I looked all around; he warn't anywhere. I says:

"Jim!"

"Here I is, Huck. Is dey out o' sight yit? Don't talk loud."

He was in the river under the stern oar, with just his nose out. I told him they were out of sight, so he come aboard. He says:

"I was a-listenin' to all de talk, en I slips into de river en was gwyne to shove for sho' if dey come aboard. Den I was gwyne to swim to de raf' agin when dey was gone. But lawsy, how you did fool 'em, Huck! Dat *wuz* de smartes' dodge! I tell you, chile, I 'speck it save' ole Jim—ole Jim ain't gwyne to forgit you for dat, honey."

Then we talked about the money. It was a pretty good raise, twenty dollars apiece. Jim said we could take deck passage on a steamboat now, and the money would last us as far as we wanted to go in the free States. He said twenty mile more warn't far for the raft to go, but he wished we was already there.

Towards daybreak we tied up, and Jim was mighty particular about hiding the raft good. Then he worked all day fixing things in bundles, and getting all ready to quit rafting.

That night about ten we hove in sight of the lights of a town away down in a left-hand bend.

I went off in the canoe, to ask about it. Pretty soon I found a man out in the river with a skiff, setting a trot-line. I ranged up and says:

"Mister, is that town Cairo?"

"Cairo? no. You must be a blame' fool."

"What town is it, mister?"

"If you want to know, go and find out. If you stay here botherin' around me for about a half a minute longer, you'll get something you won't want."

I paddled to the raft. Jim was awful disappointed, but I said never mind, Cairo would be the next place, I reckoned.

We passed another town before daylight, and I was going out again; but it was high ground, so I didn't go. No high ground about Cairo, Jim said. I had forgot it. We laid up for the day, on a tow-head tolerable close to the left-hand bank. I begun to suspicion something. So did Jim. I says:

"Maybe we went by Cairo in the fog that night."

He says:

"Doan' le's talk about it, Huck. Po' niggers can't have no luck. I awluz 'spected dat rattlesnake-skin warn't done wid its work."

"I wish I'd never seen that snake-skin, Jim—I do wish I'd never laid eyes on it."

"It ain't yo' fault, Huck; you didn' know. Don't you blame yo'self 'bout it."

When it was daylight, here was the clear Ohio water in shore, sure enough, and outside was the old regular Muddy! So it was all up with Cairo.[29]

We talked it all over. It wouldn't do to take to the shore; we couldn't take the raft up the stream, of course. There warn't no way but to wait for dark, and start back in the canoe and take the chances. So we slept all day amongst the cotton-wood thicket, so as to be fresh for the work, and when we went back to the raft about dark the canoe was gone!

We didn't say a word for a good while. There warn't anything to say. We both knowed well enough it was some more work of the rattle-snake skin; so what was the use to talk about it? It would only look like we was finding fault, and that would be bound to fetch more bad luck—and keep on fetching it, too, till we knowed enough to keep still.

By-and-by we talked about what we better do, and found there warn't no way but just to go along down with the raft till we got a chance to buy a canoe to go back in. We warn't going to borrow it when there warn't anybody around, the way pap would do, for that might set people after us.

So we shoved out, after dark, on the raft.

Anybody that don't believe yet, that it's foolishness to handle a snake-skin, after all that that snake-skin done for us, will believe it now, if they read on and see what more it done for us.

The place to buy canoes is off of rafts laying up at shore. But we didn't see no rafts laying up; so we went along during three hours and more. Well, the night got gray, and ruther thick, which is the next meanest thing to fog. You can't tell the shape of the river, and you can't see no distance. It got to be very late and still, and then along comes a steamboat up the river. We lit the lantern, and judged she would see it. Up-stream boats didn't generly come close to us; they go out and follow the bars and hunt for easy water under the reefs; but nights like this they bull right up the channel against the whole river.

We could hear her pounding along, but we didn't see her good till she was close. She aimed right for us. Often they do that and try to see how close they can come without touching; sometimes the wheel bites off a sweep, and then the pilot sticks his head out and laughs, and thinks he's

---

[29] When Jim and Huck see the clear water of the Ohio River flowing along beside the muddy water of the Mississippi, they realize that they've missed Cairo.

mighty smart. Well, here she comes, and we said she was going to try and shave us; but she didn't seem to be sheering off a bit. She was a big one, and she was coming in a hurry, too, looking like a black cloud with rows of glow-worms around it; but all of a sudden she bulged out, big and scary, with a long row of wide-open furnace doors shining like red-hot teeth, and her monstrous bows and guards hanging right over us. There was a yell at us, and a jingling of bells to stop the engines, a pow-wow of cussing, and whistling of steam—and as Jim went overboard on one side and I on the other, she come smashing straight through the raft.

I dived—and I aimed to find the bottom, too, for a thirty-foot wheel had got to go over me, and I wanted it to have plenty of room. I could always stay under water a minute; this time I reckon I staid under a minute and a half. Then I bounced for the top in a hurry, for I was nearly busting. I popped out to my arm-pits and blowed the water out of my nose, and puffed a bit. Of course there was a booming current; and of course that boat started her engines again ten seconds after she stopped them, for they never cared much for raftsmen; so now she was churning along up the river, out of sight in the thick weather, though I could hear her.

I sung out for Jim about a dozen times, but I didn't get any answer; so I grabbed a plank that touched me while I was "treading water," and struck out for shore, shoving it ahead of me. But I made out to see that the drift of the current was towards the left-hand shore, which meant that I was in a crossing; so I changed off and went that way.

It was one of these long, slanting, two-mile crossings; so I was a good long time in getting over. I made a safe landing, and clumb up the bank. I couldn't see but a little ways, but I went poking along over rough ground for a quarter of a mile or more, and then I run across a big old-fashioned double log-house before I noticed it. I was going to rush by and get away, but a lot of dogs jumped out and went to howling and barking at me, and I knowed better than to move another peg.

Chapter XVII
An Evening Call—The Farm in Arkansaw—
Interior Decorations—Stephen Dowling Bots—
Poetical Effusions

In about half a minute somebody spoke out of a window, without putting his head out, and says:

"Be done, boys! Who's there?"

"WHO'S THERE?"

I says:

"It's me."

"Who's me?"

"George Jackson, sir." *lie*

"What do you want?"

"I don't want nothing, sir. I only want to go along by, but the dogs won't let me."

"What are you prowling around here this time of night, for—hey?"

"I warn't prowling around, sir; I fell overboard off of the steamboat."

"Oh, you did, did you? Strike a light there, somebody. What did you say your name was?"

"George Jackson, sir. I'm only a boy." *what?*

"Look here; if you're telling the truth, you needn't be afraid—nobody'll hurt you. But don't try to budge; stand right where you are. Rouse out Bob and Tom, some of you, and fetch the guns. George Jackson, is there anybody with you?"

"No, sir, nobody."

I heard the people stirring around in the house now, and see a light. The man sung out:

"Snatch that light away, Betsy, you old fool—ain't you got any sense? Put it on the floor behind the front door. Bob, if you and Tom are ready, take your places."

"All ready."

"Now, George Jackson, do you know the Shepherdsons?"

"No, sir—I never heard of them."

"Well, that may be so, and it mayn't. Now, all ready. Step forward, George Jackson. And mind, don't you hurry—come mighty slow. If there's anybody with you, let him keep back—if he shows himself he'll be shot. Come along, now. Come slow; push the door open, yourself—just enough to squeeze in, d' you hear?"

I didn't hurry, I couldn't if I'd a wanted to. I took one slow step at a *ok* time, and there warn't a sound, only I thought I could hear my heart. The dogs were still as the humans, but they followed a little behind me. When I got to the three log door-steps I heard them unlocking and unbarring and unbolting. I put my hand on the door and pushed it a little and a little more, till somebody said, "There, that's enough—put your head in." I done it, but I judged they would take it off.

The candle was on the floor, and there they all was, looking at me, and me at them, for about a quarter of a minute. Three big men with guns pointed at me, which made me wince, I tell you; the oldest, gray and about sixty, the other two thirty or more—all of them fine and handsome—and the sweetest old gray-headed lady, and back of her two young women which I couldn't see right well. The old gentleman says:

"There—I reckon it's all right. Come in."

As soon as I was in, the old gentleman he locked the door and barred it and bolted it, and told the young men to come in with their guns, and they all went in a big parlor that had a new rag carpet on the floor, and got together in a corner that was out of the range of the front windows— there warn't none on the side. They held the candle, and took a good look at me, and all said, "Why, *he* ain't a Shepherdson—no, there ain't any Shepherdson about him." Then the old man said he hoped I wouldn't mind being searched for arms, because he didn't mean no harm by it—it was only to make sure. So he didn't pry into my pockets, but only felt outside with his hands, and said it was all right. He told me to make myself easy and at home, and tell all about myself; but the old lady says:

"Why bless you, Saul, the poor thing's as wet as he can be; and don't you reckon it may be he's hungry?"

"True for you, Rachel—I forgot."

So the old lady says:

"Betsy" (this was a nigger woman), "you fly around and get him something to eat, as quick as you can, poor thing; and one of you girls go and wake up Buck and tell him—Oh, here he is himself. Buck, take this little stranger and get the wet clothes off from him and dress him up in some of yours that's dry."

Buck looked about as old as me—thirteen or fourteen or along there, though he was a little bigger than me. He hadn't on anything but a shirt, and he was very frowsy-headed. He come in gaping and digging one fist into his eyes, and he was dragging a gun along with the other one. He says:

"Ain't they no Shepherdsons around?"

They said, no, 'twas a false alarm.

"Well," he says, "if they'd a ben some, I reckon I'd a got one."

They all laughed, and Bob says:

"Why, Buck, they might have scalped us all, you've been so slow in coming."

"Well, nobody come after me, and it ain't right. I'm always kep' down; I don't get no show."

"Never mind, Buck, my boy," says the old man, "you'll have show enough, all in good time, don't you fret about that. Go 'long with you now, and do as your mother told you."

When we got up-stairs to his room, he got me a coarse shirt and a round-about and pants of his, and I put them on. While I was at it he asked me what my name was, but before I could tell him, he started to telling me about a blue jay and a young rabbit he had catched in the woods day before yesterday, and he asked me where Moses was when the candle went out. I said I didn't know; I hadn't heard about it before, no way.

"Well, guess," he says.

"How'm I going to guess," says I, "when I never heard tell about it before?"

"But you can guess, can't you? It's just as easy."

"*Which* candle?" I says.

"Why, any candle," he says.

"I don't know where he was," says I; "where was he?"

"Why he was in the *dark!* That's where he was!"

"Well, if you knowed where he was, what did you ask me for?"

"Why, blame it, it's a riddle, don't you see? Say, how long are you going to stay here? You got to stay always. We can just have booming times—they don't have no school now. Do you own a dog? I've got a dog—and he'll go in the river and bring out chips that you throw in. Do you like to comb up, Sundays, and all that kind of foolishness? You bet I don't, but ma she makes me. Confound these ole britches, I reckon I'd better put 'em on, but I'd ruther not, it's so warm. Are you all ready? All right—come along, old hoss."

Cold corn-pone, cold corn-beef, butter and butter-milk—that is what they had for me down there, and there ain't nothing better that ever I've come across yet. Buck and his ma and all of them smoked cob pipes, except the nigger woman, which was gone, and the two young women. They all smoked and talked, and I eat and talked. The young women had quilts around them, and their hair down their backs. They all asked me questions, and I told them how pap and me and all the family was living on a little farm down at the bottom of Arkansaw, and my sister Mary Ann run off and got married and never was heard of no more, and Bill went to hunt them and he warn't heard of no more, and Tom and Mort died, and then there warn't nobody but just me and pap left, and he was just trimmed down to nothing, on account of his troubles; so when he died I took what there was left, because the farm didn't belong to us, and started up the river, deck passage, and fell overboard; and that was how I come to be here. So they said I could have a home there as long as I wanted it. Then it was most daylight, and everybody went to bed, and I went to bed with

Buck, and when I waked up in the morning, drat it all, I had forgot what my name was. So I laid there about an hour trying to think, and when Buck waked up, I says:

"Can you spell, Buck?"

"Yes," he says.

"I bet you can't spell my name," says I.

"I bet you what you dare I can," says he.

"All right," says I, "go ahead."

"G-o-r-g-e J-a-x-o-n—there now," he says.

"Well," says I, "you done it, but I didn't think you could. It ain't no slouch of a name to spell—right off without studying."

I set it down, private, because somebody might want *me* to spell it, next, and so I wanted to be handy with it and rattle it off like I was used to it.

It was a mighty nice family, and a mighty nice house, too. I hadn't seen no house out in the country before that was so nice and had so much style.[30] It didn't have an iron latch on the front door, nor a wooden one with a buckskin string, but a brass knob to turn, the same as houses in town. There warn't no bed in the parlor, not a sign of a bed; but heaps of parlors in towns has beds in them. There was a big fire place that was bricked on the bottom, and the bricks was kept clean and red by pouring water on them and scrubbing them with another brick; sometimes they washed them over with red water-paint that they call Spanish-brown, same as they do in town. They had big brass dog-irons that could hold up a saw-log. There was a clock on the middle of the mantel-piece, with a picture of a town painted on the bottom half of the glass front, and a round place in the middle of it for the sun, and you could see the pendulum swing behind it. It was beautiful to hear that clock tick; and sometimes when one of these peddlers had been along and scoured her up and got her in good shape, she would start in and strike a hundred and fifty before she got tuckered out. They wouldn't took any money for her.

Well, there was a big outlandish parrot on each side of the clock, made out of something like chalk, and painted up gaudy. By one of the parrots was a cat made of crockery, and a crockery dog by the other; and when

---

[30] The Grangerfords' house is decorated in a style that Twain's audiences would recognize as typical of fashionable, well-to-do nineteenth-century citizens. Twain parodies this artificial and excessive decor. Claudia Durst Johnson writes of Twain's cultural satire: "The way in which this so-called stylish decor fits into the whole story of the Grangerfords' lives emphasizes the tragedy of their story. . . . On the outside is a thin veneer of fashionable and stylish society with its self-conscious display of polite manners, Christian books, churchgoing, and elegant parties. At the core, however, is not civilized society at all, but savagery, as they slaughter their neighbors" (231).

you pressed down on them they squeaked, but didn't open their mouths nor look different nor interested. They squeaked through underneath. There was a couple of big wild-turkey-wing fans spread out behind those things. On a table in the middle of the room was a kind of a lovely crockery basket that had apples and oranges and peaches and grapes piled up in it which was much redder and yellower and prettier than real ones is, but they warn't real because you could see where pieces had got chipped off and showed the white chalk or whatever it was, underneath.

This table had a cover made out of beautiful oil-cloth, with a red and blue spread-eagle painted on it, and a painted border all around. It come all the way from Philadelphia, they said. There was some books too, piled up perfectly exact, on each corner of the table. One was a big family Bible, full of pictures. One was "Pilgrim's Progress," [31] about a man that left his family it didn't say why. I read considerable in it now and then. The statements was interesting, but tough. Another was "Friendship's Offering," full of beautiful stuff and poetry; but I didn't read the poetry. Another was Henry Clay's Speeches, and another was Dr. Gunn's Family Medicine, which told you all about what to do if a body was sick or dead. There was a Hymn Book, and a lot of other books. And there was nice split-bottom chairs, and perfectly sound, too—not bagged down in the middle and busted, like an old basket.

They had pictures hung on the walls—mainly Washingtons and Lafayettes, and battles, and Highland Marys, and one called "Signing the Declaration." There was some that they called crayons, which one of the daughters which was dead made her own self when she was only fifteen years old. They was different from any pictures I ever see before; blacker, mostly, than is common. One was a woman in a slim black dress, belted small under the arm-pits, with bulges like a cabbage in the middle of the sleeves, and a large black scoop-shovel bonnet with a black veil, and white slim ankles crossed about with black tape, and very wee black slippers, like a chisel, and she was leaning pensive on a tombstone on her right elbow, under a weeping willow, and her other hand hanging down her side holding a white handkerchief and a reticule, and underneath the picture it said "Shall I Never See Thee More Alas." Another one was a young lady with her hair all combed up straight to the top of her head, and knotted there in front of a comb like a chair-back, and she was crying into a handker-

[31] Written by John Bunyan in 1678, *The Pilgrim's Progress from This World, to That Which Is to Come* is a religious allegory about the search for salvation. It is arguably the most well-known allegory in English literature. Huck's journey with Jim may be read in terms of Bunyan's work.

chief and had a dead bird laying on its back in her other hand with its heels up, and underneath the picture it said "I Shall Never Hear Thy Sweet Chirrup More Alas." There was one where a young lady was at a window looking up at the moon, and tears running down her cheeks; and she had an open letter in one hand with black sealing-wax showing on one edge of it, and she was mashing a locket with a chain to it against her mouth, and underneath the picture it said "And Art Thou Gone Yes Thou Art Gone Alas." These was all nice pictures, I reckon, but I didn't somehow seem to take to them, because if ever I was down a little, they always give me the fan-tods. Everybody was sorry she died, because she had laid out a lot more of these pictures to do, and a body could see by what she had done what they had lost. But I reckoned, that with her disposition, she was having a better time in the graveyard. She was at work on what they said was her greatest picture when she took sick, and every day and every night it was her prayer to be allowed to live till she got it done, but she never got the chance. It was a picture of a young woman in a long white gown, standing on the rail of a bridge all ready to jump off, with her hair all down her back, and looking up to the moon, with the tears running down her face, and she had two arms folded across her breast, and two arms stretched out in front, and two more reaching up towards the moon—and the idea was to see which pair would look best and then scratch out all the other arms; but, as I was saying, she died before she got her mind made up, and now they kept this picture over the head of the bed in her room, and every time her birthday come they hung flowers on it. Other times it was hid with a little curtain. The young woman in the picture had a kind of a nice sweet face, but there was so many arms it made her look too spidery, seemed to me.

This young girl kept a scrap-book when she was alive, and used to paste obituaries and accidents and cases of patient suffering in it out of the *Presbyterian Observer,* and write poetry after them out of her own head. It was very good poetry. This is what she wrote about a boy by the name of Stephen Dowling Bots that fell down a well and was drownded:

ODE TO STEPHEN DOWLING BOTS, DEC'D.[32]

And did young Stephen sicken,
   And did young Stephen die?
And did the sad hearts thicken,
   And did the mourners cry?

---

[32] Twain satirizes nineteenth-century society's obsession with death. This preoccupation was exemplified by the popularity of "mourning pictures" and sentimental verse commissioned for obituaries. Emmeline's poetry is from the "Graveyard School" of verse.

5   No; such was not the fate of
          Young Stephen Dowling Bots;
     Though sad hearts round him thickened,
          'Twas not from sickness' shots.

     No whooping-cough did rack his frame,
10   Nor measles drear, with spots;
     Not these impaired the sacred name
          Of Stephen Dowling Bots.

     Despised love struck not with woe
          That head of curly knots,
15   Nor stomach troubles laid him low,
          Young Stephen Dowling Bots.

     O no. Then list with tearful eye,
          Whilst I his fate do tell.
     His soul did from this cold world fly,
20   By falling down a well.

     They got him out and emptied him;
          Alas it was too late;
     His spirit was gone for to sport aloft
          In the realms of the good and great.

If Emmeline Grangerford could make poetry like that before she was
fourteen, there ain't no telling what she could a done by-and-by. Buck said
she could rattle off poetry like nothing. She didn't ever have to stop to
think. He said she would slap down a line, and if she couldn't find anything to rhyme with it she would just scratch it out and slap down another
one, and go ahead. She warn't particular, she could write about anything
you choose to give her to write about, just so it was sadful. Every time a
man died, or a woman died, or a child died, she would be on hand with
her "tribute" before he was cold. She called them tributes. The neighbors
said it was the doctor first, then Emmeline, then the undertaker—the undertaker never got in ahead of Emmeline but once, and then she hung fire
on a rhyme for the dead person's name, which was Whistler. She warn't
ever the same, after that; she never complained, but she kind of pined away
and did not live long. Poor thing, many's the time I made myself go up to
the little room that used to be hers and get out her poor old scrap-book
and read in it when her pictures had been aggravating me and I had soured
on her a little. I liked all that family, dead ones and all, and warn't going
to let anything come between us. Poor Emmeline made poetry about all the
dead people when she was alive, and it didn't seem right that there warn't

nobody to make some about her, now she was gone; so I tried to sweat out a verse or two myself, but I couldn't seem to make it go, somehow. They kept Emmeline's room trim and nice and all the things fixed in it just the way she liked to have them when she was alive, and nobody ever slept there. The old lady took care of the room herself, though there was plenty of niggers, and she sewed there a good deal and read her Bible there, mostly.

Well, as I was saying about the parlor, there was beautiful curtains on the windows: white, with pictures painted on them, of castles with vines all down the walls, and cattle coming down to drink. There was a little old piano, too, that had tin pans in it, I reckon, and nothing was ever so lovely as to hear the young ladies sing, "The Last Link is Broken" and play "The Battle of Prague" on it. The walls of all the rooms was plastered, and most had carpets on the floors, and the whole house was whitewashed on the outside.

It was a double house, and the big open place betwixt them was roofed and floored, and sometimes the table was set there in the middle of the day, and it was a cool, comfortable place. Nothing couldn't be better. And warn't the cooking good, and just bushels of it too!

Chapter XVIII
Col. Grangerford—Aristocracy—Feuds—
The Testament—Recovering the Raft—
The Wood-pile—Pork and Cabbage

Col. Grangerford was a gentleman, you see. He was a gentleman all over; and so was his family. He was well born, as the saying is, and that's worth as much in a man as it is in a horse, so the Widow Douglas said, and nobody ever denied that she was of the first aristocracy in our town; and pap he always said it, too, though he warn't no more quality than a mudcat, himself. Col. Grangerford was very tall and very slim, and had a darkish-paly complexion, not a sign of red in it anywheres; he was clean-shaved every morning, all over his thin face, and he had the thinnest kind of lips, and the thinnest kind of nostrils, and a high nose, and heavy eyebrows, and the blackest kind of eyes, sunk so deep back that they seemed like they was looking out of caverns at you, as you may say. His forehead was high, and his hair was black and straight, and hung to his shoulders. His hands was long and thin, and every day of his life he put on a clean shirt and a full suit from head to foot made out of linen so white it hurt your eyes to look at it; and on Sundays he wore a blue tail-coat with brass buttons on it. He carried a mahogany cane with a silver head to it. There warn't no

COL. GRANGERFORD.

frivolishness about him, not a bit, and he warn't ever loud. He was as kind as he could be—you could feel that, you know, and so you had confidence. Sometimes he smiled, and it was good to see; but when he straightened himself up like a liberty-pole, and the lightning begun to flicker out from under his eyebrows you wanted to climb a tree first, and find out what the matter was afterwards. He didn't ever have to tell anybody to mind their manners—everybody was always good mannered where he was. Everybody loved to have him around, too; he was sunshine most always—I mean he made it seem like good weather. When he turned into a cloud-bank it was awful dark for half a minute and that was enough; there wouldn't nothing go wrong again for a week.

When him and the old lady come down in the morning, all the family got up out of their chairs and give them good-day, and didn't set down again till they had set down. Then Tom and Bob went to the sideboard where the decanters was, and mixed a glass of bitters and handed it to him, and he held it in his hand and waited till Tom's and Bob's was mixed, and then they bowed and said, "Our duty to you, sir, and madam;" and *they* bowed the least bit in the world and said thank you, and so they drank, all three, and Bob and Tom poured a spoonful of water on the sugar and the mite of whisky or apple brandy in the bottom of their tumblers, and give it to me and Buck, and we drank to the old people too.

Bob was the oldest, and Tom next. Tall, beautiful men with very broad shoulders and brown faces, and long black hair and black eyes. They dressed in white linen from head to foot, like the old gentleman, and wore broad Panama hats.

Then there was Miss Charlotte, she was twenty-five, and tall and proud and grand, but as good as she could be, when she warn't stirred up;

but when she was, she had a look that would make you wilt in your tracks, like her father. She was beautiful.

So was her sister, Miss Sophia, but it was a different kind. She was gentle and sweet, like a dove, and she was only twenty.

Each person had their own nigger to wait on them—Buck, too. My nigger had a monstrous easy time, because I warn't used to having anybody do anything for me, but Buck's was on the jump most of the time.

This was all there was of the family, now; but there used to be more— three sons; they got killed; and Emmeline that died.

The old gentleman owned a lot of farms, and over a hundred niggers. Sometimes a stack of people would come there, horseback, from ten or fifteen mile around, and stay five or six days, and have such junketings round about and on the river, and dances and picnics in the woods daytimes, and balls at the house, nights. These people was mostly kin-folks of the family. The men brought their guns with them. It was a handsome lot of quality, I tell you.

There was another clan of aristocracy around there—five or six families—mostly of the name of Shepherdson. They was as high-toned, and well born, and rich and grand, as the tribe of Grangerfords. The Shepherdsons and the Grangerfords used the same steamboat landing, which was about two mile above our house; so sometimes when I went up there with a lot of our folks I used to see a lot of the Shepherdsons there, on their fine horses.

One day Buck and me was away out in the woods, hunting, and heard a horse coming. We was crossing the road. Buck says:

"Quick! Jump for the woods!"

We done it, and then peeped down the woods through the leaves. Pretty soon a splendid young man come galloping down the road, setting his horse easy and looking like a soldier. He had his gun across his pommel. I had seen him before. It was young Harney Shepherdson. I heard Buck's gun go off at my ear, and Harney's hat tumbled off from his head. He grabbed his gun and rode straight to the place where we was hid. But we didn't wait. We started through the woods on a run. The woods warn't thick, so I looked over my shoulder, to dodge the bullet, and twice I seen Harney cover Buck with his gun; and then he rode away the way he come—to get his hat, I reckon, but I couldn't see. We never stopped running till we got home. The old gentleman's eyes blazed a minute—'twas pleasure, mainly, I judged—then his face sort of smoothed down, and he says, kind of gentle:

"I don't like that shooting from behind a bush. Why didn't you step into the road, my boy?"

"The Shepherdsons don't, father. They always take advantage."

Miss Charlotte she held her head up like a queen while Buck was telling his tale, and her nostrils spread and her eyes snapped. The two young men looked dark, but never said nothing. Miss Sophia she turned pale, but the color come back when she found the man warn't hurt.

Soon as I could get Buck down by the corn-cribs under the trees by ourselves, I says:

"Did you want to kill him, Buck?"

"Well, I bet I did."

"What did he do to you?"

"Him? He never done nothing to me."

"Well, then, what did you want to kill him for?"

"Why, nothing—only it's on account of the feud."[33]

"What's a feud?"

"Why, where was you raised? Don't you know what a feud is?"

"Never heard of it before—tell me about it."

"Well," says Buck, "a feud is this way. A man has a quarrel with an-other man, and kills him; then that other man's brother kills *him;* then the other brothers, on both sides, goes for one another; then the *cousins* chip in—and by-and-by everybody's killed off, and there ain't no more feud. But it's kind of slow, and takes a long time."

"Has this one been going on long, Buck?"

"Well, I should *reckon!* it started thirty year ago, or som'ers along there. There was trouble 'bout something and then a lawsuit to settle it; and the suit went agin one of the men, and so he up and shot the man that won the suit—which he would naturally do, of course. Anybody would."

"What was the trouble about, Buck?—land?"

"I reckon maybe—I don't know."

"Well, who done the shooting?—was it a Grangerford or a Shep-herdson?"

"Laws, how do *I* know? It was so long ago."

"Don't anybody know?"

"Oh, yes, pa knows, I reckon, and some of the other old folks; but they don't know, now, what the row was about in the first place."

---

[33] Twain bases the Grangerford and Shepherdson feud on the real feud between the Dar-nalls and the Watsons described in *Life on the Mississippi*. Feuds provide an example of ritualized violence in the nineteenth-century South and Southwest. "The evidence on which the reputation of the honorable man rested included overt acts of bravery in de-fending himself and his own kind against verbal insult. Other evidence consisted of ex-ternal signs: high social position, property in land and slaves, proper attire, close adher-ence to rules of etiquette, proper accent ... [etc.]" (Claudia Johnson 181). Twain satirizes the Southern code of honor and the romanticism of violence, revealing the bloody, tragic outcome of these extended battles.

"Has there been many killed, Buck?"

"Yes—right smart chance of funerals. But they don't always kill. Pa's got a few buck-shot in him; but he don't mind it 'cuz he don't weigh much anyway. Bob's been carved up some with a bowie, and Tom's been hurt once or twice."

"Has anybody been killed this year, Buck?"

"Yes, we got one and they got one. 'Bout three months ago, my cousin Bud, fourteen year old, was riding through the woods on t'other side of the river, and didn't have no weapon with him, which was blame' foolishness, and in a lonesome place he hears a horse a-coming behind him, and sees old Baldy Shepherdson a-linkin' after him with his gun in his hand and his white hair a-flying in the wind; and 'stead of jumping off and taking to the brush, Bud 'lowed he could outrun him; so they had it, nip and tuck, for five mile or more, the old man a-gaining all the time; so at last Bud seen it warn't any use, so he stopped and faced around so as to have the bullet holes in front, you know, and the old man he rode up and shot him down. But he didn't git much chance to enjoy his luck, for inside of a week our folks laid *him* out."

"I reckon that old man was a coward, Buck."

"I reckon he *warn't* a coward. Not by a blame' sight. There ain't a coward amongst them Shepherdsons—not a one. And there ain't no cowards amongst the Grangerfords, either. Why, that old man kep' up his end in a fight one day, for a half an hour, against three Grangerfords, and come out winner. They was all a-horseback; he lit off of his horse and got behind a little wood-pile, and kep' his horse before him to stop the bullets; but the Grangerfords staid on their horses and capered around the old man, and peppered away at him, and he peppered away at them. Him and his horse both went home pretty leaky and crippled, but the Grangerfords had to be *fetched* home—and one of 'em was dead, and another died the next day. No, sir, if a body's out hunting for cowards, he don't want to fool away any time amongst them Shepherdsons, becuz they don't breed any of that *kind*."

Next Sunday we all went to church, about three mile, everybody a-horseback. The men took their guns along, so did Buck, and kept them between their knees or stood them handy against the wall. The Shepherdsons done the same. It was pretty ornery preaching—all about brotherly love, and such-like tiresomeness; but everybody said it was a good sermon, and they all talked it over going home, and had such a powerful lot to say about faith, and good works, and free grace, and preforeordestination,[34]

---

[34] Huck combines the Presbyterian concepts of predestination and foreordination.

and I don't know what all, that it did seem to me to be one of the roughest Sundays I had run across yet.

About an hour after dinner everybody was dozing around, some in their chairs and some in their rooms, and it got to be pretty dull. Buck and a dog was stretched out on the grass in the sun, sound asleep. I went up to our room, and judged I would take a nap myself. I found that sweet Miss Sophia standing in her door, which was next to ours, and she took me in her room and shut the door very soft, and asked me if I liked her, and I said I did; and she asked me if I would do something for her and not tell anybody, and I said I would. Then she said she'd forgot her Testament, and left it in the seat at church, between two other books and would I slip out quiet and go there and fetch it to her, and not say nothing to nobody. I said I would. So I slid out and slipped off up the road, and there warn't anybody at the church, except maybe a hog or two, for there warn't any lock on the door, and hogs likes a puncheon floor in summer-time because it's cool. If you notice, most folks don't go to church only when they've got to; but a hog is different.

Says I to myself, something's up—it ain't natural for a girl to be in such a sweat about a Testament; so I give it a shake, and out drops a little piece of paper with *"Half-past two"* wrote on it with a pencil. I ransacked it, but couldn't find anything else. I couldn't make anything out of that, so I put the paper in the book again, and when I got home and up stairs, there was Miss Sophia in her door waiting for me. She pulled me in and shut the door; then she looked in the Testament till she found the paper, and as soon as she read it she looked glad; and before a body could think, she grabbed me and give me a squeeze, and said I was the best boy in the world, and not to tell anybody. She was mighty red in the face, for a minute, and her eyes lighted up and it made her powerful pretty. I was a good deal astonished, but when I got my breath I asked her what the paper was about, and she asked me if I had read it, and I said no, and she asked me if I could read writing, and I told her "no, only coarse-hand," and then she said the paper warn't anything but a book-mark to keep her place, and I might go and play now.

I went off down to the river, studying over this thing, and pretty soon I noticed that my nigger was following along behind. When we was out of sight of the house, he looked back and around a second, and then comes a-running, and says:

"Mars Jawge, if you'll come down into de swamp, I'll show you a whole stack o' water-moccasins."

Thinks I, that's mighty curious; he said that yesterday. He oughter know a body don't love water-moccasins enough to go around hunting for them. What is he up to, anyway? So I says—

"All right, trot ahead."

I followed a half a mile, then he struck out over the swamp and waded ankle deep as much as another half mile. We come to a little flat piece of land which was dry and very thick with trees and bushes and vines, and he says—

"You shove right in dah, jist a few steps, Mars Jawge, dah's whah dey is. I's seed 'm befo', I don't k'yer to see 'em no mo'."

Then he slopped right along and went away, and pretty soon the trees hid him. I poked into the place a-ways, and come to a little open patch as big as a bedroom, all hung around with vines, and found a man laying there asleep—and by jings it was my old Jim!

I waked him up, and I reckoned it was going to be a grand surprise to him to see me again, but it warn't. He nearly cried, he was so glad, but he warn't surprised. Said he swum along behind me, that night, and heard me yell every time, but dasn't answer, because he didn't want nobody to pick *him* up, and take him into slavery again. Says he—

"I got hurt a little, en couldn't swim fas', so I wuz a considable ways behine you, towards de las'; when you landed I reck'ned I could ketch up wid you on de lan' 'dout havin' to shout at you, but when I see dat house I begin to go slow. I 'uz off too fur to hear what dey say to you—I wuz 'fraid o' de dogs—but when it 'uz all quiet agin, I knowed you's in de house, so I struck out for de woods to wait for day. Early in de mawnin' some er de niggers come along, gwyne to de fields, en dey tuk me en showed me dis place, whah de dogs can't track me on accounts o' de water, en dey brings me truck to eat every night, en tells me how you's a gitt'n along."

"Why didn't you tell my Jack to fetch me here sooner, Jim?"

"Well, 'twarn't no use to 'sturb you, Huck, tell we could do sumfn—but we's all right, now. I ben a-buyin' pots en pans en vittles, as I got a chanst, en a patchin' up de raf', nights, when—"

"*What* raft, Jim?"

"Our ole raf'."

"You mean to say our old raft warn't smashed all to flinders?"

"No, she warn't. She was tore up a good deal—one en' of her was—but dey warn't no great harm done, on'y our traps was mos' all los'. Ef we hadn' dive' so deep en swum so fur under water, en de night hadn' ben so dark, en we warn't so sk'yerd, en ben sich punkin-heads, as de sayin' is, we'd a seed de raf'. But it's jis' as well we didn't, 'kase now she's all fixed up agin mos' as good as new, en we's got a new lot o' stuff, too, in de place o' what 'uz los'."

"Why, how did you get hold of the raft again, Jim—did you catch her?"

"How I gwyne to ketch her, en I out in de woods? No, some er de niggers foun' her ketched on a snag, along heah in de ben', en dey hid her in a crick, 'mongst de willows, en dey wuz so much jawin' 'bout which un 'um she b'long to de mos', dat I come to heah 'bout it pooty soon, so I ups en settles de trouble by tellin' 'um she don't b'long to none uv um, but to you en me; en I ast 'm if dey gwyne to grab a young white genlman's propaty, en git a hid'n for it? Den I gin 'm ten cents apiece, en dey 'uz mighty well satisfied, en wisht some mo' raf's 'ud come along en make 'm rich agin. Dey's mighty good to me, dese niggers is, en whatever I wants 'm to do fur me, I doan' have to ast 'm twice, honey. Dat Jack's a good nigger, en pooty smart."

"Yes, he is. He ain't ever told me you was here; told me to come, and he'd show me a lot of water-moccasins. If anything happens, *he* ain't mixed up in it. He can say he never seen us together, and it'll be the truth."

I don't want to talk much about the next day. I reckon I'll cut it pretty short. I waked up about dawn, and was agoing to turn over and go to sleep again, when I noticed how still it was—didn't seem to be anybody stirring. That warn't usual. Next I noticed that Buck was up and gone. Well, I gets up, a-wondering, and goes down stairs—nobody around; everything as still as a mouse. Just the same outside; thinks I, what does it mean? Down by the wood-pile I comes across my Jack, and says:

"What's it all about?"

Says he:

"Don't you know, Mars Jawge?"

"No," says I, "I don't."

"Well, den, Miss Sophia's run off! 'deed she has. She run off in de night, sometime—nobody don't know jis' when—run off to get married to dat young Harney Shepherdson, you know—leastways, so dey 'spec. De fambly foun' it out, 'bout half an hour ago—maybe a little mo'—en' I *tell* you dey warn't no time los'. Sich another hurryin' up guns en hosses *you* never see! De women folks has gone for to stir up de relations, en ole Mars Saul en de boys tuck dey guns en rode up de river road for to try to ketch dat young man en kill him 'fo' he kin git acrost de river wid Miss Sophia. I reck'n dey's gwyne to be mighty rough times."

"Buck went off 'thout waking me up."

"Well, I reck'n he *did!* Dey warn't gwyne to mix you up in it. Mars Buck he loaded up his gun en 'lowed he's gwyne to fetch home a Shepherdson or bust. Well, dey'll be plenty un 'm dah, I reck'n, en you bet you he'll fetch one ef he gits a chanst."

I took up the river road as hard as I could put. By-and-by I begin to hear guns a good ways off. When I come in sight of the log store and the wood-pile where the steamboats lands, I worked along under the trees and brush till I got to a good place, and then I clumb up into the forks of a cotton-wood that was out of reach, and watched. There was a wood-rank four foot high, a little ways in front of the tree, and first I was going to hide behind that; but maybe it was luckier I didn't.

There was four or five men cavorting around on their horses in the open place before the log store, cussing and yelling, and trying to get at a couple of young chaps that was behind the wood-rank alongside of the steamboat landing—but they couldn't come it. Every time one of them showed himself on the river side of the wood-pile he got shot at. The two boys was squatting back to back behind the pile, so they could watch both ways.

By-and-by the men stopped cavorting around and yelling. They started riding towards the store; then up gets one of the boys, draws a steady bead over the wood-rank, and drops one of them out of his saddle. All the men jumped off of their horses and grabbed the hurt one and started to carry him to the store; and that minute the two boys started on the run. They got half-way to the tree I was in before the men noticed. Then the men see them, and jumped on their horses and took out after them. They gained on the boys, but it didn't do no good, the boys had too good a start; they got to the wood-pile that was in front of my tree, and slipped in behind it, and so they had the bulge on the men again. One of the boys was Buck, and the other was a slim young chap about nineteen years old.

The men ripped around awhile, and then rode away. As soon as they was out of sight, I sung out to Buck and told him. He didn't know what to make of my voice coming out of the tree, at first. He was awful surprised. He told me to watch out sharp and let him know when the men come in sight again; said they was up to some devilment or other—wouldn't be gone long. I wished I was out of that tree, but I dasn't come down. Buck begun to cry and rip, and 'lowed that him and his cousin Joe (that was the other young chap) would make up for this day, yet. He said his father and his two brothers was killed, and two or three of the enemy. Said the Shepherdsons laid for them, in ambush. Buck said his father and brothers ought to waited for their relations—the Shepherdsons was too strong for them. I asked him what was become of young Harney and Miss Sophia. He said they'd got across the river and was safe. I was glad of that; but the way Buck did take on because he didn't manage to kill Harney that day he shot at him—I hain't ever heard anything like it.

All of a sudden, bang! bang! bang! goes three or four guns—the men had slipped around through the woods and come in from behind without their horses! The boys jumped for the river—both of them hurt—and as they swum down the current the men run along the bank shooting at them and singing out, "Kill them, kill them!" It made me so sick I most fell out of the tree. I ain't agoing to tell all that happened—it would make me sick again if I was to do that. I wished I hadn't ever come ashore that night, to see such things. I ain't ever going to get shut of them—lots of times I dream about them.

I staid in the tree till it begun to get dark, afraid to come down. Sometimes I heard guns away off in the woods; and twice I seen little gangs of men gallop past the log store with guns; so I reckoned the trouble was still a-going on. I was mighty downhearted; so I made up my mind I wouldn't ever go anear that house again, because I reckoned I was to blame, somehow. I judged that that piece of paper meant that Miss Sophia was to meet Harney somewheres at half-past two and run off; and I judged I ought to told her father about that paper and the curious way she acted, and then maybe he would a locked her up, and this awful mess wouldn't ever happened.

When I got down out of the tree, I crept along down the river bank a piece, and found the two bodies laying in the edge of the water, and tugged at them till I got them ashore; then I covered up their faces, and got away as quick as I could. I cried a little when I was covering up Buck's face, for he was mighty good to me.

It was just dark, now. I never went near the house, but struck through the woods and made for the swamp. Jim warn't on his island, so I tramped off in a hurry for the crick, and crowded through the willows, red-hot to jump aboard and get out of that awful country—the raft was gone! My souls, but I was scared! I couldn't get my breath for most a minute. Then I raised a yell. A voice not twenty-five foot from me, says—

"Good lan'! is dat you, honey? Doan' make no noise."

It was Jim's voice—nothing ever sounded so good before. I run along the bank a piece and got aboard, and Jim he grabbed me and hugged me, he was so glad to see me. He says—

"Laws bless you, chile, I 'uz right down sho' you's dead agin. Jack's been heah; he say he reck'n you's ben shot, kase you didn' come home no mo'; so I's jes' dis minute a startin' de raf' down towards de mouf er de crick, so's to be all ready for to shove out en leave soon as Jack comes agin en tells me for certain you *is* dead. Lawsy, I's mighty glad to git you back agin, honey."

I says—

"All right—that's mighty good; they won't find me, and they'll think I've been killed, and floated down the river—there's something up there that'll help them to think so—so don't you lose no time, Jim, but just shove off for the big water as fast as ever you can."

I never felt easy till the raft was two mile below there and out in the middle of the Mississippi. Then we hung up our signal lantern, and judged that we was free and safe once more. I hadn't had a bite to eat since yesterday, so Jim he got out some corn-dodgers and buttermilk, and pork and cabbage, and greens—there ain't nothing in the world so good, when it's cooked right—and whilst I eat my supper we talked, and had a good time. I was powerful glad to get away from the feuds, and so was Jim to get away from the swamp. We said there warn't no home like a raft, after all. Other places do seem so cramped up and smothery, but a raft don't. You feel mighty free and easy and comfortable on a raft.

Chapter XIX
Tying Up Day-times—An Astronomical Theory—Running a Temperance Revival—The Duke of Bridgewater—The Troubles of Royalty

Two or three days and nights went by; I reckon I might say they swum by, they slid along so quiet and smooth and lovely. Here is the way we put in the time. It was a monstrous big river down there—sometimes a mile and a half wide; we run nights, and laid up and hid day-times; soon as night was most gone, we stopped navigating and tied up—nearly always in the dead water under a tow-head; and then cut young cottonwoods and willows and hid the raft with them. Then we set out the lines. Next we slid into the river and had a swim, so as to freshen up and cool off; then we set down on the sandy bottom where the water was about knee deep, and watched the daylight come. Not a sound, anywheres—perfectly still—just like the whole world was asleep, only sometimes the bull-frogs a-cluttering, maybe. The first thing to see, looking away over the water, was a kind of dull line—that was the woods on t'other side—you couldn't make nothing else out; then a pale place in the sky; then more paleness, spreading around; then the river softened

HIDING DAY-TIMES.

up, away off, and warn't black any more, but gray; you could see little dark spots drifting along, ever so far away—trading scows, and such things; and long black streaks—rafts; sometimes you could hear a sweep screaking; or jumbled up voices, it was so still, and sounds come so far; and by-and-by you could see a streak on the water which you know by the look of the streak that there's a snag there in a swift current which breaks on it and makes that streak look that way; and you see the mist curl up off of the water, and the east reddens up, and the river, and you make out a log cabin in the edge of the woods, away on the bank on t'other side of the river, being a wood-yard, likely, and piled by them cheats so you can throw a dog through it anywheres; then the nice breeze springs up, and comes fanning you from over there, so cool and fresh, and sweet to smell, on ac-count of the woods and the flowers; but sometimes not that way, because they've left dead fish laying around, gars, and such, and they do get pretty rank; and next you've got the full day, and everything smiling in the sun, and the song-birds just going it!

A little smoke couldn't be noticed, now, so we would take some fish off of the lines, and cook up a hot breakfast. And afterwards we would watch the lonesomeness of the river, and kind of lazy along, and by-and-by lazy off to sleep. Wake up, by-and-by, and look to see what done it, and maybe see a steamboat, coughing along up stream, so far off towards the other side you couldn't tell nothing about her only whether she was a stern-wheel or side-wheel; then for about an hour there wouldn't be noth-ing to hear nor nothing to see—just solid lonesomeness. Next you'd see a raft sliding by, away off yonder, and maybe a galoot on it chopping, be-cause they're most always doing it on a raft; you'd see the axe flash and come down—you don't hear nothing; you see that axe go up again, and by the time it's above the man's head then you hear the *k'chunk!*—it had took all that time to come over the water. So we would put in the day, lazy-ing around, listening to the stillness. Once there was a thick fog, and the rafts and things that went by was beating tin pans so the steamboats wouldn't run over them. A scow or a raft went by so close we could hear them talking and cussing and laughing—heard them plain; but we couldn't see no sign of them; it made you feel crawly, it was like spirits carrying on that way in the air. Jim said he believed it was spirits; but I says:

"No, spirits wouldn't say, 'dern the dern fog.'"

Soon as it was night, out we shoved; when we got her out to about the middle, we let her alone, and let her float wherever the current wanted her to; then we lit the pipes, and dangled our legs in the water and talked about all kinds of things—we was always naked, day and night, whenever the mosquitoes would let us—the new clothes Buck's folks made for me was too good to be comfortable, and besides I didn't go much on clothes, no-how.

Sometimes we'd have that whole river all to ourselves for the longest time. Yonder was the banks and the islands, across the water; and maybe a spark—which was a candle in a cabin window—and sometimes on the water you could see a spark or two—on a raft or a scow, you know; and maybe you could hear a fiddle or a song coming over from one of them crafts. It's lovely to live on a raft. We had the sky, up there, all speckled with stars, and we used to lay on our backs and look up at them, and discuss about whether they was made, or only just happened—Jim he allowed they was made, but I allowed they happened; I judged it would have took too long to *make* so many. Jim said the moon could a *laid* them; well, that looked kind of reasonable, so I didn't say nothing against it, because I've seen a frog lay most as many, so of course it could be done. We used to watch the stars that fell, too, and see them streak down. Jim allowed they'd got spoiled and was hove out of the nest.

Once or twice of a night we would see a steamboat slipping along in the dark, and now and then she would belch a whole world of sparks up out of her chimbleys, and they would rain down in the river and look awful pretty; then she would turn a corner and her lights would wink out and her pow-wow shut off and leave the river still again; and by-and-by her waves would get to us, a long time after she was gone, and joggle the raft a bit, and after that you wouldn't hear nothing for you couldn't tell how long, except maybe frogs or something.

After midnight the people on shore went to bed, and then for two or three hours the shores was black—no more sparks in the cabin windows. These sparks was our clock—the first one that showed again meant morning was coming, so we hunted a place to hide and tie up, right away.

One morning about day-break, I found a canoe and crossed over a chute to the main shore—it was only two hundred yards—and paddled about a mile up a crick amongst the cypress woods, to see if I couldn't get some berries. Just as I was passing a place where a kind of a cow-path crossed the crick, here comes a couple of men tearing up the path as tight as they could foot it. I thought I was a goner, for whenever anybody was after anybody I judged it was *me*—or maybe Jim. I was about to dig out from there in a hurry, but they was pretty close to me then, and sung out and begged me to save their lives—said they hadn't been doing nothing, and was being chased for it—said there was men and dogs a-coming. They wanted to jump right in, but I says—

"Don't you do it. I don't hear the dogs and horses yet; you've got time to crowd through the brush and get up the crick a little ways; then you take to the water and wade down to me and get in—that'll throw the dogs off the scent."

They done it, and soon as they was aboard I lit out for our tow-head, and in about five or ten minutes we heard the dogs and the men away off, shouting. We heard them come along towards the crick, but couldn't see them; they seemed to stop and fool around a while; then, as we got further and further away all the time, we couldn't hardly hear them at all; by the time we had left a mile of woods behind us and struck the river, everything was quiet, and we paddled over to the tow-head and hid in the cotton-woods and was safe.

One of these fellows was about seventy, or upwards, and had a bald head and very gray whiskers. He had an old battered-up slouch hat on, and a greasy blue woolen shirt, and ragged old blue jeans britches stuffed into his boot tops, and home-knit galluses—no, he only had one. He had an old long-tailed blue jeans coat with slick brass buttons, flung over his arm, and both of them had big fat ratty-looking carpet-bags.

The other fellow was about thirty and dressed about as ornery. After breakfast we all laid off and talked, and the first thing that come out was that these chaps didn't know one another.

"What got you into trouble?" says the baldhead to t'other chap.

"Well, I'd been selling an article to take the tartar off the teeth—and it does take it off, too, and generly the enamel along with it—but I staid about one night longer than I ought to, and was just in the act of sliding out when I ran across you on the trail this side of town, and you told me they were coming, and begged me to help you to get off. So I told you I was expecting trouble myself and would scatter out *with* you. That's the whole yarn—what's yourn?"

"Well, I'd ben a-runnin' a little temperance revival thar 'bout a week, and was the pet of the women-folks, big and little, for I was makin' it mighty warm for the rummies, I *tell* you, and takin' as much as five or six dollars a night—ten cents a head, children and niggers free—and business a growin' all the time; when somehow or another a little report got around, last night, that I had a way of puttin' in my time with a private jug, on the sly. A nigger rousted me out this mornin', and told me the people was getherin' on the quiet, with their dogs and horses, and they'd be along pretty soon and give me 'bout half an hour's start, and then run me down, if they could; and if they got me they'd tar and feather me and ride me on a rail, sure. I didn't wait for no breakfast—I warn't hungry."

"Old man," said the young one, "I reckon we might double-team it together; what do you think?"

"I ain't undisposed. What's your line—mainly?"

"Jour printer, by trade; do a little in patent medicines; theater-actor—
tragedy, you know; take a turn at mesmerism and phrenology when there's
a chance; teach singing-geography school for a change; sling a lecture,
sometimes—oh, I do lots of things—most anything that comes handy, so
it ain't work. What's your lay?"

"I've done considerble in the doctoring way in my time. Layin' on
o' hands is my best holt—for cancer, and paralysis, and sich things; and I
k'n tell a fortune pretty good, when I've got somebody along to find out
the facts for me. Preachin's my line, too; and workin' camp-meetin's; and
missionaryin' around."

Nobody never said anything for a while; then the young man hove a
sigh and says—

"Alas!"

"What're you alassin' about?" says the baldhead.

"To think I should have lived to be leading such a life, and be degraded down into such company." And he begun to wipe the corner of his
eye with a rag.

"Dern your skin, ain't the company good enough for you?" says the
baldhead, pretty pert and uppish.

" Yes, it *is* good enough for me; it's as good as I deserve; for who
fetched me so low, when I was so high? *I* did myself. I don't blame *you,*
gentlemen—far from it; I don't blame anybody. I deserve it all. Let the cold
world do its worst; one thing I know—there's a grave somewhere for me.
The world may go on just as it's always done, and take everything from
me—loved ones, property, everything—but it can't take that. Some day
I'll lie down in it and forget it all, and my poor broken heart will be at
rest." He went on a-wiping.

"Drot your pore broken heart," says the baldhead; "what are you
heaving your pore broken heart at *us* f'r? *We* hain't done nothing."

"No, I know you haven't. I ain't blaming you, gentlemen. I brought
myself down—yes, I did it myself. It's right I should suffer—perfectly
right—I don't make any moan."

"Brought you down from whar? Whar was you brought down from?"

"Ah, you would not believe me; the world never believes—let it
pass—'tis no matter. The secret of my birth—"

"The secret of your birth! Do you mean to say—"

"Gentlemen," says the young man, very solemn, "I will reveal it to
you, for I feel I may have confidence in you. By rights I am a duke!"

Jim's eyes bugged out when he heard that; and I reckon mine did, too.
Then the baldhead says: "No! you can't mean it?"

"Yes. My great-grandfather, eldest son of the Duke of Bridgewater,
fled to this country about the end of the last century, to breathe the pure

air of freedom; married here, and died, leaving a son, his own father dying about the same time. The second son of the late duke seized the title and estates—the infant real duke was ignored. I am the lineal descendant of that infant—I am the rightful Duke of Bridgewater; and here am I, forlorn, torn from my high estate, hunted of men, despised by the cold world, ragged, worn, heart-broken, and degraded to the companionship of felons on a raft!"

Jim pitied him ever so much, and so did I. We tried to comfort him, but he said it warn't much use, he couldn't be much comforted; said if we was a mind to acknowledge him, that would do him more good than most anything else; so we said we would, if he would tell us how. He said we ought to bow, when we spoke to him, and say "Your Grace," or "My Lord," or "Your Lordship"—and he wouldn't mind it if we called him plain "Bridgewater," which he said was a title, anyway, and not a name; and one of us ought to wait on him at dinner, and do any little thing for him he wanted done.

Well, that was all easy, so we done it. All through dinner Jim stood around and waited on him, and says, "Will yo' Grace have some o' dis, or some o' dat?" and so on, and a body could see it was mighty pleasing to him.

But the old man got pretty silent, by-and-by—didn't have much to say, and didn't look pretty comfortable over all that petting that was going on around that duke. He seemed to have something on his mind. So, along in the afternoon, he says:

"Looky here, Bilgewater," he says, "I'm nation sorry for you, but you ain't the only person that's had troubles like that."

"No?"

"No, you ain't. You ain't the only person that's ben snaked down wrongfully out'n a high place."

"Alas!"

"No, you ain't the only person that's had a secret of his birth." And by jings, *he* begins to cry.

"Hold! What do you mean?"

"Bilgewater, kin I trust you?" says the old man, still sort of sobbing.

"To the bitter death!" He took the old man by the hand and squeezed it, and says, "That secret of your being: speak!"

"Bilgewater, I am the late Dauphin!" [35]

---

[35] "Louis XVII's ambiguous death inspired rumors concerning his whereabouts in the Louisiana region of the Mississippi River" (Lemaster and Wilson 235). Twain uses the King and the Duke to satirize not only royalty but the fraudulence in the exalted manners and preoccupations of Southern society.

You bet you Jim and me stared, this time. Then the duke says:
"You are what?"

"Yes, my friend, it is too true—your eyes is lookin' at this very moment on the pore disappeared Dauphin, Looy the Seventeen, son of Looy the Sixteen and Marry Antonette."

"You! At your age! No! You mean you're the late Charlemagne; you must be six or seven hundred years old, at the very least."

"Trouble has done it, Bilgewater, trouble has done it; trouble has brung these gray hairs and this premature balditude. Yes, gentlemen, you see before you, in blue jeans and misery, the wanderin', exiled, trampled-on, and sufferin' rightful King of France."

Well, he cried and took on so, that me and Jim didn't know hardly what to do, we was so sorry—and so glad and proud we'd got him with us, too. So we set in, like we done before with the duke, and tried to comfort *him*. But he said it warn't no use, nothing but to be dead and done with it all could do him any good; though he said it often made him feel easier and better for a while if people treated him according to his rights, and got down on one knee to speak to him, and always called him "Your Majesty," and waited on him first at meals, and didn't set down in his presence till he asked them. So Jim and me set to majestying him, and doing this and that and t'other for him, and standing up till he told us we might set down. This done him heaps of good, and so he got cheerful and comfortable. But the duke kind of soured on him, and didn't look a bit satisfied with the way things was going; still, the king acted real friendly towards him, and said the duke's great-grandfather and all the other Dukes of Bilgewater was a good deal thought of by *his* father and was allowed to come to the palace considerable; but the duke staid huffy a good while, till by-and-by the king says:

"Like as not we got to be together a blamed long time, on this h-yer raft, Bilgewater, and so what's the use o' your bein' sour? It'll only make things oncomfortable. It ain't my fault I warn't born a duke, it ain't your fault you warn't born a king—so what's the use to worry? Make the best o' things the way you find 'em, says I—that's my motto. This ain't no bad thing that we've struck here—plenty grub and an easy life—come, give us your hand, Duke, and le's all be friends."

The duke done it, and Jim and me was pretty glad to see it. It took away all the uncomfortableness, and we felt mighty good over it, because it would a been a miserable business to have any unfriendliness on the raft; for what you want, above all things, on a raft, is for everybody to be satisfied, and feel right and kind towards the others.

It didn't take me long to make up my mind that these liars warn't no kings nor dukes, at all, but just low-down humbugs and frauds. But I never

said nothing, never let on; kept it to myself; it's the best way; then you
don't have no quarrels, and don't get into no trouble. If they wanted us to
call them kings and dukes, I hadn't no objections, 'long as it would keep
peace in the family; and it warn't no use to tell Jim, so I didn't tell him. If
I never learnt nothing else out of pap, I learnt that the best way to get along
with his kind of people is to let them have their own way.

Chapter XX
Huck Explains—Laying Out a Campaign—
Working the Camp-meeting—A Pirate at the
Camp-meeting—The Duke as a Printer

They asked us considerable many questions; wanted to know what we
covered up the raft that way for, and laid by in the day-time instead of
running—was Jim a runaway nigger? Says I—
 "Goodness sakes, would a runaway nigger run *south?*"

ON THE RAFT.

No, they allowed he
wouldn't. I had to account for
things some way, so I says:
 "My folks was living in Pike
County, in Missouri, where I was
born, and they all died off but me
and pa and my brother Ike. Pa,
he 'lowed he'd break up and go
down and live with Uncle Ben,
who's got a little one-horse place
on the river, forty-four mile below Orleans. Pa was pretty poor,
and had some debts; so when
he'd squared up there warn't
nothing left but sixteen dollars
and our nigger, Jim. That warn't
enough to take us fourteen hundred mile, deck passage nor no
other way. Well, when the river
rose, pa had a streak of luck
one day; he ketched this piece of
a raft; so we reckoned we'd go
down to Orleans on it. Pa's luck
didn't hold out; a steamboat run

over the forrard corner of the raft, one night, and we all went overboard and dove under the wheel; Jim and me come up, all right, but pa was drunk, and Ike was only four years old, so they never come up no more. Well, for the next day or two we had considerable trouble, because people was always coming out in skiffs and trying to take Jim away from me, saying they believed he was a runaway nigger. We don't run day-times no more now; nights they don't bother us."

The duke says—

"Leave me alone to cipher out a way so we can run in the day-time if we want to. I'll think the thing over—I'll invent a plan that'll fix it. We'll let it alone for to-day, because of course we don't want to go by that town yonder in day-light—it mightn't be healthy."

Towards night it begun to darken up and look like rain; the heat lightning was squirting around, low down in the sky, and the leaves was beginning to shiver—it was going to be pretty ugly, it was easy to see that. So the duke and the king went to overhauling our wigwam, to see what the beds was like. My bed was a straw tick—better than Jim's, which was a corn-shuck tick; there's always cobs around about in a shuck tick, and they poke into you and hurt; and when you roll over, the dry shucks sound like you was rolling over in a pile of dead leaves; it makes such a rustling that you wake up. Well, the duke allowed he would take my bed; but the king allowed he wouldn't. He says—

"I should a reckoned the difference in rank would a sejested to you that a corn-shuck bed warn't just fitten for me to sleep on. Your Grace'll take the shuck bed yourself."

Jim and me was in a sweat again, for a minute, being afraid there was going to be some more trouble amongst them; so we was pretty glad when the duke says—

"'Tis my fate to be always ground into the mire under the iron heel of oppression. Misfortune has broken my once haughty spirit; I yield, I submit; 'tis my fate. I am alone in the world—let me suffer; I can bear it."

We got away as soon as it was good and dark. The king told us to stand well out towards the middle of the river, and not show a light till we got a long ways below the town. We come in sight of the little bunch of lights by-and-by—that was the town, you know—and slid by, about a half a mile out, all right. When we was three-quarters of a mile below, we hoisted up our signal lantern; and about ten o'clock it come on to rain and blow and thunder and lighten like everything; so the king told us to both stay on watch till the weather got better; then him and the duke crawled into the wigwam and turned in for the night. It was my watch below, till twelve, but I wouldn't a turned in, anyway, if I'd had a bed; because a body don't see such a storm as that every day in the week, not by a long sight.

My souls, how the wind did scream along! And every second or two there'd come a glare that lit up the white-caps for a half a mile around, and you'd see the islands looking dusty through the rain, and the trees thrashing around in the wind; then comes a *h-wack!*—bum! bum! bumble-umble-um-bum-bum-bum-bum—and the thunder would go rumbling and grumbling away, and quit—and then *rip* comes another flash and another sockdolager. The waves most washed me off the raft, sometimes, but I hadn't any clothes on, and didn't mind. We didn't have no trouble about snags; the lightning was glaring and flittering around so constant that we could see them plenty soon enough to throw her head this way or that and miss them.

I had the middle watch, you know, but I was pretty sleepy by that time, so Jim he said he would stand the first half of it for me; he was always mighty good, that way, Jim was. I crawled into the wigwam, but the king and the duke had their legs sprawled around so there warn't no show for me; so I laid outside—I didn't mind the rain, because it was warm, and the waves warn't running too high, now. About two they come up again, though, and Jim was going to call me, but he changed his mind because he reckoned they warn't high enough yet to do any harm; but he was mistaken about that, for pretty soon all of a sudden along comes a regular ripper, and washed me overboard. It most killed Jim a-laughing. He was the easiest nigger to laugh that ever was, anyway.

I took the watch, and Jim he laid down and snored away; and by-and-by the storm let up for good and all; and the first cabin-light that showed, I rousted him out and we slid the raft into hiding-quarters for the day.

The king got out an old ratty deck of cards, after breakfast, and him and the duke played seven-up a while, five cents a game. Then they got tired of it, and allowed they would "lay out a campaign," as they called it. The duke went down into his carpet-bag and fetched up a lot of little printed bills, and read them out loud. One bill said, "The celebrated Dr. Armand de Montalban of Paris," would "lecture on the Science of Phrenology" at such and such a place, on the blank day of blank, at ten cents admission, and "furnish charts of character at twenty-five cents apiece." The duke said that was *him*. In another bill he was the "world-renowned Shaksperean tragedian, Garrick the Younger,[36] of Drury Lane, London." In other bills he had a lot of other names and done other wonderful things, like finding

---

[36] David Garrick was an eighteenth-century British Shakespearean actor. "No English actor who was thriving in the profession would willingly have taken on the rigors of 'exile' in the colonies. The great Garrick never thought of doing so" (Shattuck 3).

water and gold with a "divining-rod," "dissipating witch-spells," and so on. By-and-by he says—

"But the histrionic muse is the darling. Have you ever trod the boards, Royalty?"

"No," says the king.

"You shall, then, before you're three days older, Fallen Grandeur," says the duke. "The first good town we come to, we'll hire a hall and do the sword-fight in Richard III[37] and the balcony scene in Romeo and Juliet. How does that strike you?"

"I'm in, up to the hub, for anything that will pay, Bilgewater, but you see I don't know nothing about play-actn', and hain't ever seen much of it. I was too small when pap used to have 'em at the palace. Do you reckon you can learn me?"

"Easy!"

"All right. I'm jist a-freezn' for something fresh, anyway. Less commence, right away."

So the duke he told him all about who Romeo was, and who Juliet was, and said he was used to being Romeo, so the king could be Juliet.

"But if Juliet's such a young gal, Duke, my peeled head and my white whiskers is goin' to look oncommon odd on her, maybe."

"No, don't you worry—these country jakes won't ever think of that. Besides, you know, you'll be in costume, and that makes all the difference in the world; Juliet's in a balcony, enjoying the moonlight before she goes to bed, and she's got on her night-gown and her ruffled night-cap. Here are the costumes for the parts."

He got out two or three curtain-calico suits, which he said was meedyevil armor for Richard III and t'other chap, and a long white cotton night-shirt and a ruffled night-cap to match. The king was satisfied; so the duke got out his book and read the parts over in the most splendid spread-eagle way, prancing around and acting at the same time, to show how it had got to be done; then he give the book to the king and told him to get his part by heart.

---

[37]Performances of Shakespeare were popular on the western frontier. Players, both American and British, put on shows in hotel ballrooms and dining rooms, breweries, circus rings, small theaters, and showboats. The frontiersman's love of oratory made Shakespeare popular. Further, "he also had a 'snobbish' value. Some western dwellers, who honoured culture and craved it, were glad to see Shakespeare and imbibe a little of the sophistication and fashion of the East. To see him was an 'opportunity.' The presentation of his plays, too, proclaimed that the frontier was not abysmally ignorant" (Dunn 176).

There was a little one-horse town about three mile down the bend, and after dinner the duke said he had ciphered out his idea about how to run in daylight without it being dangersome for Jim; so he allowed he would go down to the town and fix that thing. The king allowed he would go too, and see if he couldn't strike something. We was out of coffee, so Jim said I better go along with them in the canoe and get some.

When we got there, there warn't nobody stirring; streets empty, and perfectly dead and still, like Sunday. We found a sick nigger sunning himself in a back yard, and he said everybody that warn't too young or too sick or too old, was gone to camp-meeting, about two mile back in the woods. The king got the directions, and allowed he'd go and work that camp-meeting for all it was worth, and I might go, too.

The duke said what he was after was a printing office. We found it; a little bit of a concern, up over a carpenter shop—carpenters and printers all gone to the meeting, and no doors locked. It was a dirty, littered-up place, and had ink marks, and handbills with pictures of horses and runaway niggers on them, all over the walls. The duke shed his coat and said he was all right, now. So me and the king lit out for the camp-meeting.

We got there in about a half an hour, fairly dripping, for it was a most awful hot day. There was as much as a thousand people there, from twenty mile around. The woods was full of teams and wagons, hitched everywheres, feeding out of the wagon troughs and stomping to keep off the flies. There was sheds made out of poles and roofed over with branches, where they had lemonade and gingerbread to sell, and piles of watermelons and green corn and such-like truck.

The preaching was going on under the same kinds of sheds, only they was bigger and held crowds of people. The benches was made out of outside slabs of logs, with holes bored in the round side to drive sticks into for legs. They didn't have no backs. The preachers had high platforms to stand on, at one end of the sheds. The women had on sun-bonnets; and some had linsey-woolsey frocks, some gingham ones, and a few of the young ones had on calico. Some of the young men was barefooted, and some of the children didn't have on any clothes but just a tow-linen shirt. Some of the old women was knitting, and some of the young folks was courting on the sly.

The first shed we come to, the preacher was lining out a hymn. He lined out two lines, everybody sung it, and it was kind of grand to hear it, there was so many of them and they done it in such a rousing way; then he lined out two more for them to sing—and so on. The people woke up more and more, and sung louder and louder; and towards the end, some begun to groan, and some begun to shout. Then the preacher begun to preach; and begun in earnest, too; and went weaving first to one side of the platform and then the other, and then a leaning down over the front of it, with his arms and his body going all the time, and shouting his words out with all his might; and every now and then he would hold up his Bible and spread it open, and kind of pass it around this way and that, shouting, "It's the brazen serpent in the wilderness! Look upon it and live!" And people would shout out, "Glory!—A-a-*men!*" And so he went on, and the people groaning and crying and saying amen:

"Oh, come to the mourners' bench![38] come, black with sin! (*amen!*) come, sick and sore! (*amen!*) come, lame and halt, and blind! (*amen!*) come, pore and needy, sunk in shame! (*a-a-men!*) come all that's worn, and soiled, and suffering!—come with a broken spirit! come with a contrite heart! come in your rags and sin and dirt! the waters that cleanse is free, the door of heaven stands open—oh, enter in and be at rest!" (*a-a-men! glory, glory hallelujah!*)

And so on. You couldn't make out what the preacher said, any more, on account of the shouting and crying. Folks got up, everywheres in the crowd, and worked their way, just by main strength, to the mourners' bench, with the tears running down their faces; and when all the mourners had got up there to the front benches in a crowd, they sung, and shouted, and flung themselves down on the straw, just crazy and wild.

Well, the first I knowed, the king got agoing; and you could hear him over everybody; and next he went a-charging up on to the platform and the preacher he begged him to speak to the people, and he done it. He told them he was a pirate—been a pirate for thirty years, out in the Indian Ocean, and his crew was thinned out considerable, last spring, in a fight, and he was home now, to take out some fresh men, and thanks to goodness he'd been robbed last night, and put ashore off of a steamboat without a cent, and he was glad of it, it was the blessedest thing that ever happened to him, because he was a changed man now, and happy for the first time in his life; and poor as he was, he was going to start right off and work his way back to the Indian Ocean and put in the rest of his life trying to turn the pirates into the true path; for he could do it better than anybody else, being acquainted with all pirate crews in that ocean; and

---

[38] "In the larger camp-meetings the center of interest was the mourner's bench located directly in front of the pulpit. To the godly this structure was also known as the 'altar'; to the scoffers, because of its similarity to a hog enclosure, it was the 'pen'. . . . By definition, a mourner was, 'one who, becoming alarmed about the state of his soul, began to pray and seek deliverance from the bondage and domination of sin.' Thus the sinners who wished to be 'instructed' were isolated from the saved persons and sinners not yet moved" (Charles Johnson 133).

though it would take him a long time to get there, without money, he would get there anyway, and every time he convinced a pirate he would say to him, "Don't you thank me, don't you give me no credit, it all belongs to them dear people in Pokeville camp-meeting, natural brothers and bene-factors of the race—and that dear preacher there, the truest friend a pirate ever had!"

And then he busted into tears, and so did everybody. Then somebody sings out, "Take up a collection for him, take up a collection!" Well, a half a dozen made a jump to do it, but somebody sings out, "Let *him* pass the hat around!" Then everybody said it, the preacher too.

So the king went all through the crowd with his hat, swabbing his eyes, and blessing the people and praising them and thanking them for be-ing so good to the poor pirates away off there; and every little while the prettiest kind of girls, with the tears running down their cheeks, would up and ask him would he let them kiss him, for to remember him by; and he always done it; and some of them he hugged and kissed as many as five or six times—and he was invited to stay a week; and everybody wanted him to live in their houses, and said they'd think it was an honor; but he said as this was the last day of the camp-meeting he couldn't do no good, and besides he was in a sweat to get to the Indian Ocean right off and go to work on the pirates.

When we got back to the raft and he come to count up, he found he had collected eighty-seven dollars and seventy-five cents. And then he had fetched away a three-gallon jug of whisky, too, that he found under a wagon when he was starting home through the woods. The king said, take it all around, it laid over any day he'd ever put in in the missionarying line. He said it warn't no use talking, heathens don't amount to shucks, along-side of pirates, to work a camp-meeting with.

The duke was thinking *he'd* been doing pretty well, till the king come to show up, but after that he didn't think so so much. He had set up and printed off two little jobs for farmers, in that printing office—horse bills—and took the money, four dollars. And he had got in ten dollars worth of advertisements for the paper, which he said he would put in for four dol-lars if they would pay in advance—so they done it. The price of the paper was two dollars a year, but he took in three subscriptions for half a dollar apiece on condition of them paying him in advance; they were going to pay in cord-wood and onions, as usual, but he said he had just bought the con-cern and knocked down the price as low as he could afford it, and was go-ing to run it for cash. He set up a little piece of poetry, which he made, him-self, out of his own head—three verses—kind of sweet and saddish—the name of it was, "Yes, crush, cold world, this breaking heart"—and he left that all set up and ready to print in the paper and didn't charge nothing for it. Well, he took in nine dollars and a half, and said he'd done a pretty square day's work for it.

Then he showed us another little job he'd printed and hadn't charged for, because it was for us. It had a picture of a runaway nigger, with a bundle on a stick,[39] over his shoulder, and "$200 reward" under it. The reading was all about Jim, and just described him to a dot. It said he run away from St. Jacques' plantation, forty mile below New Orleans, last winter, and likely went north, and whoever would catch him and send him back, he could have the reward and expenses.

"Now," says the duke, "after to-night we can run in the daytime if we want to. Whenever we see anybody coming, we can tie Jim hand and foot with a rope, and lay him in the wigwam and show this handbill and say we captured him up the river, and were too poor to travel on a steamboat, so we got this little raft on credit from our friends and are going down to get the reward. Handcuffs and chains would look still better on Jim, but it wouldn't go well with the story of us being so poor. Too much like jewelry. Ropes are the correct thing—we must preserve the unities, as we say on the boards."

We all said the duke was pretty smart, and there couldn't be no trouble about running daytimes. We judged we could make miles enough that night to get out of the reach of the pow-wow we reckoned the duke's work in the printing office was going to make in that little town—then we could boom right along, if we wanted to.

We laid low and kept still, and never shoved out till nearly ten o'clock; then we slid by, pretty wide away from the town, and didn't hoist our lantern till we was clear out of sight of it.

When Jim called me to take the watch at four in the morning, he says—

"Huck, does you reck'n we gwyne to run acrost any mo' kings on dis trip?"

"No," I says, "I reckon not."

---

[39] This image of an escaping male slave was popular on posters during the period. Slave traders offered large sums on these advertisements, which also featured bold lettering and eye-catching layouts. One ad from 1853 reads: "$1200 to 1250 DOLLARS! FOR NEGROES!! The undersigned wishes to purchase a large lot of NEGROES for the New Orleans market. I will pay $1200 to $1250 for No. 1 young men, and $850 to $1000 for No. 1 young women. In fact I will pay more for likely NEGROES, than any other trader in Kentucky. My office is adjoining the Broadway Hotel, on Broadway, Lexington, Ky., where I or my Agent can always be found. WM. F. TALBOTT. Lexington, July 2, 1853" (Claudia Johnson 115).

"Well," says he, "dat's all right, den. I doan' mine one er two kings, but dat's enough. Dis one's powerful drunk, en de duke ain' much better."

I found Jim had been trying to get him to talk French, so he could hear what it was like; but he said he had been in this country so long, and had so much trouble, he'd forgot it.

Chapter XXI
Sword Exercise—Hamlet's Soliloquy—
They Loafed Around Town—A Lazy Town—
Old Boggs—Dead

It was after sun-up, now, but we went right on, and didn't tie up. The king and the duke turned out, by-and-by, looking pretty rusty; but after they'd jumped overboard and took a swim, it chippered them up a good deal. After breakfast the king he took a seat on a corner of the raft, and pulled off his boots and rolled up his britches, and let his legs dangle in the water, so as to be comfortable, and lit his pipe, and went to getting his Romeo and Juliet by heart. When he had got it pretty good, him and the duke begun to practice it together. The duke had to learn him over and over again, how to say every speech; and he made him sigh, and put his hand on his heart, and after while he said he done it pretty well; "only," he says, "you mustn't bellow out *Romeo!* that way, like a bull—you must say it soft, and sick, and languishy, so—R-o-o-meo! that is the idea; for Juliet's a dear sweet mere child of a girl, you know, and she don't bray like a jackass."

PRACTICING.

Well, next they got out a couple of long swords that the duke made out of oak laths, and begun to practice the sword-fight—the duke called himself Richard III; and the way they laid on, and pranced around the raft was grand to see. But by-and-by the king tripped and fell overboard, and after that they took a rest, and had a talk about all kinds of adventures they'd had in other times along the river.

After dinner the duke says:

"Well, Capet,[40] we'll want to make this a first-class show, you know, so I guess we'll add a little more to it. We want a little something to answer encores with, anyway."

"What's onkores, Bilgewater?"

The duke told him, and then says:

"I'll answer by doing the Highland fling or the sailor's hornpipe; and you—well, let me see—oh, I've got it you can do Hamlet's soliloquy."

"Hamlet's which?"

"Hamlet's soliloquy, you know; the most celebrated thing in Shakespeare. Ah, it's sublime, sublime! Always fetches the house. I haven't got it in the book—I've only got one volume—but I reckon I can piece it out from memory. I'll just walk up and down a minute, and see if I can call it back from recollection's vaults."

So he went to marching up and down, thinking, and frowning horrible every now and then; then he would hoist up his eyebrows; next he would squeeze his hand on his forehead and stagger back and kind of moan; next he would sigh, and next he'd let on to drop a tear. It was beautiful to see him. By-and-by he got it. He told us to give attention. Then he strikes a most noble attitude, with one leg shoved forwards, and his arms stretched away up, and his head tilted back, looking up at the sky; and then he begins to rip and rave and grit his teeth; and after that, all through his speech he howled, and spread around, and swelled up his chest, and just knocked the spots out of any acting ever *I* see before. This is the speech—I learned it, easy enough, while he was learning it to the king:

To be, or not to be;[41] that is the bare bodkin
That makes calamity of so long life;
For who would fardels bear, till Birnam Wood do come to
    Dunsinane,
5   But that the fear of something after death
Murders the innocent sleep,
Great nature's second course,

---

[40] Thomas Carlyle's *History of the French Revolution,* a book from which Twain often drew, revealed that Louis XVI was addressed as Citizen Louis Capet after his dethronement.

[41] The Duke garbles Hamlet's soliloquy with lines from *Macbeth* and *Richard III.*

And makes us rather sling the arrows of outrageous fortune
Than fly to others that we know not of.
10   There's the respect must give us pause:
Wake Duncan with thy knocking! I would thou couldst;
For who would bear the whips and scorns of time,
The oppressor's wrong, the proud man's contumely,
The law's delay, and the quietus which his pangs might take,
15   In the dead waste and middle of the night, when churchyards yawn
In customary suits of solemn black,
But that the undiscovered country from whose bourne no traveler
      returns,
Breathes forth contagion on the world,
20   And thus the native hue of resolution, like the poor cat i' the adage,
Is sicklied o'er with care,
And all the clouds that lowered o'er our housetops,
With this regard their currents turn awry,
And lose the name of action.
25   'Tis a consummation devoutly to be wished. But soft you, the fair
      Ophelia:
Ope not thy ponderous and marble jaws,
But get thee to a nunnery—go!

Well, the old man he liked that speech, and he mighty soon got it so
he could do it first rate. It seemed like he was just born for it; and when he
had his hand in and was excited, it was perfectly lovely the way he would
rip and tear and rair up behind when he was getting it off.

The first chance we got, the duke he had some show bills printed;
and after that, for two or three days as we floated along, the raft was
a most uncommon lively place, for there warn't nothing but sword-
fighting and rehearsing—as the duke called it—going on all the time. One
morning, when we was pretty well down the State of Arkansaw, we
come in sight of a little one-horse town in a big bend; so we tied up about
three-quarters of a mile above it, in the mouth of a crick which was shut
in like a tunnel by the cypress trees, and all of us but Jim took the canoe and went down there to see if there was any chance in that place for
our show.

We struck it mighty lucky; there was going to be a circus there that
afternoon, and the country people was already beginning to come in, in
all kinds of old shackly wagons, and on horses. The circus would leave before night, so our show would have a pretty good chance. The duke he
hired the court house, and we went around and stuck up our bills. They
read like this:

SHAKSPEREAN REVIVAL!!!
WONDERFUL ATTRACTION!
FOR ONE NIGHT ONLY!

The world renowned tragedians,
David Garrick the younger,
of Drury Lane Theatre, London,
and
Edmund Kean the elder,[42] of the Royal Haymarket Theatre,
White-chapel, Pudding Lane, Piccadilly, London, and the
Royal Continental Theatres, in their sublime
Shaksperean Spectacle entitled

The Balcony Scene
in
Romeo and Juliet!!!

Romeo . . . . Mr. Garrick
Juliet . . . . Mr. Kean
Assisted by the whole strength of the company!
New costumes, new scenery, new appointments!
Also:
The thrilling, masterly, and blood-curdling
Broad-sword conflict
In Richard III!!!
Richard III . . . Mr. Garrick
Richmond . . . Mr. Kean
also:
(by special request)
Hamlet's Immortal Soliloquy!!
By the Illustrious Kean!
Done by him 300 consecutive nights in Paris!
For One Night Only,
On account of imperative European engagements!
Admission 25 cents; children and servants, 10 cents.

---

[42] Kean, a popular Shakespearean actor who arrived in New York in 1820, proves an interestingly appropriate alter ego for the King. In 1821 his refusal to perform *Richard III*

Then we went loafing around the town. The stores and houses was most all old shackly dried-up frame concerns that hadn't ever been painted; they was set up three or four foot above ground on stilts, so as to be out of reach of the water when the river was overflowed. The houses had little gardens around them, but they didn't seem to raise hardly anything in them but jimpson weeds, and sunflowers, and ash-piles, and old curled-up boots and shoes, and pieces of bottles, and rags, and played-out tin-ware. The fences was made of different kinds of boards, nailed on at different times; and they leaned every which-way, and had gates that didn't generly have but one hinge—a leather one. Some of the fences had been white-washed, some time or another, but the duke said it was in Clumbus's time, like enough. There was generly hogs in the garden, and people driving them out.

All the stores was along one street. They had white-domestic awnings in front, and the country people hitched their horses to the awning-posts. There was empty dry-goods boxes under the awnings, and loafers roosting on them all day long, whittling them with their Barlow knives; and chawing tobacco, and gaping and yawning and stretching—a mighty ornery lot. They generly had on yellow straw hats most as wide as an umbrella, but didn't wear no coats nor waistcoats; they called one another Bill, and Buck, and Hank, and Joe, and Andy, and talked lazy and drawly, and used considerable many cuss-words. There was as many as one loafer leaning up against every awning-post, and he most always had his hands in his britches pockets, except when he fetched them out to lend a chaw of tobacco or scratch. What a body was hearing amongst them, all the time was—

"Gimme a chaw'v tobacker, Hank."

"Cain't—I hain't got but one chaw left. Ask Bill."

Maybe Bill he gives him a chaw; maybe he lies and says he ain't got none. Some of them kinds of loafers never has a cent in the world, nor a chaw of tobacco of their own. They get all their chawing by borrowing— they say to a fellow, "I wisht you'd len' me a chaw, Jack, I jist this minute give Ben Thompson the last chaw I had"—which is a lie, pretty much every time; it don't fool nobody but a stranger; but Jack ain't no stranger, so he says—

---

to a Boston audience he deemed insultingly small (20 patrons) injured his popularity in America. In 1825 he attempted to play the lead in another Boston production of *Richard III*. This time the show sold out, with the gallery and pit packed with "anti-Keanites." "Outside, a mob milled in the streets. When Kean appeared on the stage in street clothes to make his apology he was not allowed to speak. They pelted him with nuts, cakes, bottles of 'offensive drugs,' and more insulting missiles. Kean . . . precipi-tated . . . the first really all-out theater riot in America" (Shattuck 43).

"*You* give him a chaw, did you? so did your sister's cat's grandmother. You pay me back the chaws you've awready borry'd off'n me, Lafe Buckner, then I'll loan you one or two ton of it, and won't charge you no back intrust, nuther."

"Well, I *did* pay you back some of it wunst."

"Yes, you did—'bout six chaws. You borry'd store tobacker and paid back nigger-head."

Store tobacco is flat black plug, but these fellows mostly chaws the natural leaf twisted. When they borrow a chaw, they don't generly cut it off with a knife, but they set the plug in between their teeth, and gnaw with their teeth and tug at the plug with their hands till they get it in two—then sometimes the one that owns the tobacco looks mournful at it when it's handed back, and says, sarcastic—

"Here, gimme the *chaw*, and you take the *plug*."

All the streets and lanes was just mud, they warn't nothing else but mud—mud as black as tar, and nigh about a foot deep in some places; and two or three inches deep in *all* the places. The hogs loafed and grunted around, everywheres. You'd see a muddy sow and a litter of pigs come lazying along the street and whollop herself right down in the way, where folks had to walk around her, and she'd stretch out, and shut her eyes, and wave her ears, whilst the pigs was milking her, and look as happy as if she was on salary. And pretty soon you'd hear a loafer sing out, "Hi! *so* boy! sick him, Tige!" and away the sow would go, squealing most horrible, with a dog or two swinging to each ear, and three or four dozen more a-coming; and then you would see all the loafers get up and watch the thing out of sight, and laugh at the fun and look grateful for the noise. Then they'd settle back again till there was a dog-fight. There couldn't anything wake them up all over, and make them happy all over, like a dog fight—unless it might be putting turpentine on a stray dog and setting fire to him, or tying a tin pan to his tail and see him run himself to death.

On the river front some of the houses was sticking out over the bank, and they was bowed and bent, and about ready to tumble in. The people had moved out of them. The bank was caved away under one corner of some others, and that corner was hanging over. People lived in them yet, but it was dangersome, because sometimes a strip of land as wide as a house caves in at a time. Sometimes a belt of land a quarter of a mile deep will start in and cave along and cave along till it all caves into the river in one summer. Such a town as that has to be always moving back, and back, and back, because the river's always gnawing at it.

The nearer it got to noon that day, the thicker and thicker was the wagons and horses in the streets, and more coming all the time. Families fetched their dinners with them, from the country, and eat them in the wagons. There was considerable whisky drinking going on, and I seen three fights. By-and-by somebody sings out—

"Here comes old Boggs!—in from the country for his little old monthly drunk—here he comes, boys!"

All the loafers looked glad—I reckoned they was used to having fun out of Boggs. One of them says—

"Wonder who he's a gwyne to chaw up this time. If he'd a chawed up all the men he's ben a gwyne to chaw up in the last twenty year, he'd have considerable ruputation, now."

Another one says, "I wisht old Boggs'd threaten me, 'cuz then I'd know I warn't gwyne to die for a thousan' year."

Boggs comes a-tearing along on his horse, whooping and yelling like an Injun, and singing out—

"Cler the track, thar. I'm on the waw-path, and the price uv coffins is a gwyne to raise."

He was drunk, and weaving about in his saddle; he was over fifty year old, and had a very red face. Everybody yelled at him, and laughed at him, and sassed him, and he sassed back, and said he'd attend to them and lay them out in their regular turns, but he couldn't wait now, because he'd come to town to kill old Colonel Sherburn, and his motto was, "meat first, and spoon vittles to top off on."

He see me, and rode up and says—

"Whar'd you come f'm, boy? You prepared to die?"

Then he rode on. I was scared; but a man says—

"He don't mean nothing; he's always a carryin' on like that, when he's drunk. He's the best-naturedest old fool in Arkansaw—never hurt nobody, drunk nor sober."

Boggs rode up before the biggest store in town and bent his head down so he could see under the curtain of the awning, and yells—

"Come out here, Sherburn! Come out and meet the man you've swindled. You're the houn' I'm after, and I'm agwyne to have you, too!"

And so he went on, calling Sherburn everything he could lay his tongue to, and the whole street packed with people listening and laughing and going on. By-and-by a proud-looking man about fifty-five—and he was a heap the best dressed man in that town, too—steps out of the store, and the crowd drops back on each side to let him come. He says to Boggs, mighty ca'm and slow—he says:

"I'm tired of this; but I'll endure it till one o'clock. Till one o'clock, mind—no longer. If you open your mouth against me only once, after that time, you can't travel so far but I will find you."

Then he turns and goes in. The crowd looked mighty sober; nobody stirred, and there warn't no more laughing. Boggs rode off blackguarding

Sherburn as loud as he could yell, all down the street; and pretty soon back he comes and stops before the store, still keeping it up. Some men crowded around him and tried to get him to shut up, but he wouldn't; they told him it would be one o'clock in about fifteen minutes, and so he *must* go home—he must go right away. But it didn't do no good. He cussed away, with all his might, and throwed his hat down in the mud and rode over it, and pretty soon away he went a-raging down the street again, with his gray hair a-flying. Everybody that could get a chance at him tried their best to coax him off of his horse so they could lock him up and get him sober; but it warn't no use—up the street he would tear again, and give Sherburn another cussing. By-and-by somebody says—

"Go for his daughter!—quick, go for his daughter; sometimes he'll listen to her. If anybody can persuade him, she can."

So somebody started on a run. I walked down street a ways, and stopped. In about five or ten minutes, here comes Boggs again—but not on his horse. He was a-reeling across the street towards me, bareheaded, with a friend on both sides of him aholt of his arms and hurrying him along. He was quiet, and looked uneasy; and he warn't hanging back any, but was doing some of the hurrying himself. Somebody sings out—

"Boggs!"

I looked over there to see who said it, and it was that Colonel Sherburn. He was standing perfectly still, in the street, and had a pistol raised in his right hand—not aiming it, but holding it out with the barrel tilted up towards the sky. The same second I see a young girl coming on the run, and two men with her. Boggs and the men turned round, to see who called him, and when they see the pistol the men jumped to one side, and the pistol barrel come down slow and steady to a level—both barrels cocked. Boggs throws up both of his hands, and says, "O Lord, don't shoot!" Bang! goes the first shot, and he staggers back clawing at the air—bang! goes the second one, and he tumbles backwards onto the ground, heavy and solid, with his arms spread out. That young girl screamed out, and comes rushing, and down she throws herself on her father, crying, and saying, "Oh, he's killed him, he's killed him!" The crowd closed up around them, and shouldered and jammed one another, with their necks stretched, trying to see, and people on the inside trying to shove them back, and shouting, "Back, back! give him air, give him air!"

Colonel Sherburn he tossed his pistol onto the ground, and turned around on his heels and walked off.[43]

---

[43] Twain bases this passage on the 1845 murder of Sam Smarr by William Owsley. Dueling was a common practice during the nineteenth century. In *Life on the Mississippi,*

They took Boggs to a little drug store, the crowd pressing around, just the same, and the whole town following, and I rushed and got a good place at the window, where I was close to him and could see in. They laid him on the floor, and put one large Bible under his head, and opened another one and spread it on his breast—but they tore open his shirt first, and I seen where one of the bullets went in. He made about a dozen long gasps, his breast lifting the Bible up when he drawed in his breath, and letting it down again when he breathed it out—and after that he laid still; he was dead. Then they pulled his daughter away from him, screaming and crying, and took her off. She was about sixteen, and very sweet and gentlelooking, but awful pale and scared.

Well, pretty soon the whole town was there, squirming and scrouging and pushing and shoving to get at the window and have a look, but people that had the places wouldn't give them up, and folks behind them was saying all the time, "Say, now, you've looked enough, you fellows; 'tain't right and 'tain't fair, for you to stay thar all the time, and never give nobody a chance; other folks has their rights as well as you."

There was considerable jawing back, so I slid out, thinking maybe there was going to be trouble. The streets was full, and everybody was excited. Everybody that seen the shooting was telling how it happened, and there was a big crowd packed around each one of these fellows, stretching their necks and listening. One long lanky man, with long hair and a big white fur stove-pipe hat on the back of his head, and a crooked-handled cane, marked out the places on the ground where Boggs stood, and where Sherburn stood, and the people following him around from one place to t'other and watching everything he done, and bobbing their heads to show they understood, and stooping a little and resting their hands on their thighs to watch him mark the places on the ground with his cane; and then he stood up straight and stiff where Sherburn had stood, frowning and having his hat-brim down over his eyes, and sung out, "Boggs!" and then fetched his cane down slow to a level, and says "Bang!" staggered backwards, says "Bang!" again, and fell down flat on his back. The people that had seen the thing said he done it perfect; said it was just exactly the way it all happened. Then as much as a dozen people got out their bottles and treated him.

Twain railed against such violence, fueled by the code of honor romanticized in novels by Sir Walter Scott: "The genuine and wholesome civilization of the nineteenth century is curiously confused and commingled with the Walter Scott Middle-Age sham civilization, and so you have practical common-sense progressive ideas, and progressive works, mixed up with the duel, the inflated speech, and the jejune romanticism of an absurd past that is dead, and out of charity ought to be buried" (266). See the narrative of Austin Steward in Weeks for another vivid account of dueling.

Well, by-and-by somebody said Sherburn ought to be lynched. In about a minute everybody was saying it; so away they went, mad and yelling, and snatching down every clothes-line they come to, to do the hanging with.

Chapter XXII
Sherburn—Attending the Circus—Intoxication
in the Ring—The Thrilling Tragedy

They swarmed up the street towards Sherburn's house, a-whooping and yelling and raging like Injuns, and everything had to clear the way or get run over and tromped to mush, and it was awful to see. Children was heeling it ahead of the mob, screaming and trying to get out of the way; and every window along the road was full of women's heads, and there was nigger boys in every tree, and bucks and wenches looking over every fence; and as soon as the mob would get nearly to them they would break and skaddle back out of reach. Lots of the women and girls was crying and taking on, scared most to death.

They swarmed up in front of Sherburn's palings as thick as they could jam together, and you couldn't hear yourself think for the noise. It was a little twenty-foot yard. Some sung out "Tear down the fence! tear down the fence!" Then there was a racket of ripping and tearing and smashing, and down she goes, and the front wall of the crowd begins to roll in like a wave.

Just then Sherburn steps out on to the roof of his little front porch, with a double-barrel gun in his hand, and takes his stand, perfectly ca'm and deliberate, not saying a word. The racket stopped, and the wave sucked back.

SHERBURN STEPS OUT.

Sherburn never said a word—just stood there, looking down. The stillness was awful creepy and uncomfortable. Sherburn run his eye slow along the crowd; and wherever it struck, the people tried a little to outgaze him, but they couldn't; they dropped their eyes and looked sneaky. Then pretty soon Sherburn sort of laughed; not the pleasant kind, but the kind that makes you feel like when you are eating bread that's got sand in it.

Then he says, slow and scornful:

"The idea of *you* lynching anybody![44] It's amusing. The idea of you thinking you had pluck enough to lynch a *man!* Because you're brave enough to tar and feather poor friendless cast-out women that come along here, did that make you think you had grit enough to lay your hands on a *man?* Why, a *man's* safe in the hands of ten thousand of your kind—as long as it's day-time and you're not behind him.

"Do I know you? I know you clear through. I was born and raised in the South, and I've lived in the North; so I know the average all around. The average man's a coward. In the North he lets anybody walk over him that wants to, and goes home and prays for a humble spirit to bear it. In the South one man, all by himself, has stopped a stage full of men, in the day-time, and robbed the lot. Your newspapers call you a brave people so much that you think you *are* braver than any other people—whereas you're just *as* brave, and no braver. Why don't your juries hang murderers? Because they're afraid the man's friends will shoot them in the back, in the dark—and it's just what they *would* do.

"So they always acquit; and then a *man* goes in the night, with a hundred masked cowards at his back, and lynches the rascal. Your mistake is, that you didn't bring a man with you; that's one mistake, and the other is that you didn't come in the dark, and fetch your masks. You brought *part* of a man—Buck Harkness, there—and if you hadn't had him to start you, you'd a taken it out in blowing.

"You didn't want to come. The average man don't like trouble and danger. *You* don't like trouble and danger. But if only *half* a man—like Buck Harkness, there—shouts 'Lynch him! lynch him!' you're afraid to back down—afraid you'll be found out to be what you are—*cowards*—and so you raise a yell, and hang yourselves onto that half-a-man's coat tail, and come raging up here, swearing what big things you're going to do. The pitifulest thing out is a mob; that's what an army is—a mob; they don't fight with courage that's born in them, but with courage that's bor-

---

[44] Twain uses Colonel Sherburn not only to satirize the southern code of honor, but to attack the entire violent structure of the South's social system. Twain essentially uses Sherburn as a mouthpiece in this passage, inveighing against mob violence and lynchings common to the period.

rowed from their mass, and from their officers. But a mob without any *man* at the head of it, is *beneath* pitifulness. Now the thing for *you* to do, is to droop your tails and go home and crawl in a hole. If any real lynching's going to be done, it will be done in the dark, Southern fashion; and when they come they'll bring their masks, and fetch a *man* along. Now *leave*—and take your half-a-man with you"—tossing his gun up across his left arm and cocking it, when he says this.

The crowd washed back sudden, and then broke all apart and went tearing off every which way, and Buck Harkness he heeled it after them, looking tolerable cheap. I could a staid, if I'd a wanted to, but I didn't want to.

I went to the circus, and loafed around the back side till the watchman went by, and then dived in under the tent. I had my twenty-dollar gold piece and some other money, but I reckoned I better save it, because there ain't no telling how soon you are going to need it, away from home and amongst strangers, that way. You can't be too careful. I ain't opposed to spending money on circuses, when there ain't no other way, but there ain't no use in *wasting* it on them.

It was a real bully circus. It was the splendidest sight that ever was, when they all come riding in, two and two, a gentleman and lady, side by side, the men just in their drawers and under-shirts, and no shoes nor stirrups, and resting their hands on their thighs, easy and comfortable—there must a' been twenty of them—and every lady with a lovely complexion, and perfectly beautiful, and looking just like a gang of real sure-enough queens, and dressed in clothes that cost millions of dollars, and just littered with diamonds. It was a powerful fine sight; I never see anything so lovely. And then one by one they got up and stood, and went a-weaving around the ring so gentle and wavy and graceful, the men looking ever so tall and airy and straight, with their heads bobbing and skimming along, away up there under the tent-roof, and every lady's rose-leafy dress flapping soft and silky around her hips, and she looking like the most loveliest parasol.

And then faster and faster they went, all of them dancing, first one foot stuck out in the air and then the other, the horses leaning more and more, and the ring-master going round and round the centre-pole, cracking his whip and shouting "hi!—hi!" and the clown cracking jokes behind him; and by-and-by all hands dropped the reins, and every lady put her knuckles on her hips and every gentleman folded his arms, and then how the horses did lean over and hump themselves! And so, one after the other they all skipped off into the ring, and made the sweetest bow I ever see, and then scampered out, and everybody clapped their hands and went just about wild.

Well, all through the circus they done the most astonishing things; and all the time that clown carried on so it most killed the people. The ringmaster couldn't ever say a word to him but he was back at him quick as a wink with the funniest things a body ever said; and how he ever *could* think of so many of them, and so sudden and so pat, was what I couldn't noway understand. Why, I couldn't a thought of them in a year. And by-and-by a drunk man tried to get into the ring—said he wanted to ride; said he could ride as well as anybody that ever was. They argued and tried to keep him out, but he wouldn't listen, and the whole show come to a stand-still. Then the people begun to holler at him and make fun of him, and that made him mad, and he begun to rip and tear; so that stirred up the people, and a lot of men begun to pile down off of the benches and swarm towards the ring, saying, "Knock him down! throw him out!" and one or two women begun to scream. So, then, the ring-master he made a little speech, and said he hoped there wouldn't be no disturbance, and if the man would promise he wouldn't make no more trouble, he would let him ride, if he thought he could stay on the horse. So everybody laughed and said all right, and the man got on. The minute he was on, the horse begun to rip and tear and jump and cavort around, with two circus men hanging onto his bridle trying to hold him, and the drunk man hanging onto his neck, and his heels flying in the air every jump, and the whole crowd of people standing up shouting and laughing till tears rolled down. And at last, sure enough, all the circus men could do, the horse broke loose, and away he went like the very nation, round and round the ring, with that sot laying down on him and hanging to his neck, with first one leg hanging most to the ground on one side, and then t'other one on t'other side, and the people just crazy. It warn't funny to me, though; I was all of a tremble to see his danger. But pretty soon he struggled up astraddle and grabbed the bridle, a-reeling this way and that; and the next minute he sprung up and dropped the bridle and stood! and the horse a-going like a house afire too. He just stood up there, a-sailing around as easy and comfortable as if he warn't ever drunk in his life—and then he begun to pull off his clothes and sling them. He shed them so thick they kind of clogged up the air, and altogether he shed seventeen suits. And then, there he was, slim and handsome, and dressed the gaudiest and prettiest you ever saw, and he lit into that horse with his whip and made him fairly hum—and finally skipped off, and made his bow and danced off to the dressing-room, and everybody just a-howling with pleasure and astonishment.

Then the ring-master he see how he had been fooled, and he *was* the sickest ring-master you ever see, I reckon. Why, it was one of his own men! He had got up that joke all out of his own head, and never let on to no-body. Well, I felt sheepish enough, to be took in so, but I wouldn't a been in that ring-master's place, not for a thousand dollars. I don't know; there may be bullier circuses than what that one was, but I never struck them yet. Anyways it was plenty good enough for *me;* and wherever I run across it, it can have all of *my* custom, every time.

Well, that night we had *our* show; but there warn't only about twelve people there; just enough to pay expenses. And they laughed all the time, and that made the duke mad; and everybody left, anyway, before the show was over, but one boy which was asleep. So the duke said these Arkansaw lunkheads couldn't come up to Shakspeare; what they wanted was low comedy—and may be something ruther worse than low comedy, he reckoned. He said he could size their style. So next morning he got some big sheets of wrapping-paper and some black paint, and drawed off some handbills and stuck them up all over the village. The bills said:

AT THE COURT HOUSE!

FOR 3 NIGHTS ONLY!

The World-Renowned Tragedians

DAVID GARRICK THE YOUNGER!

AND

EDMUND KEAN THE ELDER!

Of the London and Continental Theatres,

In their Thrilling Tragedy of

THE KING'S CAMELOPARD,

OR

THE ROYAL NONESUCH!!![45]

Admission 50 cents.

---

[45] Twain originally titled this skit "The Burning Shame." It was based on a story, told to Twain by Jim Gillis in 1865, which "involved a lighted candle stuck in a naked man's posterior." The version in *Huck Finn* was apparently edited for propriety's sake. The skit "follows the tradition of the 'Guyuscutus' hoax, in which the exhibit of a ferocious beast is advertised and people pay to see it. Roars and pounding are heard backstage, but when screams announce that the beast has escaped, the audience dashes for the doors and the tricksters disappear with the money" (Lemaster and Wilson 644).

Then at the bottom was the biggest line of all—which said:

LADIES AND CHILDREN NOT ADMITTED.

"There," says he, "if that line don't fetch them, I don't know Arkansaw!"

Chapter XXIII
Sold—Royal Comparisons—Jim Gets Homesick

Well, all day him and the king was hard at it, rigging up a stage, and a curtain, and a row of candles for footlights; and that night the house was jam full of men in no time. When the place couldn't hold no more, the duke he quit tending door and went around the back way and come into the stage and stood up before the curtain, and made a little speech, and praised up this tragedy, and said it was the most thrillingest one that ever was; and so he went on a-bragging about the tragedy and about Edmund Kean the Elder, which was to play the main principal part in it; and at last when he'd got everybody's expectations up high enough, he rolled up the curtain, and the next minute the king come a-prancing out on all fours, naked; and he was painted all over, ring-streaked-and-striped, all sorts of colors, as splendid as a rainbow. And—but never mind the rest of his outfit, it was just wild, but it was awful funny. The people most killed

TRAGEDY.

themselves laughing; and when the king got done capering, and capered off behind the scenes, they roared and clapped and stormed and haw-hawed till he come back and done it over again; and after that, they made him do it another time. Well, it would a made a cow laugh to see the shines that old idiot cut.

Then the duke he lets the curtain down, and bows to the people, and says the great tragedy will be performed only two nights more, on accounts of pressing London engagements, where the seats is all sold already for it in Drury Lane; and then he makes them another bow, and says if he has succeeded in pleasing them and instructing them, he will be deeply obleeged if they will mention it to their friends and get them to come and see it.

Twenty people sings out:

"What, is it over? Is that *all?*"

The duke says yes. Then there was a fine time. Everybody sings out "sold," and rose up mad, and was agoing for that stage and them tragedians. But a big fine-looking man jumps up on a bench, and shouts:

"Hold on! Just a word, gentlemen." They stopped to listen. "We are sold—mighty badly sold. But we don't want to be the laughing-stock of this whole town, I reckon, and never hear the last of this thing as long as we live. *No.* What we want, is to go out of here quiet, and talk this show up, and sell the *rest* of the town! Then we'll all be in the same boat. Ain't that sensible?" ("You bet it is!—the jedge is right!" everybody sings out.) "All right, then—not a word about any sell. Go along home, and advise everybody to come and see the tragedy."

Next day you couldn't hear nothing around that town but how splendid that show was. House was jammed again, that night, and we sold this crowd the same way. When me and the king and the duke got home to the raft, we all had a supper; and by-and-by, about midnight, they made Jim and me back her out and float her down the middle of the river and fetch her in and hide her about two mile below town.

The third night the house was crammed again—and they warn't newcomers this time, but people that was at the show the other two nights. I stood by the duke at the door, and I see that every man that went in had his pockets bulging, or something muffed up under his coat—and I see it warn't no perfumery neither, not by a long sight. I smelt sickly eggs by the barrel, and rotten cabbages, and such things; and if I know the signs of a dead cat being around, and I bet I do, there was sixty-four of them went in. I shoved in there for a minute, but it was too various for me, I couldn't stand it. Well, when the place couldn't hold no more people, the duke he give a fellow a quarter and told him to tend door for him a minute, and then he started around for the stage door, I after him; but the minute we turned the corner and was in the dark, he says:

"Walk fast, now, till you get away from the houses, and then shin for the raft like the dickens was after you!"

I done it, and he done the same. We struck the raft at the same time, and in less than two seconds we was gliding down stream, all dark and still, and edging towards the middle of the river, nobody saying a word. I reckoned the poor king was in for a gaudy time of it with the audience; but nothing of the sort; pretty soon he crawls out from under the wigwam, and says:

"Well, how'd the old thing pan out this time, Duke?"

He hadn't been up town at all.

We never showed a light till we was about ten mile below the village. Then we lit up and had a supper, and the king and the duke fairly laughed their bones loose over the way they'd served them people. The duke says:

"Greenhorns, flatheads! *I* knew the first house would keep mum and let the rest of the town get roped in; and I knew they'd lay for us the third night, and consider it was *their* turn now. Well, it *is* their turn, and I'd give something to know how much they'd take for it. I *would* just like to know how they're putting in their opportunity. They can turn it into a picnic, if they want to—they brought plenty provisions."

Them rapscallions took in four hundred and sixty-five dollars in that three nights. I never see money hauled in by the wagon-load like that, before.

By-and-by, when they was asleep and snoring, Jim says:

"Don't it 'sprise you, de way dem kings carries on, Huck?"

"No," I says, "It don't."

"Why don't it, Huck?"

"Well, it don't, because it's in the breed. I reckon they're all alike,"

"But, Huck, dese kings o' ourn is reglar rapscallions; dat's jist what dey is; dey's reglar rapscallions."

"Well, that's what I'm a-saying; all kings is mostly rapscallions, as fur as I can make out."

"Is dat so?"

"You read about them once—you'll see. Look at Henry the Eight; this'n 's a Sunday-School Superintendent to *him*. And look at Charles Second, and Louis Fourteen, and Louis Fifteen, and James Second, and Edward Second, and Richard Third, and forty more; besides all them Saxon heptarchies that used to rip around so in old times and raise Cain. My, you ought to seen old Henry the Eight when he was in bloom. He *was* a blossom. He used to marry a new wife every day, and chop off her head next morning. And he would do it just as indifferent as if he was ordering up eggs. 'Fetch up Nell Gwynn,' he says. They fetch her up. Next morning, 'Chop off her head!' And they chop it off. 'Fetch up Jane Shore,' he says; and up she comes. Next morning 'Chop off her head'—and they chop it off. 'Ring up Fair Rosamun.' Fair Rosamun answers the bell. Next morning, 'Chop off her head.' And he made every one of them tell him a tale every night; and he kept that up till he had hogged a thousand and one tales that way, and then he put them all in a book, and called it Domesday Book—which was a good name and stated the case. You don't know kings, Jim, but I know them; and this old rip of ourn is one of the cleanest I've struck in history. Well, Henry he takes a notion he wants to get up some trouble with this country. How does he go at it—give notice?—give the country a show? No. All of a sudden he heaves all the tea in Boston Harbor overboard, and whacks out a declaration of independence, and dares them to come on. That was *his* style—he never give anybody a chance. He had suspicions of his father, the Duke of Wellington. Well, what did he do?—ask him to show up? No—drownded him in a butt of mamsey, like a cat. Spose people left money laying around where he was—what did he do? He collared it. Spose he contracted to do a thing; and you paid him, and didn't set down there and see that he done it—what did he do? He always done the other thing. Spose he opened his mouth—what then? If he didn't shut it up powerful quick, he'd lose a lie, every time. That's the kind of a bug Henry was; and if we'd a had him along 'stead of our kings, he'd a fooled that town a heap worse than ourn done. I don't say that ourn is lambs, because they ain't, when you come right down to the cold facts; but they ain't nothing to *that* old ram, anyway. All I say is, kings is kings, and you got to make allowances. Take them all around, they're a mighty ornery lot. It's the way they're raised."

"But dis one do *smell* so like de nation, Huck."

"Well, they all do, Jim. We can't help the way a king smells; history don't tell no way."

"Now de duke, he's a tolerble likely man, in some ways."

"Yes, a duke's different. But not very different. This one's a middling hard lot, for a duke. When he's drunk, there ain't no near-sighted man could tell him from a king."

"Well, anyways, I doan' hanker for no mo' un um, Huck. Dese is all I kin stan'."

"It's the way I feel, too, Jim. But we've got them on our hands, and we got to remember what they are, and make allowances. Sometimes I wish we could hear of a country that's out of kings."

What was the use to tell Jim these warn't real kings and dukes? It wouldn't a done no good; and besides, it was just as I said; you couldn't tell them from the real kind.

I went to sleep, and Jim didn't call me when it was my turn. He often done that. When I waked up, just at day-break, he was setting there
with his head down betwixt his knees, moaning and mourning to himself.
I didn't take notice, nor let on. I knowed what it was about. He was thinking about his wife and his children, away up yonder, and he was low and
homesick; because he hadn't ever been away from home before in his life;
and I do believe he cared just as much for his people as white folks does
for their'n. It don't seem natural, but I reckon it's so. He was often moaning and mourning that way, nights, when he judged I was asleep, and saying, "Po' little 'Lizabeth! po' little Johnny! it's mighty hard; I spec' I ain't
ever gwyne to see you no mo', no mo'!" He was a mighty good nigger,
Jim was.

But this time I somehow got to talking to him about his wife and
young ones; and by-and-by he says:

"What makes me feel so bad dis time, 'uz bekase I hear sumpn
over yonder on de bank like a whack, er a slam, while ago, en it mine
me er de time I treat my little 'Lizabeth so ornery. She warn't on'y 'bout
fo' year ole, en she tuck de sk'yarlet-fever, en had a powful rough spell;
but she got well, en one day she was a-stannin' aroun', en I says to her,
I says:

"'Shet de do'.'

"She never done it; jis' stood dah, kiner smilin' up at me. It make me
mad; en I says agin, mighty loud, I says:

"'Doan' you hear me?—shet de do'!'

"She jis' stood de same way, kiner smilin' up. I was a-bilin'! I says:

"'I lay I *make* you mine!'

"En wid dat I fetch' her a slap side de head dat sont her a-sprawlin'.
Den I went into de yuther room, en 'uz gone 'bout ten minutes; en when I
come back, dah was dat do' a-stannin' open *yit*, en dat chile stannin' mos'
right in it, a-lookin' down and mournin', en de tears runnin' down. My,
but I *wuz* mad! I was agwyne for de chile, but jis' den—it was a do' dat
open innerds—jis' den, 'long come de wind en slam it to, behine de
chile, ker-*blam!*—en my lan', de chile never move'! My breff mos' hop
outer me; en I feel so—so—I doan' know *how* I feel. I crope out, all a-
tremblin', en crope aroun' en open de do' easy en slow, en poke my head
in behine de chile, sof' en still, en all uv a sudden I says pow! jis' as loud
as I could yell. She never budge! Oh, Huck, I bust out a-cryin' en grab her
up in my arms, en say, 'Oh, de po' little thing! de Lord God Amighty fogive po' ole Jim, kaze he never gwyne to fogive hisself as long's he live!'
Oh, she was plumb deef en dumb, Huck, plumb deef en dumb—en I'd ben
a-treat'n her so!"

Chapter XXIV
Jim in Royal Robes—They Take a Passenger—
Getting Information—Family Grief

Next day, towards night, we laid up under a little willow tow-head out in the middle, where there was a village on each side of the river, and the duke and the king begun to lay out a plan for working them towns. Jim he spoke to the duke, and said he hoped it wouldn't take but a few hours, because it got mighty heavy and tiresome to him when he had to lay all day in the wigwam tied with the rope. You see, when we left him all alone we had to tie him, because if anybody happened on him all by himself and not tied, it wouldn't look much like he was a runaway nigger, you know. So the duke said it *was* kind of hard to have to lay roped all day, and he'd cipher out some way to get around it.

HARMLESS.

He was uncommon bright, the duke was, and he soon struck it. He dressed Jim up in King Lear's outfit—it was a long curtain-calico gown, and a white horse-hair wig and whiskers; and then he took his theatre paint and painted Jim's face and hands and ears and neck all over a dead dull solid blue, like a man that's been drownded nine days. Blamed if he warn't the horriblest looking outrage I ever see. Then the duke took and wrote out a sign on a shingle so—

> Sick Arab—but harmless when not out of his head.

And he nailed that shingle to a lath, and stood the lath up four or five foot in front of the wigwam. Jim was satisfied. He said it was a sight better than lying tied a couple of years every day and trembling all over every time there was a sound. The duke told him to make himself free and easy, and if anybody ever come meddling around, he must hop out of the wigwam, and carry on a little, and fetch a howl or two like a wild beast, and he reckoned they would light out and leave him alone. Which was sound enough judgment; but you take the average man, and he wouldn't wait for him to howl. Why, he didn't only look like he was dead, he looked considerable more than that.

These rapscallions wanted to try the Nonesuch again, because there was so much money in it, but they judged it wouldn't be safe, because maybe the news might a worked along down by this time. They couldn't hit no project that suited, exactly; so at last the duke said he reckoned he'd lay off and work his brains an hour or two and see if he couldn't put up something on the Arkansaw village; and the king he allowed he would drop over to t'other village, without any plan, but just trust in Providence to lead him the profitable way—meaning the devil, I reckon. We had all bought store clothes where we stopped last; and now the king put his'n on, and he told me to put mine on. I done it, of course. The king's duds was all black, and he did look real swell and starchy. I never knowed how clothes could change a body before. Why, before, he looked like the orneriest old rip that ever was; but now, when he'd take off his new white beaver and make a bow and do a smile, he looked that grand and good and pious that you'd say he had walked right out of the ark, and maybe was old Leviticus himself.[46] Jim cleaned up the canoe, and I got my paddle ready. There was a big steamboat laying at the shore away up under the point, about three mile above town—been there a couple of hours, taking on freight. Says the king:

"Seein' how I'm dressed, I reckon maybe I better arrive down from St. Louis or Cincinnati, or some other big place. Go for the steamboat, Huckleberry; we'll come down to the village on her."

I didn't have to be ordered twice, to go and take a steamboat ride. I fetched the shore a half a mile above the village, and then went scooting along the bluff bank in the easy water. Pretty soon we come to a nice innocent-looking young country jake setting on a log swabbing the sweat

---

[46] It is Noah who departs in the ark after God destroys mankind by flood for wickedness (Gen. 8.18). Leviticus, the third book of the Old Testament, is full of laws, warnings, and offerings whereby a sinner may seek forgiveness and be cleansed. Huck conflates Noah with the book of Leviticus in his description of the king. In store-bought clothes even the king looks pious, like someone ready to make a new start.

off of his face, for it was powerful warm weather; and he had a couple of big carpet-bags by him.

"Run her nose in shore," says the king. I done it. "Wher' you bound for, young man?"

"For the steamboat; going to Orleans."

"Git aboard," says the king. "Hold on a minute, my servant 'll he'p you with them bags. Jump out and he'p the gentleman, Adolphus"— meaning me, I see.

I done so, and then we all three started on again. The young chap was mighty thankful; said it was tough work toting his baggage such weather. He asked the king where he was going, and the king told him he'd come down the river and landed at the other village this morning, and now he was going up a few mile to see an old friend on a farm up there. The young fellow says:

"When I first see you, I says to myself, 'It's Mr. Wilks, sure, and he come mighty near getting here in time.' But then I says again, 'No, I reckon it ain't him, or else he wouldn't be paddling up the river.' You *ain't* him, are you?"

"No, my name's Blodgett—Elexander Blodgett—*Reverend* Elexander Blodgett, I spose I must say, as I'm one o' the Lord's poor servants. But still I'm jist as able to be sorry for Mr. Wilks for not arriving in time, all the same, if he's missed anything by it—which I hope he hasn't."

"Well, he don't miss any property by it, because he'll get that all right; but he's missed seeing his brother Peter die—which he mayn't mind, no-body can tell as to that—but his brother would a give anything in this world to see *him* before he died; never talked about nothing else all these three weeks; hadn't seen him since they was boys together—and hadn't ever seen his brother William at all—that's the deef and dumb one— William ain't more than thirty or thirty-five. Peter and George was the only ones that come out here; George was the married brother; him and his wife both died last year. Harvey and William's the only ones that's left now; and, as I was saying, they haven't got here in time."

"Did anybody send 'em word?"

"Oh, yes; a month or two ago, when Peter was first took; because Peter said then that he sorter felt like he warn't going to get well this time. You see, he was pretty old, and George's g'yirls was too young to be much company for him, except Mary Jane the red-headed one; and so he was kinder lonesome after George and his wife died, and didn't seem to care much to live. He most desperately wanted to see Harvey— and William too, for that matter—because he was one of them kind that can't bear to make a will. He left a letter behind for Harvey, and said he'd told in it where his money was hid, and how he wanted the rest of the property divided up so George's g'yirls would be all right—for George didn't leave nothing. And that letter was all they could get him to put a pen to."

"Why do you reckon Harvey don't come? Wher' does he live?"

"Oh, he lives in England—Sheffield—preaches there—hasn't ever been in this country. He hasn't had any too much time—and besides he mightn't a got the letter at all, you know."

"Too bad, too bad he couldn't a lived to see his brothers, poor soul. You going to Orleans, you say?"

"Yes, but that ain't only a part of it. I'm going in a ship, next Wednesday, for Ryo Janeero, where my uncle lives."

"It's a pretty long journey. But it'll be lovely; wisht I was agoing. Is Mary Jane the oldest? How old is the others?"

"Mary Jane's nineteen, Susan's fifteen, and Joanna's about fourteen— that's the one that gives herself to good works and has a hare-lip."

"Poor things! to be left alone in the cold world so."

"Well, they could be worse off. Old Peter had friends, and they ain't going to let them come to no harm. There's Hobson, the Babtis' preacher; and Deacon Lot Hovey, and Ben Rucker, and Abner Shackleford, and Levi Bell, the lawyer; and Dr. Robinson, and their wives, and the widow Bartley, and—well, there's a lot of them; but these are the ones that Peter was thickest with, and used to write about sometimes, when he wrote home; so Harvey 'll know where to look for friends when he gets here."

Well, the old man he went on asking questions till he just fairly emptied that young fellow. Blamed if he didn't inquire about everybody and everything in that blessed town, and all about all the Wilkses; and about Peter's business—which was a tanner; and about George's—which was a carpenter; and about Harvey's—which was a dissentering minister; and so on, and so on. Then he says:

"What did you want to walk all the way up to the steamboat for?"

"Because she's a big Orleans boat, and I was afeard she mightn't stop there. When they're deep they won't stop for a hail. A Cincinnati boat will, but this is a St. Louis one."

"Was Peter Wilks well off?"

"Oh, yes, pretty well off. He had houses and land, and it's reckoned he left three or four thousand in cash hid up some'ers."

"When did you say he died?"

"I didn't say, but it was last night."

"Funeral to-morrow, likely?"

"Yes, 'bout the middle of the day."

"Well, it's all terrible sad; but we've all got to go, one time or another. So what we want to do is to be prepared; then we're all right."

"Yes, sir, it's the best way. Ma used to always say that."

When we struck the boat, she was about done loading, and pretty soon she got off. The king never said nothing about going aboard, so I lost my ride, after all. When the boat was gone, the king made me paddle up another mile to a lonesome place, and then he got ashore and says:

"Now hustle back, right off, and fetch the duke up here, and the new carpet-bags. And if he's gone over to t'other side go over there and git him. And tell him to git himself up regardless. Shove along, now."

I see what *he* was up to; but I never said nothing, of course. When I got back with the duke, we hid the canoe and then they set down on a log, and the king told him everything, just like the young fellow had said it—every last word of it. And all the time he was a doing it, he tried to talk like an Englishman; and he done it pretty well too, for a slouch. I can't imitate him, and so I ain't agoing to try to; but he really done it pretty good. Then he says:

"How are you on the deef and dumb, Bilgewater?"

The duke said, leave him alone for that; said he had played a deef and dumb person on the histronic boards. So then they waited for a steamboat.

About the middle of the afternoon a couple of little boats come along, but they didn't come from high enough up the river; but at last there was a big one, and they hailed her. She sent out her yawl, and we went aboard, and she was from Cincinnati; and when they found we only wanted to go four or five mile they was booming mad, and gave us a cussing, and said they wouldn't land us. But the king was ca'm. He says:

"If gentlemen kin afford to pay a dollar a mile apiece, to be took on and put off in a yawl, a steamboat kin afford to carry 'em, can't it?"

So they softened down and said it was all right; and when we got to the village, they yawled us ashore. About two dozen men flocked down, when they see the yawl a coming; and when the king says—

"Kin any of you gentlemen tell me wher' Mr. Peter Wilks lives?" they give a glance at one another, and nodded their heads, as much as to say, "What d' I tell you?" Then one of them says, kind of soft and gentle:

"I'm sorry, sir, but the best we can do is to tell you where he *did* live yesterday evening."

Sudden as winking, the ornery old cretur went all to smash, and fell up against the man, and put his chin on his shoulder, and cried down his back, and says:

"Alas, alas, our poor brother—gone, and we never got to see him; oh, it's too, *too* hard!"

Then he turns around, blubbering, and makes a lot of idiotic signs to
the duke on his hands, and blamed if *he* didn't drop a carpet-bag and bust
out a-crying. If they warn't the beatenest lot, them two frauds, that ever I
struck.

Well, the men gathered around, and sympathized with them, and
said all sorts of kind things to them, and carried their carpet-bags up
the hill for them, and let them lean on them and cry, and told the king
all about his brother's last moments, and the king he told it all over
again on his hands to the duke, and both of them took on about that
dead tanner like they'd lost the twelve disciples. Well, if ever I struck anything like it, I'm a nigger. It was enough to make a body ashamed of the
human race.

Chapter XXV
Is It Them?—Singing the "Doxologer"—Awful
Square—Funeral Orgies—A Bad Investment

The news was all over town in two minutes, and you could see the people
tearing down on the run, from every which way, some of them putting on
their coats as they come. Pretty soon we was in the middle of a crowd, and
the noise of the tramping was like a soldier-march. The windows and
door-yards was full; and every minute somebody would say, over a fence:

"Is it *them?*"

And somebody trotting along with the gang would answer back
and say,

"You bet it is."

When we got to the house, the street in front of it was packed, and the
three girls was standing in the door. Mary Jane *was* red-headed, but that
don't make no difference, she was most awful beautiful, and her face and
her eyes was all lit up like glory, she was so glad her uncles was come. The
king he spread his arms, and Mary Jane she jumped for them, and the
hare-lip jumped for the duke, and there they *had* it! Everybody most, leastways women, cried for joy to see them meet again at last and have such
good times.

Then the king he hunched the duke, private—I see him do it—and
then he looked around and see the coffin, over in the corner on two
chairs; so then, him and the duke, with a hand across each other's shoulder, and t'other hand to their eyes, walked slow and solemn over there,
everybody dropping back to give them room, and all the talk and noise
stopping, people saying "Sh!" and all the men taking their hats off and

drooping their heads, so you could a heard a pin fall. And when they got there, they bent over and looked in the coffin, and took one sight, and then they bust out a crying so you could a heard them to Orleans, most; and then they put their arms around each other's necks, and hung their chins over each other's shoulders; and then for three minutes, or maybe four, I never see two men leak the way they done. And mind you, everybody was doing the same; and the place was that damp I never see anything like it. Then one of them got on one side of the coffin, and t'other on t'other side, and they kneeled down and rested their foreheads on the coffin, and let on to pray all to theirselves. Well, when it come to that, it worked the crowd like you never see anything like it, and everybody broke down and went to sobbing right out loud—the poor girls, too; and every woman, nearly, went up to the girls, without saying a word, and kissed them, solemn, on the forehead, and then put their hand on their head, and looked up towards the sky, with the tears running down, and then busted out and went off sobbing and swabbing, and give the next woman a show. I never see anything so disgusting.

"YOU BET IT IS."

Well, by-and-by the king he gets up and comes forward a little, and works himself up and slobbers out a speech, all full of tears and flapdoodle about its being a sore trial for him and his poor brother to lose the diseased, and to miss seeing diseased alive, after the long journey of four thousand mile, but it's a trial that's sweetened and sanctified to us by this dear sympathy and these holy tears, and so he thanks them out of his heart and out of his brother's heart, because out of their mouths they can't, words being too weak and cold, and all that kind of rot and slush, till it was just sickening; and then he blubbers out a pious goody-goody Amen, and turns himself loose and goes to crying fit to bust.

And the minute the words were out of his mouth somebody over in the crowd struck up the doxolojer,[47] and everybody joined in with all their might, and it just warmed you up and made you feel as good as church letting out. Music *is* a good thing; and after all that soul-butter and hogwash, I never see it freshen up things so, and sound so honest and bully.

Then the king begins to work his jaw again, and says how him and his nieces would be glad if a few of the main principal friends of the family would take supper here with them this evening, and help set up with the ashes of the diseased; and says if his poor brother laying yonder could speak, he knows who he would name, for they was names that was very dear to him, and mentioned often in his letters; and so he will name the same, to-wit, as follows, vizz.: Rev. Mr. Hobson, and Deacon Lot Hovey, and Mr. Ben Rucker, and Abner Shackleford, and Levi Bell, and Dr. Robinson, and their wives, and the widow Bartley.

Rev. Hobson and Dr. Robinson was down to the end of the town, a-hunting together; that is, I mean the doctor was shipping a sick man to t'other world, and the preacher was pinting him right. Lawyer Bell was away up to Louisville on some business. But the rest was on hand, and so they all come and shook hands with the king and thanked him and talked to him; and then they shook hands with the duke, and didn't say nothing but just kept a-smiling and bobbing their heads like a passel of sapheads whilst he made all sorts of signs with his hands and said "Goo-goo—goo-goo-goo" all the time, like a baby that can't talk.

So the king he blatted along, and managed to inquire about pretty much everybody and dog in town, by his name, and mentioned all sorts of little things that happened one time or another in the town, or to George's family, or to Peter; and he always let on that Peter wrote him the things, but that was a lie, he got every blessed one of them out of that young flathead that we canoed up to the steamboat.

Then Mary Jane she fetched the letter her father left behind, and the king he read it out loud and cried over it. It give the dwelling-house and three thousand dollars, gold, to the girls; and it give the tanyard (which was doing a good business), along with some other houses and land (worth about seven thousand), and three thousand dollars in gold to Harvey and William, and told where the six thousand cash was hid, down cellar. So these two frauds said they'd go and fetch it up, and have everything square and above-board; and told me to come with a candle. We shut the cellar

---

[47] A doxology is a hymn of praise to God. The hymn most commonly referred to as "The Doxology" was composed by Louis Bourgeois in 1551: "Praise God, from whom all blessings flow;/ Praise him, all creatures here below;/ Praise him above, ye heav'nly hosts,/ Praise Father, Son, and Holy Ghost."

door behind us, and when they found the bag they spilt it out on the floor, and it was a lovely sight, all them yaller-boys. My, the way the king's eyes did shine! He slaps the duke on the shoulder, and says:

"Oh, *this* ain't bully, nor noth'n! Oh, no, I reckon not! Why, Biljy, it beats the Nonesuch, *don't* it?"

The duke allowed it did. They pawed the yaller-boys, and sifted them through their fingers and let them jingle down on the floor; and the king says:

"It ain't no use talkin'; bein' brothers to a rich dead man, and repre-sentatives of furrin heirs that's got left, is the line for you and me, Bilge. Thish-yer comes of trust'n to Providence. It's the best way, in the long run. I've tried 'em all, and ther' ain't no better way."

Most everybody would a been satisfied with the pile, and took it on trust; but no, they must count it. So they counts it, and it comes out four hundred and fifteen dollars short. Says the king:

"Dern him, I wonder what he done with that four hundred and fifteen dollars?"

They worried over that a while, and ransacked all around for it. Then the duke says:

"Well, he was a pretty sick man, and likely he made a mistake—I reckon that's the way of it. The best way's to let it go, and keep still about it. We can spare it."

"Oh, shucks, yes, we can *spare* it. I don't k'yer noth'n 'bout that—it's the *count* I'm thinkin' about. We want to be awful square and open and aboveboard, here, you know. We want to lug this h-yer money up stairs and count it before everybody—then ther' ain't noth'n suspicious. But when the dead man says ther's six thous'n dollars, you know, we don't want to—"

"Hold on," says the duke. "Less make up the deffisit"—and he begun to haul out yaller-boys out of his pocket.

"It's a most amaz'n' good idea, duke—you *have* got a rattlin' clever head on you," says the king. "Blest if the old Nonesuch ain't a heppin' us out agin,"—and *he* begun to haul out yaller-jackets and stack them up.

It most busted them, but they made up the six thousand clean and clear.

"Say," says the duke, "I got another idea. Le's go up stairs and count this money, and then take and *give it to the girls.*"

"Good land, duke, lemme hug you! It's the most dazzling idea 'at ever a man struck. You have cert'nly got the most astonishin' head I ever see. Oh, this is the boss dodge, ther' ain't no mistake 'bout it. Let 'em fetch along their suspicions now, if they want to—this'll lay 'em out."

When we got up stairs, everybody gethered around the table, and the king he counted it and stacked it up, three hundred dollars in a pile—twenty elegant little piles. Everybody looked hungry at it, and licked their chops. Then they raked it into the bag again, and I see the king begin to swell himself up for another speech. He says:

"Friends all, my poor brother that lays yonder, has done generous by them that's left behind in the vale of sorrers. He has done generous by these-yer poor little lambs that he loved and sheltered, and that's left fatherless and motherless. Yes, and we that knowed him, knows that he would a done *more* generous by 'em if he hadn't ben afeard o' woundin' his dear William and me. Now, *wouldn't* he? Ther' ain't no question 'bout it, in *my* mind. Well, then—what kind o' brothers would it be, that'd stand in his way at sech a time? And what kind o' uncles would it be that'd rob—yes, *rob*—sech poor sweet lambs as these 'at he loved so, at sech a time? If I know William—and I *think* I do—he—well, I'll jest ask him." He turns around and begins to make a lot of signs to the duke with his hands; and the duke he looks at him stupid and leather-headed a while, then all of a sudden he seems to catch his meaning, and jumps for the king, goo-gooing with all his might for joy, and hugs him about fifteen times before he lets up. Then the king says, "I knowed it; I reckon *that*'ll convince anybody the way *he* feels about it. Here, Mary Jane, Susan, Joanner, take the money—take it *all*. It's the gift of him that lays yonder, cold but joyful."

Mary Jane she went for him, Susan and the hare-lip went for the duke, and then such another hugging and kissing I never see yet. And everybody crowded up with the tears in their eyes, and most shook the hands off of them frauds, saying all the time:

"You *dear* good souls!—how *lovely!*—how *could* you!"

Well, then, pretty soon all hands got to talking about the diseased again, and how good he was, and what a loss he was, and all that; and before long a big iron-jawed man worked himself in there from outside, and stood a listening and looking, and not saying anything; and nobody saying anything to him either, because the king was talking and they was all busy listening. The king was saying—in the middle of something he'd started in on—

"—they bein' partickler friends o' the diseased. That's why they're invited here this evenin'; but to-morrow we want *all* to come—everybody; for he respected everybody, he liked everybody, and so it's fitten that his funeral orgies sh'd be public."

And so he went a-mooning on and on, liking to hear himself talk, and every little while he fetched in his funeral orgies again, till the duke he couldn't stand it no more; so he writes on a little scrap of paper, "*obsequies,* you old fool," and folds it up and goes to goo-gooing and reaching it over people's heads to him. The king he reads it, and puts it in his pocket, and says:

"Poor William, afflicted as he is, his *heart's* aluz right. Asks me to invite everybody to come to the funeral—wants me to make 'em all welcome. But he needn't a worried—it was jest what I was at."

Then he weaves along again, perfectly ca'm, and goes to dropping in his funeral orgies again every now and then, just like he done before. And when he done it the third time, he says:

"I say orgies, not because it's the common term, because it ain't—obsequies bein' the common term—but because orgies is the right term. Obsequies ain't used in England no more, now—it's gone out. We say orgies now, in England. Orgies is better, because it means the thing you're after, more exact. It's a word that's made up out'n the Greek *orgo*, outside, open, abroad; and the Hebrew *jeesum*, to plant, cover up; hence in*ter*. So, you see, funeral orgies is an open er public funeral."

He was the *worst* I ever struck. Well, the iron-jawed man he laughed right in his face. Everybody was shocked. Everybody says, "Why *doctor!*" and Abner Shackleford says:

"Why, Robinson, hain't you heard the news? This is Harvey Wilks."

The king he smiled eager, and shoved out his flapper, and says:

"*Is* it my poor brother's dear good friend and physician? I —"

"Keep your hands off of me!" says the doctor. "*You* talk like an Englishman, *don't* you? It's the worst imitation I ever heard. *You* Peter Wilks's brother! You're a fraud, that's what you are!"

Well, how they all took on! They crowded around the doctor, and tried to quiet him down, and tried to explain to him, and tell him how Harvey'd showed in forty ways that he *was* Harvey, and knowed everybody by name, and the names of the very dogs, and begged and *begged* him not to hurt Harvey's feelings and the poor girl's feelings, and all that; but it warn't no use, he stormed right along, and said any man that pretended to be an Englishman and couldn't imitate the lingo no better than what he did, was a fraud and a liar. The poor girls was hanging to the king and crying; and all of a sudden the doctor ups and turns on *them*. He says:

"I was your father's friend, and I'm your friend; and I warn you *as* a friend, an honest one, that wants to protect you and keep you out of harm and trouble, to turn your backs on that scoundrel, and have nothing to do with him, the ignorant tramp, with his idiotic Greek and Hebrew as he calls it. He is the thinnest kind of an impostor—has come here with a lot of empty names and facts which he picked up somewheres, and you take them for *proofs*, and are helped to fool yourselves by these foolish friends here, who ought to know better. Mary Jane Wilks, you know me for your friend, and for your unselfish friend, too. Now listen to me; turn this pitiful rascal out—I *beg* you to do it. Will you?"

Mary Jane straightened herself up, and my, but she was handsome!
She says:

"*Here* is my answer." She hove up the bag of money and put it in
the king's hands, and says, "Take this six thousand dollars, and invest it
for me and my sisters any way you want to, and don't give us no receipt
for it."

Then she put her arm around the king on one side, and Susan and the
hare-lip done the same on the other. Everybody clapped their hands and
stomped on the floor like a perfect storm, whilst the king held up his head
and smiled proud. The doctor says:

"All right; I wash *my* hands of the matter. But I warn you all that a
time's coming when you're going to feel sick whenever you think of this
day"—and away he went.

"All right, doctor," says the king, kinder mocking him; "we'll try and
get 'em to send for you"—which made them all laugh, and they said it was
a prime good hit.

Chapter XXVI
A Pious King—The King's Clergy—
She Asked His Pardon—Hiding in the Room—
Huck Takes the Money

Well, when they was all gone, the king he asks Mary Jane how they was
off for spare rooms, and she said she had one spare room, which would do
for Uncle William, and she'd give her own room to Uncle Harvey, which
was a little bigger, and she would turn into the room with her sisters and
sleep on a cot; and up garret was a little cubby, with a pallet in it. The king
said the cubby would do for his valley—meaning me.

So Mary Jane took us up, and she showed them their rooms, which
was plain but nice. She said she'd have her frocks and a lot of other traps
took out of her room if they was in Uncle Harvey's way, but he said they
warn't. The frocks was hung along the wall, and before them was a curtain made out of calico that hung down to the floor. There was an old hair
trunk in one corner, and a guitar box in another, and all sorts of little
knick-knacks and jimcracks around, like girls brisken up a room with. The
king said it was all the more homely and more pleasanter for these fixings,
and so don't disturb them. The duke's room was pretty small, but plenty
good enough, and so was my cubby.

That night they had a big supper, and all them men and women was
there, and I stood behind the king and the duke's chairs and waited on

them, and the niggers waited on the rest. Mary Jane she set at the head of the table, with Susan alongside of her, and said how bad the biscuits was, and how mean the preserves was, and how ornery and tough the fried chickens was—and all that kind of rot, the way women always do for to force out compliments; and the people all knowed everything was tiptop, and said so—said "How *do* you get biscuits to brown so nice?" and "Where, for the land's sake *did* you get these amaz'n pickles?" and all that kind of hum-bug talky-talk, just the way people always does at a supper, you know.

THE CUBBY.

And when it was all done, me and the hare-lip had supper in the kitchen off of the leavings, whilst the others was helping the niggers clean up the things. The hare-lip she got to pumping me about England, and blest if I didn't think the ice was getting mighty thin, sometimes. She says:

"Did you ever see the king?"

"Who? William Fourth? Well, I bet I have—he goes to our church." I knowed he was dead years ago, but I never let on. So when I says he goes to our church, she says:

"What—regular?"

"Yes—regular. His pew's right over opposite ourn—on t'other side the pulpit."

"I thought he lived in London?"

"Well, he does. Where *would* he live?"

"But I thought *you* lived in Sheffield?"

I see I was up a stump. I had to let on to get choked with a chicken bone, so as to get time to think how to get down again. Then I says:

"I mean he goes to our church regular when he's in Sheffield. That's only in the summer-time, when he comes there to take the sea baths."

"Why, how you talk—Sheffield ain't on the sea."

"Well, who said it was?"

"Why, you did."

"I *didn't,* nuther."

"You did!"

"I didn't."

"You did."

"I never said nothing of the kind."

"Well, what *did* you say, then?"

"Said he come to take the sea *baths*—that's what I said."

"Well, then! how's he going to take the sea baths if it ain't on the sea?"

"Looky here," I says; "did you ever see any Congress water?"

"Yes."

"Well, did you have to go to Congress to get it?"

"Why, no."

"Well, neither does William Fourth have to go to the sea to get a sea bath."

"How does he get it, then?"

"Gets it the way people down here gets Congress water—in barrels. There in the palace at Sheffield they've got furnaces, and he wants his water hot. They can't bile that amount of water away off there at the sea. They haven't got no conveniences for it."

"Oh, I see, now. You might a said that in the first place and saved time."

When she said that, I see I was out of the woods again, and so I was comfortable and glad. Next, she says:

"Do you go to church, too?"

"Yes—regular."

"Where do you set?"

"Why, in our pew."

"*Whose* pew?"

"Why, *ourn*—your Uncle Harvey's."

"His'n? What does *he* want with a pew?"

"Wants it to set in. What did you *reckon* he wanted with it?"

"Why, I thought he'd be in the pulpit."

Rot him, I forgot he was a preacher. I see I was up a stump again, so I played another chicken bone and got another think. Then I says:

"Blame it, do you suppose there ain't but one preacher to a church?"

"Why, what do they want with more?"

"What!—to preach before a king? I never did see such a girl as you. They don't have no less than seventeen."

"Seventeen! My land! Why, I wouldn't set out such a string as that, not if I *never* got to glory. It must take 'em a week."

"Shucks, they don't *all* of 'em preach the same day—only *one* of 'em."

"Well, then, what does the rest of 'em do?"

"Oh, nothing much. Loll around, pass the plate—and one thing or another. But mainly they don't do nothing."

"Well, then, what are they *for?*"

"Why, they're for *style.* Don't you know nothing?") sure Huck

"Well, I don't *want* to know no such foolishness as that. How is servants treated in England? Do they treat 'em better 'n we treat our niggers?"

"*No!* A servant ain't nobody there. They treat them worse than dogs."

"Don't they give 'em holidays, the way we do, Christmas and New Year's week, and Fourth of July?"

"Oh, just listen! A body could tell *you* hain't ever been to England, by that. Why, (Hare-l—why, Joanna,) they never see a holiday from year's end to year's end; never go to the circus, nor theatre, nor nigger shows, nor nowheres." he doesn't even listen to her

"Nor church?"

"Nor church."

"But *you* always went to church."

Well, I was gone up again. I forgot I was the old man's servant. But next minute I whirled in on a kind of an explanation how a valley was different from a common servant, and *had* to go to church whether he wanted to or not, and set with the family, on account of its being the law. But I didn't do it pretty good, and when I got done I see she warn't satisfied. She says:

"Honest injun, now, hain't you been telling me a lot of lies?") Someone found it!

"Honest injun," says I.

"None of it at all?"

"None of it at all. Not a lie in it," says I.

"Lay your hand on this book and say it."

I see it warn't nothing but a dictionary, so I laid my hand on it and said it. So then she looked a little better satisfied, and says:

"Well, then, I'll believe some of it; but I hope to gracious if I'll believe the rest."

"What is it you won't believe, Joe?" says Mary Jane, stepping in with Susan behind her. "It ain't right nor kind for you to talk so to him, and him a stranger and so far from his people. How would you like to be treated so?"

"That's always your way, Maim—always sailing in to help somebody before they're hurt. I hain't done nothing to him. He's told some stretchers, I reckon; and I said I wouldn't swallow it all; and that's every bit and grain I *did* say. I reckon he can stand a little thing like that, can't he?"

"I don't care whether 'twas little or whether 'twas big; he's here in our house and a stranger, and it wasn't good of you to say it. If you was in his place, it would make you feel ashamed; and so you oughtn't to say a thing to another person that will make *them* feel ashamed."

"Why, Maim, he said—"

"It don't make no difference what he *said*—that ain't the thing. The thing is for you to treat him *kind,* and not be saying things to make him remember he ain't in his own country and amongst his own folks."

I says to myself, *this* is a girl that I'm letting that old reptile rob her of her money!

Then Susan *she* waltzed in; and if you'll believe me, she did give Hare-lip hark from the tomb!

Says I to myself, And this is *another* one that I'm letting him rob her of her money!

Then Mary Jane she took another inning, and went in sweet and lovely again—which was her way—but when she got done there warn't hardly anything left o' poor Hare-lip. So she hollered.

"All right, then," says the other girls; "you just ask his pardon."

She done it, too. And she done it beautiful. She done it so beautiful it was good to hear; and I wished I could tell her a thousand lies, so she could do it again.

I says to myself, this is *another* one that I'm letting him rob her of her money. And when she got through, they all jest laid theirselves out to make me feel at home and know I was amongst friends. I felt so ornery and low down and mean, that I says to myself, My mind's made up; I'll hive that money for them or bust.

So then I lit out—for bed, I said, meaning some time or another. When I got by myself, I went to thinking the thing over. I says to myself, shall I go to that doctor, private, and blow on these frauds? No—that won't do. He might tell who told him; then the king and the duke would make it warm for me. Shall I go, private, and tell Mary Jane? No—I dasn't do it. Her face would give them a hint, sure; they've got the money, and they'd slide right out and get away with it. If she was to fetch in help, I'd get mixed up in the business, before it was done with, I judge. No, there ain't no good way but one. I got to steal that money, somehow; and I got to steal it some way that they won't suspicion that I done it. They've got a good thing, here; and they ain't agoing to leave till they've played this family and this town for all they're worth, so I'll find a chance time enough. I'll steal it, and hide it; and by-and-by, when I'm away down the river, I'll write a letter and tell Mary Jane where it's hid. But I better hive it to-night, if I can, because the doctor maybe hasn't let up as much as he lets on he has; he might scare them out of here, yet.

So, thinks I, I'll go and search them rooms. Up stairs the hall was dark, but I found the duke's room, and started to paw around it with my hands; but I recollected it wouldn't be much like the king to let anybody else take care of that money but his own self; so then I went to his room and begun to paw around there. But I see I couldn't do nothing without a candle, and I dasn't light one, of course. So I judged I'd got to do the other thing—lay for them, and eavesdrop. About that time, I hears their footsteps coming, and was going to skip under the bed; I reached for it, but it wasn't where I thought it would be; but I touched the curtain that hid Mary Jane's frocks, so I jumped in behind that and snuggled in amongst the gowns, and stood there perfectly still.

They come in and shut the door; and the first thing the duke done was to get down and look under the bed. Then I was glad I hadn't found the bed when I wanted it. And yet, you know, it's kind of natural to hide under the bed when you are up to anything private. They sets down, then, and the king says:

"Well, what is it? and cut it middlin' short, because it's better for us to be down there a-whoopin'-up the mournin', than up here givin' 'em a chance to talk us over."

"Well, this is it, Capet. I ain't easy; I ain't comfortable. That doctor lays on my mind. I wanted to know your plans. I've got a notion, and I think it's a sound one."

"What is it, duke?"

"That we better glide out of this, before three in the morning, and clip it down the river with what we've got. Specially, seeing we got it so easy—*given* back to us, flung at our heads, as you may say, when of course we allowed to have to steal it back. I'm for knocking off and lighting out."

That made me feel pretty bad. About an hour or two ago, it would a been a little different, but now it made me feel bad and disappointed. The king rips out and says:

"What! And not sell out the rest o' the property? March off like a passel o' fools and leave eight or nine thous'n' dollars' worth o' property layin' around jest sufferin' to be scooped in?—and all good salable stuff, too."

The duke he grumbled; said the bag of gold was enough, and he didn't want to go no deeper—didn't want to rob a lot of orphans of *everything* they had. — good hearted

"Why, how you talk!" says the king. "We sha'n't rob 'em of nothing at all but jest this money. The people that *buys* the property is the suff'rers; because as soon's it's found out 'at we didn't own it—which won't be long after we've slid—the sale won't be valid, and it'll all go back to the estate. These-yer orphans 'll git their house back agin, and that's enough for *them;* they're young and spry, and k'n easy earn a livin'. *They* ain't agoing to suffer. Why, jest think—there's thous'n's and thous'n's that ain't nigh so well off. Bless you, *they* ain't got noth'n to complain of."

Well, the king he talked him blind; so at last he give in, and said all right, but said he believed it was blame foolishness to stay, and that doctor hanging over them. But the king says:

"Cuss the doctor! What do we k'yer for *him?* Hain't we got all the fools in town on our side? and ain't that a big enough majority in any town?"

So they got ready to go down stairs again. The duke says:

"I don't think we put that money in a good place."

That cheered me up. I'd begun to think I warn't going to get a hint of no kind to help me. The king says:

"Why?"

"Because Mary Jane'll be in mourning from this out; and first you know the nigger that does up the rooms will get an order to box these duds up and put 'em away; and do you reckon a nigger can run across money and not borrow some of it?"

"Your head's level, agin, duke," says the king; and he come a fumbling under the curtain two or three foot from where I was. I stuck tight to the wall, and kept mighty still, though quivery; and I wondered what them fellows would say to me if they catched me; and I tried to think what I'd better do if they did catch me. But the king he got the bag before I could think more than about a half a thought, and he never suspicioned I was around. They took and shoved the bag through a rip in the straw tick that was under the feather bed, and crammed it in a foot or two amongst the straw and said it was all right, now, because a nigger only makes up the feather bed, and don't turn over the straw tick only about twice a year, and so it warn't in no danger of getting stole, now.

But I knowed better. I had it out of there before they was half-way down stairs. I groped along up to my cubby, and hid it there till I could get a chance to do better. I judged I better hide it outside of the house somewheres, because if they missed it they would give the house a good ransacking. I knowed that very well. Then I turned in, with my clothes all on; but I couldn't a gone to sleep, if I'd a wanted to, I was in such a sweat to get through with the business. By-and-by I heard the king and the duke come up; so I rolled off of my pallet and laid with my chin at the top of my ladder and waited to see if anything was going to happen. But nothing did.

So I held on till all the late sounds had quit and the early ones hadn't begun, yet; and then I slipped down the ladder.

Chapter XXVII
The Funeral—Satisfying Curiosity—Suspicious
of Huck—Quick Sales and Small Profits

I crept to their doors and listened; they was snoring, so I tip-toed along, and got down stairs all right. There warn't a sound anywheres. I peeped through a crack of the dining room door, and see the men that was watching the corpse all sound asleep on their chairs. The door was open into the parlor, where the corpse was laying, and there was a candle in both rooms. I passed along, and the parlor door was open; but I see there warn't nobody in there but the remainders of Peter; so I shoved on by; but the front door was locked, and the key wasn't there. Just then I heard somebody coming down the stairs, back behind me. I run in the parlor, and took a swift look around, and the only place I see to hide the bag was in the coffin. The lid was shoved along about a foot, showing the dead man's face down in there, with a wet cloth over it, and his shroud on. I tucked the money-bag in under the lid, just down beyond where his hands was crossed, which made me creep, they was so cold, and then I run back across the room and in behind the door.

A CRACK IN THE
DINING ROOM DOOR.

The person coming was Mary Jane. She went to the coffin, very soft, and kneeled down and looked in; then she put up her handkerchief and I see she begun to cry, though I couldn't hear her, and her back was to me. I slid out, and as I passed the dining room I thought I'd make sure them watchers hadn't seen me; so I looked through the crack and everything was all right. They hadn't stirred.

I slipped up to bed, feeling ruther blue, on accounts of the thing playing out that way after I had took so much trouble and run so much resk about it. Says I, if it could stay where it is, all right; because when we get down the river a hundred mile or two, I could write back to Mary Jane, and she could dig him up again and get it; but that ain't the thing that's going to happen; the thing that's going to happen is, the money'll be found when they come to screw on the lid. Then the king'll get it again, and it'll be a long day before he gives anybody another chance to smouch it from him. Of course I *wanted* to slide down and get it out of there, but I dasn't try it. Every minute it was getting earlier, now, and pretty soon some of them watchers would begin to stir, and I might get catched—catched with six thousand dollars in my hands that nobody hadn't hired me to take care of. I don't wish to be mixed up in no such business as that, I says to myself.

When I got down stairs in the morning, the parlor was shut up, and the watchers was gone. There warn't nobody around but the family and the widow Bartley and our tribe. I watched their faces to see if anything had been happening, but I couldn't tell.

Towards the middle of the day the undertaker come, with his man, and they set the coffin in the middle of the room on a couple of chairs, and then set all our chairs in rows, and borrowed more from the neighbors till the hall and the parlor and the dining room was full. I see the coffin lid was the way it was before, but I dasn't go to look in under it, with folks around.

Then the people begun to flock in, and the beats and the girls took seats in the front row at the head of the coffin, and for a half an hour the people filed around slow, in single rank, and looked down at the dead man's face a minute, and some dropped in a tear, and it was all very still and solemn, only the girls and the beats holding handkerchiefs to their eyes and keeping their heads bent, and sobbing a little. There warn't no other sound but the scraping of the feet on the floor, and blowing noses—because people always blows them more at a funeral than they do at other places except church.

When the place was packed full, the undertaker he slid around in his black gloves with his softy soothering ways, putting on the last touches, and getting people and things all ship-shape and comfortable, and making no more sound than a cat. He never spoke; he moved people around, he squeezed in late ones, he opened up passage-ways, and done it with nods, and signs with his hands. Then he took his place over against the wall. He was the softest, glidingest, stealthiest man I ever see; and there warn't no more smile to him than there is to a ham.

They had borrowed a melodeum—a sick one; and when everything was ready, a young woman set down and worked it, and it was pretty skreeky and colicky, and everybody joined in and sung, and Peter was the only one that had a good thing, according to my notion. Then the Reverend

Hobson opened up, slow and solemn, and begun to talk; and straight off the most outrageous row busted out in the cellar a body ever heard; it was only one dog, but he made a most powerful racket, and he kept it up, right along; the parson he had to stand there, over the coffin, and wait—you couldn't hear yourself think. It was right down awkward, and nobody didn't seem to know what to do. But pretty soon they see that long-legged undertaker make a sign to the preacher as much as to say, "Don't you worry—just depend on me." Then he stooped down and begun to glide along the wall, just his shoulders showing over the people's heads. So he glided along, and the pow-wow and racket getting more and more outrageous all the time; and at last, when he had gone around two sides of the room, he disappears down cellar. Then, in about two seconds we heard a whack, and the dog he finished up with a most amazing howl or two, and then everything was dead still, and the parson begun his solemn talk where he left off. In a minute or two here comes this undertaker's back and shoulders gliding along the wall again; and so he glided, and glided, around three sides of the room, and then rose up, and shaded his mouth with his hands, and stretched his neck out towards the preacher, over the people's heads, and says, in a kind of a coarse whisper, "*He had a rat!*" Then he drooped down and glided along the wall again to his place. You could see it was a great satisfaction to the people, because naturally they wanted to know. A little thing like that don't cost nothing, and it's just the little things that makes a man to be looked up to and liked. There warn't no more popular man in town than what that undertaker was.

Well, the funeral sermon was very good, but pison long and tiresome; and then the king he shoved in and got off some of his usual rubbage, and at last the job was through, and the undertaker begun to sneak up on the coffin with his screw-driver. I was in a sweat then, and watched him pretty keen. But he never meddled at all; just slid the lid along, as soft as mush, and screwed it down tight and fast. So there I was! I didn't know whether the money was in there or not. So, says I, spose somebody has hogged that bag on the sly?—now how do *I* know whether to write to Mary Jane or not? Spose she dug him up and didn't find nothing—what would she think of me? Blame it, I says, I might get hunted up and jailed; I'd better lay low and keep dark, and not write at all; the thing's awful mixed, now; trying to better it, I've worsened it a hundred times, and I wish to goodness I'd just let it alone, dad fetch the whole business!

They buried him, and we come back home, and I went to watching faces again—I couldn't help it, and I couldn't rest easy. But nothing come of it; the faces didn't tell me nothing.

The king he visited around, in the evening, and sweetened every body up, and made himself ever so friendly; and he give out the idea that his congregation over in England would be in a sweat about him, so he must hurry and settle up the estate right away, and leave for home. He was very sorry he was so pushed, and so was everybody; they wished he could stay longer, but they said they could see it couldn't be done. And he said of course him and William would take the girls home with them; and that pleased everybody too, because then the girls would be well fixed, and amongst their own relations; and it pleased the girls, too—tickled them so they clean forgot they ever had a trouble in the world; and told him to sell out as quick as he wanted to, they would be ready. Them poor things was that glad and happy it made my heart ache to see them getting fooled and lied to so, but I didn't see no safe way for me to chip in and change the general tune.

Well, blamed if the king didn't bill the house and the niggers and all the property for auction straight off—sale two days after the funeral; but anybody could buy private beforehand if they wanted to.

So the next day after the funeral, along about noontime, the girls' joy got the first jolt; a couple of nigger traders come along, and the king sold them the niggers reasonable, for three-day drafts as they called it, and away they went, the two sons up the river to Memphis, and their mother down the river to Orleans. I thought them poor girls and them niggers would break their hearts for grief; they cried around each other, and took on so it most made me down sick to see it. The girls said they hadn't ever dreamed of seeing the family separated or sold away from the town. I can't ever get it out of my memory, the sight of them poor miserable girls and niggers hanging around each other's necks and crying; and I reckon I couldn't stood it all but would a had to bust out and tell on our gang if I hadn't knowed the sale warn't no account and the niggers would be back home in a week or two.

The thing made a big stir in the town, too, and a good many come out flat-footed and said it was scandalous to separate the mother and the children that way. It injured the frauds some; but the old fool he bulled right along, spite of all the duke could say or do, and I tell you the duke was powerful uneasy.

Next day was auction day. About broad-day in the morning, the king and the duke come up in the garret and woke me up, and I see by their look that there was trouble. The king says:

"Was you in my room night before last?"

"No, your majesty"—which was the way I always called him when nobody but our gang warn't around.

"Was you in there yisterday er last night?"

"No, your majesty."

"Honor bright, now—no lies."

"Honor bright, your majesty, I'm telling you the truth. I hain't been anear your room since Miss Mary Jane took you and the duke and showed it to you."

The duke says:

"Have you seen anybody else go in there?"

"No, your grace, not as I remember, I believe."

"Stop and think."

I studied a while, and see my chance, then I says:

"Well, I see the niggers go in there several times."

Both of them gave a little jump; and looked like they hadn't ever expected it, and then like they *had*. Then the duke says:

"What, *all* of them?"

"No—leastways not all at once. That is, I don't think I ever see them all come *out* at once but just one time."

"Hello—when was that?"

"It was the day we had the funeral. In the morning. It warn't early, because I overslept. I was just starting down the ladder, and I see them."

"Well, go on, *go* on—what did they do? How'd they act?"

"They didn't do nothing. And they didn't act anyway, much, as fur as I see. They tip-toed away; so I seen, easy enough, that they'd shoved in there to do up your majesty's room, or something, sposing you was up; and found you *warn't* up, and so they was hoping to slide out of the way of trouble without waking you up, if they hadn't already waked you up."

"Great guns, *this* is a go!" says the king; and both of them looked pretty sick, and tolerable silly. They stood there a thinking and scratching their heads, a minute, and the duke he bust into a kind of little raspy chuckle, and says:

"It does beat all, how neat the niggers played their hand. They let on to be *sorry* they was going out of this region! and I believed they *was* sorry. And so did you, and so did everybody. Don't ever tell *me* any more that a nigger ain't got any histrionic talent. Why, the way they played that thing, it would fool *anybody*. In my opinion there's a fortune in 'em. If I had capital and a theatre, I wouldn't want a better lay out than that—and here we've gone and sold 'em for a song. Yes, and ain't privileged to sing the song, yet. Say, where *is* that song—that draft?"

"In the bank for to be collected. Where *would* it be?"

"Well, *that's* all right then, thank goodness."

Says I, kind of timid-like:

"Is something gone wrong?"

The king whirls on me and rips out:

"None o' your business! You keep your head shet, and mine y'r own affairs—if you got any. Long as you're in this town, don't you forget *that*, you hear?" Then he says to the duke, "We got to jest swaller it, and say noth'n': mum's the word for *us*."

As they was starting down the ladder, the duke he chuckles again and says:

"Quick sales *and* small profits! It's a good business—yes."

The king snarls around on him and says:

"I was trying to do for the best, in sellin' 'em out so quick. If the profits has turned out to be none, lackin' considable, and none to carry, is it my fault any more'n it's yourn?"

"Well, *they'd* be in this house yet, and we *wouldn't* if I could a got my advice listened to."

The king sassed back, as much as was safe for him, and then swapped around and lit into *me* again. He give me down the banks for not coming and *telling* him I see the niggers come out of his room acting that way— said any fool would a *knowed* something was up. And then waltzed in and cussed *himself* awhile; and said it all come of him not laying late and taking his natural rest that morning, and he'd be blamed if he'd ever do it again. So they went off a jawing; and I felt dreadful glad I'd worked it all off onto the niggers and yet hadn't done the niggers no harm by it.

Chapter XXVIII
The Trip to England—"The Brute!"—Mary Jane Decides to Leave—Huck Parting with Mary Jane—Mumps—The Opposition Line

By-and-by it was getting-up time; so I come down the ladder and started for down-stairs, but as I come to the girls' room, the door was open, and I see Mary Jane setting by her old hair trunk, which was open and she'd been packing things in it—getting ready to go to England. But she had stopped now, with a folded gown in her lap, and had her face in her hands, crying. I felt awful bad to see it; of course anybody would. I went in there, and says:

"Miss Mary Jane, you can't abear to see people in trouble, and *I* can't—most always. Tell me about it."

So she done it. And it was the niggers—I just expected it. She said the beautiful trip to England was most about spoiled for her; she didn't know *how* she was ever going to be happy there, knowing the mother and the children warn't ever going to see each other no more—and then busted out bitterer than ever, and flung up her hands, and says

"Oh, dear, dear, to think they ain't *ever* going to see each other any more!"

"But they *will*—and inside of two weeks—and I *know* it!" says I.

Laws it was out before I could think!—and before I could budge, she throws her arms around my neck, and told me to say it *again,* say it *again,* say it *again!*

I see I had spoke too sudden, and said too much, and was in a close place. I asked her to let me think a minute; and she set there, very impatient and excited, and handsome, but looking kind of happy and eased-up, like a person that's had a tooth pulled out. So I went to studying it out. I says to myself, I reckon a body that ups

IN TROUBLE.

and tells the truth when he is in a tight place, is taking considerable many resks, though I ain't had no experience, and can't say for certain; but it looks so to me, anyway; and yet here's a case where I'm blest if it don't look to me like the truth is better, and actuly *safer,* than a lie. I must lay it by in my mind, and think it over some time or other, it's so kind of strange and unregular. I never see nothing like it. Well, I says to myself at last, I'm agoing to chance it; I'll up and tell the truth this time, though it does seem most like setting down on a kag of powder and touching it off just to see where you'll go to. Then I says:

"Miss Mary Jane, is there any place out of town a little ways, where you could go and stay three or four days?"

"Yes—Mr. Lothrop's. Why?"

"Never mind why, yet. If I'll tell you how I know the niggers will see each other again—inside of two weeks—here in this house—and *prove* how I know it—will you go to Mr. Lothrop's and stay four days?"

"Four days!" she says; "I'll stay a year!"

"All right," I says, "I don't want nothing more out of *you* than just your word—I druther have it than another man's kiss-the-Bible." She smiled, and reddened up very sweet, and I says, "If you don't mind it, I'll shut the door—and bolt it."

Then I come back and set down again, and says:

"Don't you holler. Just set still, and take it like a man. I got to tell the truth, and you want to brace up, Miss Mary, because it's a bad kind, and going to be hard to take, but there ain't no help for it. These uncles of yourn ain't no uncles at all—they're a couple of frauds—regular dead-beats. There, now we're over the worst of it—you can stand the rest middling easy."

It jolted her up like everything, of course; but I was over the shoal water now, so I went right along, her eyes a blazing higher and higher all the time, and told her every blame thing, from where we first struck that young fool going up to the steamboat, clear through to where she flung herself onto the king's breast at the front door and he kissed her sixteen or seventeen times—and then up she jumps, with her face afire like sunset, and says:

"The brute! Come—don't waste a minute—not a *second*—we'll have them tarred and feathered, and flung in the river!"

Says I:

"Cert'nly. But do you mean, *before* you go to Mr. Lothrop's, or —"

"Oh," she says, "what am I *thinking* about!" she says, and set right down again. "Don't mind what I said—please don't—you *won't*, now, *will* you?" Laying her silky hand on mine in that kind of a way that I said I would die first. "I never thought, I was so stirred up," she says; "now go on, and I won't do so any more. You tell me what to do, and whatever you say, I'll do it."

"Well," I says, "it's a rough gang, them two frauds, and I'm fixed so I got to travel with them a while longer, whether I want to or not— I druther not tell you why—and if you was to blow on them this town would get me out of their claws, and *I'd* be all right, but there'd be another person that you don't know about who'd be in big trouble. Well, we got to save *him*, hain't we? Of course. Well, then, we won't blow on them."

Saying them words put a good idea in my head. I see how maybe I could get me and Jim rid of the frauds; get them jailed here, and then leave. But I didn't want to run the raft in day-time, without anybody aboard to answer questions but me; so I didn't want the plan to begin working till pretty late to-night. I says:

"Miss Mary Jane, I'll tell you what we'll do—and you won't have to stay at Mr. Lothrop's so long, nuther. How fur is it?"

"A little short of four miles—right out in the country, back here."

"Well, that'll answer. Now you go along out there, and lay low till nine or half-past, to-night, and then get them to fetch you home again—tell them you've thought of something. If you get here before eleven, put a candle in this window, and if I don't turn up, wait *till* eleven, and *then* if I don't turn up it means I'm gone, and out of the way, and safe. Then you come out and spread the news around, and get these beats jailed."

"Good," she says, "I'll do it."

"And if it just happens so that I don't get away, but get took up along with them, you must up and say I told you the whole thing beforehand, and you must stand by me all you can."

"Stand by you, indeed I will. They sha'n't touch a hair of your head!" she says, and I see her nostrils spread and her eyes snap when she said it, too.

"If I get away, I sha'n't be here," I says, "to prove these rapscallions ain't your uncles, and I couldn't do it if I *was* here. I could swear they was beats and bummers, that's all; though that's worth something. Well, there's others can do that better than what I can—and they're people that ain't going to be doubted as quick as I'd be. I'll tell you how to find them. Gimme a pencil and a piece of paper. There—'*Royal Nonesuch, Bricksville.*' Put it away, and don't lose it. When the court wants to find out something about these two, let them send up to Bricksville and say they've got the men that played the Royal Nonesuch, and ask for some witnesses—why, you'll have that entire town down here before you can hardly wink, Miss Mary. And they'll come a-biling, too."

I judged we had got everything fixed about right, now. So I says:

"Just let the auction go right along, and don't worry. Nobody don't have to pay for the things they buy till a whole day after the auction, on accounts of the short notice, and they ain't going out of this till they get that money—and the way we've fixed it the sale ain't going to count, and they ain't going to *get* no money. It's just like the way it was with the niggers—it warn't no sale, and the niggers will be back before long. Why, they can't collect the money for the *niggers*, yet—they're in the worst kind of a fix, Miss Mary."

"Well," she says, "I'll run down to breakfast now, and then I'll start straight for Mr. Lothrop's."

"'Deed, *that* ain't the ticket, Miss Mary Jane," I says, "by no manner of means; go *before* breakfast."

"Why?"

"What did you reckon I wanted you to go at all for, Miss Mary?"

"Well, I never thought—and come to think, I don't know. What was it?"

"Why, it's because you ain't one of these leather-face people. I don't want no better book than what your face is. A body can set down and read it off like coarse print. Do you reckon you can go and face your uncles, when they come to kiss you good-morning, and never —"

"There, there, don't! Yes, I'll go before breakfast—I'll be glad to. And leave my sisters with them?"

"Yes—never mind about them. They've got to stand it yet a while. They might suspicion something if all of you was to go. I don't want you to see them, nor your sisters, nor nobody in this town—if a neighbor was to ask how is your uncles this morning, your face would tell something. No, you go right along, Miss Mary Jane, and I'll fix it with all of them. I'll tell Miss Susan to give your love to your uncles and say you've went away for a few hours for to get a little rest and change, or to see a friend, and you'll be back to-night or early in the morning."

"Gone to see a friend is all right, but I won't have my love given to them."

"Well, then, it sha'n't be." It was well enough to tell *her* so—no harm in it. It was only a little thing to do, and no trouble; and it's the little things that smoothes people's roads the most, down here below; it would make Mary Jane comfortable, and it wouldn't cost nothing. Then I says: "There's one more thing—that bag of money."

"Well, they've got that; and it makes me feel pretty silly to think *how* they got it."

"No, you're out, there. They hain't got it."

"Why, who's got it?"

"I wish I knowed, but I don't. I *had* it, because I stole it from them; and I stole it to give to you; and I know where I hid it, but I'm afraid it ain't there no more. I'm awful sorry, Miss Mary Jane, I'm just as sorry as I can be; but I done the best I could; I did, honest. I come nigh getting caught, and I had to shove it into the first place I come to, and run—and it warn't a good place."

"Oh, stop blaming yourself—it's too bad to do it, and I won't allow it—you couldn't help it; it wasn't your fault. Where did you hide it?"

I didn't want to set her to thinking about her troubles again; and I couldn't seem to get my mouth to tell her what would make her see that corpse laying in the coffin with that bag of money on his stomach. So for a minute I didn't say nothing—then I says:

"I'd ruther not *tell* you where I put it, Miss Mary Jane, if you don't mind letting me off; but I'll write it for you on a piece of paper, and you can read it along the road to Mr. Lothrop's, if you want to. Do you reckon that'll do?"

"Oh, yes."

So I wrote: "I put it in the coffin. It was in there when you was crying there, away in the night. I was behind the door, and I was mighty sorry for you, Miss Mary Jane." *— M Gaturing*

(It made my eyes water a little) to remember her crying there all by herself in the night, and them devils laying there right under her own roof, shaming her and robbing her; and when I folded it up and give it to her, I see the water come into her eyes, too; and she shook me by the hand, hard, and says:

"*Good*-bye—I'm going to do everything just as you've told me; and if I don't ever see you again, I sha'n't ever forget you, and I'll think of you a many and a many a time, and I'll *pray* for you, too!"—and she was gone.

Pray for me! I reckoned if she knowed me she'd take a job that was more nearer her size. But I bet she done it, just the same—she was just that kind. She had the grit to pray for Judus if she took the notion—there warn't no back-down to her, I judge. You may say what you want to, but in my opinion she had more sand in her than any girl I ever see; in my opinion she was just full of sand. It sounds like flattery, but it ain't no flattery. And when it comes to beauty—and goodness too—she lays over them all. I hain't ever seen her since that time that I see her go out of that door; no, I hain't ever seen her since, but I reckon I've thought of her a many and a many a million times, and of her saying she would pray for me; and if ever I'd a thought it would do any good for me to pray for *her*, blamed if I wouldn't a done it or bust.

Well, Mary Jane she lit out the back way, I reckon; because nobody see her go. When I struck Susan and the hare-lip, I says:

"What's the name of them people over on t'other side of the river that you all goes to see sometimes?"

They says:

"There's several; but it's the Proctors, mainly."

"That's the name," I says; "I most forgot it. Well, Miss Mary Jane she told me to tell you she's gone over there in a dreadful hurry—one of them's sick."

"Which one?"

"I don't know; leastways I kinder forget; but I thinks it's—"

"Sakes alive, I hope it ain't *Hanner?*"

"I'm sorry to say it," I says, "but Hanner's the very one."

"My goodness—and she so well only last week! Is she took bad?"

"It ain't no name for it. They set up with her all night, Miss Mary Jane said, and they don't think she'll last many hours."

"Only think of that, now! What's the matter with her?"

I couldn't think of anything reasonable, right off that way, so I says:
"Mumps."

"Mumps your granny! They don't set up with people that's got the mumps."

"They don't, don't they? You better bet they do with *these* mumps. These mumps is different. It's a new kind, Miss Mary Jane said."

"How's it a new kind?"

"Because it's mixed up with other things."

"What other things?"

"Well, measles, and whooping-cough, and erysiplas, and consumption, and yaller janders, and brain fever, and I don't know what all."

"My land! And they call it the *mumps?*"

"That's what Miss Mary Jane said."

"Well, what in the nation do they call it the *mumps* for?"

"Why, because it *is* the mumps. That's what it starts with."

"Well, ther' ain't no sense in it. A body might stump his toe, and take pison, and fall down the well, and break his neck, and bust his brains out, and somebody come along and ask what killed him, and some numskull up and say, 'Why, he stumped his *toe.*' Would ther' be any sense in that? *No.* And ther' ain't no sense in *this,* nuther. Is it ketching?"

"Is it *ketching?* Why, how you talk. Is a *harrow* catching?—in the dark? If you don't hitch onto one tooth, you're bound to on another, ain't you? And you can't get away with that tooth without fetching the whole harrow along, can you? Well, these kind of mumps is a kind of a harrow, as you may say—and it ain't no slouch of a harrow, nuther, you come to get it hitched on good."

"Well, it's awful, *I* think," says the hare-lip. "I'll go to Uncle Harvey and—"

"Oh, yes," I says, "I *would.* Of *course* I would. I wouldn't lose no time."

"Well, why wouldn't you?"

"Just look at it a minute, and maybe you can see. Hain't your uncles obleeged to get along home to England as fast as they can? And do you reckon they'd be mean enough to go off and leave you to go all that journey by yourselves? *You* know they'll wait for you. So fur, so good. Your uncle Harvey's a preacher, ain't he? Very well, then; is a *preacher* going to deceive a steamboat clerk? is he going to deceive a *ship clerk?*—so as to get them to let Miss Mary Jane go aboard? Now *you* know he ain't. What *will* he do, then? Why, he'll say, 'It's a great pity, but my church matters has got to get along the best way they can; for my niece has been exposed to the dreadful pluribus-unum mumps, and so it's my bounden duty to set down here and wait the three months it takes to show on her if she's got it.' But never mind, if you think it's best to tell your uncle Harvey—"

"Shucks, and stay fooling around here when we could all be having good times in England whilst we was waiting to find out whether Mary Jane's got it or not? Why, you talk like a muggins."

"Well, anyway, maybe you'd better tell some of the neighbors."

"Listen at that, now. You do beat all, for natural stupidness. Can't you *see* that *they'd* go and tell? Ther' ain't no way but just to not tell anybody at *all*."

"Well, maybe you're right—yes, I judge you *are* right."

"But I reckon we ought to tell Uncle Harvey she's gone out a while, anyway, so he won't be uneasy about her?"

"Yes, Miss Mary Jane she wanted you to do that. She says, 'Tell them to give Uncle Harvey and William my love and a kiss, and say I've run over the river to see Mr.—Mr.—what *is* the name of that rich family your uncle Peter used to think so much of?—I mean the one that—"

"Why, you must mean the Apthorps, ain't it?"

"Of course; bother them kind of names, a body can't ever seem to remember them, half the time, somehow. Yes, she said, say she has run over for to ask the Apthorps to be sure and come to the auction and buy this house, because she allowed her uncle Peter would ruther they had it than anybody else; and she's going to stick to them till they say they'll come, and then, if she ain't too tired, she's coming home; and if she is, she'll be home in the morning anyway. She said, don't say nothing about the Proctors, but only about the Apthorps—which'll be perfectly true, because she *is* going there to speak about their buying the house; I know it, because she told me so, herself."

"All right," they said, and cleared out to lay for their uncles, and give them the love and the kisses, and tell them the message.

Everything was all right now. The girls wouldn't say nothing because they wanted to go to England; and the king and the duke would ruther Mary Jane was off working for the auction than around in reach of Doctor Robinson. I felt very good; I judged I had done it pretty neat—I reckoned Tom Sawyer couldn't a done it no neater himself. Of course he would a throwed more style into it, but I can't do that very handy, not being brung up to it.

Well, they held the auction in the public square, along towards the end of the afternoon, and it strung along, and strung along, and the old man he was on hand and looking his level piousest, up there longside of the auctioneer, and chipping in a little Scripture, now and then, or a little goody-goody saying, of some kind, and the duke he was around goo-goo-ing for sympathy all he knowed how, and just spreading himself generly. But by-and-by the thing dragged through, and everything was sold. Everything but a little old trifling lot in the graveyard. So they'd got to work *that* off—I never see such a girafft as the king was for wanting to swallow *everything*. Well, whilst they was at it, a steamboat landed, and in about two minutes up comes a crowd a whooping and yelling and laughing and carrying on, and singing out:

"*Here's* your opposition line! here's your two sets o' heirs to old Peter Wilks—and you pays your money and you takes your choice!"

Chapter XXIX
Contested Relationship—The King Explains the
Loss—A Question of Handwriting—Digging up
the Corpse—Huck Escapes

They was fetching a very nice looking old gentleman along, and a nice looking younger one, with his right arm in a sling. And my souls, how the people yelled, and laughed, and kept it up. But I didn't see no joke about it, and I judged it would strain the duke and the king some to see any. I reckoned they'd turn pale. But no, nary a pale did *they* turn. The duke he never let on he suspicioned what was up, but just went a goo-gooing around, happy and satisfied, like a jug that's googling out buttermilk; and as for the king, he just gazed and gazed down sorrowful on them new-comers like it give him the stomach-ache in his very heart to think there could be such frauds and rascals in the world. Oh, he done it admirable. Lots of the principal people gethered around the king, to let him see they was on his side. That old gentleman that had just come looked all puzzled to death. Pretty soon he begun to speak, and I see, straight off, he pronounced *like* an Englishman, not the king's way, though the king's *was* pretty good, for an imitation. I can't give the old gent's words; nor I can't imitate him; but he turned around to the crowd, and says, about like this:

"This is a surprise to me which I wasn't looking for; and I'll acknowledge, candid and frank, I ain't very well fixed to meet it and answer it; for my brother and me has had misfortunes; he's broke his arm, and our baggage got put off at a town above here, last night in the night by a mistake. I am Peter Wilks's brother Harvey, and this is his brother William, which can't hear nor speak—and can't even make signs to amount to much, now't he's only got one hand to work them with. We are who we say we are; and in a day or two, when I get the baggage, I can prove it. But, up till then, I won't say nothing more, but go to the hotel and wait."

So him and the new dummy started off; and the king he laughs, and blethers out: "Broke his arm—*very* likely *ain't* it?—and very convenient, too, for a fraud that's got to make signs, and hain't learnt how. Lost their baggage! That's *mighty* good!—and mighty ingenious—under the *circumstances!*

all switched around

So he laughed again; and so did everybody else, except three or four, or maybe half a dozen. One of these was that doctor; another one was a sharp looking gentleman, with a carpet-bag of the old-fashioned kind made out of carpet-stuff, that had just come off of the steamboat and was talking to him in a

THE TRUE BROTHERS.

low voice, and glancing towards the king now and then and nodding their heads— it was Levi Bell, the lawyer that was gone up to Louisville; and another one was a big rough husky that come along and listened to all the old gentleman said, and was listening to the king now. And when the king got done, this husky up and says:

"Say, looky here; if you are Harvey Wilks, when'd you come to this town?"

"The day before the funeral, friend," says the king.

"But what time o' day?"

"In the evenin'—'bout an hour er two before sundown."

"*How'd* you come?"

"I come down on the *Susan Powell,* from Cincinnati."

"Well, then, how'd you come to be up at the Pint in the *mornin'*—in a canoe?"

"I warn't up at the Pint in the mornin'."

"It's a lie."

Several of them jumped for him and begged him not to talk that way to an old man and a preacher.

"Preacher be hanged, he's a fraud and a liar. He was up at the Pint that mornin'. I live up there, don't I? Well, I was up there, and he was up there. I *see* him there. He come in a canoe, along with Tim Collins and a boy."

The doctor he up and says: "Would you know the boy again if you was to see him, Hines?"

"I reckon I would, but I don't know. Why, yonder he is, now. I know him perfectly easy."

It was me he pointed at. The doctor says:

"Neighbors, I don't know whether the new couple is frauds or not; but if *these* two ain't frauds, I am an idiot, that's all. I think it's our duty to see that they don't get away from here till we've looked into this thing. Come along, Hines; come along, the rest of you. We'll take these fellows to the tavern and affront them with t'other couple, and I reckon we'll find out *something* before we get through."

It was nuts for the crowd, though maybe not for the king's friends; so we all started. It was about sundown. The doctor he led me along by the hand, and was plenty kind enough, but he never let *go* my hand.

We all got in a big room in the hotel, and lit up some candles, and fetched in the new couple. First, the doctor says:

"I don't wish to be too hard on these two men, but *I* think they're frauds, and they may have complices that we don't know nothing about. If they have, won't the complices get away with that bag of gold Peter Wilks left? It ain't unlikely. If these men ain't frauds, they won't object to sending for that money and letting us keep it till they prove they're all right—ain't that so?"

Everybody agreed to that. So I judged they had our gang in a pretty tight place, right at the outstart. But the king he only looked sorrowful, and says:

"Gentlemen, I wish the money was there, for I ain't got no disposition to throw anything in the way of a fair, open, out-and-out investigation o' this misable business; but alas, the money ain't there; you k'n send and see, if you want to."

"Where is it, then?"

"Well, when my niece give it to me to keep for her, I took and hid it inside o' the straw tick o' my bed, not wishin' to bank it for the few days we'd be here, and considerin' the bed a safe place, we not bein' used to niggers, and suppos'n' 'em honest, like servants in England. The niggers stole it the very next mornin' after I had went down stairs; and when I sold 'em, I hadn't missed the money yit, so they got clean away with it. My servant here k'n tell you 'bout it gentlemen."

The doctor and several said "Shucks!" and I see nobody didn't altogether believe him. One man asked me if I see the niggers steal it. I said no, but I see them sneaking out of the room and hustling away, and I never thought nothing, only I reckoned they was afraid they had waked up my master and was trying to get away before he made trouble with them. That was all they asked me. Then the doctor whirls on me and says:

"Are *you* English, too?"

I says yes; and him and some others laughed, and said, "Stuff!"

Well, then they sailed in on the general investigation, and there we had it, up and down, hour in, hour out, and nobody never said a word about supper, nor ever seemed to think about it—and so they kept it up, and kept it up; and it *was* the worst mixed-up thing you ever see. They made the king tell his yarn, and they made the old gentleman tell his'n; and anybody but a lot of prejudiced chuckleheads would a *seen* that the old gentleman was spinning truth and t'other one lies. And by-and-by they had me up to tell what I knowed. The king he give me a left-handed look out of the corner of his eye, and so I knowed enough to talk on the right side. I begun to tell about Sheffield, and how we lived there, and all about the English Wilkses, and so on; but I didn't get pretty fur till the doctor begun to laugh; and Levi Bell, the lawyer, says:

"Set down, my boy, I wouldn't strain myself, if I was you. I reckon you ain't used to lying, it don't seem to come handy; what you want is practice. You do it pretty awkward." *he is an expert*

I didn't care nothing for the compliment, but I was glad to be let off, anyway.

The doctor he started to say something, and turns and says:

"If you'd been in town at first, Levi Bell—"

The king broke in and reached out his hand, and says:

"Why, is this my poor dead brother's old friend that he's wrote so often about?"

The lawyer and him shook hands, and the lawyer smiled and looked pleased, and they talked right along awhile, and then got to one side and talked low; and at last the lawyer speaks up and says:

"That'll fix it. I'll take the order and send it, along with your brother's, and then they'll know it's all right."

So they got some paper and a pen, and the king he set down and twisted his head to one side, and chawed his tongue, and scrawled off something; and then they give the pen to the duke—and then for the first time, the duke looked sick. But he took the pen and wrote. So then the lawyer turns to the new old gentleman and says:

"You and your brother please write a line or two and sign your names."

The old gentleman wrote, but nobody couldn't read it. The lawyer looked powerful astonished, and says:

"Well, it beats *me*—and snaked a lot of old letters out of his pocket, and examined them, and then examined the old man's writing, and then *them* again; and then says: "These old letters is from Harvey Wilks; and here's *these* two handwritings, and anybody can see *they* didn't write them" (the king and the duke looked sold and foolish, I tell you, to see how the lawyer had took them in), "and here's *this* old gentleman's handwriting, and anybody can tell, easy enough, *he* didn't write them—fact is, the scratches he makes ain't properly *writing,* at all. Now, here's some letters from—"

The new old gentleman says:

"If you please, let me explain. Nobody can read my hand but my brother there—so he copies for me. It's *his* hand you've got there, not mine."

"*Well!*" says the lawyer, "this *is* a state of things. I've got some of William's letters too; so if you'll get him to write a line or so we can com—"

"He *can't* write with his left hand," says the old gentleman. "If he could use his right hand, you would see that he wrote his own letters and mine too. Look at both, please—they're by the same hand."

The lawyer done it, and says:

"I believe it's so—and if it ain't so, there's a heap stronger resemblance than I'd noticed before, anyway. Well, well, well! I thought we was right on the track of a solution, but it's gone to grass, partly. But anyway, *one* thing is proved—*these* two ain't either of 'em Wilkses"—and he wagged his head towards the king and the duke.

Well, what do you think?—that muleheaded old fool wouldn't give in *then!* Indeed he wouldn't. Said it warn't no fair test. Said his brother William was the cussedest joker in the world, and hadn't *tried* to write— *he* see William was going to play one of his jokes the minute he put the pen to paper. And so he warmed up and went warbling and warbling right along, till he was actuly beginning to believe what he was saying, *himself*— but pretty soon the new old gentleman broke in, and says:

"I've thought of something. Is there anybody here that helped to lay out my br—helped to lay out the late Peter Wilks for burying?"

"Yes," says somebody, "me and Ab Turner done it. We're both here."

Then the old man turns towards the king, and says:

"Peraps this gentleman can tell me what was tattooed on his breast?"

Blamed if the king didn't have to brace up mighty quick, or he'd a squshed down like a bluff bank that the river has cut under, it took him so sudden—and mind you, it was a thing that was calculated to make most *anybody* sqush to get fetched such a solid one as that without any notice—because how was *he* going to know what was tattooed on the man? He whitened a little; he couldn't help it; and it was mighty still in there, and everybody bending a little forwards and gazing at him.

Says I to myself, *Now* he'll throw up the sponge—there ain't no more use. Well, did he? A body can't hardly believe it, but he didn't. I reckon he thought he'd keep the thing up till he tired them people out, so they'd thin out, and him and the duke could break loose and get away. Anyway, he set there, and pretty soon he begun to smile, and says:

"Mf! It's a *very* tough question, *ain't* it! *Yes,* sir, I k'n tell you what's tattooed on his breast. It's jest a small, thin, blue arrow—that's what it is; and if you don't look clost, you can't see it. *Now* what do you say—hey?"

Well, *I* never see anything like that old blister for clean out-and-out cheek.

The new old gentleman turns brisk towards Ab Turner and his pard, and his eye lights up like he judged he'd got the king *this* time, and says:

"There—you've heard what he said! Was there any such mark on Peter Wilks's breast?"

Both of them spoke up and says:

"We didn't see no such mark."

"Good!" says the old gentleman. "Now, what you *did* see on his breast was a small dim P, and a B (which is an initial he dropped when he was young), and a W, with dashes between them, so: P—B—W"—and he marked them that way on a piece of paper. "Come—ain't that what you saw?"

Both of them spoke up again, and says:

"No, we *didn't.* We never seen any marks at all."

Well, everybody *was* in a state of mind, now; and they sings out:

"The whole *bilin'* of 'm 's frauds! Le's duck 'em! le's drown 'em! le's ride 'em on a rail!" and everybody was whooping at once, and there was a rattling pow-wow. But the lawyer he jumps on the table and yells, and says:

"Gentlemen—gentle*men!* Hear me just a word—just a *single* word— if you PLEASE! There's one way yet—let's go and dig up the corpse and look."

That took them.

"Hooray!" they all shouted, and was starting right off; but the lawyer and the doctor sung out:

"Hold on, hold on! Collar all these four men and the boy, and fetch *them* along, too!"

"We'll do it!" they all shouted; "and if we don't find them marks we'll lynch the whole gang!"

(*I was* scared, now) I tell you. But there warn't no getting away, you know. They gripped us all, and marched us right along, straight for the graveyard, which was a mile and a half down the river, and the whole town at our heels, for we made noise enough, and it was only nine in the evening.

As we went by our house I wished I hadn't sent Mary Jane out of town; because now if I could tip her the wink, she'd light out and save me, and blow on our dead-beats.

Well, we swarmed along down the river road, just carrying on like wild-cats; and to make it more scary, the sky was darking up, and the lightning beginning to wink and flitter, and the wind to shiver amongst the leaves. *perhaps* This was the most awful trouble and most dangersome I ever was in; and I was kinder stunned; everything was going so different from what I had allowed for; stead of being fixed so I could take my own time, if I wanted to, and see all the fun, and have Mary Jane at my back to save me and set me free when the close-fit come, here was nothing in the world betwixt me and sudden death but just them tattoo-marks. If they didn't find them—

I couldn't bear to think about it; and yet, somehow, I couldn't think about nothing else. It got darker and darker, and it was a beautiful time to give the crowd the slip; but that big husky had me by the wrist—Hines—and a body might as well try to give Goliar[48] the slip. He dragged me right along, he was so excited; and I had to run to keep up.

When they got there they swarmed into the graveyard and washed over it like an overflow. And when they got to the grave, they found they had about a hundred times as many shovels as they wanted, but nobody hadn't thought to fetch a lantern. But they sailed into digging, anyway, by the flicker of the lightning, and sent a man to the nearest house a half a mile off, to borrow one.   `scaly`

So they dug and dug, like everything; and it got awful dark, and the rain started, and the wind swished and swushed along, and the lightning come brisker and brisker, and the thunder boomed; but them people never took no notice of it, they was so full of this business; and one minute you could see everything and every face in that big crowd, and the shovelfuls of dirt sailing up out of the grave, and the next second the dark wiped it all out, and you couldn't see nothing at all.

At last they got out the coffin, and begun to unscrew the lid, and then such another crowding, and shouldering, and shoving as there was, to scrouge in and get a sight, you never see; and in the dark, that way, it was awful. Hines he hurt my wrist dreadful, pulling and tugging so, and I reckon he clean forgot I was in the world, he was so excited and panting.

---

[48] 1 Sam. 17.23–51. Goliath, the Philistine champion slain by David in the Old Testament.

All of a sudden the lightning let go a perfect sluice of white glare, and somebody sings out:

"By the living jingo, here's the bag of gold on his breast!"

Hines let out a whoop, like everybody else, and dropped my wrist and give a big surge to bust his way in and get a look, and the way I lit out and shinned for the road in the dark, there ain't nobody can tell.

I had the road all to myself, and I fairly flew—leastways I had it all to myself except the solid dark, and the now-and-then glares, and the buzzing of the rain, and the thrashing of the wind, and the splitting of the thunder; and sure as you are born I did clip it along!

When I struck the town, I see there warn't nobody out in the storm, so I never hunted for no back streets, but humped it straight through the main one; and when I begun to get towards our house I aimed my eye and set it. No light there; the house all dark—which made me feel sorry and disappointed, I didn't know why. But at last, just as I was sailing by, *flash* comes the light in Mary Jane's window! and my heart swelled up sudden, like to bust; and the same second the house and all was behind me in the dark, and wasn't ever going to be before me no more in this world. (She *was* the best girl I ever see, and had the most sand.)

The minute I was far enough above the town to see I could make the towhead, I begun to look sharp for a boat to borrow; and the first time the lightning showed me one that wasn't chained, I snatched it and shoved. It was a canoe and warn't fastened with nothing but a rope. The towhead was a rattling big distance off, away out there in the middle of the river, but I didn't lose no time; and when I struck the raft at last, I was so fagged I would a just laid down to blow and gasp if I could afforded it. But I didn't. As I sprung aboard I sung out:

"Out with you Jim, and set her loose! Glory be to goodness, we're shut of them!"

Jim lit out, and was a coming for me with both arms spread, he was so full of joy; but when I glimpsed him in the lightning, my heart shot up in my mouth, and I went overboard backwards; for I forgot he was old King Lear and a drownded A-rab all in one, and it most scared the livers and lights out of me. But Jim fished me out, and was going to hug me and bless me, and so on, he was so glad I was back and we was shut of the king and the duke, but I says:

"Not now—have it for breakfast, have it for breakfast! Cut loose and let her slide!"

So, in two seconds, away we went, a sliding down the river, and it *did* seem so good to be free again and all by ourselves on the big river and no-body to bother us. I had to skip around a bit, and jump up and crack my heels a few times, I couldn't help it; but about the third crack, I noticed a sound that I knowed mighty well—and held my breath and listened and waited—and sure enough, when the next flash busted out over the water, here they come!—and just a laying to their oars and making their skiff hum! It was the king and the duke.

So I wilted right down onto the planks, then, and give up; and it was all I could do to keep from crying.) ~ not mature

Chapter XXX
The King Went for Him—A Royal Row—
Powerful Mellow

When they got aboard, the king went for me, and shook me by the collar, and says:

"Tryin' to give us the slip, was ye, you pup! Tired of our company—hey?"

I says:

"No, your majesty, we warn't—*please* don't, your majesty!"

"Quick, then, and tell us what *was* your idea, or I'll shake the insides out o' you!"

THE KING SHAKES HUCK.

"Honest, I'll tell you everything, just as it happened, your majesty. The man that had a holt of me was very good to me, and kept saying he had a boy about as big as me that died last year, and he was sorry to see a boy in such a dangerous fix; and when they was all took by surprise by finding the gold, and made a rush for the coffin, he lets go of me and whispers, 'Heel it now, or they'll hang ye, sure!' and I lit out. It didn't seem no good for *me* to stay—

I couldn't do nothing, and I didn't want to be hung if I could get away. So I never stopped running till I found the canoe; and when I got here I told Jim to hurry, or they'd catch me and hang me yet, and said I was a feard you and the duke wasn't alive, now, and I was awful sorry, and so was Jim, and was awful glad when we see you coming, you may ask Jim if I didn't."

Jim said it was so; and the king told him to shut up, and said, "Oh, yes, it's *mighty* likely!" and shook me up again, and said he reckoned he'd drownd me. But the duke says:

"Leggo the boy, you old idiot! Would *you* a done any different? Did you inquire around for *him,* when you got loose? *I* don't remember it."

So the king let go of me, and begun to cuss that town and everybody in it. But the duke says:

"You better a blame sight give *yourself* a good cussing, for you're the one that's entitled to it most. You hain't done a thing, from the start, that had any sense in it, except coming out so cool and cheeky with that imaginary blue-arrow mark. That *was* bright—it was right down bully; and it was the thing that saved us. For if it hadn't been for that, they'd a jailed us till them Englishmen's baggage come—and then—the penitentiary, you bet! But that trick took 'em to the graveyard, and the gold done us a still bigger kindness; for if the excited fools hadn't let go all holts and made that rush to get a look, we'd a slept in our cravats to-night—cravats warranted to *wear,* too—longer than *we'd* need 'em."

They was still a minute—thinking—then the king says, kind of absent-minded like:

"Mf! And we reckoned the *niggers* stole it!"

That made me squirm!

"Yes," says the duke, kinder slow, and deliberate, and sarcastic, "*We* did."

After about a half a minute, the king drawls out:

"Leastways—*I* did."

The duke says, the same way:

"On the contrary—*I* did."

The king kind of ruffles up, and says:

"Looky here, Bilgewater, what'r you referrin' to?"

The duke says, pretty brisk:

"When it comes to that, maybe you'll let me ask, what was *you* referring to?"

"Shucks!" says the king, very sarcastic; "but *I* don't know—maybe you was asleep, and didn't know what you was about."

The duke bristles up, now, and says:

"Oh, let *up* on this cussed nonsense—do you take me for a blame' fool? Don't you reckon *I* know who hid that money in that coffin?"

"Yes, sir! I know you *do* know—because you done it yourself!"

"It's a lie!"—and the duke went for him. The king sings out:

"Take y'r hands off!—leggo my throat!—I take it all back!"

The duke says:

"Well, you just own up, first, that you *did* hide that money there, intending to give me the slip one of these days, and come back and dig it up, and have it all to yourself."

"Wait jest a minute, duke—answer me this one question, honest and fair; if you didn't put the money there, say it, and I'll b'lieve you, and take back everything I said."

"You old scoundrel, I didn't, and you know I didn't. There, now!"

"Well, then, I b'lieve you. But answer me only jest this one more—now *don't* git mad; didn't you have it in your *mind* to hook the money and hide it?"

The duke never said nothing for a little bit; then he says:

"Well—I don't care if I *did*, I didn't *do* it, anyway. But you not only had it in mind to do it, but you *done* it."

"I wisht I may never die if I done it, duke, and that's honest. I won't say I warn't *goin'* to do it, because I *was;* but you—I mean somebody—got in ahead o' me."

"It's a lie! You done it, and you got to *say* you done it, or—"

The king begun to gurgle, and then he gasps out:

"'Nough!—*I own up!*"

I was very glad to hear him say that, it made me feel much more easier than what I was feeling before. So the duke took his hands off, and says:

"If you ever deny it again, I'll drown you. It's *well* for you to set there and blubber like a baby—it's fitten for you, after the way you've acted. I never see such an old ostrich for wanting to gobble everything—and I a trusting you all the time, like you was my own father. You ought to been ashamed of yourself to stand by and hear it saddled onto a lot of poor niggers and you never say a word for 'em. It makes me feel ridiculous to think I was soft enough to *believe* that rubbage. Cuss you, I can see, now, why you was so anxious to make up the deffisit—you wanted to get what money I'd got out of the Nonesuch and one thing or another, and scoop it *all!*"

The king says, timid, and still a snuffling:

"Why, duke, it was you that said make up the deffersit, it warn't me."

"Dry up! I don't want to hear no more *out* of you!" says the duke. "And *now* you see what you *got* by it. They've got all their own money back, and all of *ourn* but a shekel or two, *besides*. G'long to bed—and don't you deffersit *me* no more deffersits, long's *you* live!"

So the king sneaked into the wigwam, and took to his bottle for comfort; and before long the duke tackled *his* bottle; and so in about a half an hour they was as thick as thieves again, and the tighter they got, the lovinger they got; and went off a snoring in each other's arms. They both got powerful mellow, but I noticed the king didn't get mellow enough to forget to remember to not deny about hiding the money-bag again. That made me feel easy and satisfied. Of course when they got to snoring, we had a long gabble, and I told Jim everything.

Chapter XXXI
Ominous Plans—News from Jim—
Old Recollections—A Sheep Story—
Valuable Information

We dasn't stop again at any town, for days and days; kept right along down the river. We was down south in the warm weather, now, and a mighty long ways from home. We begun to come to trees with Spanish moss on them, hanging down from the limbs like long gray beards. It was the first I ever see it growing, and it made the woods look solemn and dismal. So now the frauds reckoned they was out of danger, and they begun to work the villages again.

First they done a lecture on temperance; but they didn't make enough for them both to get drunk on. Then in another village they started a dancing school; but they didn't know no more how to dance than a kangaroo does; so the first prance they made, the general public jumped in and pranced them out of town. Another time they tried a go at yellocution; but they didn't yellocute long till the audience got up and give them a solid good cussing and made them skip out. They tackled missionarying, and mesmerizing, and doctoring, and telling fortunes, and a little of everything; but they couldn't seem to have no luck. So at last they got just about dead broke, and laid around the raft, as she floated

SPANISH MOSS.

along, thinking, and thinking, and never saying nothing, by the half a day at a time, and dreadful blue and desperate.

And at last they took a change, and begun to lay their heads together in the wigwam and talk low and confidential two or three hours at a time. Jim and me got uneasy. We didn't like the look of it. We judged they was studying up some kind of worse deviltry than ever. We turned it over and over, and at last we made up our minds they was going to break into somebody's house or store, or was going into the counterfeit-money business, or something. So then we was pretty scared, and made up an agreement that we wouldn't have nothing in the world to do with such actions, and if we ever got the least show we would give them the cold shake, and clear out and leave them behind. Well, early one morning we hid the raft in a good safe place about two mile below a little bit of a shabby village, named Pikesville, and the king he went ashore, and told us all to stay hid whilst he went up to town and smelt around to see if anybody had got any wind of the Royal Nonesuch there yet. ("House to rob, you *mean,*" says I to myself; "and when you get through robbing it you'll come back here and wonder what has become of me and Jim and the raft—and you'll have to take it out in wondering.") And he said if he warn't back by midday, the duke and me would know it was all right, and we was to come along.

So we staid where we was. The duke he fretted and sweated around, and was in a mighty sour way. He scolded us for everything, and we couldn't seem to do nothing right; he found fault with every little thing. Something was a-brewing, sure. I was good and glad when midday come and no king; we could have a change, anyway—and maybe a chance for *the* change, on top of it. So me and the duke went up to the village, and hunted around there for the king, and by-and-by we found him in the back room of a little low doggery, very tight, and a lot of loafers bullyragging him for sport, and he a cussing and threatening with all his might, and so tight he couldn't walk, and couldn't do nothing to them. The duke he begun to abuse him for an old fool, and the king begun to sass back; and the minute they was fairly at it, I lit out, and shook the reefs out of my hind legs, and spun down the river road like a deer—for I see our chance; and I made up my mind that it would be a long day before they ever see me and Jim again. I got down there all out of breath but loaded up with joy, and sung out:

"Set her loose, Jim, we're all right, now!"

But there warn't no answer, and nobody come out of the wigwam. Jim was gone! I set up a shout—and then another—and then another one; and run this way and that in the woods, whooping and screeching; but it warn't no use—old Jim was gone. Then I set down and cried; I couldn't help it. But I couldn't set still long. Pretty soon I went out on the road, trying to think what I better do, and I run across a boy walking, and asked him if he'd seen a strange nigger, dressed so and so, and he says:

"Yes."

"Whereabouts?" says I.

"Down to Silas Phelps's place, two mile below here. He's a runaway nigger, and they've got him. Was you looking for him?"

"You bet I ain't! I run across him in the woods about an hour or two ago, and he said if I hollered he'd cut my livers out—and told me to lay down and stay where I was; and I done it. Been there ever since; afeard to come out."

"Well," he says, "you needn't be afeard no more, becuz they've got him. He run off f'm down South, som'ers."

"It's a good job they got him."

"Well, I *reckon!* There's two hunderd dollars reward on him. It's like picking up money out'n the road."

"Yes, it is—and *I* could a had it if I'd been big enough; I see him *first.* Who nailed him?"

"It was an old fellow—a stranger—and he sold out his chance in him for forty dollars, becuz he's got to go up the river and can't wait. Think o' that, now! You bet *I'd* wait, if it was seven year."

"That's me, every time," says I. "But maybe his chance ain't worth no more than that, if he'll sell it so cheap. Maybe there's something ain't straight about it."

"But it *is,* though—straight as a string. I see the handbill myself. It tells all about him, to a dot—paints him like a picture, and tells the plantation he's frum, below Newr*leans.* No-sirree-*bob,* they ain't no trouble 'bout *that* speculation, you bet you. Say, gimme a chaw tobacker, won't ye?"

I didn't have none, so he left. I went to the raft, and set down in the wigwam to think. But I couldn't come to nothing. I thought till I wore my head sore, but I couldn't see no way out of the trouble. After all this long journey, and after all we'd done for them scoundrels, here was it all come to nothing, everything all busted up and ruined, because they could have the heart to serve Jim such a trick as that, and make him a slave again all his life, and amongst strangers, too, for forty dirty dollars.

Once I said to myself it would be a thousand times better for Jim to be a slave at home where his family was, as long as he'd *got* to be a slave, and so I'd better write a letter to Tom Sawyer and tell him to tell Miss Watson where he was. But I soon give up that notion, for two things: she'd be mad and disgusted at his rascality and ungratefulness for leaving her, and so she'd sell him straight down the river again; and if she didn't, everybody naturally despises an ungrateful nigger, and they'd make Jim feel it all the time, and so he'd feel ornery and disgraced. And then think of *me!* It would get all around that Huck Finn helped a nigger to get his freedom; and if I was ever to see anybody from that town again, I'd be ready to get down and lick his boots for shame. That's just the way: a person does a low-down thing, and then he don't want to take no consequences of it. Thinks as long as he can hide it, it ain't no disgrace. That was my fix exactly. The more I studied about this, the more my conscience went to grinding me, and the more wicked and low-down and ornery I got to feeling. And at last, when it hit me all of a sudden that here was the plain hand of Providence slapping me in the face and letting me know my wickedness was being watched all the time from up there in heaven, whilst I was stealing a poor old woman's nigger that hadn't ever done me no harm, and now was showing me there's One that's always on the lookout, and ain't agoing to allow no such miserable doings to go only just so fur and no further, I most dropped in my tracks I was so scared. Well, I tried the best I could to kinder soften it up somehow for myself, by saying I was brung up wicked, and so I warn't so much to blame; but something inside of me kept saying, "There was the Sunday school, you could a gone to it; and if you'd a done it they'd a learnt you, there, that people that acts as I'd been acting about that nigger goes to everlasting fire."

It made me shiver. And I about made up my mind to pray; and see if I couldn't try to quit being the kind of a boy I was, and be better. So I kneeled down. But the words wouldn't come. Why wouldn't they? It warn't no use to try and hide it from Him. Nor from *me,* neither. I knowed very well why they wouldn't come. It was because my heart warn't right; it was because I warn't square; it was because I was playing double. I was letting *on* to give up sin, but away inside of me I was holding on to the biggest one of all. I was trying to make my mouth *say* I would do the right thing and the clean thing, and go and write to that nigger's owner and tell where he was; but deep down in me I knowed it was a lie—and He knowed it. You can't pray a lie—I found that out.

So I was full of trouble, full as I could be; and didn't know what to do. At last I had an idea; and I says, I'll go and write the letter—and then see if I can pray. Why, it was astonishing, the way I felt as light as a feather, right straight off, and my troubles all gone. So I got a piece of paper and a pencil, all glad and excited, and set down and wrote:

> *Miss Watson your runaway nigger Jim is down here two mile*
> *below Pikesville and Mr. Phelps has got him and he will give*
> *him up for the reward if you send.*
>   Huck Finn.

I felt good and all washed clean of sin for the first time I had ever felt
so in my life, and I knowed I could pray now. But I didn't do it straight off,
but laid the paper down and set there thinking—thinking how good it was
all this happened so, and how near I come to being lost and going to hell.
And went on thinking. And got to thinking over our trip down the river;
and I see Jim before me, all the time, in the day, and in the night-time, sometimes moonlight, sometimes storms, and we a floating along, talking, and
singing, and laughing. But somehow I couldn't seem to strike no places to
harden me against him, but only the other kind. I'd see him standing my
watch on top of his'n, stead of calling me, so I could go on sleeping; and see
him how glad he was when I come back out of the fog; and when I come to
him again in the swamp, up there where the feud was; and such-like times;
and would always call me honey, and pet me, and do everything he could
think of for me, and how good he always was; and at last I struck the time I
saved him by telling the men we had small-pox aboard, and he was so grateful, and said I was the best friend old Jim ever had in the world, and the *only*
one he's got now; and then I happened to look around, and see that paper.

It was a close place. I took it up, and held it in my hand. I was a
trembling, because I'd got to decide, forever, betwixt two things, and I
knowed it. I studied a minute, sort of holding my breath, and then says
to myself:

"All right, then, I'll *go* to hell"—and tore it up.

It was awful thoughts, and awful words, but they was said. And I let
them stay said; and never thought no more about reforming. I shoved the
whole thing out of my head; and said I would take up wickedness again,
which was in my line, being brung up to it, and the other warn't. And for
a starter, I would go to work and steal Jim out of slavery again; and if I
could think up anything worse, I would do that, too; because as long as I
was in, and in for good, I might as well go the whole hog.

Then I set to thinking over how to get at it, and turned over considerable many ways in my mind; and at last fixed up a plan that suited me. So
then I took the bearings of a woody island that was down the river a piece,
and as soon as it was fairly dark I crept out with my raft and went for it,
and hid it there, and then turned in. I slept the night through, and got up
before it was light, and had my breakfast, and put on my store clothes, and
tied up some others and one thing or another in a bundle, and took the
canoe and cleared for shore. I landed below where I judged was Phelps's
place, and hid my bundle in the woods, and then filled up the canoe with
water, and loaded rocks into her and sunk her where I could find her again
when I wanted her, about a quarter of a mile below a little steam sawmill
that was on the bank.

Then I struck up the road, and when I passed the mill I see a sign on it, "Phelps's Sawmill," and when I come to the farm houses, two or three hundred yards further along, I kept my eyes peeled, but didn't see nobody around, though it was good daylight, now. But I didn't mind, because I didn't want to see nobody just yet—I only wanted to get the lay of the land. According to my plan, I was going to turn up there from the village, not from below. So I just took a look, and shoved along, straight for town. Well, the very first man I see, when I got there, was the duke. He was sticking up a bill for the Royal Nonesuch—three-night performance—like that other time. *They* had the cheek, them frauds! I was right on him, before I could shirk. He looked astonished, and says:

"Hel-*lo!* Where'd *you* come from?" Then he says, kind of glad and eager, "Where's the raft?—got her in a good place?"

I says:

"Why, that's just what I was agoing to ask your grace."

Then he didn't look so joyful—and says:

"What was your idea for asking *me?*" he says.

"Well," I says, "when I see the king in that doggery yesterday, I says to myself, we can't get him home for hours, till he's soberer; so I went a loafing around town to put in the time, and wait. A man up and offered me ten cents to help him pull a skiff over the river and back to fetch a sheep, and so I went along; but when we was dragging him to the boat, and the man left me aholt of the rope and went behind him to shove him along, he was too strong for me, and jerked loose and run, and we after him. We didn't have no dog, and so we had to chase him all over the country till we tired him out. We never got him till dark, then we fetched him over, and I started down for the raft. When I got there and see it was gone, I says to myself, 'they've got into trouble and had to leave; and they've took my nigger, which is the only nigger I've got in the world, and now I'm in a strange country, and ain't got no property no more, nor nothing, and no way to make my living;' so I set down and cried. I slept in the woods all night. But what *did* become of the raft, then?—and Jim, poor Jim!"

"Blamed if *I* know—that is, what's become of the raft. That old fool had made a trade and got forty dollars, and when we found him in the doggery the loafers had matched half dollars with him and got every cent but what he'd spent for whisky; and when I got him home late last night and found the raft gone, we said, 'That little rascal has stole our raft and shook us, and run off down the river.'"

"I wouldn't shake my *nigger,* would I?—the only nigger I had in the world, and the only property."

"We never thought of that. Fact is, I reckon we'd come to consider him *our* nigger; yes, we did consider him so—goodness knows we had trouble enough for him. So when we see the raft was gone, and we flat broke, there warn't anything for it but to try the Royal Nonesuch another shake. And I've pegged along ever since, dry as a powderhorn. Where's that ten cents? Give it here."

I had considerable money, so I give him ten cents, but begged him to spend it for something to eat, and give me some, because it was all the money I had, and I hadn't had nothing to eat since yesterday. He never said nothing. The next minute he whirls on me and says:

"Do you reckon that nigger would blow on us? We'd skin him if he done that!"

"How can he blow? Hain't he run off?"

"No! That old fool sold him, and never divided with me, and the money's gone."

"*Sold* him?" I says, and begun to cry; "why, he was *my* nigger, and that was my money. Where is he?—I want my nigger."

"Well, you can't *get* your nigger, that's all—so dry up your blubbering. Looky here—do you think *you'd* venture to blow on us? Blamed if I think I'd trust you. Why, if you *was* to blow on us—"

He stopped, but I never see the duke look so ugly out of his eyes before. I went on a-whimpering, and says:

"I don't want to blow on nobody; and I ain't got no time to blow, nohow. I got to turn out and find my nigger."

He looked kinder bothered, and stood there with his bills fluttering on his arm, thinking, and wrinkling up his forehead. At last he says:

"I'll tell you something. We got to be here three days. If you'll promise you won't blow, and won't let the nigger blow, I'll tell you where to find him."

So I promised, and he says:

"A farmer by the name of Silas Ph——" and then he stopped. You see, he started to tell me the truth; but when he stopped, that way, and begun to study and think again, I reckoned he was changing his mind. And so he was. He wouldn't trust me; he wanted to make sure of having me out of the way the whole three days. So pretty soon he says: "The man that bought him is named Abram Foster—Abram G. Foster—and he lives forty mile back here in the country, on the road to Lafayette."

"All right," I says, "I can walk it in three days. And I'll start this very afternoon."

"No you won't, you'll start *now*; and don't you lose any time about it, neither, nor do any gabbling by the way. Just keep a tight tongue in your head and move right along, and then you won't get into trouble with *us,* d'ye hear?"

That was the order I wanted, and that was the one I played for. I wanted to be left free to work my plans.

"So clear out," he says; "and you can tell Mr. Foster whatever you want to. Maybe you can get him to believe that Jim *is* your nigger—some idiots don't require documents—leastways I've heard there's such down South here. And when you tell him the handbill and the reward's bogus, maybe he'll believe you when you explain to him what the idea was for getting 'em out. Go 'long, now, and tell him anything you want to; but mind you don't work your jaw any *between* here and there."

So I left, and struck for the back country. I didn't look around, but I kinder felt like he was watching me. But I knowed I could tire him out at that. I went straight out in the country as much as a mile, before I stopped; then I doubled back through the woods towards Phelps's. I reckoned I better start in on my plan straight off, without fooling around, because I wanted to stop Jim's mouth till these fellows could get away. I didn't want no trouble with their kind. I'd seen all I wanted to of them, and wanted to get entirely shut of them.

Chapter XXXII
Still and Sunday-like—Mistaken Identity—
Up a Stump—In a Dilemma

When I got there it was all still and Sunday-like, and hot and sunshiny—the hands was gone to the fields; and there was them kind of faint dronings of bugs and flies in the air that makes it seem so lonesome and like everybody's dead and gone; and if a breeze fans along and quivers the leaves, it makes you feel mournful, because you feel like it's spirits whispering—spirits that's been dead ever so many years—and you always think they're talking about *you*. As a general thing it makes a body wish *he* was dead, too, and done with it all.

Phelps's was one of these little one-horse cotton plantations; and they all look alike. A rail fence round a two-acre yard; a stile, made out of logs sawed off and up-ended, in steps, like barrels of a different length, to climb over the fence with, and for the women to stand on when they are going to jump onto a horse; some sickly grass-patches in the big yard, but mostly it was bare and smooth, like an old hat with the nap rubbed off; big double log house for the white folks—hewed logs, with the chinks stopped up with mud or mortar, and these mud-stripes been white-washed some time or another; round-log kitchen, with a big broad, open but roofed passage joining it to the house; log smoke-house back of the kitchen; three little log nigger-cabins in a row t'other side the smoke-house; one little hut all by itself away down against the back fence, and some out-buildings down a piece the other side; ash-hopper, and big kettle to bile soap in, by the little hut; bench by the kitchen door, with bucket of water and a gourd; hound asleep there, in the sun; more hounds asleep, round about; about three shade trees away off in a corner; some currant bushes and gooseberry bushes in one place by the fence; outside of the fence a garden and a watermelon patch; then the cotton fields begins; and after the fields, the woods.

STILL AND SUNDAY-LIKE.

I went around and clumb over the back stile by the ash-hopper, and started for the kitchen. When I got a little ways, I heard the dim hum of a spinning-wheel wailing along up and sinking along down again; and then I knowed for certain I wished I was dead—for that *is* the lonesomest sound in the whole world.

I went right along, not fixing up any particular plan, but just trusting to Providence to put the right words in my mouth when the time come; for I'd noticed that Providence always did put the right words in my mouth, if I left it alone.

When I got half-way, first one hound and then another got up and went for me, and of course I stopped and faced them, and kept still. And such another pow-wow as they made! In a quarter of a minute I was a kind of a hub of a wheel, as you may say—spokes made out of dogs—circle of fifteen of them packed together around me, with their necks and noses stretched up towards me, a barking and howling; and more a coming; you could see them sailing over fences and around corners from everywheres.

A nigger woman come tearing out of the kitchen with a rolling-pin in her hand, singing out, "Begone! *you* Tige! you Spot! bedone, sah!" and she fetched first one and then another of them a clip and sent them howling, and then the rest followed; and the next second, half of them come back, wagging their tails around me and making friends with me. There ain't no harm in a hound, nohow.

And behind the woman comes a little nigger girl and two little nigger boys, without anything on but tow-linen shirts, and they hung onto their mother's gown, and peeped out from behind her at me, bashful, the way they always do. And here comes the white woman running from the house, about forty-five or fifty year old, bare-headed, and her spinning-stick in her hand; and behind her comes her little white children, acting the same way the little niggers was doing. She was smiling all over so she could hardly stand—and says:

"It's *you*, at last!—*ain't* it?"

I out with a "Yes'm," before I thought.

She grabbed me and hugged me tight; and then gripped me by both hands and shook and shook; and the tears come in her eyes, and run down over; and she couldn't seem to hug and shake enough, and kept saying, "You don't look as much like your mother as I reckoned you would, but law sakes, I don't care for that, I'm *so* glad to see you! Dear, dear, it does seem like I could eat you up! Children, it's your cousin Tom!—tell him howdy."

But they ducked their heads, and put their fingers in their mouths, and hid behind her. So she run on:

"Lize, hurry up and get him a hot breakfast, right away—or did you get your breakfast on the boat?"

I said I had got it on the boat. So then she started for the house, leading me by the hand, and the children tagging after. When we got there, she set me down in a split-bottomed chair, and set herself down on a little low stool in front of me, holding both of my hands, and says:

"Now I can have a *good* look at you; and, laws-a-me, I've been hungry for it a many and a many a time, all these long years, and it's come at last! We been expecting you a couple of days and more. What kep' you?—boat get aground?"

"Yes'm—she—"

"Don't say yes'm—say Aunt Sally. Where'd she get aground?"

I didn't rightly know what to say, because I didn't know whether the boat would be coming up the river or down. But I go a good deal on instinct; and my instinct said she would be coming up—from down towards Orleans. That didn't help me much, though; for I didn't know the names of bars down that way. I see I'd got to invent a bar, or forget the name of the one we got aground on—or—Now I struck an idea, and fetched it out:

"It warn't the grounding—that didn't keep us back but a little. We blowed out a cylinder-head."

"Good gracious! anybody hurt?"

"No'm. Killed a nigger."

"Well, it's lucky; because sometimes people do get hurt. Two years ago last Christmas, your uncle Silas was coming up from Newrleans on the old *Lally Rook,* and she blowed out a cylinder-head and crippled a man. And I think he died afterwards. He was a Baptist. Your uncle Silas knowed a family in Baton Rouge that knowed his people very well. Yes, I remember, now he *did* die. Mortification set in, and they had to amputate him. But it didn't save him. Yes, it was mortification—that was it. He turned blue all over, and died in the hope of a glorious resurrection. They say he was a sight to look at. Your uncle's been up to the town every day to fetch you. And he's gone again, not more'n an hour ago; he'll be back any minute, now. You must a met him on the road, didn't you?—oldish man, with a—"

"No, I didn't see nobody, Aunt Sally. The boat landed just at daylight, and I left my baggage on the wharf-boat and went looking around the town and out a piece in the country, to put in the time and not get here too soon; and so I come down the back way."

"Who'd you give the baggage to?"

"Nobody."

"Why, child, it'll be stole!"

"Not where *I* hid it I reckon it won't," I says.

"How'd you get your breakfast so early on the boat?"

It was kinder thin ice, but I says:

"The captain see me standing around, and told me I better have something to eat before I went ashore; so he took me in the texas to the officers' lunch, and give me all I wanted."

I was getting so uneasy I couldn't listen good. I had my mind on the children all the time; I wanted to get them out to one side and pump them a little, and find out who I was. But I couldn't get no show, Mrs. Phelps kept it up and run on so. Pretty soon she made the cold chills streak all down my back, because she says:

"But here we're a running on this way, and you hain't told me a word about Sis, nor any of them. Now I'll rest my works a little, and you start up yourn; just tell me *everything*—tell me about'm all, every one of 'm; and how they are, and what they're doing, and what they told you to tell me; and every last thing you can think of."

Well, I see I was up a stump—and up it good. Providence had stood by me this fur, all right, but I was hard and tight aground, now. I see it warn't a bit of use to try to go ahead—I'd *got* to throw up my hand. So I says to myself, here's another place where I got to resk the truth. I opened my mouth to begin; but she grabbed me and hustled me in behind the bed, and says:

"Here he comes! stick your head down lower—there, that'll do; you can't be seen, now. Don't you let on you're here. I'll play a joke on him. Children, don't you say a word."

I see I was in a fix, now. But it warn't no use to worry; there warn't nothing to do but just hold still, and try and be ready to stand from under when the lightning struck.

I had just one little glimpse of the old gentleman when he come in, then the bed hid him. Mrs. Phelps she jumps for him and says:

"Has he come?"

"No," says her husband.

"Good-*ness* gracious!" she says, "what in the world *can* have become of him?"

"I can't imagine," says the old gentleman; "and I must say, it makes me dreadful uneasy."

"Uneasy!" she says; "I'm ready to go distracted! He *must* a come; and you've missed him along the road. I *know* it's so—something *tells* me so."

"Why, Sally, I *couldn't* miss him along the road—*you* know that."

"But oh, dear, dear, what *will* Sis say! He must a come! You must a missed him. He—"

"Oh, don't distress me any more'n I'm already distressed. I don't know what in the world to make of it. I'm at my wit's end, and I don't mind acknowledging 't I'm right down scared. But there's no hope that he's come; for he *couldn't* come and me miss him. Sally, it's terrible—just terrible—something's happened to the boat, sure!"

"Why, Silas! Look yonder!—up the road!—ain't that somebody coming?"

He sprung to the window at the head of the bed, and that give Mrs. Phelps the chance she wanted. She stooped down quick, at the foot of the bed, and give me a pull, and out I come; and when he turned back from the window, there she stood, a-beaming and a-smiling like a house afire, and I standing pretty meek and sweaty alongside. The old gentleman stared, and says:

"Why, who's that?"

"Who do you reckon 't is?"

"I hain't no idea. Who *is* it?"

"It's *Tom Sawyer!*" — What in the world!

By jings, I most slumped through the floor! But there warn't no time to swap knives; the old man grabbed me by the hand and shook, and kept on shaking; and all the time, how the woman did dance around and laugh and cry; and then how they both did fire off questions about Sid, and Mary, and the rest of the tribe.

But if they was joyful, it warn't nothing to what I was; for it was like being born again, I was so glad to find out who I was. Well, they froze to me for two hours; and at last when my chin was so tired it couldn't hardly go, any more, I had told them more about my family—I mean the Sawyer family—than ever happened to any six Sawyer families. And I explained all about how we blowed out a cylinder-head at the mouth of White River and it took us three days to fix it. Which was all right, and worked first rate; because *they* didn't know but what it would take three days to fix it. If I'd a called it a bolt-head it would a done just as well.

Now I was feeling pretty comfortable all down one side, and pretty uncomfortable all up the other. Being Tom Sawyer was easy and comfortable; and it stayed easy and comfortable till by-and-by I hear a steamboat coughing along down the river—then I says to myself, spose Tom Sawyer come down on that boat?—and spose he steps in here any minute, and sings out my name before I can throw him a wink to keep quiet? Well, I couldn't *have* it that way—it wouldn't do at all. I must go up the road and waylay him. So I told the folks I reckoned I would go up to the town and fetch down my baggage. The old gentleman was for going along with me, but I said no, I could drive the horse myself, and I druther he wouldn't take no trouble about me.

Chapter XXXIII
A Nigger Stealer—Southern Hospitality—
A Pretty Long Blessing—Tar and Feathers

So I started for town, in the wagon, and when I was half-way I see a wagon coming, and sure enough it was Tom Sawyer, and I stopped and waited till he come along. I says "Hold on!" and it stopped alongside, and his mouth opened up like a trunk, and staid so; and he swallowed two or three times like a person that's got a dry throat, and then says:

"I hain't ever done you no harm. You know that. So, then, what you want to come back and ha'nt *me* for?"

I says:

"I hain't come back—I hain't been *gone*."

When he heard my voice, it righted him up some, but he warn't quite satisfied yet. He says:

"Don't you play nothing on me, because I wouldn't on you. Honest injun, now, you ain't a ghost?" —wow

"Honest injun, I ain't," I says.

"Well—I—I—well, that ought to settle it, of course; but I can't somehow seem to understand it, no way. Looky here, warn't you ever murdered *at all?*"

"IT WAS TOM SAWYER."

"No. I warn't ever murdered at all—I played it on them. You come in here and feel of me if you don't believe me."

So he done it; and it satisfied him; and he was that glad to see me again, he didn't know what to do. And he wanted to know all about it right off; because it was a grand adventure, and mysterious, and so it hit him where he lived. But I said, leave it alone till by-and-by; and told his driver to wait, and we drove off a little piece, and I told him the kind of a fix I was in, and what did he reckon we better do? He said, let him alone a minute, and don't disturb him. So he thought and thought, and pretty soon he says:

"It's all right, I've got it. Take my trunk in your wagon, and let on it's your'n; and you turn back and fool along slow, so as to get to the house about the time you ought to; and I'll go towards town a piece, and take a fresh start, and get there a quarter or a half an hour after you; and you needn't let on to know me, at first."

I says:

"All right; but wait a minute. There's one more thing—a thing that *nobody* don't know but me. And that is, there's a nigger here that I'm a trying to steal out of slavery—and his name is *Jim*— old Miss Watson's Jim."

He says:

"What! Why Jim is—"

He stopped and went to studying. I says:

"*I* know what you'll say. You'll say it's dirty low-down business; but what if it is? *I'm* low down; and I'm agoing to steal him, and I want you to keep mum and not let on. Will you?"

His eye lit up, and he says:

"I'll *help* you steal him!"

Well, I let go all holts then, like I was shot. It was the most astonishing speech I ever heard—and I'm bound to say Tom Sawyer fell, considerable, in my estimation. Only I couldn't believe it. Tom Sawyer a *nigger stealer!*

"Oh, shucks!" I says, "you're joking."

"I ain't joking, either."

"Well, then," I says, "joking or no joking, if you hear anything said about a runaway nigger, don't forget to remember that *you* don't know nothing about him, and *I* don't know nothing about him."

Then we took the trunk and put it in my wagon, and he drove off his way, and I drove mine. But of course I forgot all about driving slow, on accounts of being glad and full of thinking; so I got home a heap too quick for that length of a trip. The old gentleman was at the door, and he says:

"Why, this is wonderful! Who ever would a thought it was in that mare to do it. I wish we'd a timed her. And she hain't sweated a hair—not a hair. It's wonderful. Why, I wouldn't take a hundred dollars for that horse now; I wouldn't, honest; and yet I'd a sold her for fifteen before, and thought 'twas all she was worth."

That's all he said. He was the innocentest, best old soul I ever see. But it warn't surprising; because he warn't only just a farmer, he was a preacher, too, and had a little one-horse log church down back of the plantation, which he built it himself at his own expense, for a church and school house, and never charged nothing for his preaching, and it was worth it, too. There was plenty other farmer-preachers like that, and done the same way, down South.

In about half an hour Tom's wagon drove up to the front stile, and Aunt Sally she see it through the window, because it was only about fifty yards, and says:

"Why, there's somebody come! I wonder who 'tis? Why, I do believe it's a stranger. Jimmy" (that's one of the children), "run and tell Lize to put on another plate for dinner."

Everybody made a rush for the front door, because, of course, a stranger don't come *every* year, and so he lays over the yaller fever, for interest, when he does come. Tom was over the stile and starting for the house; the wagon was spinning up the road for the village, and we was all bunched in the front door. Tom had his store clothes on, and an audience—and that was always nuts for Tom Sawyer. In them circumstances it warn't no trouble to him to throw in an amount of style that was suitable. He warn't a boy to meeky along up that yard like a sheep; no, he come ca'm and important, like the ram. When he got afront of us, he lifts his hat ever so gracious and dainty, like it was the lid of a box that had butterflies asleep in it and he didn't want to disturb them, and says:

"Mr. Archibald Nichols, I presume?"

"No, my boy," says the old gentleman, "I'm sorry to say 't your driver has deceived you; Nichols's place is down a matter of three mile more. Come in, come in."

Tom he took a look back over his shoulder, and says, "Too late—he's out of sight."

"Yes, he's gone, my son, and you must come in and eat your dinner with us; and then we'll hitch up and take you down to Nichols's."

"Oh, I *can't* make you so much trouble; I couldn't think of it. I'll walk—I don't mind the distance."

"But we won't *let* you walk—it wouldn't be Southern hospitality to do it. Come right in."

"Oh, *do,*" says Aunt Sally; "it ain't a bit of trouble to us, not a bit in the world. You *must* stay. It's a long, dusty three mile, and we *can't* let you walk. And, besides, I've already told 'em to put on another plate, when I see you coming; so you mustn't disappoint us. Come right in, and make yourself at home."

So Tom he thanked them very hearty and handsome, and let himself be persuaded, and come in; and when he was in, he said he was a stranger from Hicksville, Ohio, and his name was William Thompson—and he made another bow.

Well, he run on, and on, and on, making up stuff about Hicksville and everybody in it he could invent, and I getting a little nervous, and wondering how this was going to help me out of my scrape; and at last, still talking along, he reached over and kissed Aunt Sally right on the mouth, and then settled back again in his chair, comfortable, and was going on talking; but she jumped up and wiped it off with the back of her hand, and says:

"You owdacious puppy!"

He looked kind of hurt, and says:

"I'm surprised at you, m'am."

"You're s'rp—Why, what do you reckon *I* am? I've a good notion to take and—say, what do you mean by kissing me?"

He looked kind of humble, and says:

"I didn't mean nothing, m'am. I didn't mean no harm. I—I—thought you'd like it."

"Why, you born fool!" She took up the spinning-stick, and it looked like it was all she could do to keep from giving him a crack with it. "What made you think I'd like it?"

"Well, I don't know. Only, they—they—told me you would."

"*They* told you I would. Whoever told you's *another* lunatic. I never heard the beat of it. Who's *they?*"

"Why—everybody. They all said so, m'am."

It was all she could do to hold in; and her eyes snapped, and her fingers worked like she wanted to scratch him; and she says:

"Who's 'everybody?' Out with their names—or ther'll be an idiot short."

He got up and looked distressed, and fumbled his hat, and says:

"I'm sorry, and I warn't expecting it. They told me to. They all told me to. They all said kiss her; and said she'd like it. They all said it—every one of them. But I'm sorry, m'am, and I won't do it no more—I won't, honest."

"You won't, won't you? Well, I sh'd *reckon* you won't!"

"No'm, I'm honest about it; I won't ever do it again. Till you ask me."

"Till I *ask* you! Well, I never see the beat of it in my born days! I lay you'll be the Methusalem-numskull of creation before ever *I* ask you—or the likes of you."

"Well," he says, "it does surprise me so. I can't make it out, somehow. They said you would, and I thought you would. But —" He stopped and looked around slow, like he wished he could run across a friendly eye, somewhere's; and fetched up on the old gentleman's, and says, "Didn't *you* think she'd like me to kiss her, sir?"

"Why, no; I—I—well, no, I b'lieve I didn't."

Then he looks on around, the same way, to me—and says:

"Tom, didn't *you* think Aunt Sally'd open out her arms and say, 'Sid Sawyer—'"

"My land!" she says, breaking in and jumping for him, "you impudent young rascal, to fool a body so —" and was going to hug him, but he fended her off, and says:

"No, not till you've asked me, first."

So she didn't lose no time, but asked him; and hugged him and kissed him, over and over again, and then turned him over to the old man, and he took what was left. And after they got a little quiet again, she says:

"Why, dear me, I never see such a surprise. We warn't looking for *you*, at all, but only Tom. Sis never wrote to me about anybody coming but him."

"It's because it warn't *intended* for any of us to come but Tom," he says; "but I begged and begged, and at the last minute she let me come, too; so, coming down the river, me and Tom thought it would be a first-rate surprise for him to come here to the house first, and for me to by-and-by tag along and drop in and let on to be a stranger. But it was a mistake, Aunt Sally. This ain't no healthy place for a stranger to come."

"No—not impudent whelps, Sid. You ought to had your jaws boxed; I hain't been so put out since I don't know when. But I don't care, I don't mind the terms—I'd be willing to stand a thousand such jokes to have you here. Well, to think of that performance! I don't deny it, I was most putrified with astonishment when you give me that smack."

We had dinner out in that broad open passage betwixt the house and the kitchen; and there was things enough on that table for seven families— and all hot, too; none of your flabby tough meat that's laid in a cupboard in a damp cellar all night and tastes like a hunk of old cold cannibal in the morning. Uncle Silas he asked a pretty long blessing over it, but it was worth it; and it didn't cool it a bit, neither, the way I've seen them kind of interruptions do, lots of times.

There was a considerable good deal of talk, all the afternoon, and me and Tom was on the lookout all the time, but it warn't no use, they didn't happen to say nothing about any runaway nigger, and we was afraid to try to work up to it. But at supper, at night, one of the little boys says:

"Pa, mayn't Tom and Sid and me go to the show?"

"No," says the old man, "I reckon there ain't going to be any; and you couldn't go if there was; because the runaway nigger told Burton and me all about that scandalous show, and Burton said he would tell the people; so I reckon they've drove the owdacious loafers out of town before this time."

So there it was!—but *I* couldn't help it. Tom and me was to sleep in the same room and bed; so, being tired, we bid good-night and went up to bed, right after supper, and clumb out of the window and down the lightning rod, and shoved for the town; for I didn't believe anybody was going to give the king and the duke a hint, and so, if I didn't hurry up and give them one they'd get into trouble sure.

On the road Tom he told me all about how it was reckoned I was mur-dered, and how pap disappeared, pretty soon, and didn't come back no more, and what a stir there was when Jim run away; and I told Tom all about our Royal Nonesuch rapscallions, and as much of the raft-voyage as I had time to; and as we struck into the town and up through the middle of it—it was as much as half after eight, then—here comes a raging rush of people, with torches, and an awful whooping and yelling, and banging tin pans and blowing horns; and we jumped to one side to let them go by; and as they went by, I see they had the king and the duke astraddle of a rail—that is, I knowed it *was* the king and the duke, though they was all over tar and feathers, and didn't look like nothing in the world that was human—just looked like a couple of monstrous big soldier-plumes. Well, it made me sick to see it; and I was sorry for them poor pitiful rascals, it seemed like I couldn't ever feel any hardness against them any more in the world. It was a dreadful thing to see. Human beings *can* be awful cruel to one another.

We see we was too late—couldn't do no good. We asked some strag-glers about it, and they said everybody went to the show looking very in-nocent; and laid low and kept dark till the poor old king was in the middle of his cavortings on the stage; then somebody give a signal, and the house rose up and went for them.

So we poked along back home, and I warn't feeling so brash as I was before, but kind of ornery, and humble, and to blame, somehow—though *I* hadn't done nothing. But that's always the way; it don't make no difference whether you do right or wrong, a person's conscience ain't got no sense, and just goes for him *anyway*. If I had a yaller dog that didn't know no more than a person's conscience does, I would pison him. It takes up more room than all the rest of a person's insides, and yet ain't no good, nohow. Tom Sawyer he says the same.

Chapter XXXIV
The Hut by the Ash-Hopper—
Outrageous—Climbing the Lightning Rod—
Troubled with Witches

We stopped talking, and got to thinking. By-and-by Tom says:

"Looky here, Huck, what fools we are, to not think of it before! I bet I know where Jim is."

"No! Where?"

"In that hut down by the ash-hopper. Why, looky here. When we was at dinner, didn't you see a nigger man go in there with some vittles?"

"Yes."

"What did you think the vittles was for?"

"For a dog."

"So'd I. Well, it wasn't for a dog."

"Why?"

"Because part of it was watermelon."

"So it was—I noticed it. Well, it does beat all, that I never thought about a dog not eating watermelon. It shows how a body can see and don't see at the same time."

"Well, the nigger unlocked the padlock when he went in, and he locked it again when he came out. He fetched uncle a key, about the time we got up from table—same key, I bet. Watermelon shows man; lock shows prisoner; and it ain't likely there's two prisoners on such a little plantation, and where the

VITTLES.

people's all so kind and good. Jim's the prisoner. All right—I'm glad we found it out detective fashion; I wouldn't give shucks for any other way. Now you work your mind and study out a plan to steal Jim, and I will study out one, too; and we'll take the one we like the best."

envy — (What a head for just a boy to have! If I had Tom Sawyer's head, I wouldn't trade it off to be a duke, nor mate of a steamboat, nor clown in a circus, nor nothing I can think of.)I went to thinking out a plan, but only just to be doing something; I knowed very well where the right plan was

wow! — going to come from. Pretty soon, Tom says:

"Ready?"

"Yes," I says.

"All right—bring it out."

"My plan is this," I says. "We can easy find out if it's Jim in there. Then get up my canoe to-morrow night, and fetch my raft over from the island. Then the first dark night that comes, steal the key out of the old man's britches, after he goes to bed, and shove off down the river on the raft, with Jim, hiding daytimes and running nights, the way me and Jim used to do before. Wouldn't that plan work?"

"*Work?* Why cert'nly, it would work, like rats a fighting. But it's too blame' simple; there ain't nothing *to* it. What's the good of a plan that ain't no more trouble than that? It's as mild as goose-milk. Why, Huck, it wouldn't make no more talk than breaking into a soap factory."

I never said nothing, because I warn't expecting nothing different; but I knowed mighty well that whenever he got *his* plan ready it wouldn't have none of them objections to it.

And it didn't. He told me what it was, and I see in a minute it was worth fifteen of mine, for style, and would make Jim just as free a man as mine would, and maybe get us all killed besides. So I was satisfied, and said we would waltz in on it. I needn't tell what it was, here, because I knowed it wouldn't stay the way it was. I knowed he would be changing it around, every which way, as we went along, and heaving in new bullinesses wherever he got a chance. And that is what he done.

Well, one thing was dead sure; and that was, that Tom Sawyer was in earnest and was actuly going to help steal that nigger out of slavery. That was the thing that was too many for me. Here was a boy that was respectable, and well brung up; and had a character to lose; and folks at home that had characters; and he was bright and not leather-headed; and knowing and not ignorant; and not mean, but kind; and yet here he was, without any more pride, or rightness, or feeling, than to stoop to this business, and make himself a shame, and his family a shame, before everybody. I *couldn't* understand it no way at all. It was outrageous, and I knowed I ought to just up and tell him so; and so be his true friend, and let him quit the thing right where he was, and save himself. And I *did* start to tell him; but he shut me up, and says:

"Don't you reckon I know what I'm about? Don't I generly know what I'm about?"

"Yes."

"Didn't I *say* I was going to help steal the nigger?"

"Yes."

"*Well* then."

That's all he said, and that's all I said. It warn't no use to say any more; because when he said he'd do a thing, he always done it. But *I* couldn't make out how he was willing to go into this thing; so I just let it go, and never bothered no more about it. If he was bound to have it so, *I* couldn't help it.

When we got home, the house was all dark and still; so we went on down to the hut by the ash-hopper, for to examine it. We went through the yard, so as to see what the hounds would do. They knowed us, and didn't make no more noise than country dogs is always doing when anything comes by in the night. When we got to the cabin, we took a look at the front and the two sides; and on the side I warn't acquainted with—which was the north side—we found a square window-hole, up tolerable high, with just one stout board nailed across it. I says:

"Here's the ticket. This hole's big enough for Jim to get through, if we wrench off the board."

Tom says:

"It's as simple as tit-tat-toe, three-in-a-row, and as easy as playing hooky. I should *hope* we can find a way that's a little more complicated than *that*, Huck Finn."

"Well, then," I says, "how'll it do to saw him out, the way I done before I was murdered, that time?"

"That's more *like*," he says. "It's real mysterious, and troublesome, and good," he says; "but I bet we can find a way that's twice as long. There ain't no hurry; le's keep on looking around."

Betwixt the hut and the fence, on the back side, was a lean-to, that joined the hut at the eaves, and was made out of plank. It was as long as the hut, but narrow—only about six foot wide. The door to it was at the south end, and was padlocked. Tom he went to the soap kettle, and searched around and fetched back the iron thing they lift the lid with; so he took it and prized out one of the staples. The chain fell down, and we opened the door and went in, and shut it, and struck a match, and see the shed was only built against the cabin and hadn't no connection with it; and there warn't no floor to the shed, nor nothing in it but some old rusty played-out hoes, and spades, and picks, and a crippled plow. The match went out, and so did we, and shoved in the staple again, and the door was locked as good as ever. Tom was joyful. He says;

"Now we're all right. We'll *dig* him out. It'll take about a week!"

Then we started for the house, and I went in the back door—you only have to pull a buckskin latch-string, they don't fasten the doors—but that warn't romantical enough for Tom Sawyer: no way would do him but he must climb up the lightning rod. But after he got up half-way about three times, and missed fire and fell every time, and the last time most busted his brains out, he thought he'd got to give it up; but after he was rested, he allowed he would give her one more turn for luck, and this time he made the trip.

In the morning we was up at break of day, and down to the nigger cabins to pet the dogs and make friends with the nigger that fed Jim—if it *was* Jim that was being fed. The niggers was just getting through breakfast and starting for the fields; and Jim's nigger was piling up a tin pan with bread and meat and things; and whilst the others was leaving, the key come from the house.

This nigger had a good-natured, chuckle-headed face, and his wool was all tied up in little bunches with thread. That was to keep witches off. He said the witches was pestering him awful, these nights, and making him see all kinds of strange things, and hear all kinds of strange words and noises, and he didn't believe he was ever witched so long, before, in his life. He got so worked up, and got to running on so about his troubles, he forgot all about what he'd been agoing to do. So Tom says:

"What's the vittles for? Going to feed the dogs?"

The nigger kind of smiled around gradually over his face, like when you heave a brickbat in a mud puddle, and he says:

"Yes, Mars Sid, *a* dog. Cur'us dog, too. Does you want to go en look at 'im?"

"Yes."

I hunched Tom, and whispers:

"You going, right here in the day-break? *That* warn't the plan."

"No, it warn't—but it's the plan *now*."

So, drat him, we went along, but I didn't like it much. When we got in, we couldn't hardly see anything, it was so dark; but Jim was there, sure enough, and could see us; and he sings out:

"Why, *Huck!* En good *lan'!* ain' dat Misto Tom?"

I just knowed how it would be; I just expected it. *I* didn't know nothing to do; and if I had, I couldn't a done it, because that nigger busted in and says:

"Why, de gracious sakes! do he know you genlmen?"

We could see pretty well, now. Tom he looked at the nigger, steady and kind of wondering, and says:

"Does *who* know us?"

"Why, dish-yer runaway nigger."

"I don't reckon he does; but what put that into your head?"

"What *put* it dar? Didn' he jis' dis minute sing out like he knowed you?"

Tom says, in a puzzled-up kind of way:

"Well, that's mighty curious. *Who* sung out? *When* did he sing out? *What* did he sing out?" And turns to me, perfectly ca'm, and says, "Did *you* hear anybody sing out?"

Of course there warn't nothing to be said but the one thing; so I says:

"No; *I* ain't heard nobody say nothing."

Then he turns to Jim, and looks him over like he never see him before; and says:

"Did you sing out?"

"No, sah," says Jim; "*I* hain't said nothing, sah."

"Not a word?"

"No, sah, I hain't said a word."

"Did you ever see us before?"

"No, sah; not as *I* knows on."

So Tom turns to the nigger, which was looking wild and distressed, and says, kind of severe:

"What do you reckon's the matter with you, anyway? What made you think somebody sung out?"

"Oh, it's de dad-blame' witches, sah, en I wisht I was dead, I do. Dey's awluz at it, sah, en dey do mos' kill me, dey sk'yers me so. Please to don't tell nobody 'bout it sah, er ole Mars Silas he'll scole me; 'kase he say dey *ain't* no witches. I jis' wish to goodness he was heah now—*den* what would he say! I jis' bet he couldn' fine no way to git aroun' it *dis* time. But it's awluz jis' so; people dat's *sot*, stays sot; dey won't look into nothn' en fine it out f'r deyselves, en when *you* fine it out en tell um 'bout it, dey doan' b'lieve you."

Tom give him a dime, and said we wouldn't tell nobody; and told him to buy some more thread to tie up his wool with; and then looks at Jim, and says:

"I wonder if Uncle Silas is going to hang this nigger. If I was to catch a nigger that was ungrateful enough to run away, *I* wouldn't give him up, I'd hang him." And whilst the nigger stepped to the door to look at the dime and bite it to see if it was good, he whispers to Jim, and says:

"Don't ever let on to know us. And if you hear any digging going on nights, it's us; we're going to set you free."

Jim only had time to grab us by the hand and squeeze it, then the nigger come back, and we said we'd come again some time if the nigger wanted us to; and he said he would, more particular if it was dark, because the witches went for him mostly in the dark, and it was good to have folks around then.

Chapter XXXV
Escaping Properly—Dark Schemes—
Discrimination in Stealing—A Deep Hole

It would be most an hour, yet, till breakfast, so we left, and struck down into the woods; because Tom said we got to have *some* light to see how to dig by, and a lantern makes too much, and might get us into trouble;

GETTING WOOD.

what we must have was a lot of them rotten chunks that's called fox-fire and just makes a soft kind of a glow when you lay them in a dark place. We fetched an armful and hid it in the weeds, and set down to rest, and Tom says, kind of dissatisfied:

"Blame it, this whole thing is just as easy and awkward as it can be. And so it makes it so rotten difficult to get up a difficult plan. There ain't no watchman to be drugged—now there *ought* to be a watchman. There ain't even a dog to give a sleeping-mixture to. And there's Jim chained by one leg, with a ten-foot chain, to the leg of his bed: why, all you got to do is to lift up the bedstead and slip off the chain. And Uncle Silas he trusts everybody; sends the key to the punkin-headed nigger, and don't send nobody to watch the nigger. Jim could a got out of that window-hole before this, only there wouldn't be no use trying to travel with a ten-foot chain on his leg. Why, drat it, Huck, it's the stupidest arrangement

I ever see. You got to invent *all* the difficulties. Well, we can't help it, we got to do the best we can with the materials we've got. Anyhow, there's one thing—there's more honor in getting him out through a lot of difficulties and dangers, where there warn't one of them furnished to you by the people who it was their duty to furnish them, and you had to contrive them all out of your own head. Now look at just that one thing of the lantern. When you come down to the cold facts, we simply got to *let on* that a lantern's resky. Why, we could work with a torchlight procession if we wanted to, *I* believe. Now, whilst I think of it, we got to hunt up something to make a saw out of, the first chance we get."

"What do we want of a saw?"

"What do we *want* of a saw? Hain't we got to saw the leg of Jim's bed off, so as to get the chain loose?"

"Why, you just said a body could lift up the bedstead and slip the chain off."

"Well, if that ain't just like you, Huck Finn. You *can* get up the infant-schooliest ways of going at a thing. Why, hain't you ever read any books at all?—Baron Trenck, nor Casanova, nor Benvenuto Chelleeny, nor Henri IV, nor none of them heroes? Whoever heard of getting a prisoner loose in such an old-maidy way as that? No; the way all the best authorities does, is to saw the bed-leg in two, and leave it just so, and swallow the sawdust, so it can't be found, and put some dirt and grease around the sawed place so the very keenest seneskal can't see no sign of it's being sawed, and thinks the bed-leg is perfectly sound. Then, the night you're ready, fetch the leg a kick, down she goes; slip off your chain, and there you are. Nothing to do but hitch your rope-ladder to the battlements, shin down it, break your leg in the moat—because a rope-ladder is nineteen foot too short, you know—and there's your horses and your trusty vassles, and they scoop you up and fling you across a saddle and away you go, to your native Langudoc, or Navarre, or wherever it is. It's gaudy, Huck. I wish there was a moat to this cabin. If we get time, the night of the escape, we'll dig one."

I says:

"What do we want of a moat, when we're going to snake him out from under the cabin?"

But he never heard me. He had forgot me and everything else. He had his chin in his hand, thinking. Pretty soon, he sighs, and shakes his head; then sighs again, and says:

"No, it wouldn't do—there ain't necessity enough for it."

"For what?" I says.

"Why, to saw Jim's leg off," he says.

"Good land!" I says, "why, there ain't *no* necessity for it. And what would you want to saw his leg off for, anyway?"

"Well, some of the best authorities has done it. They couldn't get the chain off, so they just cut their hand off, and shoved. And a leg would be better still. But we got to let that go. There ain't necessity enough in this case; and besides, Jim's a nigger and wouldn't understand the reasons for it, and how it's the custom in Europe; so we'll let it go. But there's one thing—he can have a rope-ladder; we can tear up our sheets and make him a rope-ladder easy enough. And we can send it to him in a pie; it's mostly done that way. And I've et worse pies."

"Why, Tom Sawyer, how you talk," I says; "Jim ain't got no use for a rope-ladder."

"He *has* got use for it. How *you* talk, you better say; you don't know nothing about it. He's *got* to have a rope-ladder; they all do."

"What in the nation can he *do* with it?"

"*Do* with it? He can hide it in his bed, can't he?" That's what they all do; and *he's* got to, too. Huck, you don't ever seem to want to do anything that's regular; you want to be starting something fresh all the time. Spose he *don't* do nothing with it? ain't it there in his bed, for a clew, after he's gone? and don't you reckon they'll want clews? Of course they will. And you wouldn't leave them any? That would be a *pretty* howdy-do, *wouldn't* it! I never heard of such a thing."

"Well," I says, "if it's in the regulations, and he's got to have it, all right, let him have it; because I don't wish to go back on no regulations; but there's one thing, Tom Sawyer—if we go to tearing up our sheets to make Jim a rope-ladder, we're going to get into trouble with Aunt Sally, just as sure as you're born. Now, the way I look at it, a hickry bark ladder don't cost nothing, and don't waste nothing, and is just as good to load up a pie with, and hide in a straw tick, as any rag ladder you can start; and as for Jim, he ain't had no experience, and so *he* don't care what kind of a—"

"Oh, shucks, Huck Finn, if I was as ignorant as you, I'd keep still—that's what *I'd* do. Who ever heard of a state prisoner escaping by a hickry-bark ladder? Why, it's perfectly ridiculous."

"Well, all right, Tom, fix it your own way; but if you'll take my advice, you'll let me borrow a sheet off of the clothes-line."

He said that would do. And that gave him another idea, and he says:

"Borrow a shirt, too."

"What do we want of a shirt, Tom?"

"Want it for Jim to keep a journal on."

"Journal your granny—*Jim* can't write."

"Spose he *can't* write—he can make marks on the shirt, can't he, if we make him a pen out of an old pewter spoon or a piece of an old iron barrel-hoop?"

"Why, Tom, we can pull a feather out of a goose and make him a better one; and quicker, too."

"*Prisoners* don't have geese running around the donjon-keep to pull pens out of, you muggins. They *always* make their pens out of the hardest, toughest, troublesomest piece of old brass candlestick or something like that they can get their hands on; and it takes them weeks and weeks, and months and months to file it out, too, because they've got to do it by rubbing it on the wall. *They* wouldn't use a goose-quill if they had it. It ain't regular."

"Well, then, what'll we make him the ink out of?"

"Many makes it out of iron-rust and tears; but that's the common sort and women; the best authorities uses their own blood. Jim can do that; and when he wants to send any little common ordinary mysterious message to let the world know where he's captivated, he can write it on the bottom of a tin plate with a fork and throw it out of the window. The Iron Mask always done that, and it's a blame' good way, too."

"Jim ain't got no tin plates. They feed him in a pan."

"That ain't anything; we can get him some."

"Can't nobody *read* his plates."

"That ain't got anything to *do* with it, Huck Finn. All *he's* got to do is to write on the plate and throw it out. You don't *have* to be able to read it. Why, half the time you can't read anything a prisoner writes on a tin plate, or anywhere else."

"Well, then, what's the sense in wasting the plates?"

"Why, blame it all, it ain't the *prisoner's* plates."

"But it's *somebody's* plates, ain't it?"

"Well, spos'n it is? What does the *prisoner* care whose—"

He broke off there, because we heard the breakfast horn blowing. So we cleared out for the house.

Along during that morning I borrowed a sheet and a white shirt off of the clothes-line; and I found an old sack and put them in it, and we went down and got the fox-fire, and put that in too. I called it borrowing, because that was what pap always called it; but Tom said it warn't borrowing, it was stealing. He said we was representing prisoners; and prisoners don't care how they get a thing so they get it, and nobody don't blame them for it, either. It ain't no crime in a prisoner to steal the thing he needs to get away with, Tom said; it's his right; and so, as long as we was representing a prisoner, we had a perfect right to steal anything on this place

we had the least use for, to get ourselves out of prison with. He said if
we warn't prisoners it would be a very different thing, and nobody but a
mean ornery person would steal when he warn't a prisoner. So we allowed
we would steal everything there was that come handy. And yet he made
a mighty fuss, one day, after that, when I stole a watermelon out of the
nigger patch and eat it; and he made me go and give the niggers a dime,
without telling them what it was for. Tom said that what he meant was,
we could steal anything we *needed*. Well, I says, I needed the watermelon.
But he said I didn't need it to get out of prison with, there's where the difference was. He said if I'd a wanted it to hide a knife in, and smuggle it to
Jim to kill the seneskal with, it would a been all right. So I let it go at that,
though I couldn't see no advantage in my representing a prisoner, if I got
to set down and chaw over a lot of gold-leaf distinctions like that, every
time I see a chance to hog a watermelon.

Well, as I was saying, we waited that morning till everybody was
settled down to business, and nobody in sight around the yard; then Tom
he carried the sack into the lean-to whilst I stood off a piece to keep watch.
By-and-by he come out, and we went and set down on the wood-pile, to
talk. He says:

"Everything's all right, now, except tools; and that's easy fixed."

"Tools?" I says.

"Yes."

"Tools for what?"

"Why, to dig with. We ain't agoing to *gnaw* him out, are we?"

"Ain't them old crippled picks and things in there good enough to dig
a nigger out with?" I says.

He turns on me looking pitying enough to make a body cry, and says:

"Huck Finn, did you *ever* hear of a prisoner having picks and shovels,
and all the modern conveniences in his wardrobe to dig himself out with?
Now I want to ask you—if you got any reasonableness in you at all—
what kind of a show would *that* give him to be a hero? Why, they might
as well lend him the key, and done with it. Picks and shovels—why they
wouldn't furnish 'em to a king."

"Well, then," I says, "if we don't want the picks and shovels, what do
we want?"

"A couple of case-knives."

"To dig the foundations out from under that cabin with?"

"Yes."

"Confound it, it's foolish, Tom."

"It don't make no difference how foolish it is, it's the *right* way—and
it's the regular way. And there ain't no *other* way, that ever *I* heard of, and

I've read all the books that gives any information about these things. They always dig out with a case-knife—and not through dirt, mind you; generly it's through solid rock. And it takes them weeks and weeks and weeks, and for ever and ever. Why, look at one of them prisoners in the bottom dungeon of the Castle Deef, in the harbor of Marseilles, that dug himself out that way; how long was *he* at it, you reckon?"

"I don't know."

"Well, guess."

"I don't know. A month and a half."

"*Thirty-seven year*—and he come out in China. *That's* the kind. I wish the bottom of *this* fortress was solid rock."

"*Jim* don't know nobody in China."

"What's *that* got to do with it? Neither did that other fellow. But you're always a-wandering off on a side issue. Why can't you stick to the main point?"

"All right—*I* don't care where he comes out, so he *comes* out; and Jim don't, either, I reckon. But there's one thing, anyway—Jim's too old to be dug out with a case-knife. He won't last."

"Yes he will *last*, too. You don't reckon it's going to take thirty-seven years to dig out through a *dirt* foundation, do you?"

"How long will it take, Tom?"

"Well, we can't resk being as long as we ought to, because it mayn't take very long for Uncle Silas to hear from down there by New Orleans. He'll hear Jim ain't from there. Then his next move will be to advertise Jim, or something like that. So we can't resk being as long digging him out as we ought to. By rights I reckon we ought to be a couple of years; but we can't. Things being so uncertain, what I recommend is this: that we really dig right in, as quick as we can; and after that, we can let *on*, to ourselves, that we was at it thirty-seven years. Then we can snatch him out and rush him away the first time there's an alarm. Yes, I reckon that'll be the best way."

"Now, there's *sense* in that," I says. "Letting on don't cost nothing; letting on ain't no trouble; and if it's any object, I don't mind letting on we was at it a hundred and fifty year. It wouldn't strain me none, after I got my hand in. So I'll mosey along now, and smouch a couple of case-knives."

"Smouch three," he says; "we want one to make a saw out of."

"Tom, if it ain't unregular and irreligious to sejest it," I says, "there's an old rusty saw-blade around yonder sticking under the weatherboarding behind the smoke-house."

He looked kind of weary and discouraged-like, and says:

"It ain't no use to try to learn you nothing, Huck. Run along and smouch the knives—three of them." So I done it.

— Tom is crazy!

Chapter XXXVI
The Lightning Rod—His Level Best—
A Bequest to Posterity—A High Figure

As soon as we reckoned everybody was asleep, that night, we went down the lightning rod, and shut ourselves up in the lean-to, and got out our pile of fox-fire, and went to work. We cleared everything out of the way, about four or five foot along the middle of the bottom log. Tom said he was right behind Jim's bed now, and we'd dig in under it, and when we got through there couldn't nobody in the cabin ever know there was any hole there, because Jim's counterpin hung down most to the ground, and you'd have to raise it up and look under to see the hole. So we dug and dug, with the case-knives, till most midnight; and then we was dog-tired, and our hands was blistered, and yet you couldn't see we'd done anything, hardly. At last I says:

GOING DOWN
THE LIGHTNING ROD.

"This ain't no thirty-seven year job, this is a thirty-eight year job, Tom Sawyer."

He never said nothing. But he sighed, and pretty soon he stopped digging, and then for a good little while I knowed he was thinking. Then he says:

"It ain't no use, Huck, it ain't agoing to work. If we was prisoners it would, because then we'd have as many years as we wanted, and no hurry; and we wouldn't get but a few minutes to dig, every day, while they was changing watches, and so our hands wouldn't get blistered, and we could keep it up right along, year in and year out, and do it right, and the way it ought to be done. But *we* can't fool along, we got to rush; we ain't got no time to spare. If we was to put in another night this way, we'd have to knock off for a week to let our hands get well—couldn't touch a case-knife with them sooner."

"Well, then, what we going to do, Tom?"

"I'll tell you. It ain't right, and it ain't moral, and I wouldn't like it to get out—but there ain't only just the one way; we got to dig him out with the picks, and *let on* it's case-knives."— *Finally some sense*

"*Now* you're *talking!*" I says; "your head gets leveler and leveler all the time, Tom Sawyer," I says. "Picks is the thing, moral or no moral; and as for me, I don't care shucks for the morality of it, nohow. When I start in to steal a nigger, or a watermelon, or a Sunday school book, I ain't no ways particular how it's done so it's done. What I want is my nigger; or what I want is my watermelon; or what I want is my Sunday school book; and if a pick's the handiest thing, that's the thing I'm agoing to dig that nigger or that watermelon or that Sunday school book out with; and I don't give a dead rat what the authorities thinks about it nuther."

"Well," he says, "there's excuse for picks and letting-on in a case like this; if it warn't so, I wouldn't approve of it, nor I wouldn't stand by and see the rules broke—because right is right, and wrong is wrong, and a body ain't got no business doing wrong when he ain't ignorant and knows better. It might answer for *you* to dig Jim out with a pick, *without* any letting-on, because you don't know no better; but it wouldn't for me, because I do know better. Gimme a case-knife."

He had his own by him, but I handed him mine. He flung it down, and says:

"Gimme a *case-knife.*"

Not! I didn't know just what to do—but then I thought. I scratched around amongst the old tools, and got a pick-axe and give it to him, and he took it and went to work, and never said a word.

He was always just that particular. Full of principle.

So then I got a shovel, and then we picked and shoveled, turn about, and made the fur fly. We stuck to it about a half an hour, which was as long as we could stand up; but we had a good deal of a hole to show for it. When I got up stairs, I looked out at the window and see Tom doing his level best with the lightning rod, but he couldn't come it, his hands was so sore. At last he says:

"It ain't no use, it can't be done. What you reckon I better do? Can't you think of no way?"

"Yes," I says, "but I reckon it ain't regular. Come up the stairs, and let on it's a lightning rod."

So he done it.

Next day Tom stole a pewter spoon and a brass candlestick in the house, for to make some pens for Jim out of, and six tallow candles; and I hung around the nigger-cabins, and laid for a chance, and stole three tin plates. Tom said it wasn't enough; but I said nobody wouldn't ever see the

plates that Jim throwed out, because they'd fall in the dog-fennel and jimpson weeds under the window-hole—then we could tote them back and he
could use them over again. So Tom was satisfied. Then he says:

"Now, the thing to study out is, how to get the things to Jim."

"Take them in through the hole," I says, "when we get it done."

He only just looked scornful, and said something about nobody ever
heard of such an idiotic idea, and then he went to studying. By-and-by he
said he had ciphered out two or three ways, but there warn't no need to
decide on any of them yet. Said we'd got to post Jim first.

That night we went down the lightning rod a little after ten, and
took one of the candles along, and listened under the window-hole, and
heard Jim snoring; so we pitched it in, and it didn't wake him. Then we
whirled in with the pick and shovel, and in about two hours and a half the
job was done. We crept in under Jim's bed and into the cabin, and pawed
around and found the candle and lit it, and stood over Jim a while, and
found him looking hearty and healthy, and then we woke him up gentle
and gradual. He was so glad to see us he most cried; and called us honey,
and all the pet names he could think of; and was for having us hunt up a
cold chisel to cut the chain off of his leg with, right away, and clearing out
without losing any time. But Tom he showed him how unregular it would
be, and set down and told him all about our plans, and how we could alter them in a minute any time there was an alarm; and not to be the least
afraid, because we would see he got away, *sure*. So Jim he said it was all
right, and we set there and talked over old times a while, and then Tom
asked a lot of questions, and when Jim told him Uncle Silas come in every
day or two to pray with him, and Aunt Sally come in to see if he was comfortable and had plenty to eat, and both of them was kind as they could
be, Tom says:

"*Now* I know how to fix it. We'll send you some things by them."

I said, "Don't do nothing of the kind; it's one of the most jackass ideas
I ever struck;" but he never paid no attention to me; went right on. It was
his way when he'd got his plans set.

So he told Jim how we'd have to smuggle in the rope-ladder pie, and
other large things, by Nat, the nigger that fed him, and he must be on the
lookout, and not be surprised, and not let Nat see him open them; and we
would put small things in uncle's coat pockets and he must steal them out;
and we would tie things to aunt's apron strings or put them in her apron
pocket, if we got a chance; and told him what they would be and what they
was for. And told him how to keep a journal on the shirt with his blood,
and all that. He told him everything. Jim he couldn't see no sense in the
most of it, but he allowed we was white folks and knowed better than him;
so he was satisfied, and said he would do it all just as Tom said.

Jim had plenty corn-cob pipes and tobacco; so we had a right down good sociable time; then we crawled out through the hole, and so home to bed, with hands that looked like they'd been chawed. Tom was in high spirits. He said it was the best fun he ever had in his life, and the most intellectural; and said if he only could see his way to it we would keep it up all the rest of our lives and leave Jim to our children to get out; for he believed Jim would come to like it better and better the more he got used to it. He said that in that way it could be strung out to as much as eighty year, and would be the best time on record. And he said it would make us all celebrated that had a hand in it.

In the morning we went out to the wood-pile and chopped up the brass candlestick into handy sizes, and Tom put them and the pewter spoon in his pocket. Then we went to the nigger-cabins, and while I got Nat's notice off, Tom shoved a piece of candlestick into the middle of a corn-pone that was in Jim's pan, and we went along with Nat to see how it would work, and it just worked noble; when Jim bit into it it most mashed all his teeth out; and there warn't ever anything could a worked better. Tom said so himself. Jim he never let on but what it was only just a piece of rock or something like that that's always getting into bread, you know; but after that he never bit into nothing but what he jabbed his fork into it in three or four places, first.

And whilst we was a standing there in the dimmish light, here comes a couple of the hounds bulging in, from under Jim's bed; and they kept on piling in till there was eleven of them, and there warn't hardly room in there to get your breath. By jings, we forgot to fasten that lean-to door. The nigger Nat he only just hollered "witches!" once, and keeled over onto the floor amongst the dogs, and begun to groan like he was dying. Tom jerked the door open and flung out a slab of Jim's meat, and the dogs went for it, and in two seconds he was out himself and back again and shut the door, and I knowed he'd fixed the other door too. Then he went to work on the nigger, coaxing him and petting him, and asking him if he'd been imagining he saw something again. He raised up, and blinked his eyes around, and says:

"Mars Sid, you'll say I's a fool, but if I didn't b'lieve I see most a million dogs, er devils, er some'n, I wisht I may die right heah in dese tracks. I did, mos' sholy. Mars Sid, I *felt* um—I *felt* um, sah; dey was all over me. Dad fetch it, I jis' wisht I could git my han's on one er dem witches jis' wunst—on'y jis' wunst—it's all I'd ast. But mos'ly I wisht dey'd lemme 'lone, I does."

Tom says:

"Well, I tell you what *I* think. What makes them come here just at this runaway nigger's breakfast-time? It's because they're hungry; that's the reason. You make them a witch pie; that's the thing for *you* to do."

"But my lan', Mars Sid, how's I gwyne to make 'm a witch pie? I doan' know how to make it. I hain't ever hearn er sich a thing b'fo'."

"Well, then, I'll have to make it myself."

"Will you do it, honey?—will you? I'll wusshup de groun' und' yo' foot, I will!"

"All right, I'll do it, seeing it's you, and you've been good to us and showed us the runaway nigger. But you got to be mighty careful. When we come around, you turn your back; and then whatever we've put in the pan, don't you let on you see it at all. And don't you look, when Jim unloads the pan—something might happen, I don't know what. And above all, don't you *handle* the witch-things."

"*Hannel* 'm, Mars Sid? What *is* you a talkin' 'bout? I wouldn' lay de weight er my finger on um, not f'r ten hund'd thous'n billion dollars, I wouldn't."

Chapter XXXVII
The Last Shirt—Mooning Around—
Sailing Orders—The Witch Pie

That was all fixed. So then we went away and went to the rubbage pile in the back yard where they keep the old boots, and rags, and pieces of bottles, and wore-out tin things, and all such truck, and scratched around and found an old tin wash-pan and stopped up the holes as well as we could, to bake the pie in, and took it down cellar and stole it full of flour, and started for breakfast and found a couple of shingle-nails that Tom said would be handy for a prisoner to scrabble his name and sorrows on the dungeon walls with, and dropped one of them in Aunt Sally's apron pocket which was hanging on a chair, and t'other we stuck in the band of Uncle Silas's hat, which was on the bureau, because we heard the children say their pa and ma was going to the runaway nigger's house this morning, and then went to breakfast, and Tom dropped the pewter spoon in Uncle Silas's coat pocket, and Aunt Sally wasn't come yet, so we had to wait a little while.

And when she come she was hot, and red, and cross, and couldn't hardly wait for the blessing; and then she went to sluicing out coffee with one hand and cracking the handiest child's head with her thimble with the other, and says:

"I've hunted high, and I've hunted low, and it does beat all, what *has* become of your other shirt."

My heart fell down amongst my lungs and livers and things, and a hard piece of corn-crust started down my throat after it and got met on

the road with a cough and
was shot across the table and
took one of the children in the
eye and curled him up like a
fishing-worm, and let a cry out
of him the size of a war-whoop,
and Tom he turned kinder
blue around the gills, and it
all amounted to a considerable
state of things for about a quarter of a minute or as much as
that, and I would a sold out for
half price if there was a bidder.
But after that we was all right
again—it was the sudden surprise of it that knocked us so
kind of cold. Uncle Silas he says:

"It's most uncommon curi-
ous, I can't understand it. I
know perfectly well I took it
off, because—"

"Because you hain't got but
one *on.* Just *listen* at the man! I
know you took it off, and know

THE RUBBAGE PILE.

it by a better way than your wool-gethering memory, too, because it was
on the clo'es-line yesterday—I see it there myself. But it's gone—that's the
long and the short of it, and you'll just have to change to a red flann'l one
till I can get time to make a new one. And it'll be the third I've made in two
years; it just keeps a body on the jump to keep you in shirts; and whatever
you do manage to *do* with 'm all, is more'n I can make out. A body'd think
you *would* learn to take some sort of care of 'em, at your time of life."

"I know it, Sally, and I do try all I can. But it oughtn't to be altogether
my fault, because you know I don't see them nor have nothing to do with
them except when they're on me; and I don't believe I've ever lost one of
them *off* of me."

"Well, it ain't *your* fault if you haven't, Silas—you'd a done it if you
could, I reckon. And the shirt ain't all that's gone, nuther. Ther's a spoon
gone; and *that* ain't all. There was ten, and now ther's only nine. The calf
got the shirt I reckon, but the calf never took the spoon, *that's* certain."

"Why, what else is gone, Sally?"

"There's six *candles* gone—that's what. The rats could a got the
candles, and I reckon they did; I wonder they don't walk off with the whole

place, the way you're always going to stop their holes and don't do it; and if they warn't fools they'd sleep in your hair, Silas—*you'd* never find it out; but you can't lay the *spoon* on the rats, and that I *know*."

"Well, Sally, I'm in fault, and I acknowledge it; I've been remiss; but I won't let to-morrow go by without stopping up them holes."

"Oh, I wouldn't hurry, next year'll do. Matilda Angelina Araminta *Phelps!*"

Whack comes the thimble, and the child snatches her claws out of the sugarbowl without fooling around any. Just then, the nigger woman steps onto the passage, and says:

"Missus, dey's a sheet gone."

"A *sheet* gone! Well, for the land's sake!"

"I'll stop up them holes *to-day,*" says Uncle Silas, looking sorrowful.

"Oh, *do* shet up!—spose the rats took the *sheet? Where's* it gone, Lize?"

"Clah to goodness I hain't no notion, Miss Sally. She wuz on de clo's-line yistiddy, but she done gone; she ain' dah no mo,' now."

"I reckon the world *is* coming to an end. I *never* see the beat of it, in all my born days. A shirt, and a sheet, and a spoon, and six can—"

"Missus," comes a young yaller wench, "dey's a brass cannelstick miss'n."

"Cler out from here, you hussy, er I'll take a skillet to ye!"

Well, she was just a biling. I begun to lay for a chance; I reckoned I would sneak out and go for the woods till the weather moderated. She kept a raging right along, running her insurrection all by herself, and every-body else mighty meek and quiet; and at last Uncle Silas, looking kind of foolish, fishes up that spoon out of his pocket. She stopped, with her mouth open and her hands up; and as for me, I wished I was in Jeruslem or somewheres. But not long; because she says:

"It's *just* as I expected. So you had it in your pocket all the time; and like as not you've got the other things there, too. How'd it get there?"

"I reely don't know, Sally," he says, kind of apologizing, "or you know I would tell. I was a-studying over my text in Acts Seventeen, before break-fast, and I reckon I put it in there, not noticing, meaning to put my Testa-ment in, and it must be so, because my Testament ain't in, but I'll go and see, and if the Testament is where I had it, I'll know I didn't put it in, and that will show that I laid the Testament down and took up the spoon, and—"

"Oh, for the land's sake! Give a body a rest! Go 'long now, the whole kit and biling of ye; and don't come nigh me again till I've got back my peace of mind."

I'd a heard her, if she'd a said it to herself, let alone speaking it out; and I'd a got up and obeyed her, if I'd a been dead. As we was passing through the setting-room, the old man he took up his hat, and the shingle-nail fell out on the floor, and he just merely picked it up and laid it on the mantel-shelf, and never said nothing, and went out. Tom see him do it, and remembered about the spoon, and says:

"Well, it ain't no use to send things by *him* no more, he ain't reliable." Then he says: "But he done us a good turn with the spoon, anyway, without knowing it, and so we'll go and do him one without *him* knowing it—stop up his rat-holes."

There was a noble good lot of them, down cellar, and it took us a whole hour, but we done the job tight and good, and ship-shape. Then we heard steps on the stairs, and blowed out our light, and hid; and here comes the old man, with a candle in one hand and a bundle of stuff in t'other, looking as absent-minded as year before last. He went a mooning around, first to one rat-hole and then another, till he'd been to them all. Then he stood about five minutes, picking tallow-drip off of his candle and thinking. Then he turns off slow and dreamy towards the stairs, saying:

"Well, for the life of me I can't remember when I done it. I could show her now that I warn't to blame on account of the rats. But never mind—let it go. I reckon it wouldn't do no good."

And so he went on a mumbling up stairs, and then we left. He was a mighty nice old man. And always is.

Tom was a good deal bothered about what to do for a spoon, but he said we'd got to have it; so he took a think. When he had ciphered it out, he told me how we was to do; then we went and waited around the spoon-basket till we see Aunt Sally coming, and then Tom went to counting the spoons and laying them out to one side, and I slid one of them up my sleeve, and Tom says:

"Why, Aunt Sally, there ain't but nine spoons, *yet.*"

She says:

"Go 'long to your play, and don't bother me. I know better, I counted 'm myself."

"Well, I've counted them twice, Aunty, and I can't make but nine."

She looked out of all patience, but of course she come to count—anybody would.

"I declare to gracious ther' *ain't* but nine!" she says. "Why, what in the world—plague *take* the things, I'll count 'm again."

So I slipped back the one I had, and when she got done counting, she says:

"Hang the troublesome rubbage, ther's *ten,* now!" and she looked huffy and bothered both. But Tom says:

"Why, Aunty, I don't think there's ten."

"You numskull, didn't you see me *count* 'm?"

"I know, but—"

"Well, I'll count 'm *again.*"

So I smouched one, and they come out nine same as the other time. Well, she *was* in a tearing way—just a trembling all over, she was so mad. But she counted and counted, till she got that addled she'd start to count-in the *basket* for a spoon, sometimes; and so, three times they come out right, and three times they come out wrong. Then she grabbed up the bas-ket and slammed it across the house and knocked the cat galley-west; and she said cle'r out and let her have some peace, and if we come bothering around her again betwixt that and dinner, she'd skin us. So we had the odd spoon; and dropped it in her apron pocket whilst she was a giving us our sailing-orders, and Jim got it all right, along with her shingle-nail, be-fore noon. We was very well satisfied with this business, and Tom allowed it was worth twice the trouble it took, because he said *now* she couldn't ever count them spoons twice alike again to save her life; and wouldn't be-lieve she'd counted them right, if she *did;* and said that after she'd about counted her head off, for the next three days, he judged she'd give it up and offer to kill anybody that wanted her to ever count them any more.

So we put the sheet back on the line, that night, and stole one out of her closet; and kept on putting it back and stealing it again, for a couple of days, till she didn't know how many sheets she had, any more, and said she didn't *care,* and warn't agoing to bullyrag the rest of her soul out about it, and wouldn't count them again not to save her life, she druther die first.

So we was all right now, as to the shirt and the sheet and the spoon and the candles, by the help of the calf and the rats and the mixed-up counting; and as to the candlestick, it warn't no consequence, it would blow over by-and-by.

But that pie was a job; we had no end of trouble with that pie. We fixed it up away down in the woods, and cooked it there; and we got it done at last, and very satisfactory, too; but not all in one day; and we had to use up three washpans full of flour, before we got through, and we got burnt pretty much all over, in places, and eyes put out with the smoke; because, you see, we didn't want nothing but a crust, and we couldn't prop it up right, and she would always cave in. But of course we thought of the right way at last; which was to cook the ladder, too, in the pie. So then we laid in with Jim, the second night, and tore up the sheet all in little strings, and twisted them together, and long before daylight we had a lovely rope, that you could a hung a person with. We let on it took nine months to make it.

And in the forenoon we took it down to the woods, but it wouldn't go in the pie. Being made of a whole sheet, that way, there was rope enough for forty pies, if we'd a wanted them, and plenty left over for soup, or sausage, or anything you choose. We could a had a whole dinner.

But we didn't need it. All we needed was just enough for the pie, and so we throwed the rest away. We didn't cook none of the pies in the washpan, afraid the solder would melt; but Uncle Silas he had a noble brass warming-pan which he thought considerable of, because it belonged to one of his ancestors with a long wooden handle that come over from England with William the Conqueror in the *Mayflower* or one of them early ships and was hid away up garret with a lot of other old pots and things that was valuable, not on account of being any account because they warn't, but on account of them being relicts, you know, and we snaked her out, private, and took her down there, but she failed on the first pies, because we didn't know how, but she come up smiling on the last one. We took and lined her with dough, and set her in the coals, and loaded her up with rag-rope, and put on a dough roof, and shut down the lid, and put hot embers on top, and stood off five foot, with the long handle, cool and comfortable, and in fifteen minutes she turned out a pie that was a satisfaction to look at. But the person that et it would want to fetch a couple of kags of toothpicks along, for if that rope-ladder wouldn't cramp him down to business, I don't know nothing what I'm talking about, and lay him in enough stomach-ache to last him till next time, too.

Nat didn't look, when we put the witch-pie in Jim's pan; and we put the three tin plates in the bottom of the pan under the vittles; and so Jim got everything all right, and as soon as he was by himself he busted into the pie and hid the rope-ladder inside of his straw tick, and scratched some marks on a tin plate and throwed it out of the window-hole.

Chapter XXXVIII
The Coat of Arms—A Skilled Superintendent—
Unpleasant Glory—A Tearful Subject

Making them pens was a distressid tough job, and so was the saw; and Jim allowed the inscription was going to be the toughest of all. That's the one which the prisoner has to scrabble on the wall. But we had to have it; Tom said we'd *got* to; there warn't no case of a state prisoner not scrabbling his inscription to leave behind, and his coat of arms.

"Look at Lady Jane Grey," he says; "look at Gilford Dudley; look at old Northumberland! Why, Huck, spose it *is* considerble trouble?—what you going to do?—how you going to get around it? Jim's *got* to do his in-scription and coat of arms. They all do."

Jim says:

JIM'S COAT OF ARMS.

"Why, Mars Tom, I hain't got no coat o' arms; I hain't got nuffn but dish-yer ole shirt, en you knows I got to keep de journal on dat."

"Oh, you don't understand, Jim; a coat of arms is very different."

"Well," I says, "Jim's right, anyway, when he says he ain't got no coat of arms, because he hain't."

"I reckon *I* knowed that," Tom says, "but you bet he'll have one before he goes out of this—because he's going out *right,* and there ain't going to be no flaws in his record."

So whilst me and Jim filed away at the pens on a brickbat apiece, Jim a making his'n out of the brass and I making mine out of the spoon, Tom set to work to think out the coat of arms. By-and-by he said he'd struck so many good ones he didn't hardly know which to take, but there was one which he reckoned he'd decide on. He says:

"On the scutcheon we'll have a bend *or* in the dexter base a saltire murrey in the fess, with a dog, couchant, for common charge, and under his foot a chain embattled, for slavery, with a chevron *vert* in a chief engrailed, and three invected lines on a field *azure,* with the nombril points rampant on a dancette indented; crest, a runaway nigger, *sable,* with his bundle over his shoulder on a bar sinister; and a couple of gules for supporters, which is you and me; motto, *Maggiore fretta, minore atto.* Got it out of a book—means, the more haste, the less speed."

"Geewhillikins," I says, "but what does the rest of it mean?"

"We ain't got no time to bother over that," he says, "we got to dig in like all git-out."

"Well, anyway," I says, "what's *some* of it? What's a fess?"

"A fess—a fess is—*you* don't need to know what a fess is. I'll show him how to make it when he gets to it."

"Shucks, Tom," I says, "I think you might tell a person. What's a bar sinister?"

"Oh, *I* don't know. But he's got to have it. All the nobility does."
That was just his way. If it didn't suit him to explain a thing to you,
he wouldn't do it. You might pump at him a week, it wouldn't make no
difference.

He'd got all that coat of arms business fixed, so now he started in to
finish up the rest of that part of the work, which was to plan out a mournful inscription—said Jim got to have one, like they all done. He made up
a lot, and wrote them out on a paper, and read them off, so:

1. *Here a captive heart busted.*
2. *Here a poor prisoner, forsook by the world and friends, fretted out
   his sorrowful life.*
3. *Here a lonely heart broke, and a worn spirit went to its rest, after
   thirty-seven years of solitary captivity.*
4. *Here, homeless and friendless, after thirty-seven years of bitter
   captivity, perished a noble stranger, natural son of Louis XIV.*

Tom's voice trembled, whilst he was reading them, and he most broke
down. When he got done, he couldn't no way make up his mind which one
for Jim to scrabble onto the wall, they was all so good; but at last he allowed he would let him scrabble them all on. Jim said it would take him a
year to scrabble such a lot of truck onto the logs with a nail, and he didn't
know how to make letters, besides; but Tom said he would block them out
for him, and then he wouldn't have nothing to do but just follow the lines.
Then pretty soon he says:

"Come to think, the logs ain't agoing to do; they don't have log walls
in a dungeon: we got to dig the inscriptions into a rock. We'll fetch a rock."

Jim said the rock was worse than the logs; he said it would take him
such a pison long time to dig them into a rock, he wouldn't ever get out.
But Tom said he would let me help him do it. Then he took a look to see
how me and Jim was getting along with the pens. It was most pesky tedious hard work and slow, and didn't give my hands no show to get well
of the sores, and we didn't seem to make no headway, hardly. So Tom says:

"I know how to fix it. We got to have a rock for the coat of arms and
mournful inscriptions, and we can kill two birds with that same rock.
There's a gaudy big grindstone down at the mill, and we'll smouch it, and
carve the things on it, and file out the pens and the saw on it, too."

It warn't no slouch of an idea; and it warn't no slouch of a grindstone
nuther; but we allowed we'd tackle it. It warn't quite midnight, yet, so we
cleared out for the mill, leaving Jim at work. We smouched the grindstone, and set out to roll her home, but it was a most nation tough job.
Sometimes, do what we could, we couldn't keep her from falling over, and

she come mighty near mashing us, every time. Tom said she was going to get one of us, sure, before we got through. We got her half way; and then we was plumb played out, and most drownded with sweat. We see it warn't no use, we got to go and fetch Jim. So he raised up his bed and slid the chain off of the bed-leg, and wrapt it round and round his neck, and we crawled out through our hole and down there, and Jim and me laid into that grindstone and walked her along like nothing; and Tom superin-tended. He could out-superintend any boy I ever see. He knowed how to do everything.

Our hole was pretty big, but it warn't big enough to get the grindstone through; but Jim he took the pick and soon made it big enough. Then Tom marked out them things on it with the nail, and set Jim to work on them, with the nail for a chisel and an iron bolt from the rubbage in the lean-to for a hammer, and told him to work till the rest of his candle quit on him, and then he could go to bed, and hide the grindstone under his straw tick and sleep on it. Then we helped him fix his chain back on the bed-leg, and was ready for bed ourselves. But Tom thought of something, and says:

"You got any spiders in here, Jim?"

"No, sah, thanks to goodness I hain't, Mars Tom."

"All right, we'll get you some."

"But bless you, honey, I doan' *want* none. I's afeard un um. I jis' 's soon have rattlesnakes aroun'."

Tom thought a minute or two, and says:

"It's a good idea. And I reckon it's been done. It *must* a been done; it stands to reason. Yes, it's a prime good idea. Where could you keep it?"

"Keep what, Mars Tom?"

"Why, a rattlesnake."

"De goodness gracious alive, Mars Tom! Why, if dey was a rattlesnake to come in heah, I'd take en bust right out thoo dat log wall, I would, wid my head."

"Why, Jim, you wouldn't be afraid of it, after a little. You could tame it."

"*Tame* it!"

"Yes—easy enough. Every animal is grateful for kindness and petting, and they wouldn't *think* of hurting a person that pets them. Any book will tell you that. You try—that's all I ask; just try for two or three days. Why, you can get him so, in a little while, that he'll love you; and sleep with you; and won't stay away from you a minute; and will let you wrap him round your neck and put his head in your mouth."

"*Please*, Mars Tom—*doan'* talk so! I can't *stan'* it! He'd *let* me shove his head in my mouf—fer a favor, hain't it? I lay he'd wait a pow'ful long time 'fo' I *ast* him. En mo' en dat, I doan' *want* him to sleep wid me."

[handwritten marginalia: "and Tom" / "isn't foolish?"]

"Jim, don't act so foolish). A prisoner's *got* to have some kind of a dumb pet, and if a rattlesnake hain't ever been tried, why, there's more glory to be gained in your being the first to ever try it than any other way you could ever think of to save your life."

"Why, Mars Tom, I doan' *want* no sich glory. Snake take 'n bite Jim's chin off, den *whah* is de glory? No, sah, I doan' want no sich doin's."

"Blame it, can't you *try?* I only *want* you to try—you needn't keep it up if it don't work."

"But de trouble all *done,* ef de snake bite me while I's a tryin' him. Mars Tom, I's willin' to tackle mos' anything 'at ain't onreasonable, but ef you en Huck fetches a rattlesnake in heah for me to tame, I's gwyne to *leave,* dat's *shore.*"

"Well, then, let it go, let it go, if you're so bullheaded about it. We can get you some garter-snakes, and you can tie some buttons on their tails, and let on they're rattlesnakes, and I reckon that 'll have to do."

"I k'n stan' *dem,* Mars Tom, but blame' 'f I couldn' get along widout um, I tell you dat. I never knowed b'fo', 't was so much bother and trouble to be a prisoner."

"Well, it *always* is, when it's done right. You got any rats around here?"

"No, sah, I hain't seed none."

"Well, we'll get you some rats."

"Why, Mars Tom, I doan' *want* no rats. Dey's de dad-blamedest cre-turs to sturb a body, en rustle roun' over 'im, en bite his feet, when he's tryin' to sleep, I ever see. No, sah, gimme g'yarter-snakes, 'f I's got to have 'm, but doan' gimme no rats, I ain't got no use f'r um, skasely."

"But, Jim, you *got* to have 'em—they all do. So don't make no more fuss about it. Prisoners ain't ever without rats. There ain't no instance of it. And they train them, and pet them, and learn them tricks, and they get to be as sociable as flies. But you got to play music to them. You got any-thing to play music on?" *[handwritten marginalia: "no they don't"]*

"I ain' got nuffn but a coase comb en a piece o' paper, en a juice-harp; but I reck'n dey wouldn' take no stock in a juice-harp."

"Yes they would. *They* don't care what kind of music 'tis. A jews-harp's plenty good enough for a rat. All animals like music—in a prison they dote on it. Specially, painful music; and you can't get no other kind out of a jews-harp. It always interests them; they come out to see what's the matter with you. Yes, you're all right; you're fixed very well. You want to set on your bed, nights, before you go to sleep, and early in the morn-ings, and play your jews-harp; play 'The Last Link is Broken'—that's the thing that'll scoop a rat, quicker'n anything else: and when you've played about two minutes, you'll see all the rats, and the snakes, and spiders, and things begin to feel worried about you, and come. And they'll just fairly swarm over you, and have a noble good time."

"Yes, *dey* will, I reck'n, Mars Tom, but what kine er time is *Jim* havin'? Blest if I kin see de pint. But I'll do it ef I got to. I reck'n I better keep de animals satisfied, en not have no trouble in de house."

Tom waited to think it over, and see if there wasn't nothing else; and pretty soon he says:

"Oh—there's one thing I forgot. Could you raise a flower here, do you reckon?"

"I doan' know but maybe I could, Mars Tom; but it's tolable dark in heah, en I ain' got no use f'r no flower, nohow, en she'd be a pow'ful sight o' trouble."

"Well, you try it, anyway. Some other prisoners has done it."

"One er dem big cat-tail-lookin' mullen-stalks would grow in heah, Mars Tom, I reck'n, but she wouldn't be wuth half de trouble she'd coss."

"Don't you believe it. We'll fetch you a little one, and you plant it in the corner, over there, and raise it. And don't call it mullen, call it Pitchiola—that's its right name, when it's in a prison. And you want to water it with your tears."

"Why, I got plenty spring water, Mars Tom."

"You don't *want* spring water; you want to water it with your tears. It's the way they always do."

"Why, Mars Tom, I lay I kin raise one er dem mullen-stalks twyste wid spring water whiles another man's a *start'n* one wid tears."

"That ain't the idea. You got to do it with tears."

"She'll die on my han's, Mars Tom, she sholy will; kase I doan' skasely ever cry."

So Tom was stumped. But he studied it over, and then said Jim would have to worry along the best he could with an onion. He promised he would go to the nigger-cabins and drop one, private, in Jim's coffee-pot, in the morning. Jim said he would "jis' 's soon have tobacker in his coffee;" and found so much fault with it, and with the work and bother of raising the mullen, and jews-harping the rats, and petting and flattering up the snakes and spiders and things, on top of all the other work he had to do on pens, and inscriptions, and journals, and things, which made it more trouble and worry and responsibility to be a prisoner than anything he ever undertook, that Tom most lost all patience with him; and said he was just loadened down with more gaudier chances than a prisoner ever had in the world to make a name for himself, and yet he didn't know enough to appreciate them, and they was just about wasted on him. So Jim he was sorry, and said he wouldn't behave so no more, and then me and Tom shoved for bed.

Chapter XXXIX
Rats—Lively Bed-fellows—The Straw Dummy

In the morning we went up to the village and bought a wire rat trap and fetched it down, and unstopped the best rat hole, and in about an hour we had fifteen of the bulliest kind of ones; and then we took it and put it in a safe place under Aunt Sally's bed. But while we was gone for spiders, little Thomas Franklin Benjamin Jefferson Elexander Phelps found it there, and opened the door of it to see if the rats would come out, and they did; and Aunt Sally she come in, and when we got back she was a standing on top of the bed raising Cain, and the rats was doing what they could to keep off the dull times for her. So she took and dusted us both with the hickry, and we was as much as two hours catching another fifteen or sixteen, drat that meddlesome cub, and they warn't the likeliest, nuther, because the first haul was the pick of the flock. I never see a likelier lot of rats than what that first haul was.

KEEPING OFF DULL TIMES.

We got a splendid stock of sorted spiders, and bugs, and frogs, and caterpillars, and one thing or another; and we like-to got a hornet's nest, but we didn't. The family was at home. We didn't give it right up, but staid with them as long as we could; because we allowed we'd tire them out or they'd got to tire us out, and they done it. Then we got allycumpain and rubbed on the places, and was pretty near all right again, but couldn't set down convenient. And so we went for the snakes, and grabbed a couple of dozen garters and housesnakes, and put them in a bag, and put it in our room, and by that time it was supper time, and a rattling good honest day's work; and hungry?—oh, no, I reckon not! And there warn't a blessed snake up there, when we went back—we didn't half tie the sack, and they worked out, somehow, and left. But it didn't matter much, because they was still on the premises somewhere. So we judged we could get some of them again. No, there warn't no real scarcity of snakes about the house for a considerable spell. You'd see them dripping from the rafters and places, every now and then; and they generly landed in your plate, or down the back of your neck, and most of the time where you didn't want them. Well, they was handsome and striped, and there warn't no harm in a million of them; but that never made no difference to Aunt Sally, she despised snakes, be the breed what they might, and she couldn't stand them no way you could fix it; and every time one of them flopped down on her, it didn't make no difference what she was doing, she would just lay that work down and light out. I never see such a woman. And you could hear her whoop to Jericho. You couldn't get her to take aholt of one of them with the tongs. And if she turned over and found one in bed, she would scramble out and lift a howl that you would think the house was afire. She disturbed the old man so, that he said he could most wish there hadn't ever been no snakes created. Why, after every last snake had been gone clear out of the house for as much as a week, Aunt Sally warn't over it yet; she warn't near over it; when she was setting thinking about something, you could touch her on the back of her neck with a feather and she would jump right out of her stockings. It was very curious. But Tom said all women was just so. He said they was made that way; for some reason or other.

We got a licking every time one of our snakes come in her way; and she allowed these lickings warn't nothing to what she would do if we ever loaded up the place again with them. I didn't mind the lickings, because they didn't amount to nothing; but I minded the trouble we had, to lay in another lot. But we got them laid in, and all the other things; and you never see a cabin as blithesome as Jim's was when they'd all swarm out for music and go for him. Jim didn't like the spiders, and the spiders didn't like Jim; and so they'd lay for him and make it mighty warm for him. And he said that between the rats, and the snakes, and the grindstone, there warn't no room in bed for him, skasely; and when there was, a body couldn't sleep, it was so lively, and it was always lively, he said, because *they* never all slept at one time, but took turn about, so when the snakes was asleep the rats was on deck, and when the rats turned in the snakes come on watch, so he always had one gang under him, in his way, and t'other gang having a circus over him, and if he got up to hunt a new place, the spiders would take a chance at him as he crossed over. He said if he ever got out, this time, he wouldn't ever be a prisoner again, not for a salary.

Well, by the end of three weeks, everything was in pretty good shape. The shirt was sent in early, in a pie, and every time a rat bit Jim he would get up and write a little in his journal whilst the ink was fresh; the pens was made, the inscriptions and so on was all carved on the grindstone; the bed-leg was sawed in two, and we had et up the sawdust, and it give us a most amazing stomach-ache. We reckoned we was all going to die, but didn't. It was the most undigestible sawdust I ever see; and Tom said the same. But as I was saying, we'd got all the work done, now, at last; and we was all pretty much fagged out, too, but mainly Jim. The old man had wrote a couple of times to the plantation below Orleans to come and get their runaway nigger, but hadn't got no answer, because there warn't no such plantation; so he allowed he would advertise Jim in the St. Louis and New Orleans papers; and when he mentioned the St. Louis ones, it give me the cold shivers, and I see we hadn't no time to lose. So Tom said, now for the nonnamous letters.

"What's them?" I says.

"Warnings to the people that something is up. Sometimes it's done one way, sometimes another. But there's always somebody spying around, that gives notice to the governor of the castle. When Louis XVI was going to light out of the Tooleries, a servant-girl done it. It's a very good way, and so is the nonnamous letters. We'll use them both. And it's usual for the prisoner's mother to change clothes with him, and she stays in, and he slides out in her clothes. We'll do that too."

"But looky here, Tom, what do we want to *warn* anybody for, that something's up? Let them find it out for themselves—it's their lookout."

"Yes, I know; but you can't depend on them. It's the way they've acted from the very start—left us to do *everything*. They're so confiding and mullet-headed they don't take notice of nothing at all. So if we don't *give* them notice, there won't be nobody nor nothing to interfere with us, and so after all our hard work and trouble this escape'll go off perfectly flat: won't amount to nothing—won't be nothing *to* it."

"Well, as for me, Tom, that's the way I'd like."

"Shucks!" he says, and looked disgusted. So I says:

"But I ain't going to make no complaint. Any way that suits you suits me. What you going to do about the servant-girl?"

"You'll be her. You slide in, in the middle of the night, and hook that yaller girl's frock."

"Why, Tom, that'll make trouble next morning; because of course she prob'bly hain't got any but that one."

"I know; but you don't want it but fifteen minutes, to carry the nonnamous letter and shove it under the front door."

"All right, then, I'll do it; but I could carry it just as handy in my own togs."

"You wouldn't look like a servant-girl *then*, would you?"

"No, but there won't be nobody to see what I look like, *anyway*."

"That ain't got nothing to do with it. The thing for us to do, is just to do our *duty*, and not worry about whether anybody *sees* us do it or not. Hain't you got no principle at all?"

"All right, I ain't saying nothing; I'm the servant-girl. Who's Jim's mother?"

"I'm his mother. I'll hook a gown from Aunt Sally."

"Well, then, you'll have to stay in the cabin when me and Jim leaves."

"Not much. I'll stuff Jim's clothes full of straw and lay it on his bed to represent his mother in disguise, and Jim 'll take Aunt Sally's gown off of me and wear it, and we'll all evade together. When a prisoner of style escapes, it's called an evasion. It's always called so when a king escapes, frinstance. And the same with a king's son; it don't make no difference whether he's a natural one or an unnatural one."

So Tom he wrote the nonnamous letter, and I smouched the yaller wench's frock, that night, and put it on, and shoved it under the front door, the way Tom told me to. It said:

Beware. Trouble is brewing. Keep a sharp lookout.
                                      UNKNOWN FRIEND.

Next night we stuck a picture which Tom drawed in blood, of a skull and crossbones, on the front door; and next night another one of a coffin, on the back door. I never see a family in such a sweat. They couldn't a been worse scared if the place had a been full of ghosts laying for them behind everything and under the beds and shivering through the air. If a door banged, Aunt Sally she jumped, and said "ouch!" if anything fell, she jumped and said "ouch!" if you happened to touch her, when she warn't noticing, she done the same; she couldn't face noway and be satisfied, because she allowed there was something behind her every time—so she was always a whirling around, sudden, and saying "ouch," and before she'd get two-thirds around, she'd whirl back again, and say it again; and she was afraid to go to bed, but she dasn't set up. So the thing was working very well, Tom said; he said he never see a thing work more satisfactory. He said it showed it was done right.

So he said, now for the grand bulge! So the very next morning at the streak of dawn we got another letter ready, and was wondering what we better do with it, because we heard them say at supper they was going to have a nigger on watch at both doors all night. Tom he went down the lightning rod to spy around; and the nigger at the back door was asleep, and he stuck it in the back of his neck and come back. This letter said:

Don't betray me, I wish to be your friend. There is a desprate gang of cutthroats from over in the Ingean Territory going to steal your runaway nigger to-night, and they have been trying to scare you so as you will stay in the house and not bother

*them. I am one of the gang, but have got religgion and wish to
quit it and lead a honest life again, and will betray the helish design. They will sneak down from northards, along the fence, at
midnight exact, with a false key, and go in the nigger's cabin to
get him. I am to be off a piece and blow a tin horn if I see any
danger; but stead of that, I will* BA *like a sheep soon as they get
in and not blow at all; then whilst they are getting his chains
loose, you slip there and lock them in, and can kill them at your
leasure. Don't do anything but just the way I am telling you, if
you do they will suspicion something and raise whoopjamboree-
hoo. I do not wish any reward but to know I have done the
right thing.*

UNKNOWN FRIEND.

Chapter XL
Fishing—The Vigilance Committee—
A Lively Run—Jim Advises a Doctor

We was feeling pretty good, after breakfast, and took my canoe and went
over the river a fishing, with a lunch, and had a good time, and took a look
at the raft and found her all right, and got home late to supper, and found
them in such a sweat and worry they didn't know which end they was
standing on, and made us go right off to bed the minute we was done supper, and wouldn't tell us what the trouble was, and never let on a word
about the new letter, but didn't need to, because we knowed as much
about it as anybody did, and as soon as we was half up stairs and her back
was turned, we slid for the cellar cubboard and loaded up a good lunch
and took it up to our room and went to bed, and got up about half-past
eleven, and Tom put on Aunt Sally's dress that he stole and was going to
start with the lunch, but says:

"Where's the butter?"

"I laid out a hunk of it," I says, "on a piece of a corn-pone."

"Well, you *left* it laid out, then—it ain't here."

"We can get along without it," I says.

"We can get along *with* it, too," he says; "just you slide down cellar and fetch it. And then mosey right down the lightning rod and
come along. I'll go and stuff the straw into Jim's clothes to represent his
mother in disguise, and be ready to *ba* like a sheep and shove soon as you
get there."

FISHING.

So out he went, and down cellar went I. The hunk of butter, big as a person's fist, was where I had left it, so I took up the slab of corn-pone with it on, and blowed out my light, and started up stairs, very stealthy, and got up to the main floor all right, but here comes Aunt Sally with a candle, and I clapped the truck in my hat, and clapped my hat on my head, and the next second she see me; and she says:

"You been down cellar?"

"Yes'm."

"What you been doing down there?"

"Noth'n."

"Noth'n!"

"No'm."

"Well, then, what possessed you to go down there this time of night?"

"I don't know'm."

"You don't *know*? Don't answer me that way, Tom, I want to know what you been *doing* down there."

"I hain't been doing a single thing, Aunt Sally, I hope to gracious if I have."

I reckoned she'd let me go now, and as a generl thing she would; but I spose there was so many strange things going on she was just in a sweat about every little thing that warn't yard-stick straight; so she says, very decided:

"You just march into that setting-room and stay there till I come. You been up to something you no business to, and I lay I'll find out what it is before *I'm* done with you."

So she went away as I opened the door and walked into the setting-room. My, but there was a crowd there! Fifteen farmers, and every one of them had a gun. I was most powerful sick, and slunk to a chair and set down. They was setting around, some of them talking a little, in a low voice, and all of them fidgety and uneasy, but trying to look like they warn't; but I knowed they was, because they was always taking off their hats, and putting them on, and scratching their heads, and changing their seats, and fumbling with their buttons. I warn't easy myself, but I didn't take my hat off, all the same.

I did wish Aunt Sally would come, and get done with me, and lick me, if she wanted to, and let me get away and tell Tom how we'd overdone this thing, and what a thundering hornet's nest we'd got ourselves into, so we could stop fooling around, straight off, and clear out with Jim before these rips got out of patience and come for us.

At last she come, and begun to ask me questions, but I *couldn't* answer them straight, I didn't know which end of me was up; because these men was in such a fidget now, that some was wanting to start right *now* and lay for them desperadoes, and saying it warn't but a few minutes to midnight; and others was trying to get them to hold on and wait for the sheep-signal; and here was aunty pegging away at the questions, and me a shaking all over and ready to sink down in my tracks I was that scared; and the place getting hotter and hotter, and the butter beginning to melt and run down my neck and behind my ears; and pretty soon, when one of them says, "*I'm* for going and getting in the cabin *first*, and right *now*, and catching them when they come," I most dropped; and a streak of butter come a trickling down my forehead, and Aunt Sally she see it, and turns white as a sheet, and says:

"For the land's sake, what *is* the matter with the child?—he's got the brain fever as shore as you're born, and they're oozing out!"

And everybody runs to see, and she snatches off my hat, and out comes the bread, and what was left of the butter, and she grabbed me, and hugged me, and says:

"Oh, what a turn you did give me! and how glad and grateful I am it ain't no worse; for luck's against us, and it never rains but it pours, and when I see that truck I thought we'd lost you, for I knowed by the color and all, it was just like your brains would be if—Dear, dear whyd'nt you *tell* me that was what you'd been down there for, *I* wouldn't a cared. Now cler out to bed, and don't lemme see no more of you till morning!"

I was up stairs in a second, and down the lightning rod in another one, and shinning through the dark for the lean-to. I couldn't hardly get my words out, I was so anxious; but I told Tom as quick as I could, we must jump for it, now, and not a minute to lose—the house full of men, yonder, with guns!

His eyes just blazed; and he says:

"No!—is that so? *Ain't* it bully! Why, Huck, if it was to do over again, I bet I could fetch two hundred! If we could put it off till—"

"Hurry! *hurry!*" I says. "Where's Jim?"

"Right at your elbow; if you reach out your arm you can touch him. He's dressed, and everything's ready. Now we'll slide out and give the sheep-signal."

But then we heard the tramp of men, coming to the door, and heard them begin to fumble with the padlock; and heard a man say:

"I *told* you we'd be too soon; they haven't come—the door is locked. Here, I'll lock some of you into the cabin and you lay for 'em in the dark and kill 'em when they come; and the rest scatter around a piece, and listen if you can hear 'em coming."

So in they come, but couldn't see us in the dark, and most trod on us whilst we was hustling to get under the bed. But we got under all right, and out through the hole, swift but soft—Jim first, me next, and Tom last, which was according to Tom's orders. Now we was in the lean-to, and heard trampings close by outside. So we crept to the door, and Tom stopped us there and put his eye to the crack, but couldn't make out nothing, it was so dark; and whispered and said he would listen for the steps to get further, and when he nudged us Jim must glide out first, and him last. So he set his ear to the crack and listened, and listened, and listened, and the steps a scraping around, out there, all the time; and at last he nudged us, and we slid out, and stooped down, not breathing, and not making the least noise, and slipped stealthy towards the fence, in Injun file, and got to it, all right, and me and Jim over it; but Tom's britches catched fast on a splinter on the top rail, and then he hear the steps coming, so he had to pull loose, which snapped the splinter and made a noise; and as he dropped in our tracks and started, somebody sings out:

"Who's that? Answer, or I'll shoot!"

But we didn't answer; we just unfurled our heels and shoved. Then there was a rush, and a *bang, bang, bang!* and the bullets fairly whizzed around us! We heard them sing out:

"Here they are! They've broke for the river! after 'em, boys! And turn loose the dogs!"

So here they come, full tilt. We could hear them, because they wore boots, and yelled, but we didn't wear no boots, and didn't yell. We was in the path to the mill; and when they got pretty close onto us, we dodged into the bush and let them go by, and then dropped in behind them. They'd had all the dogs shut up, so they wouldn't scare off the robbers; but by this time somebody had let them loose, and here they come, making pow-wow enough for a million; but they was our dogs; so we stopped in our tracks till they catched up; and when they see it warn't nobody but us, and no excitement to offer them, they only just said howdy, and tore right ahead towards the shouting and clattering; and then we up steam again and whizzed along after them till we was nearly to the mill, and then struck up through the bush to where my canoe was tied, and hopped in and pulled for dear life towards the middle of the river, but didn't make no more noise than we was obleeged to. Then we struck out, easy and comfortable, for the island where my raft was; and we could hear them yelling and barking at each other all up and down the bank, till we was so far away the sounds got dim and died out. And when we stepped onto the raft, I says:

"Now, old Jim, you're a free man *again,* and I bet you won't ever be a slave no more."

"En a mighty good job it wuz, too, Huck. It 'uz planned beautiful, en it 'uz *done* beautiful; en dey ain't *nobody* kin git up a plan dat's mo' mixed-up en splendid den what dat one wuz."

We was all as glad as we could be, but Tom was the gladdest of all, because he had a bullet in the calf of his leg. *— that's horrible!*

When me and Jim heard that, we didn't feel so brash as what we did before. It was hurting him considerable, and bleeding; so we laid him in the wigwam and tore up one of the duke's shirts for to bandage him, but he says:

"Gimme the rags, I can do it myself. Don't stop, now; don't fool around here, and the evasion booming along so handsome; man the sweeps, and set her loose! Boys, we done it elegant!—'deed we did. I wish *we'd* a had the handling of Louis XVI, there wouldn't a been no 'Son of Saint Louis, ascend to heaven!' wrote down in *his* biography: no, sir, we'd a whooped him over the *border*—that's what we'd a done with *him*—and done it just as slick as nothing at all, too. Man the sweeps—man the sweeps!"

But me and Jim was consulting—and thinking. And after we'd thought a minute, I says:

"Say it, Jim."

So he says:

"Well, den, dis is de way it look to me, Huck. Ef it wuz *him* dat 'uz bein' sot free, en one er de boys wuz to git shot, would he say, 'Go on en save me, nemmine 'bout a doctor f'r to save dis one?' Is dat like Mars Tom Sawyer? Would he say dat? You *bet* he wouldn't! *Well,* den, is *Jim* gywne to say it? No, sah—I doan' budge a step out'n dis place, 'dout a *doctor;* not if it's forty year!"

I knowed he was white inside, and I reckoned he'd say what he did say—so it was all right, now, and I told Tom I was agoing for a doctor. He raised considerable row about it, but me and Jim stuck to it and wouldn't budge; so he was for crawling out and setting the raft loose himself; but we wouldn't let him. Then he give us a piece of his mind—but it didn't do no good.

So when he see me getting the canoe ready, he says:

"Well, then, if you're bound to go, I'll tell you the way to do, when you get to the village. Shut the door, and blindfold the doctor tight and fast, and make him swear to be silent as the grave, and put a purse full of gold in his hand, and then take and lead him all around the back alleys and everywheres, in the dark, and then fetch him here in the canoe, in a round-about way amongst the islands, and search him and take his chalk away from him, and don't give it back to him till you get him back to the vil-lage, or else he will chalk this raft so he can find it again. It's the way they all do."

So I said I would, and left, and Jim was to hide in the woods when he see the doctor coming, till he was gone again.

Chapter XLI
The Doctor—Uncle Silas—Sister Hotchkiss—
Aunt Sally in Trouble

The doctor was an old man; a very nice, kind-looking old man, when I got him up. I told him me and my brother was over on Spanish Island hunting, yesterday afternoon, and camped on a piece of a raft we found, and about midnight he must a kicked his gun in his dreams, for it went off and shot him in the leg, and we wanted him to go over there and fix it and not say nothing about it, nor let any-body know, because we wanted to come home this evening and sur-prise the folks.

"Who is your folks?" he says.

"The Phelpses, down yonder."

"Oh," he says. And after a minute, he says: "How'd you say he got shot?"

"He had a dream," I says, "and it shot him." that makes no sense

"Singular dream," he says.

So he lit up his lantern, and got his saddle-bags, and we started. But when he sees the canoe, he didn't like the look of her—said she was big enough for one, but didn't look pretty safe for two. I says:

Kemble

THE DOCTOR.

"Oh, you needn't be afeard, sir, she carried the three of us, easy enough."

that was stupid

"What three?"

"Why, me and Sid, and—and—and *the guns;* that's what I mean."

"Oh," he says.

But he put his foot on the gunnel, and rocked her; and shook his head, and said he reckoned he'd look around for a bigger one. But they was all locked and chained; so he took my canoe, and said for me to wait till he come back, or I could hunt around further, or maybe I better go down home and get them ready for the surprise, if I wanted to. But I said I didn't; so I told him just how to find the raft, and then he started.

I struck an idea, pretty soon. I says to myself, spos'n he can't fix that leg just in three shakes of a sheep's tail, as the saying is? spos'n it takes him three or four days? What are we going to do?—lay around there till he lets the cat out of the bag? No, sir, I know what *I'll* do. I'll wait, and when he comes back, if he says he's got to go any more, I'll get down there, too, if I swim; and we'll take and tie him, and keep him, and shove out down the river; and when Tom's done with him, we'll give him what it's worth, or all we got, and then let him get ashore.

So then I crept into a lumber pile to get some sleep; and next time I waked up the sun was away up over my head! I shot out and went for the doctor's house, but they told me he'd gone away in the night, some time or other, and warn't back yet. Well, thinks I, that looks powerful bad for Tom, and I'll dig out for the island, right off. So away I shoved, and turned the corner, and nearly rammed my head into Uncle Silas's stomach! He says:

uh oh!

"Why, *Tom!* Where you been, all this time, you rascal?"

"*I* hain't been nowheres," I says, "only just hunting for the runaway nigger—me and Sid."

"Why, where ever did you go?" he says. "Your aunt's been mighty uneasy."

"She needn't," I says, "because we was all right. We followed the men and the dogs, but they out-run us, and we lost them; but we thought we heard them on the water, so we got a canoe and took out after them, and crossed over but couldn't find nothing of them; so we cruised along up-shore till we got kind of tired and beat out; and tied up the canoe and went to sleep, and never waked up till about an hour ago, then we paddled over here to hear the news, and Sid's at the post-office to see what he can hear, and I'm a branching out to get something to eat for us, and then we're going home."

So then we went to the post-office to get "Sid"; but just as I suspicioned, he warn't there; so the old man he got a letter out of the office, and we waited a while longer but Sid didn't come; so the old man said come along, let Sid foot it home, or canoe-it, when he got done fooling around—

but we would ride. I couldn't get him to let me stay and wait for Sid; and he said there warn't no use in it, and I must come along, and let Aunt Sally see we was all right.

When we got home, Aunt Sally was that glad to see me she laughed and cried both, and hugged me, and give me one of them lickings of hern that don't amount to shucks, and said she'd serve Sid the same when he come.

And the place was plum full of farmers and farmers' wives, to dinner; and such another clack a body never heard. Old Mrs. Hotchkiss was the worst; her tongue was agoing all the time. She says:

"Well, Sister Phelps, I've ransacked that-air cabin over an' I b'lieve the nigger was crazy. I says so to Sister Damrell—didn't I, Sister Damrell?—s'I, he's crazy, s'I—them's the very words I said. You all hearn me: he's crazy, s'I; everything shows it, s'I. Look at that-air grindstone, s'I; want to tell *me*'t any cretur 'ts in his right mind 's agoin' to scrabble all them crazy things onto a grindstone, s'I? Here sich 'n' sich a person busted his heart; 'n' here so 'n' so pegged along for thirty-seven year, 'n' all that—natcherl son o' Louis somebody, 'n' sich everlast'n rubbage. He's plumb crazy, s'I; it's what I says in the fust place, it's what I says in the middle, 'n' it's what I says last 'n' all the time—the nigger's crazy—crazy's Nebokoodneezer, s'I." [49]

"An' look at that-air ladder made out'n rags, Sister Hotchkiss," says old Mrs. Damrell; "what in the name o' goodness *could* he ever want of—"

"The very words I was a-sayin' no longer ago th'n this minute to Sister Utterback, 'n' she'll tell you so herself. Sh-she, look at that-air rag ladder, sh-she; 'n' s'I, yes, *look* at it, s'I—what *could* he a-wanted of it, s'I. Sh-she, Sister Hotchkiss, sh-she—"

"But how in the nation'd they ever *git* that grindstone *in* there, *any-way?* 'n' who dug that-air *hole?* 'n' who—"

"My very *words*, Brer Penrod! I was a-sayin'—pass that-air sasser o' m'lasses, won't ye?—I was a-sayin' to Sister Dunlap, jist this minute, how *did* they git that grindstone in there, s'I. Without *help*, mind you—'thout *help! That's* wher' 'tis. Don't tell *me*, s'I; there *wuz* help, s'I; 'n' ther' wuz a *plenty* help, too, s'I; ther's ben a *dozen* a-helpin' that nigger, 'n' I lay I'd skin every last nigger on this place, but *I'd* find out who done it, s'I; 'n' moreover, s'I—"

---

[49] Dan. 4.33. In the Old Testament, Nebuchadnezzar, King of Babylon, "was driven from men, and did eat grass as oxen, and his body was wet with the dew of heaven, till his hairs were grown like eagles' feathers, and his nails like birds' claws."

too much'

s' I

"A *dozen* says you!—*forty* couldn't a done everything that's been done. Look at them case-knife saws and things, how tedious they've been made; look at that bed-leg sawed off with 'm, a week's work for six men; look at that nigger made out'n straw on the bed; and look at—"

"You may *well* say it, Brer Hightower! It's jist as I was a-sayin' to Brer Phelps, his own self. S'e, what do *you* think of it, Sister Hotchkiss, s'e? think o' what, Brer Phelps, s'I? think o' that bed-leg sawed off that a way, s'e? *think* of it, s'I? I lay it never sawed *itself* off, s'I—somebody *sawed* it, s'I; that's my opinion, take it or leave it, it mayn't be no 'count, s'I, but sich as 't is, it's my opinion, s'I, 'n' if anybody k'n start a better one, s'I, let him *do* it, s'I, that's all. I says to Sister Dunlap, s'I—"

"Why, dog my cats, they must a ben a house-full o' niggers in there every night for four weeks, to a done all that work, Sister Phelps. Look at that shirt—every last inch of it kivered over with secret African writ'n done with blood! Must a ben a raft uv 'm at it right along, all the time, amost. Why, I'd give two dollars to have it read to me; 'n' as for the niggers that wrote it, I 'low I'd take 'n' lash 'm t'll—"

"People to *help* him, Brother Marples! Well, I reckon you'd *think* so, if you'd a been in this house for a while back. Why, they've stole everything they could lay their hands on—and we a watching, all the time, mind you. They stole that shirt right off o' the line! and as for that sheet they made the rag ladder out of ther' ain't no telling how many times they *didn't* steal that; and flour, and candles, and candlesticks, and spoons, and the old warming-pan, and most a thousand things that I disremember, now, and my new calico dress; and me, and Silas, and my Sid and Tom on the constant watch day *and* night, as I was a telling you, and not a one of us could catch hide nor hair, nor sight nor sound of them; and here at the last minute, lo and behold you, they slides right in under our noses, and fools us, and not only fools *us* but the Injun Territory robbers too, and actuly gets *away* with that nigger, safe and sound, and that with sixteen men and twenty-two dogs right on their very heels at that very time! I tell you, it just bangs anything I ever *heard* of. Why, *sperits* couldn't a done better, and been no smarter. And I reckon they must a *been* sperits—because, *you* know our dogs, and ther' ain't no better; well, them dogs never even got on the *track* of 'm once! You explain *that* to me, if you can!—*any* of you!"

"Well, it does beat—"

"Laws alive, I never—"

"So help me, I wouldn't a be—"

"*House* thieves as well as—"

"Goodnessgracioussakes, I'd a ben afeard to *live* in sich a—"

"'Fraid to *live!*—why, I was that scared I dasn't hardly go to bed, or get up, or lay down, or *set* down, Sister Ridgeway. Why, they'd steal the very—why, goodness sakes, you can guess what kind of a fluster *I* was in by the time midnight come, last night. I hope to gracious if I warn't afraid they'd steal some o' the family! I was just to that pass, I didn't have no reasoning faculties no more. It looks foolish enough, *now,* in the day-time; but I says to myself, there's my two poor boys asleep, 'way up stairs in that lonesome room, and I declare to goodness I was that uneasy 't I crep' up there and locked 'em in! I *did.* And anybody would. Because, you know, when you get scared, that way, and it keeps running on, and getting worse and worse, all the time, and your wits gets to addling, and you get to doing all sorts o' wild things, and by-and-by you think to yourself, spos'n *I* was a boy, and was away up there, and the door ain't locked, and you—" She stopped, looking kind of wondering, and then she turned her head around slow, and when her eye lit on me—I got up and took a walk.

Says I to myself, I can explain better how we come to not be in that room this morning, if I go out to one side and study over it a little. So I done it. But I dasn't go fur, or she'd a sent for me. And when it was late in the day, the people all went, and then I come in and told her the noise and shooting waked up me and "Sid," and the door was locked, and we wanted to see the fun, so we went down the lightning rod, and both of us got hurt a little, and we didn't never want to try *that* no more. And then I went on and told her all what I told Uncle Silas before; and then she said she'd forgive us, and maybe it was all right enough anyway, and about what a body might expect of boys, for all boys was a pretty harum-scarum lot, as fur as she could see; and so, as long as no harm hadn't come of it, she judged she better put in her time being grateful we was alive and well and she had us still, stead of fretting over what was past and done. So then she kissed me, and patted me on the head, and dropped into a kind of a brown study; and pretty soon jumps up, and says:

"Why, lawsamercy, it's most night, and Sid not come yet! What *has* become of that boy?"

I see my chance; so I skips up and says:

"I'll run right up to town and get him," I says.

"No you won't," she says. "You'll stay right wher' you are; *one's* enough to be lost at a time. If he ain't here to supper, your uncle 'll go."

Well, he warn't there to supper; so right after supper uncle went.

He come back about ten, a little bit uneasy; hadn't run across Tom's track. Aunt Sally was a good *deal* uneasy; but Uncle Silas he said there warn't no occasion to be—boys will be boys, he said, and you'll see this one turn up in the morning, all sound and right. So she had to be satisfied.

But she said she'd set up for him a while, anyway, and keep a light burning, so he could see it.

And then when I went up to bed she come up with me and fetched her candle, and tucked me in, and mothered me so good I felt mean, and like I couldn't look her in the face; and she set down on the bed and talked with me a long time, and said what a splendid boy Sid was, and didn't seem to want to ever stop talking about him; and kept asking me every now and then, if I reckoned he could a got lost, or hurt, or maybe drownded, and might be laying at this minute, somewheres, suffering or dead, and she not by him to help him, and so the tears would drip down, silent, and I would tell her that Sid was all right, and would be home in the morning, sure; and she would squeeze my hand, or maybe kiss me, and tell me to say it again, and keep on saying it, because it done her good, and she was in so much trouble. And when she was going away, she looked down in my eyes, so steady and gentle, and says:

"The door ain't going to be locked, Tom; and there's the window and the rod; but you'll be good, *won't* you? And you won't go? For *my* sake."

Laws knows I *wanted* to go, bad enough, to see about Tom, and was all intending to go; but after that, I wouldn't a went, not for kingdoms.

But she was on my mind, and Tom was on my mind; so I slept very restless. And twice I went down the rod, away in the night, and slipped around front, and see her setting there by her candle in the window with her eyes towards the road and the tears in them; and I wished I could do something for her, but I couldn't, only to swear that I wouldn't never do nothing to grieve her any more. And the third time, I waked up at dawn, and slid down, and she was there yet, and her candle was most out, and her old gray head was resting on her hand, and she was asleep.

Chapter XLII
Tom Sawyer Wounded—The Doctor's Story—
Tom Confesses—Aunt Polly Arrives—
Hand Out Them Letters

The old man was up town again, before breakfast, but couldn't get no track of Tom; and both of them set at the table, thinking, and not saying nothing, and looking mournful, and their coffee getting cold, and not eating anything. And by-and-by the old man says:

"Did I give you the letter?"

"What letter?"

TOM SAWYER WOUNDED.

"The one I got yesterday out of the post-office."

"No, you didn't give me no letter."

"Well, I must a forgot it."

So he rummaged his pockets, and then went off somewheres where he had laid it down, and fetched it, and give it to her. She says:

"Why, it's from St. Petersburg—it's from Sis."

I allowed another walk would do me good; but I couldn't stir. But before she could break it open, she dropped it and run—for she see something. And so did I. It was Tom Sawyer on a mattress; and that old doctor; and Jim, in *her* calico dress, with his hands tied behind him; and a lot of people. I hid the letter behind the first thing that come handy, and rushed. She flung herself at Tom, crying, and says:

"Oh, he's dead, he's dead, I know he's dead!"

And Tom he turned his head a little, and muttered something or other, which showed he warn't in his right mind; then she flung up her hands, and says:

"He's alive, thank God! And that's enough!" and she snatched a kiss of him, and flew for the house to get the bed ready, and scattering orders right and left at the niggers and everybody else, as fast as her tongue could go, every jump of the way.

I followed the men to see what they was going to do with Jim; and the old doctor and Uncle Silas followed after Tom into the house. The men was very huffy, and some of them wanted to hang Jim, for an example to all the other niggers around there, so they wouldn't be trying to run away, like Jim done, and making such a raft of trouble, and keeping a whole family scared most to death for days and nights. But the others said, don't do it, it wouldn't answer at all, he ain't our nigger, and his owner would turn up and make us pay for him, sure. So that cooled them down a little, because the people that's always the most anxious for to hang a nigger that hain't done just right, is always the very ones that ain't the most anxious to pay for him when they've got their satisfaction out of him. — *that's sick*

They cussed Jim considerble, though, and give him a cuff or two, side the head, once in a while, but Jim never said nothing, and he never let on to know me, and they took him to the same cabin, and put his own clothes on him, and chained him again, and not to no bed-leg, this time, but to a big staple drove into the bottom log, and chained his hands, too, and both legs, and said he warn't to have nothing but bread and water to eat, after this, till his owner come or he was sold at auction, because he didn't come in a certain length of time, and filled up our hole, and said a couple of farmers with guns must stand watch around about the cabin every night, and a bulldog tied to the door in the day-time; and about this time they was through with the job and was tapering off with a kind of generl good-bye cussing, and then the old doctor comes and takes a look, and says:

"Don't be no rougher on him than you're obleeged to, because he ain't a bad nigger. When I got to where I found the boy, I see I couldn't cut the bullet out without some help, and he warn't in no condition for me to leave, to go and get help; and he got a little worse and a little worse, and after a long time he went out of his head, and wouldn't let me come anigh him, any more, and said if I chalked his raft he'd kill me, and no end of wild foolishness like that, and I see I couldn't do anything at all with him; so I says, I got to have *help,* somehow; and the minute I says it, out crawls this nigger from somewheres, and says he'll help, and he done it, too, and done it very well. Of course I judged he must be a runaway nigger, and there I *was!* and there I had to stick, right straight along all the rest of the day, and all night. It was a fix, I tell you! I had a couple of patients with the chills, and of course I'd of liked to run up to town and see them, but I dasn't, because the nigger might get away, and then I'd be to blame; and yet never a skiff come close enough for me to hail. So there I had to stick, plumb till daylight this morning; and I never see a nigger that was a better *Jim is a good person* nuss or faithfuller, and yet he was risking his freedom to do it, and was all tired out, too, and I see plain enough he'd been worked main hard, lately. I liked the nigger for that; I tell you, gentlemen, a nigger like that is worth a thousand dollars — and kind treatment, too. I had everything I needed, and the boy was doing as well there as he would a done at home — better, maybe, because it was so quiet; but there I *was,* with both of 'm on my hands, and there I had to stick, till about dawn this morning; then some men in a skiff come by, and as good luck would have it, the nigger was setting by the pallet with his head propped on his knees, sound asleep; so I motioned them in, quiet, and they slipped up on him and grabbed him and tied him before he knowed what he was about, and we never had no trouble. And the boy being in a kind of a flighty sleep, too, we muffled the oars and hitched the raft on, and towed her over very nice and quiet, and the nigger never made the least row nor said a word, from the start. He ain't no bad nigger, gentlemen; that's what I think about him."

Somebody says:

"Well, it sounds very good, doctor, I'm obleeged to say."

Then the others softened up a little, too, and I was mighty thankful to that old doctor for doing Jim that good turn; and I was glad it was according to my judgment of him, too; because I thought he had a good heart in him and was a good man, the first time I see him. Then they all agreed that Jim had acted very well, and was deserving to have some notice took of it, and reward. So every one of them promised, right out and hearty, that they wouldn't cuss him no more. — respect for a slave?

Then they come out and locked him up. I hoped they was going to say he could have one or two of the chains took off, because they was rotten heavy, or could have meat and greens with his bread and water, but they didn't think of it, and I reckoned it warn't best for me to mix in, but I judged I'd get the doctor's yarn to Aunt Sally, somehow or other, as soon as I'd got through the breakers that was laying just ahead of me. Explanations, I mean, of how I forgot to mention about Sid being shot, when I was telling how him and me put in that dratted night paddling around hunting the runaway nigger.

But I had plenty time. Aunt Sally she stuck to the sick-room all day and all night; and every time I see Uncle Silas mooning around, I dodged him.

Next morning I heard Tom was a good deal better, and they said Aunt Sally was gone to get a nap. So I slips to the sick-room, and if I found him awake I reckoned we could put up a yarn for the family that would wash. But he was sleeping, and sleeping very peaceful, too; and pale, not fire-faced the way he was when he come. So I set down and laid for him to wake. In about a half an hour, Aunt Sally comes gliding in, and there I was, up a stump again! She motioned me to be still, and set down by me, and begun to whisper, and said we could all be joyful now, because all the symptoms was first rate, and he'd been sleeping like that for ever so long, and looking better and peacefuller all the time, and ten to one he'd wake up in his right mind.

So we set there watching, and by-and-by he stirs a bit, and opens his eyes very natural, and takes a look, and says:

"Hello, why I'm at *home!* How's that? Where's the raft?"

"It's all right," I says.

"And *Jim?*"

"The same," I says, but couldn't say it pretty brash. But he never noticed, but says:

"Good! Splendid! *Now* we're all right and safe! Did you tell Aunty?"
I was going to say yes; but she chipped in and says:

"About what, Sid?"

"Why, about the way the whole thing was done."

"What whole thing?"

"Why, *the* whole thing. There ain't but one; how we set the runaway
nigger free—me and Tom."

"Good land! Set the run—What *is* the child talking about! Dear, dear,
out of his head again!"

"No, I ain't out of my HEAD; I know all what I'm talking about. We
did set him free—me and Tom. We laid out to do it, and we *done* it. And
we done it elegant, too." He'd got a start, and she never checked him up,
just set and stared and stared, and let him clip along, and I see it warn't no
use for *me* to put in. "Why, Aunty, it cost us a power of work—weeks of
it—hours and hours, every night, whilst you was all asleep. And we had
to steal candles, and the sheet, and the shirt, and your dress, and spoons,
and tin plates, and case-knives, and the warming-pan, and the grindstone,
and flour, and just no end of things, and you can't think what work it was
to make the saws, and pens, and inscriptions, and one thing or another,
and you can't think *half* the fun it was. And we had to make up the pictures of coffins and things, and nonnamous letters from the robbers, and
get up and down the lightning rod, and dig the hole into the cabin, and
make the rope-ladder and send it in cooked up in a pie, and send in spoons
and things to work with, in your apron pocket—"

"Mercy sakes!"

"—and load up the cabin with rats and snakes and so on, for company for Jim; and then you kept Tom here so long with the butter in his
hat that you come near spiling the whole business, because the men come
before we was out of the cabin, and we had to rush, and they heard us and
let drive at us, and I got my share, and we dodged out of the path and let
them go by, and when the dogs come they warn't interested in us, but
went for the most noise, and we got our canoe, and made for the raft, and
was all safe, and Jim was a free man, and we done it all by ourselves, and
wasn't it bully, Aunty!"

"Well, I never heard the likes of it in all my born days! So it was *you,*
you little rapscallions, that's been making all this trouble, and turned
everybody's wits clean inside out and scared us all most to death. I've as
good a notion as ever I had in my life, to take it out o' you this very minute.
To think, here I've been, night after night, a—*you* just get well once, you
young scamp, and I lay I'll tan the Old Harry out o' both o' ye!"

But Tom, he *was* so proud and joyful, he just *couldn't* hold in, and his tongue just *went* it—she a-chipping in, and spitting fire all along, and both of them going it at once, like a cat-convention; and she says:

"*Well*, you get all the enjoyment you can out of it *now*, for mind I tell you if I catch you meddling with him again—"

"Meddling with *who?*" Tom says, dropping his smile and looking surprised.

"With *who?* Why, the runaway nigger, of course. Who'd you reckon?"

Tom looks at me very grave, and says:

"Tom, didn't you just tell me he was all right? Hasn't he got away?"

"Him?" says Aunt Sally; "the runaway nigger? 'Deed he hasn't. They've got him back, safe and sound, and he's in that cabin again, on bread and water, and loaded down with chains, till he's claimed or sold!"

Tom rose square up in bed, with his eye hot, and his nostrils opening and shutting like gills, and sings out to me:

"They hain't no *right* to shut him up! *Shove!*—and don't you lose a minute. Turn him loose! he ain't no slave; he's as free as any cretur that walks this earth!"[50]

"What *does* the child mean?"

"I mean every word I *say*, Aunt Sally, and if somebody don't go, I'll go. I've knowed him all his life, and so has Tom, there. Old Miss Watson died two months ago, and she was ashamed she ever was going to sell him down the river, and *said* so; and she set him free in her will."

"Then what on earth did *you* want to set him free for, seeing he was already free?"

"Well, that *is* a question, I must say; and *just* like women! Why, I wanted the *adventure* of it; and I'd a waded neck-deep in blood to—goodness alive, AUNT POLLY!"

---

[50] Many have written about the disappointing nature of *Huckleberry Finn*'s ending and the cruelty of Tom's hoax. However, Jim's false enslavement at the Phelpses' symbolizes his position as a free black man. Missouri slave narratives suggest that bondage of African Americans continued even after emancipation. Former slave Louis Hill notes, "I was too young to know what to expect from freedom. My mother picked up and left de white folks in de night and took us kids with her. Dat was after we was free but dey wouldn't let her get away in de daytime very handy" (Rawick 186). Former slave Susan Rhodes states, "Den my old Miss told my sister dat all de niggers was free now, go for herself, but she was going to keep de two youngest niggers. Dat was me and my baby sister, I don't know how old I was but I was big 'nough to do any kind of work most" (Rawick 285). Even if not illegally held, former slaves' economic conditions helped trap them in servitude. Tom Sawyer's declaration, under these circumstances, rings hollow.

If she warn't standing right there, just inside the door, looking as sweet and contented as an angel half-full of pie, I wish I may never!

Aunt Sally jumped for her, and most hugged the head off of her, and cried over her, and I found a good enough place for me under the bed, for it was getting pretty sultry for *us,* seemed to me. And I peeped out, and in a little while Tom's Aunt Polly shook herself loose and stood there looking across at Tom over her spectacles—kind of grinding him into the earth, you know. And then she says:

"Yes, you *better* turn y'r head away—I would if I was you, Tom."

"Oh, deary me!" says Aunt Sally; "*is* he changed so? Why, that ain't *Tom* it's Sid; Tom's—Tom's—why, where is Tom? He was here a minute ago."

"You mean where's Huck *Finn*—that's what you mean! I reckon I hain't raised such a scamp as my Tom all these years, not to know him when I *see* him. That *would* be a pretty howdy-do. Come out from under that bed, Huck Finn."

So I done it. But not feeling brash.

Aunt Sally she was one of the mixed-upest looking persons I ever see; except one, and that was Uncle Silas, when he come in, and they told it all to him. It kind of made him drunk, as you may say, and he didn't know nothing at all the rest of the day, and preached a prayer-meeting sermon that night that gave him a rattling ruputation, because the oldest man in the world couldn't a understood it. So Tom's Aunt Polly, she told all about who I was, and what; and I had to up and tell how I was in such a tight place that when Mrs. Phelps took me for Tom Sawyer—she chipped in and says, "Oh, go on and call me Aunt Sally, I'm used to it, now, and 'tain't no need to change"—that when Aunt Sally took me for Tom Sawyer, I had to stand it—there warn't no other way, and I knowed he wouldn't mind, because it would be nuts for him, being a mystery, and he'd make an adventure out of it and be perfectly satisfied. And so it turned out, and he let on to be Sid, and made things as soft as he could for me.

And his Aunt Polly she said Tom was right about old Miss Watson setting Jim free in her will; and so, sure enough, Tom Sawyer had gone and took all that trouble and bother to set a free nigger free! and I couldn't ever understand, before, until that minute and that talk, how he *could* help a body set a nigger free, with his bringing-up.

Well, Aunt Polly she said that when Aunt Sally wrote to her that Tom and *Sid* had come, all right and safe, she says to herself:

"Look at that, now! I might have expected it, letting him go off that way without anybody to watch him. So now I got to go and trapse all the way down the river, eleven hundred mile, and find out what that creetur's up to, *this* time; as long as I couldn't seem to get any answer out of you about it."

"Why, I never heard nothing from you," says Aunt Sally.

"Well, I wonder! Why, I wrote you twice, to ask you what you could mean by Sid being here."

"Well, I never got 'em, Sis."

Aunt Polly, she turns around slow and severe, and says:

"You, Tom!"

"Well—*what?*" he says, kind of pettish.

"Don't you what *me*, you impudent thing—hand out them letters."

"What letters?"

"*Them* letters. I be bound, if I have to take aholt of you I'll—"

"They're in the trunk. There, now. And they're just the same as they was when I got them out of the office. I hain't looked into them, I hain't touched them. But I knowed they'd make trouble, and I thought if you warn't in no hurry, I'd—"

"Well, you *do* need skinning, there ain't no mistake about it. And I wrote another one to tell you I was coming; and I spose he—"

"No, it come yesterday; I hain't read it yet, but *it's* all right, I've got that one."

I wanted to offer to bet two dollars she hadn't, but I reckoned maybe it was just as safe to not to. So I never said nothing.

Chapter the Last
Out of Bondage—Paying the Captive—
Yours Truly, Huck Finn

The first time I catched Tom, private, I asked him what was his idea, time of the evasion?—what it was he'd planned to do if the evasion worked all right and he managed to set a nigger free that was already free before? And he said, what he had planned in his head, from the start, if we got Jim out all safe, was for us to run him down the river, on the raft, and have adventures plumb to the mouth of the river, and then tell him about his being free, and take him back up home on a steamboat, in style, and pay him for his lost time, and write word ahead and get out all the niggers around, and have them waltz him into town with a torchlight procession and a brass band, and then he would be a hero, and so would we. But I reckoned it was about as well the way it was.

We had Jim out of the chains in no time, and when Aunt Polly and Uncle Silas and Aunt Sally found out how good he helped the doctor nurse Tom, they made a heap of fuss over him, and fixed him up prime, and give him all he wanted to eat, and a good time, and nothing to do. And we had him up to the sick-room; and had a high talk; and Tom give Jim forty dollars for being prisoner for us so patient, and doing it up so good, and Jim was pleased most to death, and busted out, and says:

OUT OF BONDAGE.

"*Dah,* now, Huck, what I tell you?—what I tell you up dah on Jackson islan'? I *tole* you I got a hairy breas', en what's de sign un it; en I *tole* you I ben rich wunst, en gwineter to be rich *agin;* en it's come true; en heah she *is! Dah,* now! doan' talk to *me*—signs is *signs,* mine I tell you; en I knowed jis' 's well 'at I 'uz gwineter be rich agin as I's a-stannin' heah dis minute!"

And then Tom he talked along, and talked along, and says, le's all three slide out of here, one of these nights, and get an outfit, and go for howling adventures amongst the Injuns, over in the Territory, for a couple of weeks or two; and I says, all right, that suits me, but I ain't got no money for to buy the outfit, and I reckon I couldn't get none from home, because it's likely pap's been back before now, and got it all away from Judge Thatcher and drunk it up.

"No he hain't," Tom says; "it's all there, yet—six thousand dollars and more; and your pap hain't ever been back since. Hadn't when I come away, anyhow."

Jim says, kind of solemn:

"He ain't a comin' back no mo', Huck."

I says:

"Why, Jim?"

"Nemmine why, Huck—but he ain't comin' back no mo'."

But I kept at him; so at last he says:

"Doan' you 'member de house dat was float'n down de river, en dey wuz a man in dah, kivered up, en I went in en unkivered him and didn' let you come in? Well, den, you k'n git yo' money when you wants it; kase dat wuz him."

Tom's most well, now, and got his bullet around his neck on a watch-guard for a watch, and is always seeing what time it is, and so there ain't nothing more to write about, and I am rotten glad of it, because if I'd a knowed what a trouble it was to make a book I wouldn't a tackled it and ain't agoing to no more. But I reckon I got to light out for the Territory ahead of the rest, because Aunt Sally she's going to adopt me and sivilize me and I can't stand it. I been there before.

THE END. YOURS TRULY, HUCK FINN.

1884

Readings

INTRODUCTION
to *Adventures of Huckleberry Finn* (1958)

Henry Nash Smith

Most of the fifty thousand people who bought *Adventures of Huckleberry Finn* upon its publication in 1885 probably welcomed the book simply as another amusing specimen of the work of the post–Civil War literary comedians like Orpheus C. Kerr and Josh Billings and Bill Nye with whom Mark Twain was habitually associated in the public mind. On the other hand, readers who prided themselves on being refined considered these humorists rather vulgar. When the Concord Library Committee characterized *Huckleberry Finn* as "the veriest trash," the denunciation was widely echoed in the press.[1] There was some basis for each of these views. The book does come out of the far from squeamish tradition of native American humor, and some things in it, such as the effort to make comedy out of Joanna Wilks's harelip, represent undeniable lapses in taste. But in our day critical opinion has vindicated the judgment of the few perceptive readers like William Dean Howells and Joel Chandler Harris who saw that whatever traits Mark Twain's novel might share, for better or for worse, with the buffoonery of the popular humorists, it was a literary masterpiece.[2]

A book so clearly great, yet with such evident defects, poses a difficult critical problem. There is little profit in making a mere checklist of faults and beauties. We must try to see the book integrally. How well has Mark Twain succeeded in organizing his material into a coherent and unified whole? And what does this whole mean? Let us begin by recalling the main outlines of the plot. Huck Finn, the thirteen- or fourteen-year-old son of the town drunkard of St. Petersburg, Missouri, a boy accustomed to sleep in an empty sugar hogshead and to eat the food chance brings within his reach, decides to run away. He needs to escape from the efforts of certain good women to "sivilize" him and from the sadistic beatings of his Pap. On uninhabited Jackson's Island in the Mississippi he encounters the runaway slave, Jim. They join forces and are lucky enough to find a lumberraft brought down by the spring flood. The ostensible narrative pattern of

---

Adventures of Huckleberry Finn. Boston: Houghton, 1958.

[1] Arthur L. Vogelback, "The Publication and Reception of *Huckleberry Finn* in America," *American Literature*, XI 260–72, November, 1939.

[2] Recent discussion of *Huckleberry Finn* is listed by Harry H. Clark in *Eight American Authors: A Review of Research and Criticism*, ed. Floyd Stovall, New York, 1956, pp. 347–55.

the story is provided by the journey of Huck and Jim some eleven hundred miles, as the River flows, from St. Petersburg to the "one-horse" plantation of Silas Phelps near Pikesville, Arkansas.

In a broad sense, the form of the narrative is thus picaresque. Like Gil Blas, the *pícaro* or rascally hero of a celebrated story by Le Sage that Mark Twain had in mind as a possible model for a sequel to *Tom Sawyer*,[3] Huck and Jim are involved in a series of adventures more or less self-contained, and at the end of each they move on until they become involved in a fresh adventure. They are fugitives from the law, living by their wits, and Huck has an easy way with watermelons and chickens, as well as a marked propensity for lying. Yet the story is not basically picaresque. The difference becomes clear if we compare Huck with the Duke and the King, who are perfect examples of the literary *pícaro,* but who are of course not the central characters. Huck does not have the *pícaro's* callousness; on the contrary, he is easily touched by the sufferings of others. And unlike the unscrupulous Gil Blas, he is "engaged"—he is helping Jim escape from slavery.

The implied denunciation of slavery in *Huckleberry Finn* is more damaging than the frontal attack delivered by *Uncle Tom's Cabin* because Jim is so much more convincing as a character than is Mrs. Stowe's Uncle Tom, who is almost an allegorical figure—a Black Christ. Yet if we read *Huckleberry Finn* simply as the story of Huck's and Jim's quest for freedom we run into difficulties. For in the last section (Chapters XXXIII–XLIII) Mark Twain seems to be burlesquing his own plot. Huck's efforts to help Jim escape, involving real danger and anguished inner conflict with the boy's conscience, give way to the elaborate foolishness of Tom Sawyer's schemes for conducting an Evasion according to rules he has deduced from *The Count of Monte Cristo* and other melodramatic works of fiction. Jim is reduced to the status of a "darkey" in a minstrel show; the reader is evidently expected to laugh at his discomforts from the rats and spiders Tom introduces as stage properties. And at the last moment it is revealed that Jim was freed two months before through the highly implausible deathbed repentance of his owner, Miss Watson. We feel as badly sold as did the audience for the Duke's and the King's presentation of *The Royal Nonesuch*.

The puzzling change of attitude toward Jim results from the presence of Tom Sawyer, whose conventional imagination cannot embrace the full recognition of Jim's humanity. He conceives the Evasion (which he knows to be unnecessary) as a means of achieving fame for himself and Jim through the artistic perfection of the scheme. When Tom re-enters the story at the

---

[3] Mark Twain to William Dean Howells, Hartford, July 5, 1875, in *Mark Twain's Letters,* ed. Albert B. Paine, 2 vols., New York, 1917, I, 258.

beginning of Chapter XXXIII, he causes an abrupt change in the perspective from which Jim is viewed. The runaway slave imprisoned in the cabin on the Phelps plantation has little in common with the Jim of the great middle section of the story. After the final escape, when Jim emerges from his hiding place and gives up his chance of freedom because he will not desert the wounded Tom, it is as if he has been underground. The reader is gratified that in the end Mark Twain consummates Jim's dignity by giving him an opportunity to make a heroic sacrifice of himself comparable to Huck's decision to go to hell for the sake of his friend. But this return to the earlier perspective on Jim cannot fully redeem the long chapters in which Tom Sawyer has been allowed to play pranks on him.

Indeed, Jim's quest for freedom receives such cavalier treatment in the Phelps plantation sequence that one is forced to ask whether it is the true imaginative center of the story. If we examine the place which the theme of Jim's escape occupies in the book as a whole, we discover that it is by no means always central to the action. The first seven chapters, where the author has to manage the transition from the state of affairs at the end of *Tom Sawyer* to the quite different atmosphere of the sequel, offered no occasion for dealing with the new problem. Not until Huck makes his Robinson-Crusoe–like discovery of Jim's campfire in Chapter VIII does the reader know that Jim has run away. We then have eight chapters during which the two friends make their way southward on the raft, with pauses for such episodes as the exploration of the "House of Death" and the wrecked steamboat *Walter Scott*. But at the end of Chapter XVI Mark Twain faced a crisis in the management of his plot, for at this point he must have discovered that the original plan of his narrative would no longer serve his purposes.

Early in Chapter XVI Huck and Jim are approaching the mouth of the Ohio at Cairo, Illinois. Jim is understandably excited. He has conceived the idea that "he'd be a free man the minute he seen it [Cairo], but if he missed it he'd be in the slave country again and no more show for freedom." Jim's notion that he would be free as soon as he entered the mouth of the Ohio was oversimplified, but that river was certainly his pathway to freedom.[4] It made no sense for Huck and Jim to move a single mile farther past the mouth of the Ohio than they were forced to. If Mark Twain took

---

[4] It is not clear how thoroughly Clemens had understood the legal status of runaway slaves in Illinois when he was a boy, or what he remembered about this complex subject when he wrote *Huckleberry Finn*. But everyone in Hannibal must have been generally familiar with the state of affairs just across the River. In the 1840s Cairo, in southern Illinois, was rather less safe for a runaway slave than would have been the Illinois shore just opposite Hannibal. To be sure, the farther the fugitive traveled in any direction the

Jim down the Mississippi he committed himself to a narrative plan that was very unlikely to lead Jim to freedom. His only alternatives would be to leave Jim in slavery (which, however faithful to historical probability, would have created a somber ending quite out of keeping with the comic tone of the book), or to free him by some such *deus ex machina* device as the supposed deathbed repentance of Miss Watson.

Why then did Mark Twain not cause Huck and Jim to make their way up the Ohio? To ask this question is to answer it: he did not know the Ohio. But he had known the lower Mississippi intimately for four years as cub and pilot. As Huck and Jim float past Cairo, Mark Twain's desire to write a story drawing upon his memories of the lower Mississippi comes into conflict with the idea of telling the story of Jim's escape from slavery. When he wrote Chapter XVI he apparently did not see any escape from the dilemma. "By-and-by," says Huck, "we talked about what we better do, and found there warn't no way but just to go along down with the raft till we got a chance to buy a canoe to go back in."

This plan represents a dead end for the original plan of escape. The destruction of the raft at the end of Chapter XVI registers the author's recognition of the fact. As Walter Blair has demonstrated recently in a brilliant study of the composition of the novel,[5] Mark Twain broke off his manuscript in 1876 near the end of Chapter XVI and laid it aside for at least two years. He took it up again—probably during the winter of 1870–1880—and added the two chapters (XVII and XVIII) dealing with the Grangerford feud. Huck and Jim are separated during this sequence, and no travel farther south is involved. Thus there was no need to solve

---

harder it was for agents sent out by his owner to overtake him. But in the 1840s a system of "indentured labor" hardly distinguishable from slavery was in full legal force in Illinois, and the laws of the state directed county officials to arrest any Negro who could not show freedom papers signed by his former master. Generally speaking, pro-slavery sentiment and the eagerness of sheriffs to capture runaway slaves increased as one moved southward in the state (Norman D. Harris, *History of the Negro Slave in Illinois and of the Slavery Agitation in That State,* Chicago, 1906, esp. pp. 22–23, 53, 109–10). Jim seems to have been familiar with the status of Negroes in Illinois, for in calmer moments he and Huck had wisely planned to go far up the Ohio River by steamboat, perhaps as far as the state of Ohio, where they might have established contact with the Underground Railway. With this sort of help they would have had a good chance to reach Canada, in the manner of Eliza and George Harris in *Uncle Tom's Cabin.* Only in Canada would Jim be immune from arrest and delivery back to his mistress.
[5] "When Was *Huckleberry Finn* Written?", *American Literature* XXX, 1–25, March, 1958. I wish to acknowledge Mr. Blair's kindness in offering me expert advice on other matters connected with *Huckleberry Finn.*

here the larger problem of how Huck and Jim could be plausibly represented as floating on down the river. Near the end of Chapter XVIII Mark
Twain again laid his manuscript aside, and did not return to it for some
months—apparently not before the summer of 1880, when the evidence
suggests that he wrote Chapters XIX, XX, and XXI.

He was now able to carry the narrative beyond the end of the feud sequence because he had at last thought of a plan which, without sacrific-
ing plausibility, would allow Huck and Jim to float down the River indefi-
nitely. This plan called for the resurrection of the raft (a note of Mark
Twain's written in 1879 or 1880 shows that he had not meant to use the
raft again when he related how it was destroyed by the steamboat[6]) and
the introduction of the Duke and the King. When these immortal rascals
come aboard, each fleeing a mob of outraged townspeople, they dominate
the raft by virtue of their superior cunning and their sheer physical superiority to Huck, who is rightly afraid of violence from them. The raft, carried downstream by the current, is the ideal mode of transportation for the
Duke and the King because they are constantly in need of a means of escape from one imbroglio and of approach to another. It is an additional
advantage for them that Huck and Jim can be made into servants. And in
the end, Jim can always be turned in for some kind of reward.

Bringing the Duke and the King into the story was a master stroke.
Not only are they themselves comic and satiric creations of the highest order, but their mode of life makes plausible a narrative pattern which allows
Mark Twain to deal with any desired aspect of life on the River or along
the shore. From the beginning of Chapter XIX to the disappearance of the
two rogues appropriately "astraddle of a rail" and "all over tar and feathers," at the end of Chapter XXXIII, the narrative consists of a series of episodes dominated by the Duke and the King. In between, the raft floats ever
southward.

But the journey which begins in Chapter XIX is quite different from
the journey described in Chapters XII–XVI, for it has nothing to do with
Jim's escape and therefore no purpose in the sense that the journey from
St. Petersburg to Cairo had a purpose. Once Mark Twain had worked out
in his mind a plausible device for taking Huck and Jim downstream, he
seems to have forgotten about the original plan of escape up the Ohio.
Even before the Duke and the King enter the story, when Huck and Jim
set out on the raft from the Grangerford plantation, the earlier plan has
sunk from sight. Huck now says that as soon as the raft had got out to
the middle of the River, "we . . . judged that we was free and safe once

---

[6] Quoted by Bernard De Voto in *Mark Twain at Work,* Cambridge, Mass., 1942, p. 67.

more . . . We said there warn't no home like a raft, after all. Other places do seem so cramped up and smothery, but a raft don't. You feel mighty free and easy and comfortable on a raft." When Huck goes ashore in Chapter XIX to look for berries, just before he meets the Duke and the King, he mentions finding a canoe without giving any indication that this is precisely what he and Jim need to make their way upstream. It should be emphasized that these incidents occur before Mark Twain has actually brought into play his device of subjecting Huck and Jim to the coercion of the Duke and the King. Thereafter, although theoretically Huck and Jim might be expected to seize the first opportunity of escaping from their captors in order to head back upstream, we are not surprised that they fail to do so. When they momentarily elude the Duke and the King after the Wilks episode (at the end of Chapter XXIX), Huck says: ". . . away we went, a sliding down the river, and it *did* seem so good to be free again and all by ourselves on the big river and nobody to bother us."

In these moments of spontaneous reflection Huck has simply forgotten Jim's assertion that below Cairo "he'd be in the slave country again and no more show for freedom." What has happened is that Mark Twain has abandoned his original narrative plan and has substituted for it a different structural principle. During the journey from the Grangerford plantation to Pikesville, the action is not dictated by the reasonable if risky plan for Jim's escape but by the powerful image of Huck and Jim's "a sliding down the river," "free and easy" on the raft.[7] This image now embodies the only meaning which freedom and safety have in the narrative. It becomes the positive value replacing the original goal of actual freedom for Jim. The new goal is a subjective state, having its empirical basis in the solitude of the friends in their "home" on "the big river" but consisting in a mode of experience rather than an outward condition. There is some suggestion, to be sure, of a pastoral sanction for the state of mind attained by Huck and Jim when they are alone on the raft. The physical setting, the River, sometimes becomes vaguely but powerfully benign, as in the ecstatic opening of Chapter XIX. But the journey considered as movement from one

---

[7]The pattern is repeated at the beginning of the Phelps plantation sequence when Tom asks Huck what his proposal for rescuing Jim is. Huck says they should simply take Jim out of the cabin at night and "shove off down the river on the raft, with Jim, hiding daytimes and running nights, the way me and Jim used to do before." But he welcomes Tom's more splendid and complicated plan for the rescue, recognizing with unconscious irony that it "would make Jim just as free a man as mine would, and maybe get us all killed besides" (Chapter XXXIV). Again, in the last chapter Tom says he had intended, after the Evasion, "for us to run [Jim] down the river, on the raft, and have adventures plumb to the mouth of the river, and then tell him about his being free."

determinate place to another has lost its meaning. It literally leads nowhere. The Phelps plantation where it ends, from the standpoint of geog-
raphy eleven hundred miles downstream from St. Petersburg, is from the
standpoint of Mark Twain's imagination very near the starting-point of
Huck's and Jim's journey. It is his fictional rendering of the farm of his
uncle John Quarles, thirty miles inland from Hannibal, where he spent
summers as a child.

The new structural principle which supplants the original linear
movement toward freedom is bipolar. It is a contrast between the raft—
connoting freedom, security, happiness, and harmony with physical nature—and the society of the towns along the shore, connoting vulgarity
and malice and fraud and greed and violence. The raft, when those invaders from the shore, the Duke and King, can be got out of the way or
even just put to sleep, is always the same. The towns are very much alike
also: Pokeville, Bricksville, and Peter Wilks's home town all embody Mark
Twain's memories of Hannibal. Huck is drawn ashore repeatedly, and repeatedly returns to the raft, but this apparent movement is merely an os-
cillation between two modes of experience, and the successive episodes are
restatements, with variations, of the same theme: the raft versus the town,
the River versus the Shore. Yet this thematic plan is not so different as it
might seem at first glance from the original narrative plan of linear movement toward a geographical goal. The book has a basic unity of theme despite Mark Twain's pronounced shift in overt structure. For not only does
the River connote freedom; the Shore connotes slavery, bondage in a more
general sense than the actual servitude of Jim. Huck and Jim share a common quest, not merely because Huck is helping Jim, but because Huck too
is fleeing from slavery. On occasion it is implied that the contrast between
freedom and slavery is even more general, that Jim's and Huck's predica-
ment is that of every man, and their quest a universal human undertaking.

In the six or seven years between the time when Mark Twain wrote
the opening chapters and the time when he wrote the last half of his book,
he had become aware of a meaning in Huck's and Jim's situation that transcended (while still including) his original concern with Jim's escape from
slavery. Slavery in the actual pre–Civil War South had come to seem to him
only an extreme example of the constraints imposed by that society on all
its members, white as well as black. And the historical South itself, remembered with such unexampled vividness from Mark Twain's boyhood,
had tended to become a metaphor for the human condition. This general-
izing of the concrete situation is strikingly evident in Colonel Sherburn's
speech to the mob, which comes significantly at the beginning of the
final continuous spurt of composition in the summer of 1883. Sherburn's
speech, as Mr. Blair has pointed out, is very close in ideas to a passage

Mark Twain had written in his own person earlier in the same year for inclusion in *Life on the Mississippi*. The passage was omitted from that book, but Mark Twain did not abandon his opinion that the "civilization" of the United States (the reference here, as in Sherburn's speech, is not limited to the South) amply deserved Mrs. Trollope's criticisms, "being slavery, rowdyism, 'chivalrous' assassinations, sham godliness, and several other devilishnesses. . . ." "She was holily hated for her 'prejudices,'" Mark Twain continued; "but they seem to have been simply the prejudices of a humane spirit against inhumanities; of an honest nature against humbug; of a clean breeding against grossness; of a right heart against unright speech and deed." [8]

One is reminded of Eric Auerbach's remark that Rousseau by contrasting the natural condition of man with existing social reality made this reality a problem for the writer and thus provided the intellectual basis for literary realism. [9] We can see in Mark Twain's description of the river towns a coming-into-being of realism as a fictional mode, even though the novel as a whole is not realistic but symbolic in structure. Lionel Trilling has advanced a similar generalization, recalling Wordsworth's boys "upon whom the shades of the prison house are inevitably to fall," and noting the constant recurrence of the image of a prison in fiction of the past century and a half. The image, he thinks, implies a new recognition of society as coercion—by the family, by the professions, by the code of respectability with its ideas of faith and duty, by the very language men speak. "The modern self," he concludes, "like Little Dorrit, was born in a prison. It assumed its nature and fate the moment it perceived, named, and denounced its oppressor." In contrast with the image of society as a prison, of course, Huck's and Jim's way of life on the raft is an embodiment of what Mr. Trilling calls "the modern imagination of autonomy and delight, of surprise and elevation, of selves conceived in opposition to the general culture." [10]

The middle section of *Huckleberry Finn*, with its superb series of little towns along the River, is rich in passages illustrating the thematic opposition between the bondage imposed by society and the freedom (at least the potential freedom) of the raft. Let us glance at the most elaborate of the interludes on shore, the sequence laid in the nameless Tennessee town where Peter Wilks the tanner has just died and the King and the Duke are trying to make away with his considerable property. In the early part of this

---

[8] *Life on the Mississippi*, New York, 1944 (Heritage Press edition), p. 392.
[9] *Mimesis, The Representation of Reality in Western Literature*, trans. Willard R. Trask, Princeton, 1953, p. 467.
[10] *The Opposing Self: Nine Essays in Criticism*, New York, 1955, Preface, pp. x–xiv.

episode Huck is a passive observer feeling almost equal distaste for the
"scamps" who are bent on gulling the townspeople and for their victims—
"a lot of prejudiced chuckle-heads" eager to be deceived and exploited.
The arrival of the adventurers in the guise of the long-awaited Wilks brothers from England produces a sensation that is described with the broad
strokes of caricature. "The news," Huck says (at the beginning of Chapter
XXV), "was all over town in two minutes . . ."; people came "tearing
down on the run"; by the time the newcomers reach the Wilks house, "the
street in front of it was packed." Through Huck's unconscious exaggera-
tions, Mark Twain passes judgment on the villagers. He condemns two
traits: their greed for sensation, a kind of tropism that focuses all their attention on any event that breaks the monotony of everyday life; and their
sentimentality, their tendency to luxuriate in emotion for its own sake.
Both these traits bespeak a lack of freedom, and both are outgrowths of a
mob spirit. The townspeople are shown in deliberately grotesque postures
(putting on their coats as they run toward the Wilks house), and are compared to soldiers obeying the commands of a drill master. A condensed
metaphor even likens them to animals in a herd (they are "trotting along
with the gang").

The evil in the culture of the village results from the deference paid by
the people to a false set of values, a collection of approved and prescribed
attitudes which derive from an outworn Calvinism and from the eighteenth-
century cult of feeling. The King is able to impose himself on the people by
pretending to be a clergyman and addressing them in a burlesque of pulpit rhetoric. He "works himself up and slobbers out a speech, all full of
tears and flapdoodle" about the "sore trial" (that is, the death of his supposed brother) which is however "sweetened and sanctified to us by this
dear sympathy and these holy tears." Then he "blubbers out a pious goody-
goody Amen, and turns himself loose and goes to crying fit to bust."

Although Huck does not analyze the situation in abstract terms, his
narrative suggests to the reader that the King's hearers are helpless because
they do not react to situations spontaneously but according to stereotyped
patterns of feeling and behavior. The town's culture does not express the
true feelings of the people, and since they are not aware of what their true
feelings are they lie at the mercy of an impostor who can manipulate the
dead symbols to which they are bound by habit and by the desire for status. In a telling metaphor, Huck remarks that the ostentatious grief of the
King and the Duke "worked the crowd"—like a strong physic.

The only skepticism and common sense in the town are represented
by Dr. Robinson and the lawyer Levi Bell, the nearest approach to intel-
lectuals among the populace, and "a big rough husky" named Hines from
up the River who happened to see the King's party board the steamboat

only a few miles above the village and thus knows for certain that they are lying about their supposed arrival straight from England. For a time the skeptics seem to be free of the conditioning that binds everyone else in the community. Lawyer Bell proposes settling the question of identity by comparing specimens of handwriting, and when this plan is frustrated suggests digging up Peter Wilks's corpse in order to examine the tattoo mark. Yet even these men are in the end controlled by the same tropisms that control the crowd. Hines, who is holding Huck by the wrist, loses his head when the bag of gold is discovered in Wilks's coffin; he "let out a whoop, like everybody else," says Huck, "and dropped my wrist and give a big surge to bust his way in and get a look. . . ." Robinson and Bell apparently make the same mistake: the King and the Duke also escape when "the excited fools . . . let go all holts and made that rush to get a look. . . ."

The implication of this passage is that Huck is not subject to the social pressures holding the townspeople in bondage. But the situation is not so simple as this. With respect to the great issue of the overt action, Jim's escape from slavery, Huck is divided against himself. His inner freedom is menaced by attitudes imposed upon him by society. The culture of the Shore had invaded his personality by implanting in him a conscience which is the internalized mores of the community. When Huck faces a crisis of decision about his loyalty to Jim, his conscience significantly addresses him in the language of the official culture, a tawdry and faded effort at a high style that is the rhetorical equivalent of the ornaments of the Grangerford parlor. The following sentence, for example (in Chapter XXXI), has a complexity of structure which is foreign to Huck's own mode of speech, as are the cant theological phrases: "And at last, when it hit me all of a sudden that here was the plain hand of Providence slapping me in the face and letting me know my wickedness was being watched all the time from up there in heaven, whilst I was stealing a poor old woman's nigger that hadn't ever done me no harm, and now was showing me there's One that's always on the lookout, and ain't agoing to allow no such miserable doings to go only just so fur and no further, I most dropped in my tracks I was so scared." Parallel clauses are built up to a monitory climax in a pattern Huck must have heard used by preachers and politicians: "It was because my heart warn't right; it was because I warn't square; it was because I was playing double. I was letting *on* to give up sin, but away inside of me I was holding on to the biggest one of all. I was trying to make my mouth *say* I would do the right thing and the clean thing, and go and write to that nigger's owner and tell where he was; but deep down in me I knowed it was a lie—and He knowed it. You can't pray a lie—I found that out."

In passages such as these, the polar opposition between the River and the Shore, between freedom and bondage, is restated as a division within Huck's own mind. The intuitive self, the spontaneous impulse from the deepest levels of the personality, is placed in opposition to the acquired conscience, the overlayer of prejudice and false valuation imposed upon all members of society in the name of religion, morality, law, and culture. Huck's triumph over his conscience is his most nearly heroic moment, falling short of grandeur only because his youth and ignorance prevent him from undertaking a decisive action.

What is the source of the power by which the true self triumphs over the false conscience? It is conveyed indirectly a few lines later, in a passage which is the emotional and thematic climax of the book, and one of its supremely beautiful moments. This is the voice of freedom, spontaneity, autonomy of the individual; of brotherhood, of the River as opposed to the Shore. Huck actually writes a letter to Miss Watson giving Jim away; but then he "laid the paper down and set there thinking . . . . And went on thinking. And got to thinking over our trip down the river; and I see Jim before me, all the time, in the day, and in the night-time, sometimes moonlight, sometimes storms, and we a floating along, talking, and singing, and laughing." There is more of this, but the quotation will suggest the extraordinary intensity of emotion together with the convincing representation in words of the free flow of reminiscence and emotion, devoid of the artifices of official rhetoric, undisciplined by syntax (although cunningly controlled in rhythm), and overwhelmingly concrete: a torrent of emotionally charged images.

The Huck who could not harden himself against Jim is the "real" or "true" Huck, the boy who has, as Mark Twain said when he described the book ten years later, a "sound heart." [11] The depraved conscience is unreal; it is an intrusion from without, just as the Duke and the King on the raft are invaders from the shore, and its threat is overcome. The narrator of the story, looking back over his experiences, knows that he has been victorious in his struggle with his conscience. The remembered struggle merely lends richness and depth to his character. Basically this character is natural man, pure and spontaneously good. But we must remember the pattern of values Mark Twain has established for his story: the contrast

---

[11] Notebook #28a [I], TS, p. 35 (1895), Mark Twain Papers, University of California Library, Berkeley. The entry refers to *Huckleberry Finn* as "a book of mine where a sound heart & a deformed conscience come into collision & conscience suffers defeat."

between the River and the Shore. Huck's goodness has to be defined in opposition to the standards of propriety and respectability that prevail in organized society. He is the Bad Boy—he is dirty and ungrammatical, he steals chickens and watermelons, he is an accomplished liar, he runs away and lives a vagabond existence with an escaped slave. In the moral system of the novel, these traits of the Bad Boy simply establish his innocence and purity. It is a scheme having something in common with the heart-of-gold formula popularized by Bret Harte, but more profound because much more serious, more deeply felt by the author.

Yet this disreputable vagabond with a good heart beneath his rags, although a fully realized character, is after all a character, not an actual person. He is conceived by Mark Twain deliberately for a specific technical purpose. He establishes a point of view, a perspective from which the events of the story can be observed and described. And since the author identifies himself with Huck by using the first person, Huck is evidently a mask, a narrative persona. In this respect Huck derives from a series of narrative personae devised by Mark Twain experimentally for earlier books: the persona of the ignorant tourist (innocent mainly because of his ignorance) in *The Innocents Abroad;* that of the tenderfoot undergoing initiation in *Roughing It;* that of the inspired idiot in *A Tramp Abroad* who professes to have come to Europe to study painting and the German language, to make pedestrian tours (which always lead him to the first vehicle he can catch), to climb the Alps (by means of a telescope). Yet earlier literary ancestors of Huck are Simon Wheeler, who tells the story of "The Celebrated Jumping Frog of Calaveras County," and other characters in Mark Twain's sketches who represent his apprentice efforts to reproduce in written prose the effect of the deadpan manner cultivated by oral storytellers in the American backwoods tradition.

Late in his career Mark Twain composed the ars poetica of the oral humorous tale, which he pronounced a native American genre entirely distinct from the comic story of the English or the witty story of the French. "The humorous story is told gravely," he asserted; "the teller does his best to conceal the fact that he even dimly suspects that there is anything funny about it. . . ." Mark Twain mentions as masters of the technique Artemus Ward (the mentor and guide he met in Nevada) and James Whitcomb Riley. He describes how in telling a certain story Riley assumed "the character of a dull-witted old farmer" and "perfectly simulated" the farm-

---

[12] "How to Tell a Story," in *The Writings of Mark Twain,* Definitive Edition, 37 vols., New York, 1922–25, XXIV, 263–70, esp. 266–67.

er's "simplicity and innocence and sincerity and unconsciousness. . . ." [12]
Artemus Ward had used a similar technique, well indicated by the title
which he always announced for his humorous "lectures" without regard
to their wildly irrelevant and rambling content: "The Babes in the Wood."
The art which Mark Twain praised in Artemus Ward and Riley was, of
course, the art he brought to perfection in his own platform appearances.
A perceptive newspaper reporter once characterized it as the pose of
"Innocence victimized by the world, flesh, and devil" [13]

Huck Finn is the literary culmination of this deadpan manner.
Through Mark Twain's use of Huck as narrator he is able to wear the mask
of innocence—not only in the sense of unspotted goodness, but also in the
sense of ignorance, inexperience, and a simple-mindedness not in the least
impaired by Huck's evident native shrewdness. Because the narrator of the
story is represented as being less sophisticated than the author and the
reader, the reader is made to perceive virtually every incident on two levels: that of Huck, and that of the author. The contrast between the two levels of perception creates an almost unbroken irony. Sometimes the effect is
rather simple comedy, as when Huck says that after he and Jim found a
wooden leg in the deserted house floating down the river, they "hunted
all around" for the other one. A more complex passage—in which comedy blends with a kind of naïve lyricism—is Huck's description of the circus (introduced rather incongruously into Chapter XXII). Huck himself
never realizes that the antics of the acrobat disguised as a drunken tramp
have been carefully rehearsed with the ringmaster. Indeed, when he proves
unable to grasp the point of Buck Grangerford's prehistoric riddle about
where Moses was when the light went out, we are forced to recognize
that the comedy of the book, while it is conveyed to us in Huck's words, is
lost on Huck himself. The narrative persona is a character without a sense
of humor.

In its simplest form, this device reinforces comic effects by contrast (as
Mark Twain noted in his description of Artemus Ward's and Riley's technique of oral story-telling). But in Mark Twain's hands it proves to have
capabilities quite beyond the range of the earlier humorists. For example,
Huck's imperviousness to comedy deepens into a predominantly melancholy cast of temperament. Wise beyond his years in the mischances of life,
he has the imagination of disaster. The thumbnail autobiographies he in-
vents, usually as a means of getting himself out of a tight place, but often
carried beyond the demands of utility for sheer love of the art, are uniformly

[13] *Washington Post,* November 25, 1884.

somber. When he plans his escape from Pap (Chapter VII), he does so by imagining his own death and planting clues that convince everyone in St. Petersburg, including Tom Sawyer, that he has actually been murdered.[14] In the crisis of Chapter XVI, when Huck overcomes the temptation to betray Jim, his heightened emotion leads him to produce on the spur of the moment a harrowing tale to the effect that his father and mother and sister are suffering from smallpox on a raft adrift in mid-river, and he is unable to tow the raft ashore by himself. The slave-hunters he encounters are so touched by the story that they give him forty dollars in gold and careful instructions about how to seek help—farther downstream. Huck tells the Grangerfords "how pap and me and all the family was living on a little farm down at the bottom of Arkansaw, and my sister Mary Ann run off and got married and never was heard of no more, and Bill went to hunt them and he warn't heard of no more, and Tom and Mort died, and then there warn't nobody but just me and pap left, and he was just trimmed down to nothing, on account of his troubles; so when he died I took what there was left, because the farm didn't belong to us, and started up the river, deck passage, and fell overboard. . . ." (Chapter XVII).

These yarns—and others like them, for Huck uses the device often—are improvisations on the themes of his own life. Although comic because they are fabrications, making the hearers into dupes, they reinforce the narrative by adding a kind of resonance to it; they make Huck's experience seem of a piece with many other lives of farmer-folk along the river. As projections of Huck's unconscious, they reveal the gloomy substratum of his personality. His memory is stored with images of violence and calamity, bereavement, sickness, separation of families, and especially of boys left alone in the world by the death of parents.

Yet another use to which Mark Twain perceived the deadpan mask of the oral story-teller could be put is satire. In one sense the maneuver was familiar: Goldsmith's Chinese Citizen of the World and Voltaire's Ingénu from the wilds of North America are only two among dozens of deliberately naïve observers who had described Europe from an external point of view during the eighteenth century. Huck's description of the Grangerford-Shepherdson feud, which has few comic touches, is close to the traditional technique. But no one had used the device for such a brilliant blending of comedy and satire as Mark Twain achieves in Huck's celebrated descrip-

---

[14] Mr. Franklin Rogers, in "The Role of Literary Burlesque in the Development of Mark Twain's Structural Patterns, 1855–1885" (unpublished dissertation, University of California, Berkeley, 1958), suggests that at one time Mark Twain had in mind a plot for the novel involving Jim's being brought to trial for the supposed murder of Huck.

tion of the Grangerford parlor (Chapter XVII). This passage gains much of its effect from the fact that Huck sincerely admires the taste of the Grangerfords and is genuinely humble in his statement that *The Pilgrim's Progress* is "about a man that left his family it didn't say why." He even tries to "sweat out a verse or two" in memory of Emmeline Grangerford because her diligence as an elegist entitles her to an elegy of her own.

It is remarkable how consistently Mark Twain maintains Huck's point of view. When the book was published in 1885, Henry James had hardly begun to be aware of the technical effects to be achieved by excluding the author from the novel, and Howells, for all his critical sophistication concerning other men's work and his admiration for both Mark Twain and James, never did perceive that management of point-of-view was the central technical development in modern fiction. If we accept (as we must) the arbitrary convention that Huck as narrator is able to recall the exact words he has heard other characters utter, we can find only the most trifling departures from plausibility in *Huckleberry Finn,* with the one significant exception of Sherburn's speech to the mob in Chapter XXII which has been mentioned earlier. Here the mask drops, the narrative persona is forgotten, if only for a moment, and the illusion is for that moment dispelled.

Elsewhere, however, it is Huck, not Mark Twain, who speaks. The point is worth making because of its bearing on the much-discussed declaration of Huck which ends the novel: ". . . I reckon I got to light out for the Territory ahead of the rest, because Aunt Sally she's going to adopt me and sivilize me, and I can't stand it. I been there before." This is a deliberate echo of the opening pages of the story, where Huck has told the reader: "The Widow Douglas, she took me for her son, and allowed she would sivilize me; but it was rough living in the house all the time, considering how dismal regular and decent the widow was in all her ways; and so when I couldn't stand it no longer, I lit out. I got into my old rags, and my sugar-hogshead again, and was free and satisfied. But Tom Sawyer, he hunted me up and said he was going to start a band of robbers, and I might join if I would go back to the widow and be respectable. So I went back." Huck is merely summarizing here the last pages of *Tom Sawyer,* and as far as plot is concerned the opening chapters of the sequel are a continuation of the earlier book. When Huck's Pap forces him to leave the Widow Douglas's house for the cabin across the River, Huck quickly resumes his old ways and for two months is quite content. "I didn't want to go back no more," he says. "It was pretty good times up in the woods there, take it all around." This escape is purely negative in meaning: he is glad not to have Miss Watson "pecking" at him. It is true that he is presently forced to escape from a more serious menace, his Pap's drunken brutality; and when he joins forces with Jim his flight takes on a still deeper meaning. But when the Evasion from the Phelps plantation under Tom Sawyer's leadership restores the mood of the opening chapters, Huck's desire to escape is stripped of the meaning it had acquired in the middle section of the book. We are brought back to the situation at the end of *Tom Sawyer*. Even the robber gang reappears, for Tom's imagination peoples the territory with robbers in his "nonnamous letters" of warning. It is Tom, again, who conceives the plan to "go for howling adventures amongst the Injuns, over in the Territory, for a couple of weeks or two." When Huck says he means to set out ahead of the others, there is nothing in the text to indicate that his intention is more serious than Tom's.

This reading of Huck's last sentence contradicts a view that has been gaining in popularity among critics, a view which sees a portentous meaning in Huck's final escape on the theory that he has become disgusted with a society that tolerates slavery and is making a drastic, final gesture of alienation and rejection. Such a reading of the passage presupposes first, that the question of slavery as an actual institution in the Old South is central to the entire novel, and second, that Huck has matured in the course of the narrative so that his last decision has a depth not characteristic of his attitudes and actions at the beginning. Huck's maturity, according to this view, now enables him to perceive that slavery is evil.

But what is the evidence that Huck has arrived at such an insight? We can recognize that he made a thrilling step toward emotional maturity when he humbled himself to ask Jim's forgiveness for deceiving him, at the end of Chapter XV. But some if not all of this emotional growth has been sacrificed when Huck accepted Tom's leadership during the Evasion sequence, without any indication that he perceived the consequent degradation of Jim. And he is still living in Tom's fantasy-world of robber gangs and literary Indians at the end of the book. What he is trying to escape from is not a society corrupted by slavery, but the same petty harassments he had fled from at the end of *Tom Sawyer*.

The diminished Huck of the last chapters, then, is decidedly inferior to the character who had been capable of such a profound loyalty to his friend Jim in the middle section. But not even then had he been capable of arriving at the abstract proposition, "Slavery is wrong." The depth and strength of his character lie in integrity of emotion, not in intellectual acuteness. Indeed, Mark Twain's depiction of Huck's inner life suggests a contrast between thought and feeling that to some degree parallels the contrast between the Shore and the River. Huck's conscience, spokesman for the official culture, tries to beguile him with the abstractions of sin and property, the abstractions which underwrite institutions and thus provide society with the means of enslaving people in the towns. His loyalty to Jim

enables him to evade these sophistries, but he does not have enough intellectual sophistication to deny them. He acts in defiance of a doctrine which
he never ceases, on the intellectual level, to accept. Mark Twain makes this
clear in his comment on *Huckleberry Finn* written ten years after it was
published: ". . . the whole community was agreed as to one thing—the
awful sacredness of slave property." This view, he added, was held not
only by slave-owners, but by "the paupers, the loafers the tag-rag & bob-
tail of the community, & in a passionate & uncompromising form. . . ." It
was only natural that "Huck & his father the worthless loafer should feel
it" also; for "the conscience—that unerring monitor—can be trained to
approve any wild thing you *want* it to approve if you begin its education
early & stick to it."[15] Huck's spontaneously good heart has dictated his
actions, but his conscience has remained depraved, for it represents the
community. And Huck is not able to think his way toward the perception
that the community is mistaken.

Several topics touched upon earlier have led, by different routes, to
the question of the language of *Huckleberry Finn*. Huck criticizes Peter
Wilks's fellow-townsmen by means of derogatory metaphors embodied in
his diction; the King is represented as perpetrating his fraud upon them
by rhetoric; Huck's conscience tries to persuade him to betray Jim by the
same means; vernacular speech is the principal device for maintaining the
dead pan innocence of Huck as a narrative persona; the style of Emmeline
Grangerford's verse burlesques nineteenth-century sentimental literature;
Huck is prevented from seeing through the fallacies of the conventional attitude toward slavery because the lack of abstract terms in his vocabulary
makes conceptual thought difficult for him. Beyond question, Mark Twain
uses language in a variety of ways in this book to build up his meaning.
He himself calls attention to the language in his prefatory note, emphasizing the care with which he has discriminated seven dialects. "The
shadings have not been done in a haphazard fashion, or by guess-work,"
he asserts; "but pains-takingly, and with the trustworthy guidance and
support of personal familiarity with these several forms of speech." His
claim to care in the representation of dialects is borne out by a comparison
between the manuscript of about two-thirds of the novel (now in the Buffalo
Public Library) and the published text, which reveals thousands of changes
in spelling and diction evidently made for the sake of accuracy of transcrip-
tion. But even if we could prove that the dialects are accurately rendered
(which we could do only by a difficult historical inquiry into the language

---

[15] Notebook #28a [I], TS, pp. 34–36.

actually spoken along the banks of the Mississippi in the 1840s), we should still have thrown very little light upon the novel as a work of art. What counts for literature is Mark Twain's success in establishing the illusion of accuracy, in making the reader accept a character's speech as lifelike. The discriminations that matter are those which differentiate characters from one another and confer individuality on them. Pap's diatribe against the "govment" (Chapter VI), the Duke's effort to call back Hamlet's soliloquy from "recollection's vaults" (Chapter XXI), old Mrs. Hotchkiss's inspired monologue on the night of the Evasion (Chapter XLI)—the novel is filled with passages of this sort which give to each character his exactly appropriate idiom.

Just as effective as the individualizing of characters by their speech is Mark Twain's device of establishing a common diction and rhetoric for all characters the moment they try to claim for themselves a false pathos (as the Duke does when he announces the secret of his birth) or an undeserved moral authority (as the King does in the Wilks sequence). Different as the characters are in their natural selves, when they fall into pretense they all sound alike because they all begin to speak in a burlesque of the exalted rhetoric of the official culture. This "high" language might be called the "alas!" or the "soul-butter" mode of speech. The Duke and the King are masters of it, and so was Emmeline Grangerford, if we are to judge from her verses and the titles she composed for her pictures. But almost any character can resort to this pompous language on occasion, even Huck's Pap (as when he takes the pledge at the end of Chapter V). When Tom Sawyer composes "mournful inscriptions" for Jim to scribble on the wall ("Here a captive heart busted," and so on, Chapter XXXVIII) "his voice trembled, whilst he was reading them, and he most broke down." And although Huck himself never reaches this level of self-deception, his conscience, as we have seen, commands no means of expression except soul-butter.

These uses of language represent an impressive accomplishment in the art of fiction. They are, however, expert management of well-established resources of the novelist rather than technical innovations. As long as Mark Twain uses Huck simply to report dialogue, whether his own or others', he is following a convention which was familiar to Mrs. Stowe, or Cooper, or Scott, or for that matter Richardson: there was nothing new about having "low" characters speak in dialect. Such a use of the vernacular implies no identification of the author with it; on the contrary, the contrast between the dialect within the quotation marks and the correct prose outside establishes a marked distance between author and character. But Mark Twain's use of Huck's vernacular speech as the narrative medium, outside quotation marks, is something new—a drastic, even a revolutionary shift in technique. For it means that the author has put on a mask, surrendering the right to express, except indirectly by means of irony, any ideas or emotions beyond Huck's range. He has made his story entirely dramatic in the sense that he has removed himself from the stage and has undertaken to say everything he has to say within the limits of a vocabulary not his own.

In *Huckleberry Finn*, as in Wordsworth's *Lyrical Ballads*, the language of literature gains a new life by being violently torn loose from its established moorings. For one thing, a new imagery becomes available. Speaking through Huck, Mark Twain can refer to "the fish-belly white" of a man's face; he can call Henry VIII a "bug"; he can say that after Pap had got drunk in the beautiful spare-room of the new judge's house, "they had to take soundings before they could navigate it." Furthermore, the systematic elimination of conventional associations removes the cake of custom from the visible universe and fosters a completely fresh treatment of landscape. A vision not distorted by inherited modes of perception, once fresh themselves but long since grown lifeless through over-use, can report sensory experience with supreme vividness. Taking as an example the description of the sunrise near the beginning of Chapter XIX, Leo Marx has skillfully demonstrated the change in Mark Twain's rendering of landscape in *Huckleberry Finn* as compared with his procedure in earlier books.[16] In *Tom Sawyer* and *Life on the Mississippi* he had not been able to free himself from a conventional vocabulary of landscape description, "the literary counterpart of the painter's picturesque." But when he "looked at the river through Huck's eyes he was suddenly free of certain arid notions of what a writer should write." Huck's ignorance, his lack of exposure to formal culture, allows him to take the world as he finds it and report his sensations directly, "without anxiously forcing meanings upon it." The lyric intensity of the passage—a quality of which there is hardly a hint in the humorous tales from which Mark Twain's style is descended—is not an inevitable result of the use of the vernacular as a narrative medium, but is the outcome of a fortunate convergence of material (the author's boyhood memories of the River), theme (the River as a symbol of freedom), narrative technique (the choice of the vernacular persona as a means of telling the story), and language. Yet the language is the medium in which this convergence becomes possible: the point of view, as Mr. Marx points out, has become a style.

---

[16] "The Pilot and the Passenger: Landscape Conventions and the Style of *Huckleberry Finn*," *American Literature*, XXVIII, 129–46, May, 1956. I wish to thank Mr. Marx for many suggestions about *Huckleberry Finn* in private correspondence.

We can justly apply to Mark Twain's achievement what Eric Auerbach says of Dante: ". . . this man used his language to discover the world anew." [17] Yet it would be misleading to imply that Mark Twain's break with literary tradition was all clear gain. The official culture (which we perhaps too easily dismiss by calling it the Genteel Tradition) had indeed lost its power to nourish vigorous literature; an act of repudiation was necessary. But if Mark Twain rejected the affirmations proposed by the cultural tradition, what positive value was left to sustain his work as an artist? The answer proposed by *Huckleberry Finn* is: innate, natural human goodness, which would flower into brotherhood if it could only be protected against the taint of society. The vision of innocence and happiness on the raft was exhilarating, as the book itself shows, but the affirmation of natural goodness was unsatisfactory in the long run because it was contradicted by Mark Twain's own observation of human character. There was no refuge from society, even on the River. The experiment could never be tried, and even if it could have been one must doubt whether Huck and Jim can be taken as representative of humanity. If one part of Mark Twain's mind could conceive of the happiness and freedom of two comrades on the raft, another part, just as true to his over-all view of life, speaks through Colonel Sherburn's denunciation of the Bricksville mob— a denunciation which is extended to include "the average all around," "the average man," and verges upon the denunciation of "the damned human race" that later became almost habitual for Mark Twain. (The persistence of the two contradictory attitudes is charmingly revealed in the Damned Human Race Luncheon Club which he founded in his lonely old age, with a membership limited to himself and three greatly loved friends).

In *Huckleberry Finn* Colonel Sherburn asserts, for the author, that the average man is cruel and cowardly, perhaps cruel because cowardly—a helpless victim of mob spirit. In his next book Mark Twain would make one more effort to refute the charge, to establish at least the imaginative validity of the innocent vernacular character. He conceived a country-born blacksmith and horse-doctor who had come to town and become a master mechanic, able "to make everything: guns, revolvers, cannon, boiler's, engines, all sorts of labor-saving machinery." [18] Hank Morgan, the Connecticut Yankee, is carefully labeled an ignoramus in matters of art and culture but is endowed with vigorous republican principles and all the power of modern technology. If no one could escape society altogether,

---

[17] *Mimesis* p. 183.
[18] *A Connecticut Yankee in King Arthur's Court,* Definitive Edition, XIV, 5.

could this grown-up Huck Finn hope to transform it so completely that decent creatures might live in it and be happy? *A Connecticut Yankee* was a genuine *roman expérimental:* the issue was in doubt and the author allowed his imagination to follow out what seemed the inevitable consequences of the given situation. The hero was defeated by prejudice and cowardice. His technology could give him limitless physical power but could not redeem a population debauched by social institutions. He came to despise the "human muck" that he had hoped to educate into manhood,[19] and his Utopian experiment ended in the stench of twenty-five thousand corpses.

In the course of this novel the alienation from society that is hinted at in Colonel Sherburn's speech is established as the author's dominant attitude. The major direction of this thought thereafter takes him with increasing bitterness through "The Man That Corrupted Hadleyburg" and *Pudd'nhead Wilson* to *The Mysterious Stranger*. In this fable Satan symbolically destroys the image of Hannibal which was Mark Twain's persistent metaphor for human society. The later books enable us to recognize that the contrast in *Huckleberry Finn* between the River and the Shore contains a latent anarchism and even nihilism. This perception should be kept in mind when we consider what the novel has meant to twentieth-century American writers. Although no one has yet undertaken to spell out the details of Mark Twain's influence on the literature of our day, the magnitude of that influence is obvious. Everyone has read Ernest Hemingway's flamboyant assertion that "all modern American literature comes from one book by Mark Twain called *Huckleberry Finn. . . .*"[20] William Faulkner declared [more] recently that Mark Twain was the father of Sherwood Anderson, who in turn was "the father of my generation of American writers and the tradition of American writing which our successors will carry on"[21] T. S. Eliot has maintained that in *Huckleberry Finn* Mark Twain "reveals himself to be one of those writers, of whom there are not a great many in any literature, who have discovered a new way of writing, valid not only for themselves but for others. I should place him, in this respect, even with Dryden and Swift, as one of those rare writers who have brought their language up to date, and in so doing, 'purified the dialect of the tribe.'"[22]

---

[19] *A Connecticut Yankee,* Definitive Edition, XIV, 430.
[20] *Green Hills of Africa,* New York, 1935, p. 22.
[21] In an interview with Jean Stein, *Paris Review,* XII, 46, Spring, 1956.
[22] *American Literature and the American Language,* Washington University Studies, New Series, Language and Literature, No. 23, St. Louis, 1953, pp. 16–17.

Although Mark Twain's themes, especially his alienation from society, and the use of a deliberately naïve point of view have undoubtedly proved suggestive for later writers, Mr. Eliot's emphasis on language seems historically justified. Malcolm Cowley attempted to specify what is implied here by suggesting that a "Middle American" or Midwestern prose which Mark Twain took over from the early backwoods humorists and transmitted to the twentieth century has become the dominant language of American fiction. "It was certainly Hemingway who made it popular," continues Mr. Cowley, "but some of his contemporaries (including Fitzgerald and Dos Passos, but not Thomas Wolfe) seem to have approached it independently. It began to run riot among the novelists a little younger than Hemingway, like Steinbeck and Saroyan and Raymond Chandler.[23] Mr. Cowley places Gertrude Stein and Sherwood Anderson in this line of linguistic continuity, and the list of writers whom critics have seen as practitioners of a vernacular style derived from Mark Twain includes, among others, Sandburg, Mencken, Thurber, Agee, and Salinger.

The historical facts are not fully established, but the main outlines of the phenomenon are clear enough in the work of such acknowledged disciples as Anderson and Hemingway. Different as they are from one another, both these writers illustrate the vividness and power of a prose patterned on the vernacular. But they also illustrate the consequences of the tendency toward primitivism that is implicit in Huckleberry Finn. The vernacular style greatly limited the power of Mark Twain and his successors to deal with abstract thought and thus has fostered anti-intellectualism. The repudiation of the Western European literary tradition, while in one sense a liberation for the writer, cuts him off from the accumulated experience of the past and commits him to the often wasteful enterprise of building from the ground up. Mark Twain's career, with its false starts and its lack of continuity, reveals the disadvantages as well as the advantages of the literary pioneer. Like the actual pioneer, he had to pay a high price for his conquest of new territory, and his debt was entailed upon his heirs.

Still—if the new territory was to be occupied, someone had to pay that price. Mark Twain took the risk, possibly without always understanding what dangers he ran, and the result is *Huckleberry Finn:* for all its imperfections, a great book, not only because it worked a revolution in American literary prose, but because of what it says—against stupid conformity and for the autonomy of the individual.

---

[23] "The Middle American Style: D. Crockett to E. Hemingway," *New York Times Book Review*, July 15, 1945, p. 14.

THE FORM OF FREEDOM
IN *HUCKLEBERRY FINN* (1970)

Alan Trachtenberg

Certain literary works accumulate an aura which possesses the reader before he ventures into reading itself; it gives him a readiness to respond, and a set of expectations to guide his response. Who has come to *Adventures of Huckleberry Finn* free of associations, even of some intimacy with characters and episodes? An aura can be considered a mediation which situates the book and guides the reader toward an available interpretation. This is to say that books like *Huckleberry Finn* can be powerfully predetermined experiences; we encounter them, especially at certain stages of their career, from deep within the culture shared by reader, author, and work. How any book achieves an aura is a problem for the historian of culture: a book's career implicates the history of its readers. *Huckleberry Finn* became a cultural object of special intensity during a period after World War II when many Americans seized upon literary experiences as alternatives to an increasingly confining present. Mark Twain's idyll seemed to project an answerable image—an image of wise innocence in conflict with corruption, of natural man achieving independence of a depraved society. It seemed to project an image, in short, of freedom. But not freedom in the abstract; the values of the book were seen by readers as the precise negation of all the forces felt as oppressive in the 1950s. Common to the several major interpretations of the book was one absolute theme, that the book's most prominent meanings were, as Henry Nash Smith wrote, "against stupid conformity and for the autonomy of the individual." Autonomy vs. conformity: the terms condense a memorable passage of recent American history. The conception of freedom and individualism which pervades the criticism reveals as much of the subliminal concerns of the critics as it does the themes of the book, and should be understood in light of the political and social anxieties of the postwar period.

But does *Huckleberry Finn* deserve its celebration as a testimony to freedom? What exact place, in fact, does freedom have among the book's themes? To say that a theme does not exist apart from its verbal matrix may seem commonplace. But criticism has often addressed itself to extractable elements in this novel such as imagery, symbol, and episode rather than to the total and continuous verbal performance. Granted, the book's

From *Major Literary Characters: Huck Finn*. New York: Chelsea, 1990.

susceptibility to a variety of readings—its ability to come apart into separate scenes and passages which affect us independent of the continuous narrative—is a mark of strength. But a firm grip upon the complete and total text is necessary to understand the form freedom takes in the book.

We want first to locate the problem implied by "autonomy" and "conformity," the problem of freedom, within the text, and if possible, to identify the thematic problem with a formal problem. In the broadest sense, the theme of freedom begins to engage us at the outset: Huck feels cramped and confined in his new condition as ward of Widow Douglas and closet neophyte of Miss Watson. The early episodes with Tom Sawyer add a complicating paradox: to enjoy the freedom of being "bad"—joining Tom's gang—Huck must submit himself to his adopted household and appear "respectable." With Pap's arrival the paradox is reversed; now he can enjoy his former freedom to lounge and choose his time, but the expense is a confinement even more threatening, a virtual imprisonment. The only release is escape, flight, and effacement of the identity through which both town and Pap oppress him; he can resume autonomy only by assuming "death" for his name.

In brief and general terms, such is the inner logic of the theme of freedom as we arrive at the Jackson Island episode. With Jim's appearance as a runaway slave a new and decisive development begins. We now have two runaways, and their conjunction generates the rest of the narrative, deepens the theme, and forces nuances to the surface. Jim's situation is both simpler and more urgent than Huck's. His freedom is no more or less than escape from bondage, escape to free territory. He expects there to assume what is denied him in slave society, his identity as an adult man, husband, and father. The fact that the reader is made to share this expectation with Jim, that the novel does not allow us to anticipate a reversal of hope if Jim reaches free territory, is important; as readers we are freed of normal historical ambiguities in order to accept as a powerful given the possibility of fulfilled freedom for Jim. Thus by confining the action to the area of slave society, Mark Twain compels us (at the expense of historical accuracy, perhaps) to imagine the boundary between "slave" and "free" as real and unequivocal, and to accept that boundary as the definition of Jim's plight: on one side, enslaved; on the other, free.

Jim presents himself, then, unencumbered by the paradoxes of Huck's problem: to be free, to possess himself, to reveal a firm identity—these will be equal consequences of the single act of crossing the border. The effect of such a simplifying and unambiguous presence in the book is, first, to bring into relief the more subtle forms of denial of freedom, forms which cannot be overcome by simple geographical relocation, and second, to force Huck, once the boy commits himself to the slave, into a personal contradiction. Jim can say, as soon as he escapes from Miss Watson, "I owns myself," while Huck is still "owned" by the official values supervised by his "conscience." Once Jim's freedom becomes Huck's problem, the boy finds himself at odds with what Mark Twain called his "deformed conscience." Huck's "sound heart" may respond to Jim's desire to recover his humanity at the border, but his conscience wants to repress that response.

In light of this conflict, implicit in Huck's words at the end of Chapter 11, "They're after us!" what would constitute freedom for Huck? Clearly, getting Jim to the free states would not be enough. He would need to free himself of moral deformity before he too can say "I owns myself." Just as clearly neither issue is resolved in the novel. And the book's indecision is reflected in criticism. The controversies regarding the "Evasion" at the Phelps farm need not be reviewed here, but it is useful to point out that the question of the ending eventually becomes a question of *form*, of judgment about the book's unity of tone and intention. Those who wish for Jim's release through a heroic act by Huck tend to feel the ending flawed, and those who wish for Huck's escape from all consciences, including a "good" abolitionist conscience, tend to accept the ending. In either case the burden of both meaning and form has fallen on the question of unity, of the wholeness of the narrative as a patterned action.

The question of unity is, however, only one of the formal problems of the book. If form is understood as the shape given to the reader's consciousness, as the unique engagement the text makes available, criticism might profit by an account of that engagement, of the reader's participation in the book's flow of words. And from this point of view the first fact we encounter is that the book is the speech of a single voice. At the outset we learn that Huck is teller as well as actor, that we are listeners as well as witnesses of action.

Reading begins by acceding to the demands of the voice. "You don't know about me," Huck begins, and his accents identify him immediately as a recognizable type, a western or frontier speaker whose vernacular diction and syntax stand for a typology which includes dress and posture along with characteristic verbal strategies. Huck asks to be heard, as if he faced a live audience from a stage. . . . But if Huck is . . . a storyteller, Mark Twain is at the same time a novelist, a maker of a book which asks to be read as "literature" even if its mode is in some ways preliterary.

The book is born for us, in short, under the aegis of a dual tradition, a dual vision of art. The dualities are not always in accord with each other, and some tensions between an oral and a written, especially a "high" or sophisticated tradition, account for technical problems, problems which . . . bear on the theme of freedom. The book is marked by an uneasy accommodation between seriously differing modes of literary art. . . .

Transforming an oral art to a written one presented Mark Twain with difficulties apparent in almost all his long narratives. Consider the matter of filling out a book that wants to be the "adventures" of a vernacular voice. One difficulty is simply how to bring such a book to a close. The ending of *Huckleberry Finn* does, to be sure, bring the action to a point of general resolution: Jim is freed, masks are stripped away, misunderstandings cleared up, some sort of order restored. But the loose plot which calls for resolution has been kept out of sight during much of the narrative, and we cannot avoid feeling that the plain duration of the book has depended more upon the arbitrary postponement of any event (such as the recapture of Jim) which might end things too soon than upon an inner logic of plot. The only conclusive ending is the drop of the curtain, the final words, "The End. Yours Truly, Huck Finn," and silence. The performance of Huck's voice does not so much complete itself as exhaust itself.

To begin with, then, the problem of the ending is a technical problem of *an* ending. The source of the problem is the attempt to accommodate the opening convention of a vernacular storyteller, whose story simply unwinds, to the imperatives of a book-length written narrative. But the ending is a relatively minor matter. Of more consequence are the pressures upon the narrative voice through the entire course of its performance. An enormous burden is placed upon Huck, who must not only tell the story but enact it as the leading player. My discussion will focus on this double role, will attempt to assess Huck's role as the verbalizer of the narrative in order to assess his role as a character within the narrative. What freedom means in the book, and what form freedom takes, cannot be understood at all without such assessments.

What part of Huck's life in the book derives from the inner necessities of his "character," and what part derives from the outer necessities of his role as speaking voice? Huck has precisely the split identity this question implies. The consequent tensions within the narrative have been obscured in criticism by the great attention given to "identity" as a theme. The pervasive deployment of disguises, verbal and sartorial, through which Huck extricates himself from tight spots alerts the reader to the significance of hidden and revealed identities. When Huck is taken for Tom Sawyer in Chapter 32, he accepts the name with relief (it saves him the trouble of having to invent yet another name), "for it was like being born again, I was so glad to find out who I was." The line follows one of Huck's meditations on death, and some critics have been moved to discover a pattern of death and rebirth throughout, a pattern in which Huck's true name finds protection in the "death" of assumed identities. The motif is familiar in oral literature (see the excised "Raftsmen" passage), and the fact that Huck is legally dead through most of the book adds suggestive weight. At least as long as Pap lives, and as long as Huck is associated with Jim's escape, it seems impossible for the boy to own up to his true identity. The motif of disguise thus seems to harbor a dilemma directly related to the question of freedom: is it possible for Huck to both show and be his true self? To show himself as a runaway who has faked his own death and is aiding an escaped slave would invite disaster. This is a given of the narrative: to be himself Huck must hide himself.

What are the sources of this commanding paradox? Social reality, for one: Miss Watson, Pap, slavery, general avariciousness, all constitute an environment of treachery. Some critics argue too that the need to hide derives from deep psychic needs, from the extreme vulnerability expressed in Huck's character, especially his recurrent feelings of guilt. . . .

The issue is subtle and difficult. Do Huck's traits derive in fact from an inner life at odds with social necessity, or from, I want to add, imperatives of his role as narrator? Obviously we need not make an either/or choice. But the second alternative has been so little present in criticism it is worth considering at some length. The crux of the matter is whether Huck presents a consistent character, whether a sentient inner life is always present. Some critics have suggested not. Richard Poirier finds that after his reversal of attitude toward Jim in Chapter 15 (the "trash" episode) and the defeat of his "white" conscience in Chapter 16, Huck gradually disappears as an active agent in the narrative. Unable to continue the developing consciousness implicit in these scenes, Poirier argues, Mark Twain became absorbed in sheer "social panorama," to which Huck is a more or less passive witness. Henry Nash Smith makes a similar point. After losing Cairo in the fog, and losing the raft in Chapter 16, Mark Twain set aside the manuscript, and when he resumed several years later, he "now launched into a satiric description of the society of the prewar South." Huck becomes Mark Twain's satiric mask, which prevents him, Smith argues, from developing in his own right.

These are promising hints regarding Huck's status as a fictional character. Of course any criticism which charges Mark Twain with failing to continue a developing consciousness assumes such a development is a hallmark of fictional character. It might be countered that such a standard is inappropriate to this book, as Clemens himself may have suggested in his attack on the "cultivated-class standard," or that Huck's so-called disappearance in the middle section is actually another disguise, profoundly enforced by an increasingly hostile setting. His retreat, then, after the Grangerford episode, might be consistent with what had already developed as his character.

Even to begin to discuss this issue we need to understand what we mean by a "fictional character." Our expectations derive, in brief, from the novelistic tradition, in which character and action have a coextensive identity. Henry James insisted in "The Art of Fiction" . . . upon the inseparability of character and action by describing the novel as "a living thing, all one and continuous, like any other organism." "What is character," he wrote, "but the determination of incident? What is incident but the illustration of character?" The reciprocity of character and action implies, moreover, a process, a twofold development in which character fulfills itself just as it reveals itself to the reader. By development we expect a filling out, a discovery of possibilities and limitations. We also expect a certain degree of self-reflectiveness in character to register what is happening internally.

We need not remind ourselves that *Huckleberry Finn* is not a Jamesian novel. But it is important to know what sort of novel it is, to know what to expect of Huck as a character. What happens to Huck in the course of the narrative? Is he a changed being at the end from what he was at the beginning? In the opening scene Huck chafes at the "dismal regular and decent" routine of Widow Douglas, says he can't stand it "no longer," and "lights out" to his old rags and hogshead and "was free and satisfied." He returns only to qualify for Tom's gang. At the end of the book he again "lights out," this time for "howling adventures amongst the Injuns, over in the Territory." Has anything changed? The final words rejecting civilization, this time Aunt Sally's, do seem to register a difference: "I been there before." These are precious words for the reader; they confirm what he has discovered about civilization. But do they mean the same thing to Huck?

The difference we want to feel between the two rejections of civilization which frame the book parallels the indisputable difference between the two instances when Huck decides to go to hell rather than obey moral conscience. In Chapter 1, Miss Watson tries to frighten the child into sitting up straight by preaching about the bad place and what is in store for boys who don't behave. Huck retorts that he wishes he were there; if Miss Watson is heading for heaven, he would rather not try for it. In Chapter 31, in Huck's famous struggle with his conscience, this comedy of inverted values recurs, but with much expanded significance. In the first instance the preference for hell is expressed in a raffish, offhanded manner; it is a joke, not a serious commitment. In Chapter 31, in a much analyzed passage, we witness a genuine choice, preceded by an inward struggle. The language, first of self-condemnation ("here was the plain hand of Providence slapping me in the face"), then of self-reproach ("and he was so grateful, and said I was the best friend old Jim ever had in the world, and the *only* one he's got now"), externalizes the opposite perspectives of sound heart and deformed conscience. The feat of language itself convinces us that Huck has now earned a meaningful damnation on behalf of his friendship with

Jim. This episode has a structure of modulated feeling entirely missing in the first case. Moreover the much deeper implications for Huck's freedom in the second instance are affected by the location of the moment in the narrative, after the exposure of greed, corruption, hypocrisy, and violence in the river society. If the Grangerfords and all the others name heaven as their goal, then hell is by far a better aspiration. Huck's decisive words, "All right, then, I'll go to hell," are a release for the reader, for he too has been in "a close place." The line affirms Huck's fundamental rightness.

    In short, the deepened implications of "I'll go to hell" and "I been there before," implications which have led critics to impute to Huck a self-generated liberation from moral deformity, arise from the context of narrative action. But does Huck actually catch the same implications? Does he know and understand exactly what he is saying? Of course we might argue that the implications are finally comic precisely because Huck does not understand them. But if this is the case, can we also say that he is a conscious character? If we cannot believe that Huck shows himself just at the moment when we most approve of his words, then we necessarily claim we are superior to him. We fix him in an ironic relation to his own words: he says more than he knows. But then again, does he not by nature *feel* rather than think? If we say so, if we excuse him from an intellectual act we perform, then are we not exploiting our sense of superiority and condescending toward him? Of course Huck is clearly mindful of the seriousness of his impasse, that he is deciding "forever, betwixt two things." Even earlier in the narrative, however, Huck had settled moral dilemmas by choosing what to him is the easiest, most comfortable course; we approve his choices, and smile at his handy rationalizations (some of which he learns from Pap). A similar pattern finally emerges in Chapter 31; after his "awful thoughts, and awful words" about hell, he "shoved the whole thing out of my head; and said I would take up wickedness again, which was in my line, being brung up to it." A beautiful line; but beautiful because of its perfect ironic tone. Is Huck aware of the irony? Has he learned what we have learned as witnesses, overhearers, of his conflict? Can we be sure, here or at the end of the book, that we are not extrapolating from our own lessons in expecting Huck to share our recognitions?

    In at least one episode Huck does achieve an unequivocal self-awareness, and the scene is the measure of Huck's behavior elsewhere in the book. I refer to the colloquy with Jim that concludes Chapter 15, after Huck had played his joke on Jim during the fog. The scene is unusual in the book, in part because of its realized tension between Huck and Jim, in part because of the completely unfettered, "free" and honest speech by Jim ("What do dey stan' for? I's gwyne to tell you. . . . Dat truck dah is *trash;* en trash is what people is dat puts dirt on de head er dey fren's en makes 'em

ashamed"). Huck is forced by the speech to reckon with Jim as a person who
has developed specific human expectations regarding Huck. By reckoning
with such expectations Huck must reckon with, must confront himself, as
a social being whose acts make a difference. He experiences himself through
the sense compelled by Jim's speech of how another person experiences
him. Huck once more wins our approval, but more important, he wins a
self-conception which issues into an action—his apology "to a nigger."

The implications of a deepening human relation between Huck and
Jim fail to materialize in the book; they have no other dramatic conflicts
of this sort. But perhaps one confrontation is sufficient; perhaps the implications are buried in order to return in Huck's comparably "free" speech
in Chapter 31, which recalls the circumstances of his friendship with Jim
on the raft. It is curious, however, in light of the growing consciousness of
these moments of mutual perception and self-perception, that the book,
filled as it is with so many characters, is so barren of human relationships.
The superficial quality of how people deal with each other (and themselves) is, of course, a deliberate element in Mark Twain's portrait of river
society. It is also true that in Huck's experience people usually represent
problems rather than possibilities, objects rather than subjects. . . .

The scarcity of complicating relations, of *dramatic* encounters, does in
fact qualify the reader's relation to Huck. To repeat what I propose is the
critical issue at stake, we want to learn if these features of the narrative follow from Huck's "character," the demanding needs of his inner being, or
if they in some way reflect the double role he plays, as a narrator who tells
a story and a character who has a story. We need to look more closely at
Huck's technical and dramatic roles.

The absence of serious complications helps account for the book's
universal appeal. . . . Mark Twain could rely upon a readership already
trained to recognize and "read" a comic vernacular speaker, to place him
within its verbal universe; Huck appears within the guise of local color conventions (dialect, regional dress, essential "goodness" of heart). As a storyteller he intervenes very little between the events and the reader; he rarely
projects a mind that calls attention to itself apart from the immediate experiences it records. Verbally, Huck displays a prepositional exactness in defining himself in space, but more or less imprecision in regard to time; . . .

But if sequential time matters little in the narrative structure, "tim-
ing," the arch device of the oral storyteller, does. In "How to Tell a Story"
Mark Twain speaks of the importance of a studied nonchalance, an appearance of rambling purposelessness, and of the strategic pause. The storyteller holds his listener in a relation which has a strict temporal order of its
own. Within that order, generated by the verbal posture of casualness, the
placement or the withholding of details is of first importance. Thus the

comic story tends to appear within longer narratives as a set piece, such as Huck's account of the Grangerford household, or his colloquy with Jim about "Sollermun." Within these pieces, Huck's role follows what Clemens called "the first virtue of a comedian"—to "do humorous things with grave decorum and without seeming to know they are funny." Grave decorum and seeming humorlessness well describe Huck's appearance. But is he so guileful as to dissemble his appearance for the reader? Who is the controlling comedian of the book, Huck or Mark Twain? Is humorlessness, the dead pan, Huck's trick on us, or Mark Twain's? Is grave decorum a feature of Huck's own character, or of Mark Twain's deployed mask?

We need to consider dead pan, not only as a mode operative in specific passages, but as the dominant mode of the entire narrative, even when it does not lead to a punch line or reversal. The mode is based on a form of trickery, of saying less than one means. . . .

Dead pan exists in a complex relation to lies. It too is a falsehood, a manipulated appearance. But it is a lie in the service of truth or "reality," an honest lie whose effect as humor is based on our ultimate recognition of its falseness. As James Cox writes of the tall tale—a variant of dead pan—it "is true in that it is the only lie in a world of lies which reveals itself to be a lie." Commonly the procedure is to dramatize in the comic voice an apparently unrecognized discrepancy between what is perceived (the awful gimcrackery of the Grangerford sitting room) and what is felt (Huck's sentimental approval). The reader is allowed to accept the feelings as provisionally his own, only to be thwarted by the details which normally arouse a contrary response; he is released from the false feelings by recognizing their cause to be ludicrously inadequate. The reader is initially taken in by Huck's manner so that he may, so to speak, be saved from Huck's foolish approval.

But does Huck really approve? If so, he is indeed a fool, and we laugh at him as well as the complacent Grangerfords. In the convention of dead pan the teller is only apparently a fool. We permit him to practice deception on us because in the end some absurdity will be exposed to the light of universal common sense; we will gain an advantage over the world. The teller's manner is a mask which steadily, deliberately, misleads us, until at the critical moment the mask falls. Behind the mask we might expect to find the real Huck, sharing our laughter, perhaps laughing at us for being momentarily taken in. The revealed comedian becomes at least our equal. But is this model at work here? Again we face Huck's paradoxical situation, as teller and as character. If we say that Huck's manner is a deliberate guise on his part, what happens to his gravity, his solemnity, his innocence, which we have normally taken as traits of character? Apart from depriving, or freeing, him of these elements of personality, such a reading would seriously upset the balance established between reader and narrative voice established at the outset. The voice presents itself as genuinely literal-minded; it presents itself as inferior in its own mind to the civilization of Widow Douglas and Tom Sawyer. We quickly make the judgment Huck seems unable to make for himself, that literal-mindedness is notably superior to the respectable lies of the town. The obvious superiority of Huck's frankness frees the reader from the deceptions of a world where respectability is the qualification for membership in a gang of robbers. To assign duplicity to Huck (by claiming he knows more than he is saying) would disturb this effect. To serve as our liberator Huck must remain ignorant and solemn. He must remain so in order to serve as Mark Twain's comic mask. In short, Mark Twain may have removed himself from the frame of the book, as the guileful, controlling voice, but the control remains in force, internalized and sublimated. The outside speaker who in earlier versions of vernacular presentation appeared, as in the Sut Lovingood stories, as a colloquist, now hides in the mask, a secret character in the book.

Dead pan predominates, and with it, Mark Twain's use of Huck's surface manner to reach the reader on a level of common values. But Huck's speech periodically escapes studied solemnity to become either lyrical, as in the sunrise passage which opens Chapter 19, or dramatic, as when he faces up to himself after Jim's "trash" speech. Such moments usually occur after actions which begin within the comic mode. Dead pan in part neutralizes the world, holds it at bay, seems to remove the threat of harm. But genuine harm frequently springs up to threaten the comic mode itself. One of many instances occurs in Chapter 18; the deadpan technique exposes Huck's explanation of the feud as absurd (the scene parallels the exposure of Tom's absurdities in trying to enforce an oath upon his fellow robbers in Chapter 2). Before long the slaughter begins and we hear "Kill them, kill them!" The sunrise passage and the idyllic account of the raft follow in Chapter 19. Huck's lyric-dramatic voice seems to require a violation of his surface deadpan manner for release. The book alternates between a voice given over to deadpan trickery and narrative, and undisguised, direct feeling. The second voice generates needs for dramatic realization the author does not accommodate. Mark Twain's own needs, perhaps for some revenge against Southern river society, seemed to require a Huck Finn who is ignorant, half-deformed, and permanently humorless. To put the case strongly, we might say that Huck's character is stunted by his creator's need for him to serve as a technical device. The same devices of irony which liberate the reader by instructing him about civilization and human nature also repress Huck by using him; they prevent his coming into his own.

Huck's freedom, I want finally to argue, requires that he achieve a conscious moral identity. Huck cannot be free in this sense unless Mark Twain

permits him a credible and articulate inner being, with dramatic opportu-
nities to realize his self. Of course this is to make perhaps impossible and
therefore inappropriate demands upon this novel. But I think Mark Twain
came close enough to such a realization for us to judge the book by its own
best moments. Consider, for example, the raft, often taken as the symbol
of freedom. The ethic of the raft is stated eloquently "You feel mighty free
and easy and comfortable on a raft." Yes; but this mood is possible because Huck had earlier humbled himself before Jim and decided to give up
the pleasure of playing tricks. The raft has a tacit code, what we might call
its own conscience. When the Duke and King arrive, that code bends to accommodate the rascals, for, as Huck tells himself as justification for not
letting on to Jim that the men are frauds, "what you want, above all things,
on a raft, is for everybody to be satisfied, and feel right and kind towards
the others . . . it's the best way; then you don't have no quarrels, and don't
get into no trouble." "Free and easy" of the first passage has become
"satisfied" and "no quarrels . . . no trouble." The difference is subtle but
crucial. The raft is no longer free. Dissembling has returned. . . .

The raft cannot defend itself against imposture. In the end imposture
itself seems the only resort for Huck and Jim. From this point of view the
elaborate theatricals at the Phelps farm seem an appropriate conclusion:
how else might the two fugitives be returned to a possible world without
real harm, without damaging the comic expectations of the novel? But
what then can we say about freedom? Are we to judge the vulnerability of
the raft, the necessity of a concluding "Evasion" (necessary to have any
conclusion at all), to mean that by *its* nature the difficult freedom of own-
ing oneself is impossible? Are we too hard with this book to blame it for
failing to sustain the self-consciousness and process of self-discovery implicit in several scenes? Or more to the point, is that failure part of Mark
Twain's design, or a result of technical limitations? Does the book project
a fully realized vision, or is the vision blocked by the author's inability to
sustain a novelistic development? These questions characterize the critic's
dilemma in assessing the book.

Of course a vision and the verbal means of its realization and execu-
tion are virtually inseparable. Mark Twain saw the world the best he was
able to, given his special verbal resources. My argument has meant to say
that the formal problems which proceed from the initial conception of a
book-length narrative in a mainly deadpan vernacular voice themselves enforce a certain vision. Mark Twain's work as a whole suggests that he seriously doubted the possibilities of personal freedom within a social setting.
He seems to have taken freedom as true only when absolute and abstract,
outside time. The imagery of drift in this novel is invested with such longing
perhaps because it represents a condition already lost and insubstantial the

moment it is imagined. The other side of the image reveals the fully invul-
nerable trickster, whose cynicism releases him from the control of any conscience. The dream voyages and mysterious strangers which obsessed
Mark Twain's later years are anticipated in *Huckleberry Finn*.

The book is finally more persuasive as a document of enslavement, of
the variety of imprisonments within verbal styles and fictions than as a testimony to freedom. Of course its negativity implies an ideal. I would like
to identify that ideal with the "free" speech of Huck and Jim at the moments of engagement. I have tried to explain why such speech breaks out
so rarely, why moral identity was so difficult to attain given the technical
resources of the book. But we should recognize that the limits placed
upon Huck's character are also forceful imperatives from the society
within which Mark Twain portrays him. Moral character requires that
social roles be credible to young people about to assume them. The society rendered in *Huckleberry Finn* deprives all roles of credibility when
viewed from a literal-minded vernacular perspective. Rationalization and
improvisation have convincing survival value, and virtuosity of disguise
earns our admiration. Pap, after all, did bequeath a fatherly heritage by
teaching Huck how to cheat and get away with no more than a bruised
conscience. Perhaps the book's Americanness is most profoundly revealed
in this heritage of eluding fixed definitions, in the corrosive decreation of
established roles. Jim's presence reminds us, however, of the cost history
has exacted from a society which drives its children to negativity. The cost
is charged most heavily against Huck; he pays with his chance to grow up.

HUCK, JIM, AND AMERICAN
RACIAL DISCOURSE (1984)

David L. Smith

They [blacks] are at least as brave, and more adventuresome [com-
pared with whites]. But this may perhaps proceed from a want of fore-
thought, which prevents their seeing a danger till it be present. . . . They
are more ardent after their female: but love seems with them to be more
an eager desire, than a tender delicate mixture of sentiment and sensa-
tion. Their griefs are transient. Those numberless afflictions, which ren-

From *Mark Twain: A Collection of Critical Essays*. Englewood Cliffs: Prentice-
Hall, 1984.

der it doubtful whether heaven has given life to us in mercy or in wrath,
are less felt, and sooner forgotten with them. In general, their existence
appears to participate more of sensation than reflection. To this must be
ascribed their disposition to sleep when abstracted from their diver-
sions, and unemployed in labor.
—Thomas Jefferson, *Notes on the State of Virginia*

Almost any Euro-American intellectual of the nineteenth century could have written the preceding words. The notion of Negro inferiority was so deeply pervasive among those heirs of "The Enlightenment" that the categories and even the vocabulary of Negro inferiority were formalized into a tedious, unmodulated litany. This uniformity increased rather than diminished during the course of the century. As Leon Litwack and others have shown, even the abolitionists, who actively opposed slavery, frequently regarded blacks as inherently inferior. This helps to explain the widespread popularity of colonization schemes among abolitionists and other liberals.[1] As for Jefferson, it is not surprising that he held such ideas, but it is impressive that he formulated so clearly at the end of the eighteenth century what would become the dominant view of the Negro in the nineteenth century. In many ways this father of American democracy— and quite possibly of five mulatto children—was a man of his time and ahead of his time.

In July 1876, exactly one century after the American Declaration of Independence, Mark Twain began writing *Adventures of Huckleberry Finn*, a novel that illustrates trenchantly the social limitations that American "civilization" imposes on individual freedom.[2] The book takes special note of ways in which racism impinges upon the lives of Afro-Americans, even when they are legally "free." It is therefore ironic that *Huckleberry*

---

[1] The literature on the abolition movement and on antebellum debates regarding the Negro is, of course, voluminous. George M. Fredrickson's excellent *The Black Image in the White Mind* (New York: Harper Torchbooks, 1971) is perhaps the best general work of its kind. Fredrickson's *The Inner Civil War* (New York: Harper Torchbooks, 1971) is also valuable, especially pp. 53–64. Leon Litwack, in *North of Slavery* (Chicago: U of Chicago P, 1961) 214–46, closely examines the ambivalence of abolitionists regarding racial intermingling. Benjamin Quarles presents the most detailed examination of black abolitionists in *Black Abolitionists* (New York: Oxford UP, 1969), although Vincent Harding offers a more vivid (and overtly polemical) account of their relationships to white abolitionists; see *There Is a River* (New York: Harcourt, Brace, Jovanovich, 1981).
[2] For dates of composition, see Walter Blair, "When Was *Huckleberry Finn* Written?" *American Literature* 30 (Mar. 1958): 1–25.

Finn has often been attacked and even censored as a racist work. I would argue, on the contrary, that except for Melville's work, *Huckleberry Finn* is without peer among major Euro-American novels for its explicitly anti-racist stance. Those who brand the book racist generally do so without having considered the specific form of racial discourse to which the novel responds. Furthermore, *Huckleberry Finn* offers much more than the typical liberal defenses of "human dignity" and protests against cruelty. Though it contains some such elements, it is more fundamentally a critique of those socially constituted fictions—most notably romanticism, religion, and the concept of "the Negro"—which serve to justify and disguise selfish, cruel, and exploitative behavior.

When I speak of "racial discourse," I mean more than simply attitudes about race or conventions of talking about race. Most importantly, I mean that race itself is a discursive formation which delimits social relations on the basis of alleged physical differences.[3] "Race" is a strategy for relegating a segment of the population to a permanent inferior status. It functions by insisting that each "race" has specific, definitive, inherent behavioral tendencies and capacities which distinguish it from other races. Though scientifically specious, race has been powerfully effective as an ideology and as a form of social definition that serves the interests of Euro-American hegemony. In America, race has been deployed against numerous groups, including Native Americans, Jews, Asians, and even—for brief periods— an assortment of European immigrants.

For obvious reasons, however, the primary emphasis historically has been on defining "the Negro" as a deviant from Euro-American norms. "Race" in America means white supremacy and black inferiority,[4] and

---

[3] My use of "racial discourse" has some affinities to Foucault's conception of "discourse." This is not, however, a strictly Foucaultian reading. I prefer an account of power which allows for consideration of interest and hegemony. Theorists such as Marshall Berman, *All That Is Solid Melts into Air* (New York: Simon & Schuster, 1982) 34–35, and Catherine A. MacKinnon, "Feminism, Marxism, Method, and the State: An Agenda for Theory," *Signs* 7.3 (1982): 526, have indicated similar reservations. However, Frank Lentricchia ("Reading Foucault [Punishment, Labor, Resistance]," *Raritan* 1.4 [1981]: 5–32; 2.1 [1982]: 41–70) has made a provocative effort to modify Foucaultian analysis, drawing upon Antonio Gramsci's analysis of hegemony in *Selections from the Prison Notebooks* (New York: International Publishers, 1971). See Foucault, *The Archaeology of Knowledge, Power/Knowledge*, ed. Colin Gordon (New York: Pantheon, 1980) esp. 92–108; and *The History of Sexuality*, vol. 1 (New York: Vintage, 1980) esp. 92–102.

[4] This is not to discount the sufferings of other groups. But historically, the philosophical basis of Western racial discourse—which existed even before the European "discovery" of America—has been the equation of "good" and "evil" with light and dark-

"the Negro," a socially constituted fiction, is a generalized, one-dimensional surrogate for the historical reality of Afro-American people. It is this reified fiction that Twain attacks in *Huckleberry Finn*.

Twain adopts a strategy of subversion in his attack on race. That is, he focuses on a number of commonplaces associated with "the Negro" and then systematically dramatizes their inadequacy. He uses the term "nigger," and he shows Jim engaging in superstitious behavior. Yet he portrays Jim as a compassionate, shrewd, thoughtful, self-sacrificing, and even wise man. Indeed, his portrayal of Jim contradicts every claim presented in Jefferson's description of "the Negro." Jim is cautious, he gives excellent advice, he suffers persistent anguish over separation from his wife and children, and he even sacrifices his own sleep so that Huck may rest. Jim, in short, exhibits all the qualities that "the Negro" supposedly lacks. Twain's conclusions do more than merely subvert the justifications of slavery, which was already long since abolished. Twain began his book during the final disintegration of Reconstruction, and his satire on antebellum southern bigotry is also an implicit response to the Negrophobic climate of the post-Reconstruction era.[5] It is troubling, therefore, that so many readers have completely misunderstood Twain's subtle attack on racism.

Twain's use of the term "nigger" has provoked some readers to reject the novel.[6] As one of the most offensive words in our vocabulary, "nigger" remains heavily shrouded in taboo. A careful assessment of this term within the context of American racial discourse, however, will allow us to understand the particular way in which the author uses it. If we attend closely to Twain's use of the word, we may find in it not just a trigger to outrage but, more important, a means of understanding the precise nature of American racism and Mark Twain's attack on it.

---

ness (or white and black). See Jacques Derrida, "White Mythology," *New Literary History* 6 (1974): 5–74; Winthrop Jordan, *White over Black* (New York: Norton, 1968) 1–40; and Cornel West, *Prophesy Deliverance* (Philadelphia: Westminster P, 1982) 47–65. Economically, the slave trade, chattel slavery, agricultural peonage, and color-coded wage differentials have made the exploitation of African Americans the most profitable form of racism.

[5] See Lawrence I. Berkove, "The Free Man of Color in *The Grandissimes* and Works by Harris and Mark Twain," *Southern Quarterly* 18.4 (1981): 60–73; Richard Gollin and Rita Gollin, "*Huckleberry Finn* and the Time of Evasion," *Modern Language Studies* 9 (Spring 1979): 5–15; Michael Egan, *Mark Twain's Huckleberry Finn: Race, Class and Society* (Atlantic Highlands, N.J.: Humanities P, 1977) esp. 66–102.

[6] See Nat Hentoff's series of four columns in the *Village Voice* 27 (1982): "Huck Finn Better Get out of Town by Sundown" (May 4); "Is Any Book Worth the Humiliation of Our Kids?" (May 11); "Huck Finn and the Shortchanging of Black Kids" (May 18); and "These Are Little Battles Fought in Remote Places" (May 25).

Most obviously, Twain uses "nigger" throughout the book as a syn-
onym for "slave." There is ample evidence from other sources that this
corresponds to one usage common during the antebellum period. We first
encounter it in reference to "Miss Watson's big nigger, named Jim"
(chap. 2). This usage, like the term "nigger stealer," clearly designates the
"nigger" as an item of property: a commodity, a slave. This passage also
provides the only textual justification for the common critical practice of
labeling Jim "Nigger Jim," as if "nigger" were a part of his proper name.
This loathsome habit goes back at least as far as Albert Bigelow Paine's biography of Twain (1912).[7] In any case, "nigger" in this sense connotes an
inferior, even subhuman, creature who is properly owned by and subservient to Euro-Americans.

Both Huck and Jim use the word in this sense. For example, when
Huck fabricates his tale about the riverboat accident, the following exchange occurs between him and Aunt Sally:

"Good gracious! anybody hurt?"
"No'm. Killed a nigger."
"Well, it's lucky; because sometimes people do get hurt." (chap. 32)

Huck has never met Aunt Sally prior to this scene, and in spinning a lie
which this stranger will find unobjectionable, he correctly assumes that the
common notion of Negro subhumanity will be appropriate. Huck's off-
hand remark is intended to exploit Aunt Sally's attitudes, not to express
Huck's own. A nigger, Aunt Sally confirms, is not a person. Yet this exchange is hilarious precisely because we know that Huck is playing on her
glib and conventional bigotry. We know that Huck's relationship to Jim
has already invalidated for him such obtuse racial notions. The conception
of the "nigger" is a socially constituted and sanctioned fiction, and it is just
as false and absurd as Huck's explicit fabrication, which Aunt Sally also
swallows whole.

In fact, the exchange between Huck and Aunt Sally reveals a great
deal about how racial discourse operates. Its function is to promulgate a
conception of "the Negro" as a subhuman and expendable creature who
is by definition feeble-minded, immoral, lazy, and superstitious. One
crucial purpose of this social fiction is to justify the abuse and exploitation of Afro-American people by substituting the essentialist fiction of
"Negroism" for the actual character of individual Afro-Americans. Hence,
in racial discourse every Afro-American becomes just another instance of

---

[7] *Mark Twain: A Biography* (New York: Harper, 1912).

"the Negro"—just another "nigger." Twain recognizes this invidious tendency of race thinking, however, and he takes every opportunity to expose the mismatch between racial abstractions and real human beings. For example, when Pap drunkenly inveighs against the free mulatto from Ohio, he is outraged by what appears to him to be a crime against natural laws (chap. 6). In the first place, a "free nigger" is, for Pap, a contradiction in terms. Indeed, the man's clothes, his demeanor, his education, his profession, and even his silver-headed cane bespeak a social status normally achieved by only a small elite of white men. He is, in other words, a "nigger" who refuses to behave like one. Pap's ludicrous protestations discredit both himself and other believers in "the Negro," as many critics have noted. But it has not been sufficiently stressed that Pap's racial views correspond very closely to those of most of his white southern contemporaries, in substance if not in manner of expression. Such views were held not only by poor whites but by all "right-thinking" southerners, regardless of their social class. Indeed, not even the traumas of the Civil War could cure southerners of this folly. Furthermore, Pap's indignation at the Negro's right to vote is precisely analogous to the southern backlash against the enfranchisement of Afro-Americans during Reconstruction. Finally, Pap's comments are rather mild compared with the anti-Negro diatribes that were beginning to emerge among politicians even as Twain was writing *Huckleberry Finn*. He began writing this novel during the final days of Reconstruction, and it seems more than reasonable to assume that the shameful white supremacist bluster of that epoch—exemplified by Pap's tirade—informed Twain's critique of racism in *Huckleberry Finn*.[8]

Pap's final description of this Ohio gentleman as "a prowling, thieving, infernal, white-shirted free nigger" (chap. 6) almost totally contradicts his previous description of the man as a proud, elegant, dignified figure. Yet this contradiction is perfectly consistent with Pap's need to reassert "the Negro" in lieu of social reality. Despite the vulgarity of Pap's personal character, his thinking about race is highly conventional, and therefore respectable. But most of us cannot respect Pap's views, and when we reject them, we reject the standard racial discourse of both 1840 and 1880.

A reader who objects to the word "nigger" might still insist that Twain could have avoided using it. But it is difficult to imagine how Twain could have debunked a discourse without using the specific terms of that discourse. Even when Twain was writing his book, "nigger" was universally recognized as an insulting, demeaning word. According to Stuart Berg

---

[8] See Arthur G. Pettit, *Mark Twain and the South* (Lexington: U of Kentucky P, 1974).

Flexner, "Negro" was generally pronounced "nigger" until about 1825, at which time abolitionists began objecting to that term.[9] They preferred "colored person" or "person of color." Hence, W. E. B. Du Bois reports that some black abolitionists of the early 1830s declared themselves united "as men, . . . not as slaves; as 'people of color,' not as 'Negroes.'"[10] Writing a generation later in *Army Life in a Black Regiment* (1869), Thomas Wentworth Higginson deplored the common use of "nigger" among freedmen, which he regarded as evidence of low self-esteem.[11] The objections to "nigger," then, are not a consequence of the modern sensibility but had been common for a half century before *Huckleberry Finn* was published. The specific function of this term in the book, however, is neither to offend nor merely to provide linguistic authenticity. Much more importantly, it establishes a context against which Jim's specific virtues may emerge as explicit refutations of racist presuppositions.

Of course, the concept of "nigger" entails far more than just the deployment of certain vocabulary. Most of the attacks on the book focus on alleged perpetuation of racial stereotypes. Twain does indeed use stereotypes here. That practice could be excused as characteristic of the genre of humor within which Twain works. Frontier humor relies upon the use of stock types, and consequently racial stereotypes are just one of many types present in *Huckleberry Finn*. Yet while valid, such an appeal to generic convention would be unsatisfactory because it would deny Twain the credit he deserves for the sophistication of his perceptions.[12]

As a serious critic of American society, Twain recognized that racial discourse depends upon the deployment of a system of stereotypes which constitute "the Negro" as fundamentally different from and inferior to Euro-Americans. As with his handling of "nigger," Twain's strategy with racial stereotypes is to elaborate them in order to undermine them. . . .

One aspect of *Huckleberry Finn* that has elicited copious critical commentary is Twain's use of superstition.[13] In nineteenth-century racial

---

[9] *I Hear America Talking* (New York: Van Nostrand Reinhold, 1976) 57.

[10] *The Souls of Black Folk,* in *Three Negro Classics,* ed. John Hope Franklin (New York: Avon, 1965) 245.

[11] (Boston: Beacon, 1962) 28.

[12] See Ralph Ellison, "Change the Joke and Slip the Yoke" in *Shadow and Act* (New York: Random House, 1964) 45–59; Chadwick Hansen, "The Character of Jim and the Ending of *Huckleberry Finn,*" *Massachusetts Review* 5 (Autumn 1963): 45–66; Kenneth S. Lynn, *Mark Twain and Southwestern Humor* (Boston: Little, Brown, 1959).

[13] See especially Daniel Hoffman, "Jim's Magic: Black or White?" *American Literature* 32 (Mar. 1960): 47–54.

discourse, "the Negro" was always defined as inherently superstitious.[14] Many critics, therefore, have cited Jim's superstitious behavior as an instance of negative stereotyping. One cannot deny that in this respect Jim closely resembles the entire tradition of comic darkies,[15] but in some instances apparent similarities conceal fundamental differences. The issue is: does Twain merely reiterate clichés, or does he use these conventional patterns to make an unconventional point? A close examination will show that, in virtually every instance, Twain uses Jim's superstition to make points that undermine rather than revalidate the dominant racial discourse.

The first incident of this superstitious behavior occurs in chapter 2, as a result of one of Tom Sawyer's pranks. When Jim falls asleep under a tree, Tom hangs Jim's hat on a branch. Subsequently Jim concocts an elaborate tale about having been hexed and ridden by witches. The tale grows more grandiose with each repetition, and eventually Jim becomes a local celebrity, sporting a five-cent piece on a string around his neck as a talisman. "Niggers would come miles to hear Jim tell about it, and he was more looked up to than any nigger in that country," the narrator reports. Jim's celebrity finally reaches the point that "Jim was most ruined, for a servant, because he got so stuck up on account of having seen the devil and been rode by witches." That is, no doubt, amusing. Yet whether Jim believes his own tale or not—and the "superstitious Negro" thesis requires us to assume that he does—the fact remains that Jim clearly benefits from becoming more a celebrity and less a "servant." It is his owner, not Jim, who suffers when Jim reduces the amount of his uncompensated labor.[16]

This incident has often been interpreted as an example of risible Negro gullibility and ignorance as exemplified by blackface minstrelsy. Such a reading has more than a little validity, but it can only partially account

---

[14] Even the allegedly scientific works on the Negro focused on superstition as a definitive trait. See, for example, W. D. Weatherford. *Negro Life in the South* (New York: Young Men's Christian Association P, 1910); and Jerome Dowd, *Negro Races* (New York: Macmillan, 1907). No one has commented more scathingly on Negro superstitions than William Hannibal Thomas in *The American Negro* (1901; New York: Negro Universities P, 1969); by American definitions he was himself a Negro.

[15] See Fredrick Woodard and Donnarae MacCann, "*Huckleberry Finn* and the Traditions of Blackface Minstrelsy," *Interracial Books for Children Bulletin* 15.1–2 (1984): 4–13.

[16] Daniel Hoffman, in *Form and Fable in American Fiction* (New York: Oxford UP, 1961), reveals an implicit understanding of Jim's creativity, but he does not pursue the point in detail (331).

for the implications of this scene. If not for the final sentence, such an account might seem wholly satisfactory, but the information that Jim becomes, through his own story telling, unsuited for life as a slave introduces unexpected complications. Is it likely that Jim has been deceived by his own creative prevarications—especially given what we learn about his character subsequently? Or has he cleverly exploited the conventions of "Negro superstition" in order to turn a silly boy's prank to his own advantage?

Regardless of whether we credit Jim with forethought in this matter, it is undeniable that he turns Tom's attempt to humiliate him into a major personal triumph. In other words, Tom gives him an inch, and he takes an ell. It is also obvious that he does so by exercising remarkable skills as a rhetorician. By constructing a fictitious narrative of his own experience, Jim elevates himself above his prescribed station in life. By becoming, in effect, an author, Jim writes himself a new destiny. Jim's triumph may appear to be dependent upon the gullibility of other "superstitious" Negroes, but since we have no direct encounter with them, we cannot know whether they are unwitting victims of Jim's ruse or not. A willing audience need not be a totally credulous one. In any case, it is intelligence, not stupidity, that facilitates Jim's triumph. Tom may have had his chuckle, but the last laugh clearly belongs to Jim. . . .

In another instance of explicitly superstitious behavior, Jim uses a hair ball to tell Huck's fortune. One may regard this scene as a comical example of Negro ignorance and credulity, acting in concert with the ignorance and credulity of a fourteen-year-old white boy. That reading would allow one an unambiguous laugh at Jim's expense. If one examines the scene carefully, however, the inadequacy of such a reductive reading becomes apparent. Even if Jim does believe in the supernatural powers of this hair ball, the fact remains that most of the transaction depends upon Jim's quick wits. The soothsaying aside, much of the exchange between Huck and Jim is an exercise in wily and understated economic bartering. In essence, Jim wants to be paid for his services, while Huck wants free advice. . . .

In this transaction, Jim serves his own interest while appearing to serve Huck's interest. He takes a slug which is worthless to Huck, and through the alchemy of his own cleverness contrives to make it worth twenty-five cents to himself. That, in antebellum America, is not a bad price for telling a fortune. But more important, Twain shows Jim self-consciously subverting the prescribed definition of "the Negro," even as he performs within the limitations of that role. He remains the conventional "Negro" by giving the white boy what he wants, at no real cost, and by consistently appearing to be passive and subservient to the desires of Huck and the hair ball. But in fact, he serves his own interests all along. Such resourcefulness

is hardly consistent with the familiar one-dimensional concept of "the
superstitious Negro." . . .

In this . . . and other incidents, Jim emerges as an astute and sensitive
observer of human behavior. . . . Jim clearly possesses a subtlety and intelligence which "the Negro" allegedly lacks. Twain makes this point more
clearly in the debate scene in chapter 14. True enough, most of this debate
is, as several critics have noted, conventional minstrel-show banter. Nevertheless, Jim demonstrates impressive reasoning abilities, despite his
factual ignorance. For instance, in their argument over "Poly-voo-franzy,"
Huck makes a category error by implying that the difference between languages is analogous to the difference between human language and cat language. While Jim's response—that a man should talk like a man—betrays
his ignorance of cultural diversity, his argument is otherwise perceptive
and structurally sound. The humor in Huck's conclusion, "you can't learn
a nigger to argue," arises precisely from our recognition that Jim's argument is better than Huck's.

Throughout the novel Twain presents Jim in ways which render ludicrous the conventional wisdom about "Negro character." As an intelligent, sensitive, wily, and considerate individual, Jim demonstrates that
race provides no useful index of character. . . . By presenting us with a series of glimpses which penetrate the "Negro" exterior and reveal the person beneath it, Twain debunks American racial discourse. For racial discourse maintains that the "Negro" exterior is all that a Negro really has.

This insight in itself is a notable accomplishment. Twain, however, did
not view racism as an isolated phenomenon, and his effort to place racism
within the context of other cultural traditions produced the most problematic aspect of his novel. For it is in the final chapters—the Tom Sawyer
section—which most critics consider the weakest part of the book, that
Twain links his criticisms of slavery and southern romanticism, condemn-
ing the cruelties that both of these traditions entail.[17] Critics have objected
to these chapters on various grounds. Some of the most common are that
Jim becomes reduced to a comic darky,[18] that Tom's antics undermine the
seriousness of the novel, and that these burlesque narrative developments
destroy the structural integrity of the novel. Most critics see this conclusion as an evasion of the difficult issues the novel has raised. There is no
space here for a discussion of the structural issues, but it seems to me that

---

[17] See Lynn Altenbernd, "Huck Finn, Emancipator," *Criticism* 1 (1959): 298–307.
[18] See, for example, Leo Marx, "Mr. Eliot, Mr. Trilling, and *Huckleberry Finn*," *American Scholar* 22 (Autumn 1953): 423–40; and Neil Schmitz, "Twain, *Huckleberry Finn*,
and the Reconstruction," *American Studies* 12 (Spring 1971): 59–67.

as a critique of American racial discourse, these concluding chapters offer a harsh, coherent, and uncompromising indictment.

Tom Sawyer's absurd scheme to "rescue" Jim offends because the section has begun with Huck's justly celebrated crisis of conscience culminating in his resolve to free Jim, even if doing so condemns him to hell. The passage that leads to Huck's decision, familiar as it is, merits reexamination:

> I'd see him standing my watch on top of his'n—stead of calling me, so I could go on sleeping; and see him how glad he was when I come back out of the fog; and when I come to him again in the swamp, up there where the feud was; and such-like times; and would always call me honey, and pet me, and do everything he could think of for me, and how good he always was; and at last I struck the time I saved him by telling the men we had small-pox aboard, and he was so grateful, and said I was the best friend old Jim ever had in the world, and the *only* one he's got now; and then I happened to look around, and see that paper. . . . I studied a minute, sort of holding my breath, and then says to myself: "All right, then, I'll *go* to hell"—and tore it up. (chap. 31)

The issue here is not just whether or not Huck should return a fugitive slave to its lawful owner. More fundamentally, Huck must decide whether to accept the conventional wisdom, which defines "Negroes" as subhuman commodities, or the evidence of his own experience, which has shown Jim to be a good and kind man and a true friend.

Huck makes what is obviously the morally correct decision, but his doing so represents more than simply a liberal choice of conscience over social convention. Twain explicitly makes Huck's choice a sharp attack on the southern church. Huck scolds himself: "There was the Sunday school, you could a gone to it; and if you'd a done it they'd a learnt you, there, that people that acts as I'd been acting about that nigger goes to everlasting fire" (chap. 31). Yet despite Huck's anxiety, he transcends the moral limitations of his time and place. By the time Twain wrote these words, more than twenty years of national strife, including the Civil War and Reconstruction, had established Huck's conclusion regarding slavery as a dominant national consensus; not even reactionary southerners advocated a reinstitution of slavery. But since the pre–Civil War southern church taught that slavery was God's will, Huck's decision flatly repudiates the church's teachings regarding slavery. And implicitly, it also repudiates the church as an institution by suggesting that the church functions to undermine, not to encourage, a reliance on one's conscience. To define "Negroes" as subhuman removes them from moral consideration and therefore justifies their callous exploitation. This view of religion is consistent with the cynical iconoclasm that Twain expressed in *Letters from the Earth* and other "dark" works.[19]

In this context, Tom Sawyer appears to us as a superficially charming but fundamentally distasteful interloper. His actions are governed not by conscience but rather by romantic conventions and literary "authorities." Indeed, while Tom may appear to be a kind of renegade, he is in essence thoroughly conventional in his values and proclivities. . . .

To examine Tom's role in the novel, let us begin at the end. Upon learning of the failed escape attempt and Jim's recapture, Tom cries out, self-righteously: "Turn him loose! he ain't no slave; he's as free as any cre-tur that walks this earth!" (chap. 42). Tom has known all along that his cruel and ludicrous scheme to rescue the captured "prisoner" was being enacted upon a free man; and indeed, only his silence regarding Jim's status allowed the scheme to proceed with Jim's cooperation. Certainly, neither Huck nor Jim would otherwise have indulged Tom's foolishness. Tom's gratuitous cruelty here in the pursuit of his own amusement corresponds to his less vicious prank against Jim in chapter 2. And just as before, Twain converts Tom's callous mischief into a personal triumph for Jim.

Not only has Jim suffered patiently, which would, in truth, represent a doubtful virtue (Jim is not Uncle Tom); he demonstrates his moral supe-riority by surrendering himself in order to assist the doctor in treating his wounded tormentor. This is hardly the behavior one would expect from a commodity, and it is *precisely* Jim's status—man or chattel—that has been fundamentally at issue throughout the novel. It may be true that the lengthy account of Tom's juvenile antics subverts the tone of the novel, but they also provide the necessary backdrop for Jim's noble act. Up to this point we have been able to admire Jim's good sense and to respond senti-mentally to his good character. This, however, is the first time that we see him making a significant (and wholly admirable) moral decision. His act sets him apart from everyone else in the novel except Huck. And modestly (if not disingenuously), he claims to be behaving just as Tom Sawyer would. Always conscious of his role as a "Negro," Jim knows better than to claim personal credit for his good deed. Yet the contrast between Jim's behavior and Tom's is unmistakable. Huck declares that Jim is "white

---

[19] A number of critical works comment on Twain's religious views and the relation be-tween his critiques of religion and racism. See Allison Ensor, *Mark Twain and the Bible* (Lexington: U of Kentucky P, 1969); Arthur G. Pettit, "Mark Twain and the Negro, 1867–1869," *Journal of Negro History* 56 (Apr. 1971): 88–96; and Gollin and Gollin 5–15.

inside" (chap. 40). He apparently intends this as a compliment, but Tom is fortunate that Jim does not behave like most of the whites in the novel. Twain also contrasts Jim's self-sacrificing compassion with the cruel and mean-spirited behavior of his captors, emphasizing that white skin does not justify claims of superior virtue. They abuse Jim, verbally and physically, and some want to lynch him as an example to other slaves. The moderates among them resist, however, pointing out that they could be made to pay for the destruction of private property. As Huck observes, "the people that's always the most anxious for to hang a nigger that hain't done just right, is always the very ones that ain't the most anxious to pay for him when they've got their satisfaction out of him" (chap. 42). As if these enforcers of white supremacy did not appear contemptible enough already, Twain then has the doctor describe Jim as the best and most faithful nurse he has ever seen, despite Jim's "resking his freedom" and his obvious fatigue. These vigilantes do admit that Jim deserves to be rewarded, but their idea of a reward is to cease punching and cursing him. They are not even generous enough to remove Jim's heavy shackles.

Ultimately, *Huckleberry Finn* renders a harsh judgment on American society. Freedom from slavery, the novel implies, is not freedom from gratuitous cruelty; and racism, like romanticism, is finally just an elaborate justification which the adult counterparts of Tom Sawyer use to facilitate their exploitation and abuse of other human beings. Tom feels guilty, with good reason, for having exploited Jim, but his final gesture of paying Jim off is less an insult to Jim than it is Twain's commentary on Tom himself. Just as slaveholders believe that economic relations (ownership) can justify their privilege of mistreating other human beings, Tom apparently believes that an economic exchange can suffice as atonement for his misdeeds. Perhaps he finds a forty-dollar token more affordable than an apology. But then, just as Tom could only "set a free nigger free," considering, as Huck says, "his bringing-up" (chap. 42), he similarly could hardly be expected to apologize for his pranks. Huck, by contrast, is equally rich, but he *has* apologized to Jim earlier in the novel. And this is the point of Huck's final remark rejecting the prospect of civilization. To become civilized is not just to become like Aunt Sally. More immediately, it is to become like Tom Sawyer.

Jim is indeed "as free as any cretur that walks this earth." In other words, he is a man, like all men, at the mercy of other men's arbitrary cruelties. In a sense, given Twain's view of freedom, to allow Jim to escape to the North or to have Tom announce Jim's manumission earlier would have been an evasion of the novel's ethical insights. While one may escape from legal bondage there is no escape from the cruelties of this "civilization." There is no promised land where one may enjoy absolute personal freedom. An individual's freedom is always constrained by social relations to

other people. Being legally free does not spare Jim from gratuitous humiliation and suffering in the final chapters, precisely because Jim is still regarded as a "nigger." Even if he were as accomplished as the mulatto from
Ohio, he would not be exempt from mistreatment. Furthermore, since
Tom represents the hegemonic values of his society, Jim's "freedom"
amounts to little more than an obligation to live by his wits and make the
best of a bad situation, just as he has always done.

Given the subtlety of Mark Twain's approach, it is not surprising that
most of his contemporaries misunderstood or simply ignored the novel's
demystification of race. Despite their patriotic rhetoric, they, like Pap, were
unprepared to take seriously the implications of "freedom, justice, and
equality." They, after all, espoused an ideology and an explicit language of
race virtually identical to Thomas Jefferson's. Yet racial discourse flatly
contradicts and ultimately renders hypocritical the egalitarian claims of
liberal democracy. The heart of Twain's message to us is that an honest
person must reject one or the other. But hypocrisy, not honesty, is our
norm. Many of us continue to assert both racial distinction and liberal
values simultaneously. If we, a century later, continue to be confused about
Adventures of Huckleberry Finn, perhaps it is because we remain more
deeply committed to both racial discourse and a self-deluding optimism
than we care to admit.

HUCKLEBERRY FINN
Alive at 100 (1985)

Norman Mailer

Is there a sweeter tonic for the doldrums than old reviews of great novels?
In nineteenth-century Russia, *Anna Karenina* was received with the following:
"Vronsky's passion for his horse runs parallel to his passion for Anna" . . .
"Sentimental rubbish" . . . "Show me one page," says the *Odessa Courier* "that
contains an idea." *Moby-Dick* was incinerated: "Graphic descriptions of a
dreariness such as we do not remember to have met with before in marine literature" . . . "Sheer moonstruck lunacy" . . . "Sad stuff. Mr. Melville's Quak-
ers are wretched dolts and drivellers and his mad captain is a monstrous bore."

By this measure, *Huckleberry Finn* gets off lightly. The *Springfield Republican* judged it to be no worse than "a gross trifling with every fine feeling . . .

The Time of Our Time. New York: Random, 1998.

Mr. Clemens has no reliable sense of propriety," and the public library in Concord, Massachusetts, was confident enough to ban it: "the veriest trash." The *Boston Transcript* reported that "other members of the Library Committee characterize the work as rough, coarse, and inelegant, the whole book being more suited to the slums than to intelligent, respectable people."

All the same, the novel was not too unpleasantly regarded. There were no large critical hurrahs, but the reviews were, on the whole, friendly. A good tale, went the consensus. There was no sense that a great American novel had landed on the literary world of 1885. The critical climate could hardly anticipate T. S. Eliot and Ernest Hemingway's encomiums fifty years later. In the preface to the English edition, Eliot would speak of "a masterpiece . . . Twain's genius is completely realized," and Ernest went further. In *Green Hills of Africa*, after disposing of Emerson, Hawthorne, and Thoreau, and paying off Henry James and Stephen Crane with a friendly nod, he proceeded to declare, "All modern American literature comes from one book by Mark Twain called *Huckleberry Finn*. . . . It's the best book we've had. All American writing comes from that. There was nothing before. There has been nothing as good since."

Hemingway, with his nonpareil gift for nosing out the perfect *vin du pays* for an ineluctable afternoon, was more like other novelists in one dire respect: He was never at a loss to advance himself with his literary judgments. Assessing the writing of others, he used the working author's rule of thumb: If I give this book a good mark, does it help appreciation of my work? Obviously, *Huckleberry Finn* has passed the test.

A suspicion immediately arises. Mark Twain is doing the kind of writing only Hemingway can do better. Evidently, we must take a look. May I say it helps to have read *Huckleberry Finn* so long ago that it feels brand-new on picking it up again. Perhaps I was eleven when I saw it last, maybe thirteen, but now I only remember that I came to it after *Tom Sawyer* and was disappointed. I couldn't really follow *The Adventures of Huckleberry Finn*. The character of Tom Sawyer whom I had liked so much in the first book was altered, and did not seem nice anymore. Huckleberry Finn was altogether beyond me. Later, I recollect being surprised by the high regard nearly everyone who taught American Lit. lavished upon the text, but that didn't bring me back to it. Obviously, I was waiting for an assignment from the *New York Times*.

Let me offer assurances. It may have been worth the wait. I suppose I am the ten millionth reader to say that *Huckleberry Finn* is an extraordinary work. Indeed, for all I know, it is a great novel. Flawed, quirky, uneven, not above taking cheap shots and cashing far too many checks (it is rarely above milking its humor)—all the same, what a book we have here! I had the most curious sense of excitement. After a while, I understood my peculiar frame of attention. The book was so up-to-date! I was not reading a classic author so much as looking at a new work sent to me in galleys by a publisher. It was as if it had arrived with one of those rare letters that says, "We won't make this claim often, but do think we have an extraordinary first novel to send out." So it was like reading *From Here to Eternity* in galleys, back in 1950, or *Lie Down in Darkness, Catch-22*, or *The World According to Garp* (which reads like a fabulous first novel). You kept being alternately delighted, surprised, annoyed, competitive, critical, and, finally, excited. A new writer had moved onto the block. He could be a potential friend or enemy, but he most certainly was talented.

That was how it felt to read *Huckleberry Finn* a second time. I kept resisting the context until I finally surrendered. One always does surrender sooner or later to a book with a strong magnetic field. I felt as if I held the work of a young writer about thirty or thirty-five, a prodigiously talented fellow from the Midwest, from Missouri probably, who had had the audacity to write a historical novel about the Mississippi as it might have been a century and a half ago, and this young writer had managed to give us a circus of fictional virtuosities. In nearly every chapter new and remarkable characters bounded out from the printed page as if it were a tarmac on which they could perform their leaps. The author's confidence seemed so complete that he could deal with every kind of man or woman God ever gave to the middle of America. Jail-house drunks like Huck Finn's father take their bow, full of the raunchy violence that even gets into the smell of clothing. Gentlemen and river rats, young, attractive girls full of grit and "sand," and strong old ladies with aphorisms clicking like knitting needles, fools and confidence men—what a cornucopia of rabble and gentry inhabit the author's river banks.

It would be superb stuff if only the writer did not keep giving away the fact that he was a modern young American working in 1984. His anachronisms were not so much in the historical facts—those seemed accurate enough—but the point of view was too contemporary. The scenes might succeed—say it again, this young writer was talented!—but he kept betraying his literary influences. The author of *The Adventures of Huckleberry Finn* had obviously been taught a lot by such major writers as Sinclair Lewis, John Dos Passos, and John Steinbeck; he had certainly lifted from Faulkner and the mad tone Faulkner could achieve when writing about maniacal men feuding in deep swamps; he had also absorbed much of what Vonnegut and Heller could teach about the resilience of irony. If he had a surer feel for the picaresque than Saul Bellow in *Augie March*, still he felt derivative of that work. In places one could swear he had memorized *The Catcher in the Rye*, and he probably dipped into *Deliverance* and *Why Are We in Vietnam?* He might even have studied the mannerisms of movie stars. You could feel traces of John Wayne,

Victor McLaglen, and Burt Reynolds in his pages. The author had doubtless digested many a Hollywood comedy on small-town life. His instinct for life in hamlets on the Mississippi before the Civil War was as sharp as it was farcical and couldn't be more commercial.

No matter. With a talent as large as this, one could forgive the obvious eye for success. Many a large talent has to go through large borrowings in order to find his own style, and a lust for popular success while dangerous to serious writing is not necessarily fatal. Yes, one could accept the pilferings from other writers, given the scope of his work, the brilliance of the concept—to catch rural America by a trip on a raft down a great river! One could even marvel uneasily at the depth of the instinct for fiction in the author. With the boy Huckleberry Finn, this new novelist had managed to give us a character of no comfortable, measurable dimension. It is easy for characters in modern novels to seem more vivid than figures in the classics but, even so, Huckleberry Finn appeared to be more alive than Don Quixote and Julian Sorel, as naturally near to his own mind as we are to ours. But how often does a hero who is so absolutely natural on the page also succeed in acquiring convincing moral stature as his adventures develop?

It is to be repeated. In the attractive grip of this talent, one is ready to forgive the author of *Huckleberry Finn* for every influence he has so promiscuously absorbed. He has made such fertile use of his borrowings. One could even cheer his appearance on our jaded literary scene if not for the single transgression that goes too far. These are passages that do more than borrow an author's style—they copy it! Influence is mental, but theft is physical. Who can declare to a certainty that a large part of the prose in *Huckleberry Finn* is not lifted directly from Hemingway? We know that we are not reading Ernest only because the author, obviously fearful that his tone is getting too near, is careful to sprinkle his text with "a-clutterings" and "warn'ts" and "anywheres" and "t'others." But we have read Hemingway—and so we see through it—we know we are reading pure Hemingway disguised:

> We cut young cottonwoods and willows, and hid the raft with them.
> Then we set out the lines. Next we slid into the river and had a swim . . .
> then we set down on the sandy bottom where the river was knee-deep and
> watched the daylight come. Not a sound anywheres . . . the first thing to
> see, looking away over the water, was a kind of dull line—that was the
> woods on t'other side; you couldn't make nothing else out; then a pale
> place in the sky; then more paleness spreading around; then the river soft-
> ened up away off, and warn't black any more . . . by and by you could see
> a streak on the water which you know by the look of the streak that
> there's a snag there in a swift current which breaks on it and makes that
> streak look that way; and you see the mist curl up off the water and the
> east reddens up and the river.

Up to now I have conveyed, I expect, the pleasure of reading this book to-day. It is the finest compliment I can offer. We use an unspoken standard of relative judgment on picking up a classic. Secretly, we expect less reward from it than from a good contemporary novel. The average intelligent modern reader would probably, under torture, admit that *Heartburn* was more fun to read, minute for minute, than *Madame Bovary,* and maybe one even learned more. That is not to say that the first will be superior to the second a hundred years from now but that a classic novel is like a fine horse carrying an exorbi-tant impost. Classics suffer by their distance from our day-to-day gossip. The mark of how good *Huckleberry Finn* has to be is that one can compare it to a number of our best modern American novels and it stands up page for page, awkward here, sensational there—absolutely the equal of one of those rare in-credible first novels that come along once or twice in a decade. So I have spo-ken of it as kin to a first novel because it is so young and so fresh and so all-out silly in some of the chances it takes and even wins. A wiser older novelist would never play that far out when the work was already well along and so neatly in hand, but Twain does.

For the sake of literary propriety, let me not, however, lose sight of the ac-tual context. *The Adventures of Huckleberry Finn* is a novel of the nineteenth century and its grand claims to literary magnitude are also to be remarked upon. So I will say that the first measure of a great novel may be that it pre-sents—like a human of palpable charisma—an all but visible aura. Few works of literature can be so luminous without the presence of some majestic symbol. In *Huckleberry Finn* we are presented (given the possible exception of Anna Livia Plurabelle) with the best river ever to flow through a novel, our own Mis-sissippi, and in the voyage down those waters of Huck Finn and a runaway slave on their raft, we are held in the thrall of the river. Larger than a charac-ter, the river is a manifest presence, a demiurge to support the man and the boy, a deity to betray them, feed them, all but drown them, fling them apart, float them back together. The river winds like a fugue through the marrow of the true narrative, which is nothing less than the ongoing relation between Huck and the runaway slave. . . . The growth of love and knowledge between the runaway white and the runaway black is a relation equal to the relation of the men to the river, for it is also full of betrayal and nourishment, separation and return. So it manages to touch that last fine nerve of the heart where com-passion and irony speak to one another and thereby give a good turn to our most protected emotions.

Reading *Huckleberry Finn,* one comes to realize all over again that the near burned-out, throttled, hate-filled dying affair between whites and blacks is still our great national love affair, and woe to us if it ends in detestation and mutual misery. Riding the current of this novel, we are back in the happy time when the love affair was new and all seemed possible. How rich is the recollection of that emotion! What else is greatness but the indestructible wealth it leaves in the mind's recollection after hope has soured and passions are spent? It is always the hope of democracy that our wealth will be there to spend again, and the ongoing treasure of *Huckleberry Finn* is that it frees us to think of democracy and its sublime, terrifying premise: Let the passions and cupidities and dreams and kinks and ideals and greed and hopes and foul corruptions of all men and women have their day and the world will still be better off, for there is more good than bad in the sum of us and our workings. Mark Twain, whole embodiment of that democratic human, understood the premise in every turn of his pen, and how he tested it, how he twisted and tantalized and tested it until we are weak all over again with our love for the idea.

RE-MARKING TWAIN (1996)

Toni Morrison

Fear and alarm are what I remember most about my first encounter with Mark Twain's *Adventures of Huckleberry Finn*. Palpable alarm. Unlike the treasure-island excursion of *Tom Sawyer*, at no point along Huck's journey was a happy ending signaled or guaranteed. Reading *Huckleberry Finn*, chosen randomly without guidance or recommendation, was deeply disturbing. My second reading of it, under the supervision of an English teacher in junior high school, was no less uncomfortable—rather more. It provoked a feeling I can only describe now as muffled rage, as though appreciation of the work required my complicity in and sanction of something shaming. Yet the satisfactions were great: riveting episodes of flight, of cunning; the convincing commentary on adult behavior, watchful and insouciant; the authority of a child's voice in language cut for its renegade tongue and sharp intelligence. Liberating language— not baby talk for the young, nor the doggedly patronizing language of so many books on the "children's shelf." And there were interesting female characters: the clever woman undeceived by Huck's disguise; the young girl whose sorrow at the sale of slaves is grief for a family split rather than conveniences lost.

Nevertheless, for the second time, curling through the pleasure, clouding the narrative reward, was my original alarm, coupled now with a profoundly distasteful complicity.

Then, in the mid-fifties, I read it again—or sort of read it. Actually I read it through the lenses of Leslie Fiedler and Lionel Trilling. Exposed to Trilling's

New York: Oxford UP, 1996.

reverent intimacy and Fiedler's irreverent familiarity, I concluded that their criticisms served me better than the novel had, not only because they helped me see many things I had been unaware of, but precisely because they ignored or rendered trivial the things that caused my unease.

In the early eighties I read *Huckleberry Finn* again, provoked, I believe, by demands to remove the novel from the libraries and required reading lists of public schools. These efforts were based, it seemed to me, on a narrow notion of how to handle the offense Mark Twain's use of the term "nigger" would occasion for black students and the corrosive effect it would have on white ones. It struck me as a purist yet elementary kind of censorship designed to appease adults rather than educate children. Amputate the problem, band-aid the solution. A serious comprehensive discussion of the term by an intelligent teacher certainly would have benefited my eighth-grade class and would have spared all of us (a few blacks, many whites—mostly second-generation immigrant children) some grief. Name calling is a plague of childhood and a learned activity ripe for discussion as soon as it surfaces. Embarrassing as it had been to hear the dread word spoken, and therefore sanctioned, in class, my experience of Jim's epithet had little to do with my initial nervousness the book had caused. Reading "nigger" hundreds of times embarrassed, bored, annoyed— but did not faze me. In this latest reading I was curious about the source of my alarm—my sense that danger lingered after the story ended. I was powerfully attracted to the combination of delight and fearful agitation lying entwined like crossed fingers in the pages. And it was significant that this novel which had given so much pleasure to young readers was also complicated territory for sophisticated scholars.

Usually the divide is substantial: if a story that pleased us as novice readers does not disintegrate as we grow older, it maintains its value only in its retelling for other novices or to summon uncapturable pleasure as playback. Also, the books that academic critics find consistently rewarding are works only partially available to the minds of young readers. *Adventures of Huckleberry Finn* manages to close that divide, and one of the reasons it requires no leap is that in addition to the reverence the novel stimulates is its ability to transform its contradictions into fruitful complexities and to seem to be deliberately cooperating in the controversy it has excited. The brilliance of *Huckleberry Finn* is that it *is* the argument it raises.

My 1980s reading, therefore, was an effort to track the unease, nail it down, and learn in so doing the nature of my troubled relationship to this classic American work.

Although its language—sardonic, photographic, persuasively aural—and the structural use of the river as control and chaos seem to me quite the major feats of *Huckleberry Finn,* much of the novel's genius lies in its quiescence, the silences that pervade it and give it a porous quality that is by turns brooding and soothing. It lies in the approaches to and exits from action; the byways and inlets seen out of the corner of the eye; the subdued images in which the repetition of a simple word, such as "lonesome," tolls like an evening bell; the moments when nothing is said, when scenes and incidents swell the heart unbearably precisely because unarticulated, and force an act of imagination almost against the will. Some of the stillness, in the beautifully rendered eloquence of a child, is breathtaking. "The sky looks ever so deep when you lay down on your back in the moonshine." ". . . it was big trees all about, and gloomy in there amongst them. There was freckled places on the ground where the light sifted down through the leaves, and the freckled places swapped about a little." Other moments, however, are frightening meditations on estrangement and death. Huck records a conversation he overhears among happy men he cannot see but whose voices travel from the landing over the water to him. Although he details what the men say, it is how distant Huck is from them, how separated he is from their laughing male camaraderie, that makes the scene memorable. References to death, looking at it or contemplating it, are numerous. ". . . this drownded man was just his [Pap's] size, . . . but they couldn't make nothing out of the face. . . . floating on his back in the water. . . . took him and buried him on the bank. . . . I knowed mighty well that a drownded man don't float on his back, but on his face." The emotional management of death seeds the novel: Huck yearns for death, runs from its certainty and feigns it. His deepest, uncomic feelings about his status as an outsider, someone "dead" to society, are murmuring interludes of despair, soleness, isolation and unlove. A plaintive note of melancholy and dread surfaces immediately in the first chapter, after Huck sums up the narrative of his life in a prior book.

> Then I set down in a chair by the window and tried to think of something cheerful, but it warn't no use. I felt so lonesome I most wished I was dead. The stars were shining, and the leaves rustled in the woods ever so mournful; and I heard an owl, away off, who-whooing about somebody that was dead, and a whippowill and a dog crying about somebody that was going to die; and the wind was trying to whisper something to me and I couldn't make out what it was, and so it made the cold shivers run over me. Then away out in the woods I heard that kind of a sound that a ghost makes. . . . I got so downhearted and scared I did wish I had some company.

Although Huck complains bitterly of rules and regulations, I see him to be running not from external control but from external chaos. Nothing in society makes sense; all is in peril. Upper-class, churchgoing, elegantly housed families annihilate themselves in a psychotic feud, and Huck has to drag two of their corpses from the water—one of whom is a just-made friend, the boy Buck; he sees the public slaughter of a drunk; he hears the vicious plans of murderers on a wrecked steamboat; he spends a large portion of the book in the company of "[Pap's] kind of people"—the fraudulent, thieving Duke and King who wield brutal power over him, just as his father did. No wonder that when he is alone, whether safe in the Widow's house or hiding from his father, he is so very frightened and frequently suicidal.

If the emotional environment into which Twain places his protagonist is dangerous, then the leading question the novel poses for me is, What does Huck need to live without terror, melancholy and suicidal thoughts? The answer, of course, is Jim. When Huck is among society—whether respectable or deviant, rich or poor—he is alert to and consumed by its deception, its illogic, its scariness. Yet he is depressed by himself and sees nature more often as fearful. But when he and Jim become the only "we," the anxiety is outside, not within. ". . . we would watch the lonesomeness of the river . . . for about an hour . . . just solid lonesomeness." Unmanageable terror gives way to a pastoral, idyllic, intimate timelessness minus the hierarchy of age, status or adult control. It has never seemed to me that, in contrast to the entrapment and menace of the shore, the river itself provides this solace. The consolation, the healing properties Huck longs for, is made possible by Jim's active, highly vocal affection. It is in Jim's company that the dread of contemplated nature disappears, that even storms are beautiful and sublime, that real talk—comic, pointed, sad—takes place. Talk so free of lies it produces an aura of restfulness and peace unavailable anywhere else in the novel.

Pleasant as this relationship is, suffused as it is by a lightness they both enjoy and a burden of responsibility both assume, it cannot continue. Knowing the relationship is discontinuous, doomed to separation, is (or used to be) typical of the experience of white/black childhood friendships (mine included), and the cry of inevitable rupture is all the more anguished by being mute. Every reader knows that Jim will be dismissed without explanation at some point; that no enduring adult fraternity will emerge. Anticipating this loss may have led Twain to the over-the-top minstrelization of Jim. Predictable and common as the gross stereotyping of blacks was in nineteenth-century literature, here, nevertheless, Jim's portrait seems unaccountably excessive and glaring in its contradictions—like an ill-made clown suit that cannot hide the man within. Twain's black characters were most certainly based on real people. His nonfiction observations of and comments on "actual" blacks are full of references to their guilelessness, intelligence, creativity, wit, caring, etc. None is portrayed as relentlessly idiotic. Yet Jim is unlike, in many ways, the real people he must have been based on. There may be more than one reason for this extravagance. In addition to accommodating a racist readership, writing Jim so complete a buffoon solves the problem of "missing" him that would have been unacceptable at the novel's end, and helps to solve another problem: how

effectively to bury the father figure underneath the minstrel paint. The fore-
gone temporariness of the friendship urges the degradation of Jim (to divert
Huck's and our inadvertent sorrow at the close), and minstrelizing him neces-
sitates and exposes an enforced silence on the subject of white fatherhood.

The withholdings at critical moments, which I once took to be deliberate
evasions, stumbles even, or a writer's impatience with his or her material, I began to see as otherwise: as entrances, crevices, gaps, seductive invitations flash-
ing the possibility of meaning. Unarticulated eddies that encourage diving into
the novel's undertow—the real place where writer captures reader. An excellent example of what is available in this undertow is the way Twain comments
on the relationship between the antebellum period in which the narrative takes
place and the later period in which the novel was composed. The 1880s saw
the collapse of civil rights for blacks as well as the publication of *Huckleberry
Finn*. This collapse was an effort to bury the combustible issues Twain raised
in his novel. The nation, as well as Tom Sawyer, was deferring Jim's freedom
in agonizing play. The cyclical attempts to remove the novel from classrooms
extend Jim's captivity on into each generation of readers.

Or consider Huck's inability to articulate his true feelings for Jim to anybody other than the reader. When he "humbles himself" in apology to Jim for
the painful joke he plays on him, we are not given the words. Even to Tom, the
only other friend he has and the only one his own age, he must mask his emotions. Until the hell-or-heaven choice, Huck can speak of the genuine affection
and respect for Jim that blossoms throughout the narrative only aslant, or
comically to the reader—never directly to any character or to Jim himself.
While Jim repeatedly iterates his love, the depth of Huck's feelings for Jim is
stressed, underscored and rendered unimpeachable by Twain's calculated use
of speechlessness. The accumulated silences build to Huck's ultimate act of
love, in which he accepts the endangerment of his soul. These silences do not
appear to me of merely historical accuracy—a realistic portrait of how a white
child *would* respond to a black slave; they seem to be expert technical solu-
tions to the narrative's complexities and, by the way, highly prophetic descriptions of contemporary negotiations between races.

Consider the void that follows the revelation of Jim as a responsible adult
and caring parent in chapter 23. Huck has nothing to say. The chapter does
not close; it simply stops. Blanketed by eye dialect, placed auspiciously at chapter's end, held up, framed, as it were, for display by Huck's refusal to comment, it is one of the most moving remembrances in American literature. Then
comes the "meanwhile-back-at-the-ranch" first line of the next chapter. The
hush between these two chapters thunders. And its roar is enhanced by Huck's
observation on the preceding page: that although Jim's desperate love for his
wife and children "don't seem natural," Huck "reckon[s] it's so." This comment is fascinating less for its racism than for the danger it deflects from Huck

himself. Huck has never seen nor experienced a tender, caring father—yet he steps out of this well of ignorance to judge Jim's role as a father.

What I read into this observation and the hiatus that follows Jim's confirmation of his "naturalness" is that the line of thought Jim's fatherhood might provoke cannot be pursued by the author or his protagonist for fear of derailing the text into another story or destabilizing its center (this is *Huck's* adventure, not Jim's). It invites serious speculation about fatherhood—its expectations and ramifications—in the novel. First of all, it's hard not to notice that except for Judge Thatcher all of the white men who might function as father figures for Huck are ridiculed for their hypocrisy, corruption, extreme ignorance and/or violence. Thus Huck's "no comment" on Jim's status as a father works either as a comfortable evasion for or as a critique of a white readership, as well as being one of the gags Twain shoves in Huck's mouth to protect him from the line of thought neither he nor Twain can safely pursue.

As an abused and homeless child running from a feral male parent, Huck cannot dwell on Jim's confession and regret about parental negligence without precipitating a crisis from which neither he nor the text could recover. Huck's desire for a father who is adviser and trustworthy companion is universal, but he also needs something more: a father whom, unlike his own, he can control. No white man can serve all three functions. If the runaway Huck discovered on the island had been a white convict with protective paternal instincts, none of this would work, for there could be no guarantee of control and no games-playing nonsense concerning his release at the end. Only a black male slave can deliver all Huck desires. Because Jim can be controlled, it becomes possible for Huck to feel responsible for and to him—but without the onerous burden of lifelong debt that a real father figure would demand. For Huck, Jim is a father-for-free. This delicate, covert and fractious problematic is thus hidden and exposed by litotes and speechlessness, both of which are dramatic ways of begging attention.

Concerning this matter of fatherhood, there are two other instances of silence—one remarkable for its warmth, the other for its glacial coldness. In the first, Jim keeps silent for practically four-fifths of the book about having seen Pap's corpse. There seems no reason for this withholding except his concern for Huck's emotional well-being. Although one could argue that knowing the menace of his father was over might relieve Huck enormously, it could also be argued that dissipating that threat would remove the principal element of the necessity for escape—Huck's escape, that is. In any case, silence on this point persists and we learn its true motive in the penultimate paragraph in the book. And right there is the other speech void—cold and shivery in its unsaying. Jim tells Huck that his money is safe because his father is dead.

"Doan' you 'member de house dat was float'n down de river, en dey wuz a man in dah kivered up, en I went in en unkivered him and didn' let you come in? . . . dat wuz him." Huck says and thinks nothing about it. The following sentence, we are to believe, is Huck's very next thought: "Tom's most well now. . . ."

As a reader I am relieved to know Pap is no longer a menace to his son's well-being, but Huck does not share my relief. Again the father business is erased. What after all could Huck say? That he is as glad as I am? That would not do. Huck's decency prevents him from taking pleasure in anybody's death. That he is sorry? Wishes his father were alive? Hardly. The whole premise of escape while fearing and feigning death would collapse, and the contradiction would be unacceptable. Instead the crevice widens and beckons reflection on what this long-withheld information means. Any comment at this juncture, positive or negative, would lay bare the white father/white son animosity and harm the prevailing though illicit black father/white son bonding that has already taken place.

Such profoundly realized and significant moments, met with startling understatement or shocking absence of any comment at all, constitute the entrances I mentioned earlier—the invitation Twain offers that I could not refuse.

Earlier I posed the question, What does Huck need to live without despair and thoughts of suicide? My answer was, Jim. There is another question the novel poses for me: What would it take for Huck to live happily without Jim? That is the problem that gnarls the dissolution of their relationship. The freeing of Jim is withheld, fructified, top-heavy with pain, because without Jim there is no more book, no more story to tell.

There is a moment when it could have happened, when Jim, put ashore at Cairo, would have gone his way, leaving Huck to experience by himself the other adventures that follow. The reasons they miss Cairo are: there are only saplings to secure the raft; the raft tears away; Huck "couldn't budge" for half a minute; Huck forgets he has tied the canoe, can't "hardly do anything" with his hands and loses time releasing it; they are enveloped in a "solid white fog"; and for a reason even Huck doesn't understand, Jim does not do what is routine in foggy weather—beat a tin pan to signal his location. During the separation Huck notes the "dismal and lonesome" scene and searches for Jim until he is physically exhausted. Readers are as eager as he is to locate Jim, but when he does, receiving Jim's wild joy, Huck does not express his own. Rather Twain writes in the cruel joke that first sabotages the easily won relief and sympathy we feel for Jim, then leads Huck and us to a heightened restoration of his stature. A series of small accidents prevents Jim's exit from the novel, and Huck is given the gift of an assertive as well as already loving black father. It is to the father, not the nigger, that he "humbles" himself.

So there will be no "adventures" without Jim. The risk is too great. To Huck and to the novel. When the end does come, when Jim is finally, tortuously, unnecessarily freed, able now to be a father to his own children, Huck runs. Not back to the town—even if it is safe now—but a further run, for the "territory." And if there are complications out there in the world, Huck, we are to assume, is certainly ready for them. He has had a first-rate education in social and individual responsibility, and it is interesting to note that the lessons of his growing but secret activism begin to be punctuated by speech, not silence, by moves toward truth, rather than quick lies.

When the King and Duke auction Peter Wilks's slaves, Huck is moved by the sorrow of Wilks's nieces—which is caused not by losing the slaves but by the blasting of the family.

> . . . along about noon-time, the girls' joy got the first jolt. A couple of nigger-traders come along, and the king sold them the niggers reasonable, for three-day drafts as they called it, and away they went, the two sons up the river to Memphis, and their mother down the river to Orleans. I thought them poor girls and them niggers would break their hearts for grief; they cried around each other, and took on so it most made me down sick to see it. The girls said they hadn't ever dreamed of seeing the family separated or sold away from the town. . . .
> The thing made a big stir in the town, too, and a good many come out flatfooted and said it was scandalous to separate the mother and the children that way.

Later, when Huck sees Mary Jane Wilks with "her face in her hands, crying," he knows what is bothering her even before he asks her to tell him about it. "And it was the niggers—I just expected it." I think it is important to note that he is responding to the separation of parents and children. When Mary Jane sobs, "Oh, dear, dear, to think they ain't *ever* going to see each other any more!" Huck reacts so strongly he blurts out a part of the truth just to console her. "But they *will*—and inside of two weeks—and I *know* it." Her dismay over the most grotesque consequences of slavery catapults him into one of his most mature and difficult decisions—to abandon silence and chance the truth.

The change from underground activist to vocal one marks Huck's other important relationship—that between himself and Tom Sawyer, to whom Huck has always been subservient. Huck's cooperation in Jim's dehumanization is not total. It is pierced with mumbling disquiet as the degradation becomes more outré. "That warn't the plan"; "there ain't no necessity for it"; "we're going to get into trouble with Aunt Polly"; ". . . if you'll take my advice"; "what's the sense in . . ."; "Confound it, it's foolish, Tom"; "Jim's too old. . . . He won't last"; "How long will it take?"; "it's one of the most jack-ass ideas I ever struck." But these objections are not enough. Our apprehension as we follow the free fall of the father is only mildly subdued by our satisfaction at the unmanacled exit of the freedman. Tom Sawyer's silence about Jim's legal status is perverse. So perverse that the fact that Huck never speaks of or considers returning to his hometown to carry on with his erstwhile best friend (this time in safety *and* with money of his own) but wants to leave civilization altogether is more than understandable. Huck cannot have an enduring relationship with Jim; he refuses one with Tom.

The source of my unease reading this amazing, troubling book now seems clear: an imperfect coming to terms with three matters Twain addresses— Huck Finn's estrangement, soleness and morbidity as an outcast child; the disproportionate sadness at the center of Jim's and his relationship; and the secrecy in which Huck's engagement with (rather than escape from) a racist society is necessarily conducted. It is also clear that the rewards of my effort to come to terms have been abundant. My alarm, aroused by Twain's precise rendering of childhood's fear of death and abandonment, remains—as it should. It has been extremely worthwhile slogging through Jim's shame and humiliation to recognize the sadness, the tragic implications at the center of his relationship with Huck. My fury at the maze of deceit, the risk of personal harm that a white child is forced to negotiate in a race-inflected society, is dissipated by the exquisite uses to which Twain puts that maze, that risk.

Yet the larger question, the danger that sifts from the novel's last page, is whether Huck, minus Jim, will be able to stay those three monsters as he enters the "territory." Will that undefined space, so falsely imagined as "open," be free of social chaos, personal morbidity, and further moral complications embedded in adulthood and citizenship? Will it be free not only of nightmare fathers but of dream fathers too? Twain did not write Huck there. He imagined instead a reunion—Huck, Jim and Tom, soaring in a balloon over Egypt.

For a hundred years, the argument that this novel *is* has been identified, reidentified, examined, waged and advanced. What it cannot be is dismissed. It is classic literature, which is to say it heaves, manifests and lasts.

Samuel L. Clemens/
Mark Twain: Chronology

1835	Samuel Langhorne Clemens born November 30 in Florida, Missouri.
1839	Moves with family to Mississippi River town of Hannibal, Missouri.
1847	Father dies.
1848	Begins part-time apprenticeship with printer Joseph P. Ament.
1851	Begins working for brother Orion as typesetter and editorial assistant.
1853–57	Leaves Hannibal; works as journeyman printer in St. Louis, New York, and elsewhere.
1857–59	Apprenticeship on Mississippi River steamboats; licensed April 9, 1859.
1861	Brother Orion appointed secretary of Nevada Territory. Civil War disrupts river traffic; Clemens joins Orion on overland journey to the Territory and briefly serves as Orion's secretary there.
1862–64	Becomes prospector in Nevada Territory. Subsequently works as reporter for *Virginia City Territorial Enterprise* and *San Francisco Morning Call*. Adopts pen name Mark Twain.
1864–66	Works as reporter in San Francisco; publishes short story "Jim Smiley and His Jumping Frog." Visits Hawaiian Islands. Begins career as lecturer.

1867–68	Moves to East Coast; publishes *The Celebrated Jumping Frog of Calaveras County, and Other Sketches* (1867). Travels to Europe and Holy Land; publishes best-selling account of trip, *The Innocents Abroad* (1868).
1870–71	Marries Olivia Langdon of Elmira, New York, February 2; son, Langdon, born November 7, 1870. Settles in Hartford, Connecticut.
1872	Daughter, Olivia Susan (Susy), born March 19. Son Langdon dies June 2. Clemens travels to England. Publishes *Roughing It*, about adventures in Nevada, California, and Hawaii.
1873	Publishes *The Gilded Age*, written jointly with Charles Dudley Warner.
1874	Daughter, Clara Langdon, born June 8. Clemens buys a typewriter.
1876	Publishes *The Adventures of Tom Sawyer*.
1879	Installs telephone in Hartford home.
1880–83	Daughter, Jane Lampton (Jean), born July 26, 1880. Clemens begins investing in Paige typesetting machine (1880). Over these three years publishes *A Tramp Abroad* (1880), *The Prince and the Pauper* (1881), and *Life on the Mississippi* (1883).
1884	With business associate Charles Webster, founds publishing company, Charles L. Webster & Co.
1885	Publishes *Adventures of Huckleberry Finn* with Webster & Co.
1889	Publishes *A Connecticut Yankee in King Arthur's Court* with Webster & Co.
1890	Mother and mother-in-law die.
1891	Investments in Webster & Co. and Paige typesetter do badly. Moves family to Europe to decrease expenses.
1894	Publishes *The Tragedy of Pudd'nhead Wilson* and *The Comedy of Those Extraordinary Twins*. Declares bankruptcy.
1895	Makes round-the-world lecture tour to pay debts.

1896   Publishes *Personal Recollections of Joan of Arc.* Daughter
            Susy dies August 18.

1897   Publishes *Following the Equator.*

1900–01   Joins anti-imperialism movement; publishes anti-
            imperialist writings such as "To the Person Sitting in
            Darkness."

1904   Wife, Olivia Langdon Clemens, dies.

1906–07   Dictates portions of autobiography. Receives honorary
            doctorate from Oxford University.

1909   Daughter Jean dies.

1910   Clemens dies April 21.

Works Cited in Notes to *Adventures of Huckleberry Finn*

Colorado, Minnesota, Missouri, and Oregon and Washington Narratives. Vol. 2 of *The American Slave: A Composite Autobiography.* Gen. ed. George P. Rawick. Contributions in Afro-American Studies and African Studies No. 35. Series 1. Supplement. Westport: Greenwood, 1972.

Doyno, Victor. *Writing Huck Finn: Mark Twain's Creative Process.* Philadelphia: U of Pennsylvania P, 1991.

——. "The Economics of Huck's World." *Beginning to Write Huck Finn.* Philadelphia: U of Pennsylvania P, forthcoming.

Dunn, Esther Cloudman. *Shakespeare in America.* New York: Macmillan, 1939.

The Holy Bible, Containing the Old and New Testaments. Authorized, or King James Version. New York: Oxford UP, n.d.

Johnson, Charles A. *The Frontier Camp Meeting.* Dallas: Southern Methodist UP, 1955.

Johnson, Claudia Durst. *Understanding* Adventures of Huckleberry Finn. Westport: Greenwood, 1996.

LeMaster, J. R., and James D. Wilson, eds. *The Mark Twain Encyclopedia.* New York: Garland, 1993.

Shattuck, Charles H. *Shakespeare on the American Stage: From the Hallams to Edwin Booth.* Washington: Folger, 1976.

Smith, David L. "Huck, Jim, and American Racial Discourse." *Satire or Evasion? Black Perspectives on* Huckleberry Finn. Ed. James Leonard,

Thomas A. Tenny, and Thadious M. Davis. Durham: Duke UP, 1992. 103–23. Also rpt. *Mark Twain: A Collection of Critical Essays*. Ed. Eric J. Sundquist. Englewood Cliffs: Prentice, 1994. 90–102.

Trexler, Harrison Anthony. *Slavery in Missouri, 1804–1865*. Johns Hopkins U Studies in Historical and Political Science. Series 32. No. 2. Baltimore: Johns Hopkins P, 1914; rpt. *Slavery in the States: Selected Essays*. New York: Negro Universities P-Greenwood, 1969. 186–259.

Twain, Mark. [Samuel L. Clemens.] *Life on the Mississippi*. New York: New American Lib., 1961.

Weeks, Robin, ed. *Four Fugitive Slave Narratives*. Reading: Addison-Wesley, 1969.

For Further Reading

Textual

Blair, Walter. "When Was *Huckleberry Finn* Written?" *American Literature* 30 (1958): 1–25.

Doyno, Victor. *Writing* Huck Finn: *Mark Twain's Creative Process*. Philadelphia: U of Pennsylvania P, 1991

———. *Beginning to Write* Huck Finn. Philadelphia: U of Pennsylvania P, forthcoming.

Fishkin, Shelley Fisher. *Was Huck Black? Mark Twain and African-American Voices*. New York: Oxford UP, 1993.

Sewell, David R. *Mark Twain's Languages: Discourse, Dialogue, and Linguistic Variety*. Berkeley: U of California P, 1987.

Critical

Beaver, Harold. *Huckleberry Finn*. London: Allen, 1987.

Bloom, Harold, Ed. *Major Literary Characters: Huck Finn*. New York: Chelsea, 1990.

Budd, Louis. *New Essays on* Adventures of Huckleberry Finn. New York: Cambridge UP, 1985.

Chadwick-Joshua, Jocelyn. *The Jim Dilemma: Reading Race in* Huckleberry Finn. Jackson: UP of Mississippi, 1998.

Ellison, Ralph. "Twentieth-Century Fiction and the Black Mask of Humanity." *Shadow and Act*. New York: Vintage-Random, 1995. 24–44.

Graff, Gerald, and James Phelan, Eds. Adventures of Huckleberry Finn: *A Case Study in Critical Controversy*. Boston: Bedford, 1995.

Leonard, James S., et al. *Satire or Evasion? Black Perspectives on* Huckleberry Finn. Durham: Duke UP, 1992.

Quirk, Tom. *Coming to Grips with* Huckleberry Finn: *Essays on a Book, a Boy, and a Man.* Columbia: U of Missouri P, 1993.

Sattelmeyer, Robert, and J. Donald Crowley. *One Hundred Years of* Huckleberry Finn: *The Boy, His Book, and American Culture.* Columbia: U of Missouri P, 1985.

Smith, David L. "Huck, Jim, and American Racial Discourse." Sundquist. 90–102.

Sundquist, Eric J., Ed. *Mark Twain: A Collection of Critical Essays.* Englewood Cliffs: Prentice, 1994.

Trilling, Lionel. *"Huckleberry Finn." The Liberal Imagination.* New York: Viking, 1950. 106–13.

Contextual

Briden, Earl F. "Kemble's 'Specialty' and the Pictorial Countertext of *Huckleberry Finn." Mark Twain Journal* 26.2 (1988): 2–14.

Bruce, Dickson D., Jr. *Violence and Culture in the Antebellum South.* Austin: U of Texas P, 1979.

David, Beverly R. "The Pictorial *Huck Finn:* Mark Twain and His Illustrator, E. W. Kemble." *Huck Finn among the Critics: A Centennial Selection.* Ed. M. Thomas Inge. Frederick: UP of America, 1985. 269–92.

Ensor, Allison R. "The Illustrating of *Huckleberry Finn:* A Centennial Perspective." *One Hundred Years of* Huckleberry Finn: *The Boy, His Book, and American Culture.* Ed. Robert Sattelmeyer and J. Donald Crowley. Columbia: U of Missouri P, 1985.

Finkelman, Paul, Ed. *Fugitive Slaves.* New York: Garland, 1989.

Fishkin, Shelley Fisher. *Lighting Out for the Territory: Reflections on Mark Twain and American Culture.* New York: Oxford UP, 1996.

Kolin, Philip C., Ed. *Shakespeare in the South: Essays on Performance.* Jackson: UP of Mississippi, 1983.

LeMaster, J. R., and James D. Wilson, Eds. *The Mark Twain Encyclopedia.* New York: Garland, 1993.

Credits